MAN OF DEFIANCE

MAN OF DEFIANCE

A Political Biography of
ANWAR SADAT

Raphael Israeli

with Carol Bardenstein

BARNES & NOBLE BOOKS
TOTOWA, NEW JERSEY

Copyright © Raphael Israeli 1985

First published in the USA 1985 by
Barnes & Noble Books
81 Adams Drive
Totowa, New Jersey, 07512

ISBN: 0–389–20579–6

**Library of Congress Cataloging in
Publication Data**

Israeli, Raphael.
    Man of defiance.

    Bibliography: p.
    Includes index.
    1. Sadat, Anwar, 1918–1981.
    2. Egypt——Presidents——
Biography. I. Title.
DT107. 828.S23184 1985   962'.054'0924
[B]   85–7441
ISBN 0–389–20579–6

First published in Great Britain by
George Weidenfeld & Nicolson Limited

Printed in England

To the memory of my father, David Israel (1912–79), and my mother, Ruhama Amozig-Israel (1915–85)

CONTENTS

ACKNOWLEDGMENTS

Ever since my interest was aroused by the complex personality of President Anwar Sadat in the 1970s, I have been researching and studying this immensely intriguing statesman and human being. At first, I was attracted by his speeches and interviews, which I collected, translated and published; then, I attempted a systematic analysis of some of his public utterances, in order to see if a study of the contents would shed light on facets of his character. At that point, I consulted many friends and colleagues, especially psychologists, who encouraged me to delve into a non-specialist psychograph of the President. To those, and particularly Irving Alexander of Duke University, and Amiah Lieblich and Gadi Ben Ezer of the Hebrew University, I am very grateful for the many hours of talk and the numerous insights and counsels which they kindly shared with me.

While I was still struggling with this extremely complex material, I was confronted with a still greater challenge: I was offered a contract to write a complete biography of Sadat. 'Complete', because in the meantime, the President had been murdered on 6 October 1981, on the very anniversary of the October War which had made him known to the world. With trepidation I accepted the challenge. I did this for three reasons. Firstly, I decided to bring together all the research and data which I had gathered from Sadat's first term as President (1970–76) until his tragic death. Secondly, I felt that Sadat's assassination called for a summing up of his extraordinary life; it seemed futile to me to pursue a study of his character and political conduct while the momentous events which were unfolding had claimed his life. And finally, I was fortunate enough at that juncture to find a collaborator, Carol Bardenstein, who was so enthused with the project that I easily overcame my hesitation.

Carol had been my research assistant during the previous phase of this study, when the psychological study of Sadat's personality was my main concern. Then, she went to pursue her Arabic studies at the American University in Cairo, which placed her in an ideal position both to continue to collect data and to acquire an immediate and direct sense of the Egyptian environment. Together, we went to see many top Egyptian personalities who had worked closely with Sadat and knew him well, but Carol also followed up on her own and continued to search out countless numbers of former politicians, newsmen, family members, and others who had known Sadat. She also, relentlessly and enthusiastically, dug up books, articles and interviews, in Arabic and European languages, which were published in Egypt and the world over. The extent of Carol's involvement in, and shaping of, this book can, therefore, be best appreciated if she is regarded as a full collaborator rather than a mere assistant.

In addition to the massive collections of Sadat's speeches and interviews, the President's own writings, and the large number of articles written about him in the Egyptian, Arab and international press, we were fortunate enough to discover some primary material, both oral and written, which helped unravel Sadat's personality and increasingly mysterious behaviour. However, due to the political sensitivities in Egypt, and the reluctance of some personalities to be quoted, we elected to write a straightforward narrative of Sadat's story without, for the most part, quotations (except his own). The list of all interviewees is attached to the bibliography at the end of the book and our deep thanks are due collectively and severally to all of them. We owe a special gratitude to Mrs Jihan Sadat, who gracefully welcomed us to her home in Giza, shared some of her memories of the late President with us, and showed us around the house where her husband had spent much of his time; and to his daughter Rawiya, who accompanied us to Mit Abul-kum, Sadat's native village.

Following Sadat's assassination a few biographies were published, some of them rather hurriedly. While we do not wish to get into a public debate with any of the writers of these biographies, it will become evident that we deeply disagree with many of them. Our disagreements are not merely about 'facts' but also about judgements. However, while we felt in some cases that injustice was done to the late President out of political or personal bias, we could not counter those travesties by compounding them with our own bias. So, we decided to write an 'inner' and 'subjective' rather than 'outer' and 'judge-mental' biography of Sadat, the point being that it is no less important to comprehend why he acted as he acted than to pronounce a sometimes unwarranted verdict on the quality of his reasoning or the results thereof. One has to assume that Sadat, like many other statesmen, acted in good faith and that his inner concerns, shaped by innate inclinations and the circumstances in which he made his decisions, reflect the traits of his personality much more than the events which he generated, or in whose stream he was sometimes helplessly swept along.

I am indebted to many institutions and people for their generosity and encouragement. The initial collection of data had begun, some ten years ago, with the help of the Israeli Ministry of Foreign Affairs, soon to be superseded by the Harry S. Truman Research Institute of the Hebrew University, whose secretarial assistance and excellent library facilities I used extensively. The Lady Davis Institute of International Relations of the Hebrew University generously paid the salaries of my research assistants for several years. In January 1983, the Hans Seidel Foundation kindly covered the expenses of my stay in Cairo; but it was the year that I spent as a Visiting Professor at York University, Toronto (1983/4), which gave me the peace of mind, the office space and the secretarial assistance which allowed me to undertake the actual writing of this book. The autumn of 1984, which I spent as a visiting scholar at Harvard University's Middle East Center, allowed me the time to revise the manuscript and supervise the printing process.

During my working visit to Cairo I greatly benefited from the services of the Israeli Academic Center there and from the friendliness, hospitality and excellent contacts of its founder and director, Professor Shimon Shamir of Tel Aviv University. Members and staff of the Israeli Embassy in Cairo were also of great assistance to me.

Israeli statesmen, bureaucrats, diplomats and journalists, who had participated in the peace talks with Egypt and had had some personal contact with President Sadat, also offered some illuminating details on his personality, conduct under pressure, and relations with his subordinates. Much of what they had to say has been laid down in the numerous autobiographies, articles and books published following Sadat's 'peace initiative' of November 1977, the Camp David Conference of September 1978 and the signature of the peace treaty between Israel and Egypt in March 1979. All of these sources are cited in the bibliography, and my use of them will become unmistakably clear to anyone familiar with them. So, although I found no necessity in interviewing those writers for their views on Sadat, I remain deeply grateful to all of them.

Since neither Carol nor I had ever met Sadat, we thought that a meeting was desirable with someone who knew him intimately, but in whose company we would feel, at the same time, relaxed and unconstrained. Dr Eliahu Ben-Elissar, the first Israeli Ambassador to Cairo, and his wife Nitza, auspiciously filled in that gap. Both of them, long-standing friends and gracious hosts, gave us many hours of detached and unemotional, yet personal and instructive, comment on their year-long relationship with the President and his family. Other facets of the late President's personality I learned from Camellia, Sadat's daughter from his first marriage, presently living in the US; as did Carol, in her repeated encounters with Camellia's mother and sister in Cairo. To all of them we are much obliged. No less appreciative are we of the host of colleagues, librarians, secretaries, typists and go-betweens, who have helped through these years in collecting the material, arranging interviews, typing various versions of the text, sending money orders and reading through portions of the book. Special thanks go to Mr John Curtis and Miss Linda Osband of Weidenfeld and Nicolson, who patiently and enthusiastically steered this book through all stages of production. Above all, however, we acknowledge Lord Weidenfeld of London as the one whose idea it was to write this biography and so set the entire process in motion; and Mrs Venetia

ACKNOWLEDGMENTS

Pollock, who laboured through the entire manuscript and made many editorial suggestions which gave the book its final shape and readability. All mistakes and misinterpretations, however, remain the sole responsibility of the author.

Cambridge, Massachusetts
1985

A SADAT CHRONOLOGY

Early Years (1918–40)

1918 25 December	Born in Mit Abul-kum to Muhammed Sadati and Sitt-al-Barrein. Raised by his grandmother Sitt Om Muhammed.
1919	Sa'ad Zaghlul's revolution followed in 1922 by Egypt's independence.
1924	Moves with his family to Kubri al-Kubba, Cairo.
1924–36	Elementary and secondary schooling.
1936	The Anglo–Egyptian Treaty.
1937–8	Military Academy.
1937	Assigned to Manqabad in Upper Egypt.
1940	Assigned to the Signal Corps, Ma'adi.
1940	Marriage to Eqbal Mady Afifi, daughter of Mit Abul-kum's *'umda*. Four girls are born, one dies in infancy.

Early Political Activity (1939–52)

1939	Organizes discussion groups among fellow officers in Manqabad. Meets with Gamal Abd al-Nasser and establishes the 'Free Officers' against the British.
1940	Meets Hassan al-Banna, founder and head of the Muslim Brotherhood.
1941	Posted to Marsa-Matruh on the British front line against Germans and Italians. Adulation of Rommel.
1941–2	Food and anti-British riots in Cairo.
1942	Link-up with German agents to assist Nazi war effort against British. Axis defeat at Al-Alamein.
1942–4	Incarcerated by British in Cairo and Munieh jails. Escapes in October 1944 from a military hospital.
1945	Involved in unsuccessful attempt against Mustafa Nahhas, the pro-British Prime Minister.
1946 January	Caught in his attempt to assassinate Amin Osman, a member of the Nahhas Government.

1946 8 January–August	'Cell 54' experience in the Qurah al-Maydan prison. Breaks with wife Eqbal.
1948	Released from jail. Meets sixteen-year-old Jihan Raouf.
1948–9	Contracting business, driver, journalist.
1950	Divorces Eqbal, marries Jihan, taking with him his two youngest daughters, Rawiya and Camellia.
January	Reinstated as captain in armed forces. Serves for a while in Rafah, northern Sinai.
1951	Contacted by Nasser, the head of the Free Officers. Promoted to lieutenant-colonel.
December	Free Officers plan a military take-over of Egypt.
1951–2	Sadat helps train Muslim Brothers who attack British installations in Egypt.
1952 23 July	Military *coup* by Free Officers. Sadat announces on radio the take-over of the Government.

The Revolutionary Era under Nasser (1952–70)

1952 26 July	Sadat escorts General Naguib to deliver ultimatum to King Farouq and Prime Minister Maher; end of *ancien régime*. Sadat changes his name from Sadati.
1953	Founds the daily *Al-Gumhuriyya (The Republic)*, as the mouthpiece of the revolution and acts as chief editor.
1954 November	Member of 'People's Tribunal' to try Muslim Brothers for 'plot against the regime'.
1954–5	Minister of State (without portfolio) in Nasser's cabinet. Secretary General of the Islamic Congress.
1954–6	Writes several books about Nasser and the revolution.
1956 June	Evacuation of the British from Suez Canal.
July	Nationalization of the Canal and Suez crisis.
1956 October and November	The Sinai and Suez wars against Israel, Britain and France.
1958–61	Speaker of the Joint Parliament of the United Arab Republic (Egypt–Syria).
1962	Together with Field-Marshal Amer on a fact-finding mission to the Yemen. Recommends a limited involvement in the war.
1966	Speaker of the Egyptian Parliament, the National Assembly (Maglis al-Umna). Joins a delegation to the USSR (headed by Nasser). Sent by Nasser to the US to meet President Johnson.

1967 June	The Six Day War. Disaster for Egypt, Nasser resigns and comes back. Sadat participates in Nasser's meetings with Tito and top Soviet officials.
22 November	Security Council Resolution 242 is adopted.
1969	Revolutionary *coups* in the Sudan (May) and Libya (September).
December	Sadat delegated to Rabat to represent Nasser in first Islamic Summit. Appointed Vice-President of Egypt.
1969–70	War of Attrition along the Suez Canal.
1969 December	Acting President during Nasser's visit to USSR. Takes command of War of Attrition.
1970 January	Sadat allotted more power as Nasser struck down by illness. Acts for Nasser as a liaison with the Soviets.
June	Nasser again in Soviet Union, decides to adopt Rogers Plan and accept cease-fire along Canal. Sadat, uninformed, convenes ASU in Cairo, as Acting-President, and rejects the Rogers Peace Plan (officially proposed on 19 June).
July	Sadat has a mild heart attack.
7 August	American-sponsored cease-fire along the Suez Canal.
28 September	Nasser dies and Sadat steps in as Acting-President.
October	Sadat elected by ASU as sole candidate for presidency, is confirmed by the Assembly and returned by 90 per cent of the popular vote. Sworn in as President on 17 October.

Sadat's Pre-War Presidency (1970–73)

1970 7 October	Sadat's first public speech as Acting-President. Vows continued struggle against Israel and alliance with USSR.
9 November	Extends cease-fire along the Canal for three more months.
24 December	Sadat sends a message to President Nixon, protesting that he is not a Soviet satellite.
1971 4 February	Sadat announces his 'peace plan', *i.e.* non-aggression in return for total Israeli withdrawal.
15 February	Sadat answers positively to the Jarring Mission.
1–2 March	Sadat's first visit to Moscow as President.
7 March	Sadat decides not to renew Canal cease-fire agreement.
4 April	Sadat declares that he will reopen the Suez Canal if Israel withdraws to the Al-Arish–Ras Muhammed Line.

April	Travels to Benghazi, Libya, to sign the Charter of the Federated Arab Republic (FAR) – Egypt, Syria, Libya and Sudan.
24 April	Ali Sabry challenges Sadat in the ASU Secretariat.
4 May	Ali Sabry is dismissed. Thereafter other members of the 'foci of power' are either dismissed or resign.
15 May	Demonstration in support of Sadat. Onset of 'Corrective Revolution'. Liberalization of the regime, freeing of political detainees.
16 May	Ali Sabry and his group are arrested.
25–27 May	President Podgorny of the USSR visits Cairo and twists Sadat's arm into signing a fifteen-year Treaty of Friendship and Co-operation.
22 June	Sadat declares 1971 the 'Year of Decision'.
July	Sadat supports anti-Communist measures by Numeiri in the Sudan after the failure of their *coup*.
28 September	Sadat delivers a major speech on the first anniversary of Nasser's death.
1971 12–13 October	Visits Moscow to ask for weapons for the 'Year of Decision'.
November	Indo–Pakistani War and diversion of Soviet weapons to India cause Sadat to postpone the 'Year of Decision'.
11 December	Sadat asks to visit Moscow again, but is told to wait until February.
1972 15 January	Student disturbances in Cairo against Sadat's vain promises.
1–2 February	Visits Moscow to get weapons.
April	President Ceaucescu of Romania visits Sadat in Cairo. Sadat's fourth visit to Moscow, at Soviet insistence.
20 May	Nixon–Brezhnev Summit in Moscow. Joint US–USSR communiqué advocating 'relaxation' in the Middle East.
8 July	Sadat orders eviction, within a week, of all Soviet experts from Egypt.
13 July	Sadat dispatches his Prime Minister, Aziz Sidqi, to Moscow, to soothe the Soviets and ask for weapons.
17 July	Sadat makes public his decision to expel the Soviets.
24 October	Sadat convenes his National Security Council to discuss war plans.
26 October	War Minister, General Sadeq, dismissed; Ahmed Isma'il appointed in his stead.
1973 February	General Isma'il visits the USSR and brings back promises of Soviet weapons.

March	Sadat makes himself Prime Minister, Supreme Commander of the Armed Forces and Military Governor of Egypt.
April	Sadat meets with President Assad of Syria to discuss plans for forthcoming war.
May	Sadat goes to OAU Conference in Addis Ababa.
July	50,000 Libyans march to the Egyptian border to demand unity.
August	Sadat visits Saudi Arabia and the Gulf States and then goes to Syria to finalize D-Day with Assad.
22 August	Meeting in Alexandria of the joint Syrian–Egyptian Supreme Council of the Armed Forces.
30 September	Sadat tells his National Defence Council about the war plans.
4 October	Sadat informs the Soviet Union of the coming war.

The War and its Aftermath (1973–7)

1973 6 October	Surprise attack by Egypt and Syria on Israel.
13 October	Sadat rejects a cease-fire proposal by the British.
15 October	Israeli troops begin crossing the Canal westwards.
16 October	Sadat makes proposals for a peace conference in a speech to his Parliament.
16–17 October	Prime Minister Kosygin of the USSR goes to Egypt to urge Sadat to accept a cease-fire.
21 October	Security Council sponsors Resolution 338 for cease-fire on 22 October.
11 November	Six-point agreement is signed with Israel under Kissinger's mediation.
21 December	Geneva Peace Conference opens.
1974 18 January	First disengagement agreement with Israel signed.
13–15 February	Summit meeting in Algiers between Egypt, Saudi Arabia and Syria to end Arab oil embargo.
28 February	Sadat resumes diplomatic relations with US.
March	Disengagement with Israel completed.
18 April	Sadat promulgates his 'October Paper' and announces he has adopted a policy of 'diversifying sources of arms supplies'. The *infitah* (economic open-door) is launched.
12 June	Nixon pays a visit to Cairo.
25–28 October	Sadat participates at the Rabat Arab Summit Conference.

1975	January	Visits France. Workers demonstrate in Egypt against economic policy.
	February	Visits the oil-producing countries in the Gulf.
	March	Kissinger's shuttle-diplomacy for a second disengagement ends in failure.
	1–2 June	Salzburg Summit, Ford–Sadat.
	5 June	Sadat reopens the Suez Canal.
	June	Civil war erupts in Lebanon.
	July	Sadat at OAU Conference in Kampala, Uganda.
	August	Sadat at conference of the non-aligned in Colombo, Sri Lanka.
	1 September	Second disengagement with Israel is signed. Sadat breaks with Syria and the PLO.
1976	March	Sadat abrogates the Treaty of Friendship with the USSR.
	April	Sadat visits France, Germany and Austria.
	July	Sadat sends assistance to Sudan's Numeiri, who is threatened by a Libyan-instigated *coup*.
	July	*Manabir* (political platforms) are permitted to operate.
	October	Sadat re-elected to a six-year, second term of office.
	November	Sadat announces that the *manabir* will be allowed to become political parties. Left-wing students demonstrate against Sadat's reforms.
1977	January	Food riots in Egypt, Sadat is shaken by the violence. President Tito visits Egypt.
	19–24 July	Egyptian–Libyan border clashes.

The Peace Initiative and its Aftermath (1977–81)

1977	September	Sadat sends his Deputy Prime Minister, Hassan al-Tuhami, to meet with Moshe Dayan in Morocco.
	1 October	US–USSR Joint Declaration on the Middle Eaast.
	October	Sadat makes two bellicose speeches about Israel (10, 25 October).
	28 October–4 November	Sadat visits Romania, Iran and Saudi Arabia and decides to launch a peace initiative.
	9 November	Sadat declares to his People's Assembly his readiness to go to Jerusalem.
	16 November	Sadat visits Damascus to enlist Assad's support.
	19–21 November	Sadat visits Jerusalem.
	14 December	Opening of Mena House Conference in Cairo.
	25 December	Begin visits Sadat in Isma'iliyya.

26 December	The Cairo Conference ends without results.
1978 4 January	President Carter visits Sadat in Aswan.
January	The Israeli–Egyptian political and military committees meet in Jerusalem and Cairo. No results.
31 March	Sadat meets with Israeli Defence Minister, Ezer Weizman, in Cairo.
July	Sadat decides to suspend peace negotiations with Israel.
5–17 September	Camp David negotiations with Carter, Sadat and Begin.
17 September	Camp David accords are signed.
October	Mustafa Khalil appointed Prime Minister and Sadat announces the establishment of his National Democratic Party.
December	Sadat is awarded the Nobel Peace Prize.
1979 March	Carter visits Sadat and Begin.
26 March	Sadat, Begin and Carter sign the peace treaty on the White House lawn.
May	Sadat visits Al-Arish in northern Sinai following its restitution to Egypt.
September	Sadat visits Haifa.
1980 Easter	Anti-Coptic unrest in Miniah; Easter celebrations suspended.
May	Sadat appropriates extraordinary powers to himself.
4 August	Sadat exchanges messages with Begin.
Ramadan	Encounter with fundamentalist leaders.
1981 June	Zawiya al-Hamra riots. Sadat meets with Begin in Sharm al-Sheikh.
August	Sadat visits the US.
September	Sadat orders mass arrests, removes the Coptic Pope from office.
6 October	Sadat is murdered.

1
BORN PEASANT

Eqbal Afifi, Anwar Sadat's wife for ten years and the mother of his four elder daughters, is a living reminder of his peasant roots. She is to be found in downtown Cairo in a modest apartment building; a single servant attends to her needs.

'Yes, he left me, he left me,' she said, the pain of her loss unassuaged by the years. She recounted how in 1948, only ten days before she gave birth to her youngest daughter Camellia, Sadat divorced her and married Jihan. For six out of those ten years of marriage, Sadat was serving jail sentences or living incognito. Eqbal Afifi used to visit him in jail, bringing the children with her and taking him food; she has vivid recollections of the day when he ordered her not to visit him any more. She was insulted, but she obeyed. Only when he was finally released from jail in 1948 did he tell her that he had decided to divorce her.

She, like Anwar Sadat, was born in 1918 in Mit Abul-kum, one of the innumerable villages in the lush Nile Delta. Her family, she recalls proudly, was of Turkish origin. She was distantly related to the Khedive Abbas, one of the successors to the famous Muhammed Ali, which in those days gave her considerable status in the poverty-stricken countryside of Egypt. Her family also owned some land in the village, which further enhanced her social standing, and her father was 'umda (village headman), a position of prestige usually held by the socially privileged. Anwar, on the other hand, came from a poor landless family with a black Sudanese background, which placed him low on the socio-economic ladder. His surname was originally Sadati but he dropped the last letter in 1952. Eqbal Afifi remembers that when, as children, they all used to play in the dirt streets or in the village square, her parents used to caution her against the company of 'that black one'. Later on, when Sadat asked Eqbal to marry him, her family disapproved because of the great social gap between them; it was not until Anwar completed his course at the military academy in 1938 that he won favour with her family. The wedding took place two years later. Today Madame Afifi's brother is 'umda. He remembers Anwar Sadat as an ordinary child who spent most of his time in the Afifi house, almost becoming a member of the family.

Mit Abul-kum has a guest-house where Sadat used to receive visitors and hold press conferences. It consists of a large stark hall covered with straw mats and lined with sofas and chairs. The walls are still decorated with photographs of Sadat visiting his home, praying, reading from the Quran in his *abayya* (traditional garb) or strolling through the village accompanied by Egyptian VIPs. Also on the walls are decorative paintings of Sadat in elaborate costume, some tapestries, and a few gold-worked calligraphic plates made and presented to him by university students. This large room, bathed in sunshine, boasts a conspicuous throne-like chair, which is set high so that the occupant may look down on whoever is in front of it. This chair, explains the present curator of the building, was used by Sadat during news conferences.

Sadat intended to retire to Mit Abul-kum and began to build a house there, but because of his assassination it was never completed. The unfinished building looks very plain from the outside. Inside there is a large room with an entire back wall of glass which looks out onto one of the tributaries (*tar'a*) of the Nile. The tributary, Tar'a al-Burugiyya, is not very broad but is referred to by the local villagers as *al-bahr* (the sea). Surrounded on three sides by lush green fields of wheat and green feva beans (the staple protein food of Egyptians) and an orchard of orange, mango, berry and other fruit trees, Sadat's house appears serenely peaceful. The only noise that can be heard here, away from the centre of the village, is the faint rustling of a breeze. Seen from the balcony, the Nile's green waters flow gently into the far distance. On the opposite bank, large expanses of cultivated fields extend to the horizon.

Both the *'umda* of the village and Sadat's daughter, Rawiya, told how he loved to sit and meditate on this spot, long before he began to build his house, because it had significance for him as the scene of a traumatic childhood experience. The *'umda* had personally witnessed the incident he related. Anwar had had to pass a swimming test but did not know how to swim, so his friends (today's *'umda* and his brother) were trying to teach him. The *'umda* pointed to a pipe near the black well which separates the canal from the river and said: 'This is the place where Anwar jumped into the water, trying to learn how to swim, and nearly drowned. My brother Ibrahim (now living in Cairo) had to pull him out of the river to save his life.'

The *'umda* commands tremendous respect in the village, though he behaves like one of the people and his manner is always informal. He takes great pride in his position, which has been in the family for generations. When he points to the large picture on the wall of the 'Big Bey', his and Madame Afifi's father, he speaks about him with awe. This reverential attitude for those in authority, which is universal among villagers, is not only an indication of Madame Afifi's high status, but also explains Sadat's own lifetime respect for the elders of his village. Today Mit Abul-kum's villagers take great pride in Sadat, because his roots were here and because he too became a figure of authority.

Sadat's brother Esmat, against whom public charges of corruption were made after the President's murder, also maintained a large and luxurious house in Mit Abul-kum; but it has been closed since he was tried and jailed. Sadat's sister Nafisah, who provided us with considerable insight into his social background, was very friendly, even funny. She is quite ignorant, never having had any formal education, and still dresses in a traditional black *malaya* and black headgear. She joked, saying: 'Tell Begin and Carter that I love them both and I kiss both of them.' When Rawiya, Sadat's daughter, asked her aunt, 'Why do you like Begin so much?' she retorted, 'Because he understood your father.' She kept murmuring, 'The President was a great man.'

Everyone in Mit Abul-kum offered us traditional hospitality: not only coffee and tea, but at the *'umda*'s house a large meal consisting of rice, freshly cooked in milk and cream in the outdoor fire ovens, and stuffed pigeon, turkey and chicken, the birds all freshly slaughtered and prepared for us as visitors. We were amazed at the village's exhibition of abundance considering the misery evident in the surrounding area. Other peasants in the delta of the Nile still draw their water from the various tributaries of the river; but the familiar sight of the *gamoos* (water buffalo), blindfold and ever plodding round as it turns the *saqiyya* (water-wheel), is not to be seen in Mit Abul-kum.

For Mit Abul-kum was loved by the President, and he treated it as a father would a favourite child. He gave all the proceeds from his autobiography and Nobel Peace Prize to his beloved native village because he wanted it to flourish. Indeed, the contrast between the uniform brown-grey of the mud-brick houses of old Mit Abul-kum and the modern light-coloured bricks of the new village, which Sadat helped to build, is striking. In the new buildings, the original style of the *fellah*-house, with its two storeys and open rooftop, has been preserved, as have the old room plans; but the rooms are larger, the space for the animals is more clearly separated than in the old style, and there is a butagas stove and both hot and cold running water, a rare luxury even in metropolitan Cairo. Up on the roofs with the pens of chickens and rabbits, amongst the debris left behind by builders, are brand new solar heaters. Eventually, all of Mit Abul-kum's villagers are to have their homes renovated. Sadat also conceived plans for a cultural centre, which is now under construction in the middle of the village. The centre will house a library, a cinema and a hall for cultural activities. He also obtained for Mit Abul-kum special mechanized pumps from China, as well as mechanized 'Chinese ploughs', which are a thousand years ahead of the manual ploughs that are still used or the crude ploughs pulled by draft animals.

Some Egyptian intellectuals of today, especially the members of the marginal yet significant National Progressive Union Party (Hizb a-Tagammu'), who have always been critical of Sadat's conduct and policies, have also been very sarcastic about the *fellah* (peasant) image that he delighted in projecting to his people and the world. Their usual comment is, 'What kind of *fellah* is he? He may have lived in the village until he was six, but he never tilled the soil there!' Others would say, 'Why did he always have to emphasize so explicitly that he was a *fellah*, one of the people? If it were really so,' the argument would run, 'he would not have had to repeat it so often. Look at Nasser, for example. You never heard him reassure the people in any of his speeches that he was "one of them", because he really was and there was no need for him to try to prove it.'

Yet there is no doubt that the countryside played a prominent role in the imagery of Sadat's language, serving as more than a mere source of romantic nostalgia. Throughout his life, Sadat always stressed that he drew many of his basic values and models for his private and public conduct from his early experiences in the village. During those early years, he became devoted to his birthplace and learnt deep affection for, and loyalty towards, his family and clan, his friends, the community and its elders. Acceptance of the traditional hierarchy, respect for elders and admiration for local religious leaders governed every villager's thinking and conduct. Furthermore, in such a poor and close community, the *fellahin* were forced to depend heavily on each other in order to cope with both natural and political calamities. The village was the place where Sadat learned that the mobilization of collective human effort could help to achieve a common goal. Because the countryside was primitive and poor, villagers were forced to pool their resources: neighbours borrowed each other's ploughs and draft animals; they helped each other in the fields; and joined forces when someone was sick, disabled or in mourning.

In the village, Sadat had also witnessed illness, illiteracy and poverty. In his public speeches, he often cited the case of a little girl who had died because her father was unable to purchase a pound of sugar for her (Sadat was apparently referring to his own daughter, one of the four girls he had by Madame Afifi, but preferred to avoid personalization). After he became President, Sadat repeatedly pledged that he would prevent such tragedies by making social security one of the corner-stones of his rule. Indeed, subsidies for consumer goods, workers' pensions, health care, education for all, and social benefits for the poor, the handicapped, widows, orphans and the generally deprived became recurring themes in his speeches, thinking and policies.

Many of Sadat's good qualities could be ascribed to his village background, and as President he never ceased to say so. He viewed the countryside as the origin of all that was best in human endeavour. To him, the people of the land were the closest to Allah: they were the least spoiled by the trappings of modernity; and they epitomized a pristine society where relationships were natural and close, hierarchies clear and authority undisputed. The *fellahin* were generous, good-humoured, straightforward, loyal to their kin, easy-going and decent; they loved nature and saw themselves as part of it; they stood in awe before Allah and accepted his commands without protest.

All who remember Sadat today, especially his family and close associates, praise these very same qualities in him. Even Madame Afifi, who had every reason to be bitter after her husband's desertion to Jihan, explained that she felt no resentment towards him. What is more, she still keeps a huge portrait of the late President hanging on the wall in a special room of her apartment. 'No,' she said, 'I have no grudge against him. I think he was a great man. Allah have mercy on him. I have no complaints, he took care of my children, he provided for us throughout. How can I feel bitter towards him? He is the father of my children.' Rawiya, his daughter, confirms that he always provided well for them financially throughout their lives. Madame Afifi, to this day, receives a monthly pension of £150.

Rawiya told us that her father saw the children quite frequently after their parents had separated. She feels that she was her father's favourite and that she had a special relationship with him. He often took her on his travels. Rawiya cited many examples of her father giving spontaneously to people, donating money to artists and the poor. It was she who mentioned that he had given all the profits from his autobiography to his native village. She speaks of her father with genuine admiration in her voice. The most inspiring sight of her father, she recalls, was that of him at prayer: he seemed to be in direct communication with Allah, so absorbed was he. She felt he was in a truly uplifted state.

Camellia, who was born ten days after her parents divorced, is somewhat more reserved about her father, but she acknowledges his loving care and generosity to her. There is written evidence that when she was born Sadat sent a note of congratulations to her mother, later sending another note about the payments he would make to provide for his first wife and their daughters after the divorce. Camellia says that a few days before 6 October 1973 she went to Mit Abul-kum to visit her father. She and her sisters preferred to meet him outside Cairo, in one of his private residences, in order to avoid meeting his second wife Jihan; for, as Camellia explained, Sadat usually went alone to Mit Abul-kum unless some official duty necessitated Jihan's presence. On this occasion, Camellia found her father gazing at the sky, deep in troubled thought. He chatted with her, asked eagerly what she had been doing and then said goodbye. Just before she departed, he asked her whether she had enough money; when she answered yes, he murmured, 'Be sure to stock up with sugar and oil.' She left, certain that an impending economic crisis of major proportions had prompted her father's counsel. Three days later the October War broke out, and Camellia found herself one of the happy few to have provisions of sugar and oil at a time when they were quickly disappearing from the shops.

Camellia also recalls that in August 1981, before she left for Boston with her daughter Eqbal in order to pursue her graduate studies in communications, she went back to Mit Abul-kum to bid farewell to her father. She found him deeply disturbed. He posed for a photograph with her, again made sure that she had enough money for the trip and wished her well. But before she left, he embraced her and said: 'Who knows if I will ever see you again.' Two months later he was assassinated. Both Rawiya and Camellia are grateful to their father

5

for having always counselled them to be themselves and to be self-reliant. 'Do not live as the daughters of a president,' he used to tell them, 'for one day the red carpet will be pulled out from under you.'

Despite the aura surrounding Sadat's public life and the glorified image he projected to the media, he remained essentially a straightforward man with simple needs and desires. He genuinely aspired to retire to the isolation of his house in Mit Abul-kum in order to reflect and write. He loved nature and the simplicity and calm he felt in its midst. When he gave press interviews in Mit Abul-kum, perhaps sitting in traditional garb underneath a tree, indulging in peasant story-telling, he was signalling that his roots were there and that this was the source of his power. There was always a strain of asceticism in Sadat. He was well-dressed in Western-style suits, but seemed to feel most comfortable in his *abayya*. He had a pleasant residence on the Nile in Giza and luxurious offices in Cairo, but he withdrew when he could to his rather austere out-of-town residences. Sadat hated to be shut in: he preferred the countryside both for leisure and for work, official meetings and press interviews. When he was not in Mit Abul-kum, his favourite house was an old wooden one on the outskirts of Isma'iliyya. This house had once been an Egyptian engineer's summer cottage and consisted of only two modest rooms, in contrast to the more opulent official residence nearby. One of Sadat's closest associates said that he could not have borne to stay in such a bleak place, but Sadat found peace and serenity on the bank of the Suez Canal. His other hideaways in Alexandria, Aswan and elsewhere were admittedly more elaborate, but they were used for both official and private functions.

This near-idyllic picture of simplicity is marred, however, by the popular Egyptian belief that 'He dressed in the latest fashion while we slept ten in a room' (in the vernacular Egyptian, 'fashion' and 'room' rhyme); and by a seemingly credible story that we heard from various sources about Sadat's main residence at Giza. Although Jihan is usually held to have initiated events, Sadat must personally bear the responsibility. The story goes that Jihan had a craving for a beautiful house on the banks of the Nile which belonged to a teacher at Cairo University. While President Nasser was in the USSR in 1970 for medical treatment, a few months before his death, Sadat, who had been nominated Vice-President some time before, acted as President in Nasser's absence. Sadat simply forced the owner of the house to vacate the premises and then moved in himself. One version has it that the dispossessed man went to see Nasser upon his return and complained about the Vice-President's behaviour. Nasser, who was renowned for his puritanism, was shocked and reportedly burst out in fury against his deputy and sent him home, where he remained for three months because the President refused to see him. This turn of events almost cost Sadat the succession to the presidency when Nasser died.

Simplicity and austerity imply discipline and severity with oneself; Sadat was renowned for his frequent fasting and self-imposed isolation, especially when faced with crucial decisions. His widow Jihan recounted many instances when, under the weight of his responsibilities, he would come home and detach himself from his surroundings: he would sit quietly in his armchair, gaze at the ceiling or at some faraway point, say nothing, puff his pipe; he would not eat, just ask to be left alone, so that he could reflect in peace. On more than one occasion, he described the bliss he felt in solitude, either when he was in his village, or in his house by the Canal, or in the one on the Mediterranean shore, where he would watch the waves breaking in tumult against the rocks; he described the rapture he felt during the long walks he took alone, or when in the company of some intimate friend in one of his gardens, or even on his journeys abroad when he was left to himself away from the glare of the media. After one of his visits to Romania, he recalled that the part he had enjoyed most had been the few days of retreat in the Carpathian Mountains, where he had felt close to Allah, dazzled by His creation.

Sadat valued his reputation for impartiality and personal disinterest as a reflection of his 'rule by law', which was supposed to apply to everyone without distinction. Once he recounted how Nasser's daughter had been rejected by the Admissions Committee of Cairo University and had had to resign herself to enrolment in a less prestigious college. The same story, boasted Sadat, had been repeated with one of his own daughters, who had also been rejected for admission because she lacked merit. During the first Egyptian air strike in Sinai, at the opening of the October 1973 war, Sadat's younger brother Atef, who commanded an air squadron, was killed. The news was received by Sadat with equanimity, because 'all pilots are equally my sons'. One of his sons-in-law, who had been involved in some shady business deal, used part of the proceeds to purchase land and registered it in the name of his wife, who wanted the property. When Sadat was told about this, he summoned his daughter and voiced his objections to the transaction and his concern about the questionable source of money. His daughter was adamant and insisted on keeping the property, so he sent police to her house and issued an ultimatum that if she did not give up the land he would have her arrested. She yielded. This made her bitter towards him for some time, but they later made it up as she came to understand that her father had had to act like that as a matter of principle.

Later, during Sadat's presidency and in its aftermath, his image of impartiality was to suffer some blows, particularly in the case of his brother Esmat's criminal activities.

Sadat's impartiality towards his own children and his attempt to be both generous and stern show how seriously he took his family responsibilities. Village life centred around the concept of the family, both in terms of the family unit and in the broader context of the community, which was viewed as one family with the elders at its apex. The father was the key figure as he possessed an inherited authority over all members of his household. The discipline and education of his sons was a matter for his discretion; he provided for their needs and supervised their actions. Within the family, the father was the supreme judge and mediator, the ultimate source of wisdom and authority, the final arbiter of manners and morality; he was the shield and the 'face' of his family. Sadat frequently evoked an image of himself as the 'head of the Egyptian family'. He perceived Egypt as one big village, the Egyptian people as one large family, and himself as the super-patriarch upon whom were bestowed the duties and prerogatives of the father. On 20 May 1971, when there was talk in Egypt of drafting a new constitution, President Sadat presented this view to Parliament in no uncertain terms:

> When we draft the constitution, we ought to return to the village, where lie our roots, in order to remind ourselves of the rural way of life. For in the village, where we were brought up, we were taught honour and shame. We learnt that everything has a limit and that outright nihilism is impossible . . . we know from our village experience that when the head of the family is tough, we all respect that family. We also know that an atmosphere of unity prevails in the village. In case of mourning in the village, we postpone our celebrations, so as to spare the mourners our cries of joy. . . . When a man ploughs his lands, his neighbour assists him and lends his draft animals to help him. Certainly the constitution is not just for the village, but I want it to be worded in such a way as to turn the whole of Egypt into one big village.

Although Sadat did, at times, project an image of daunting formality with his impeccable dress, his propensity for pomp and ceremony and his ostensibly luxurious lifestyle, he was in fact much more at ease with small groups and could best exert his charm in *tête-à-tête* meetings. He liked to forge close personal relationships with his associates and quickly insisted on working on a first-name basis. He persisted in calling Secretary of State William Rogers 'Bill', Henry Kissinger 'Dear Henry', Prime Minister Begin 'Menachem', television star Barbara Walters 'Barbara', and so on. His interlocutors might address him deferentially as 'Mr President', but he preferred a much more cosy, personal and warm approach to the people with whom he dealt and with whom he needed to be familiar.

However awed people in his entourage were by his authority, they sensed that he treated them as members of a family of which he was the undisputed head. When he shut himself away to ponder on some major issue which required a decision, all those who worked for him stood around nervously, like children awaiting punishment, knowing that, whatever his verdict, it would have to be carried out without fail. Though he liked to create an easy-going ambiance, he always made it clear that he was in charge of the situation. He would steer events his way, treating those about him as satellites bound to follow his course. His role was that of leader, teacher, father; the people were his followers and pupils and were bound to him by ties of filial obligation. Sadat called the Egyptians 'brothers' or, when referring to students or to his troops, 'my sons'. He regarded the figure of President as the supreme representative of Egypt, the personification of its sovereignty and honour, a sort of super-*'umda* or village headman. His repeated usage of 'I' for Egypt, his conception of the state institutions as subordinate to himself, his perception of himself as the authority which granted laws, liberties, rights and privileges, all attest to the centrality of village-style paternalism in Sadat's mind. Just as the ruling prerogatives of the father were acknowledged by the members of the family, so too was the power of the President legitimized by the recognition of the Egyptian people. He thought that he represented the people and that his voice was the people's voice; his opponents were, by implication, the enemies of the people and his supporters the people's friends.

One of the major tasks of the father in the village is to protect the honour of his family. Sadat's concern for Egypt's honour, which had to be regained by eliminating the shame of defeat, was epitomized by his words, 'Better to die honourably than to live in humiliation.' Like the ancient Arab poets who sang the praise of their tribes, Sadat glorified his country and his kin, proclaiming their valour and recounting their brilliant feats in war and peace. In the process, he delighted in vilifying, castigating and menacing his foes and in placating and flattering his friends. In his speeches, he often contrasted the Egyptian people, who 'earn their bread by sweat and labour', with the Israelis, who 'get their bread, butter, phantom jets and blank cheques from the US'. Even when he had to accept or to ask for assistance, he would not 'beg'. He would simply mention his difficult plight to his 'Arab brothers' and let them 'draw their own conclusions and give what they deemed fit'. The rationale, of course, was that 'We, Egyptian peasants, are too proud to beg for assistance.'

A corollary to the concept of honour was that of 'adl (justice), which was of overwhelming importance in Sadat's thinking. For him the principle of Egypt's territorial integrity – 'Every particle of sand in our country is holy' – was analogous to the peasants' deep attachment to their own land to the point of being disposed to fight for generations over a few yards of disputed land until justice prevailed. This attitude had been reinforced in recent generations following the reintroduction before 1914 of the Bedouin ideal into Egyptian village life by the nationalist movement led by Ahmad 'Urabi: a Bedouin staked his reputation on his willingness to protect what he perceived as his rights. Sadat often likened the world to a jungle where only the strong survive: 'Only if you fight will people respect you and negotiate with you.' Only by regaining possession of what by rights belonged to him ('My territories, my oil, etc. . . .') would he be able to redress the wrong committed against him; only thus could he bring about justice, only thus redeem his honour. It was not that possession of the land in question had any intrinsic value; it was rather a question of honour, of reputation, of one's ability to defend one's rights when they were seen to be at stake.

Sadat's devoutness can also be traced back to his village origin. His writings and speeches are full of emotional references to the *kuttab* (traditional school) of his native village, where he learned the verses of the Holy Quran from

Sheikh Abdul-Hamid, and where he acquired the piety which was to pervade his life. A quick glance through his speeches shows widespread reference to Allah, the Quran, faith, believers and Islam; he also liberally interspersed his public addresses with quotations from the Holy Book. And he often explained that having to learn the Quran by heart at school had strengthened his memory, enabling him in later life to make long speeches without prepared notes.

Sadat often referred to the Holy Book as an incontestable divine history from which could be extrapolated practical directives for the conduct of contemporary politics. For example, in one of his most virulent anti-Jewish speeches, delivered on 25 April 1972 on the occasion of the birthday of the Prophet Muhammed, he related how the Prophet had negotiated with the Jews of Medina and how they had subsequently betrayed him; from this he inferred that it was pointless to talk to the Jews today. The most significant thing the Prophet had done, Sadat believed, was to evict the Jews from the Arabian Peninsula; and it therefore followed that if the Jews were expelled from 'occupied Palestine', Jerusalem and other Arab lands, it would be with the Prophet's blessing. Sadat's negative attitude towards Israelis, Zionists and Jews – terms he used interchangeably – clearly stemmed from the derogatory image of the *dhimmi* people (Jewish and Christian minorities tolerated within the Muslim community) that has become part of Islamic tradition.

In Sadat's early thinking, Islam was not merely one aspect of life but, as the sociologist R. Patai put it, 'the hub from which all radiated'. All custom and tradition was religious; every action, every abstention from action, all thoughts and feelings had a religious root. Islam determined conduct on the individual level and in the family, village, society and state. Providence, predestination and fate dictated the course of one's existence. Westernization and modernity offered a new way of life, more efficient, opulent and less taxing, but one which divorced religion from everyday secular goals and values. To consider man as the measure of reality, to mould the world to serve one's own purposes, were new notions which did not exactly square with accepting Allah's will blindly and without question.

Thus we find Sadat the statesman torn between resignation to what Allah had determined and acknowledgment that Promethean efforts were necessary to change present reality. This tension was best reflected in Sadat's maxim, 'We must create a state of faith and science.' It became imperative, in Sadat's view, that the science of the twentieth century coexist with the faith rooted in the Egyptian people since time immemorial. Egypt was an Islamic country, no one queried that; however, if Egypt did not utilize modern technology to strengthen herself, she might not be able to defend herself and her faith. She might forfeit her position as the bastion of Islam. Sadat had declared himself in favour of prohibiting alcoholic drinks in public while, at the same time, allowing foreigners, whom Egypt needed as investors, experts and tourists, to adhere to their customs.

Sadat, although a strict observer of the Five Pillars of Islam, personally forbad his troops to fast in October 1973 so that they would be in the best physical condition when battle was joined. He also enthusiastically backed the new war cry of the armed forces used during the war, '*Allah Akbar*' ('Allah is great!'), and welcomed in no uncertain terms the resurgence of Islamic orthodoxy. At the same time, however, despite Islam's strong reservations concerning usury, he invited David Rockefeller to open a branch of the Chase Manhattan Bank in Cairo. Science and technology were of prime importance for Sadat as long as they did not discount the power of faith. Sadat indeed warned his nation that he did not want the next Egyptian generation to become disorientated and lost, following Europe and the US, where technology and modernity assumed the role of a new faith. The development that Egypt was sure to experience in the coming years, Sadat repeatedly asserted, could only be undertaken if Egypt's culture and its traditional values were upheld. As President, Sadat again and again cited the example of the Vietnamese war, where the people's faith had overcome the computerized power of the mightiest nation on earth. Sadat also asserted that many of Egypt's own achievements, like the July Revolution and the 1973 war, could not be accounted for in purely scientific or rational terms. Faith and inner spiritual strength were needed if seemingly overwhelming odds were to be overcome and the impossible accomplished. The 'miracles' that Sadat so often referred to – the 'miracle of October', the 'miracle of the crossing', the 'miracle of the Israeli collapse' – could only materialize where there was faith.

Mit Abul-kum, which Sadat saw in retrospect as the formative influence on his early life, was his home for only six years. His mother, Sitt-al-Barrein (the woman of the Two Banks), the daughter of a freed slave from Africa, had lived with his father, Muhammed Sadati, in the Sudan, where he worked for a British medical team. However, when her pregnancies reached an advanced stage, her husband always sent her up the Nile to Cairo and the delta, to have her babies at his mother's home in Mit Abul-kum. Sitt Om Muhammed, Sadat's grandmother, thus witnessed the birth of her four grandchildren in her own home; mother and grandmother caring together for the new born. When they were weaned, Sitt-al-Barrein would return to the Sudan, leaving the children with their grandmother. This happened to all four babies: Tala'at, Anwar, Esmat and Nafisah, three boys and one girl. Sadat had more brothers and sisters from his father's other wives, but he does not seem to have kept in touch with them. The inconspicuous house where he was born still stands, bearing the rather presumptuous name *Dar-a-Salam* (the Abode of Peace). Sadat seems to have been particularly impressed by his grandmother, Om Muhammed, who was a strong-willed and domineering woman, making most of the major decisions for her children and grandchildren.

Sadat's father came back from the Sudan in 1922 but it was not until 1924, when Anwar was six, that the large family, including grandmother Om Muhammed and her son's three wives and children, found accommodation in a four-room house in Kubri-al-Kubba in Cairo. Sadat was enrolled in an official school, but for some reason which is not clear had to leave and to resign himself to one of the second-rate *ahli* (local) institutions of learning. With a determination that was to underlie all his deeds thereafter, Sadat, after several rejections and reapplications, made it to a high school.

In those years, Anwar Sadat also discovered his enthusiasm for acting. In response to a newspaper advertisement, he applied for a role on the stage despite his diffidence about his dark skin, which was not highly prized in bourgeois Cairo of the mid-1930s. Sadat's dream of becoming an actor never materialized, but he never lost his penchant for drama, as was clear whenever he occupied the centre-stage or attracted the limelight. Ironically, his death was a remarkable piece of drama.

Failing his first try for an actor's career, Sadat turned to the military, which at the time enjoyed a certain amount of prestige. Not without difficulty, he joined the military academy in 1937, graduating nine months later, in 1938, as a second lieutenant in the infantry. He was proud of his rank, his uniform and his swagger cane, which he brandished with dexterity. His newly-gained status won him the hand of Eqbal Afifi, whom he married in 1940. Immediately upon graduation, he was posted to a signal unit in Ma'adi, a fashionable Cairo neighbourhood. It was there, in the military setting of wartime Egypt, that he launched into the underground activity which was eventually to catapult him into politics.

2
THE GRIP OF THE PAST

Sadat was greatly preoccupied, even obsessed, by the past: his own, his nation's and the world's. There was hardly a speech, an encounter or an interview where the past was not invoked in some way, and invariably it was invoked in order to make a point, to draw a lesson, to strike an analogy or obliquely to convey a message. At times, Sadat distilled or reconstructed the past in such a way as to vindicate himself or his people; he would relate events to his audiences with vivacity and detail, even when his version defied the facts. Not that Sadat was *consciously* falsifying events; in his desire to shape a new present, in the pursuit of his vision for the future of Egypt and of the Arabs, he sensed that unless he controlled the past he might lose his grip on the generations to come. The 'generations to come', his obligation towards them and his image in their eyes were a primary consideration for him. On making his momentous decision to settle with Israel, he said that he did not 'want future generations to curse him when he was dead in his tomb'.

Sadat, like many of his Arab contemporaries, was searching for his historical identity. He was torn between his Arab–Islamic background and the rich heritage bequeathed by ancient Pharaonic Egypt. Sadat soon became disillusioned with his country's pre-revolutionary corruption and he disliked the 'history of modern Egypt' that had been taught in his youth, which treated heroes such as the pre-First World War nationalist leader, 'Urabi, as terrorists and viewed the British occupiers as saviours. But he also came to rebel against the traditional Arab–Islamic view of history, which explained all human and natural occurrences in terms of an intervening Providence. Sadat saw that this viewpoint had provided essential security to a people living permanently at the mercy of an omniscient and ubiquitous Allah, but he realized that it was inherently pessimistic about the future. Traditionally, human achievements and happiness belonged to the past, to the Golden Era of the Prophet and of the great Muslim empires that succeeded him; the further that past receded, the further one was from grace. Obsession with the past provided people with an escape from the painful events of the present; at the same time, the Arab–Muslim was committed to the restoration of past grandeur, to the retrieval of his forefathers' wisdom, knowledge, justice, values, righteousness and *savoir-faire*. Progress, then, became a process of deterioration rather than an amelioration; the best way to arrest debilitation and to avoid ultimate doom was to renounce progress, modernity and Westernization. As a result, the Arab–Muslim was left with little or no motivation for change and improvement. On the contrary, since there was nothing he could do to reverse the divinely pre-ordained decline, which had begun when Adam was chased from Paradise, he could only try to slow down decay by clinging to tradition and eschewing innovation. Stagnation was cultivated; paradoxically, as a renowned Orientalist, Von Grunebaum, once remarked, the ensuing sterility was deplored as another proof of the increasing weakness of man.

To reshape all this would require an act of will of which only revolutionaries were capable. The catchword 'revolution' became Sadat's and his contemporaries' rationale for change, progress and a future-orientated society. To break from the past while preserving it necessitated a reinterpretation of the past in a light that would make revolution palatable to the Arab–Muslim masses. It was convenient to preserve the Arab–Islamic heritage in a glass showcase where it would be safely contemplated as 'history' while history was taking a new course. Let us listen to Sadat's own words:

> If we were to consider the movement of history from the standpoint of political power, we would be committing a great mistake. . . . The revolution of 23 July 1952 was a turning point from the ruler's perspective, but it was a direct continuation of historical movement from the viewpoint of the masses. . . . (11 November 1971) Some of us mistakenly thought that we could wipe out the past. Others believe . . . that they can discredit the present. But they have proved only one thing: their inability to see the future. . . . In the past, we failed to comprehend changing circumstances and to seize the right opportunities . . . (14 April 1975) We ought to spare our new generation from confusion by providing them with the true facts. For this reason, I have set up the History Commission. We have no intention of rewriting history. I have instructed the commission just to collect evidence . . . from people who lived through those events. . . . Interpretations will be left to coming generations (26 July 1976).

Past and future were thus part of Sadat's intellectual dilemma. On the one hand, he was preoccupied with the Arab–Muslim and Pharaonic past, which provided both a rationale for present-day problems, a pretext for laying the blame on others, and a reason for praising his own heritage; on the other hand, as a statesman, he felt a compelling commitment to the present and the future and used history as a tool for building the future – positively by extracting lessons and negatively by avoiding past mistakes – even to the extent of manipulating the past in order to promote a better future.

Sadat, the statesman-historian, felt he had a providential mission and regarded the recording of 'history' as part of that mission. He was, therefore, prone not only to do the telling, but also to demonstrate his own role as a key link in the chain of successive 'revolutionaries' from 'Urabi to his own days and beyond. In addition, the more he could prove his reign to have its roots in ancient history, the more credibility and significance it acquired. The Pharaonic age and the Arab–Islamic period, to which Sadat repeatedly alluded, constituted in his mind the antecedents which gave rise to his own rule. Iconoclasm was not a prerequisite for change, in his thinking; boasting about Egypt's '7,000-year-old state bureaucracy, the first of its kind in world history', or about the models established by the Prophet Muhammed or Muhammed Ali, in no way detracted from the institutions of his own Government.

The British, then the Israelis and the Soviets, had all impinged upon Egypt's glorious past and present history-in-the-making, so they became for Sadat, and for many of his contemporaries, the objects of bitter resentment and deep hatred. Any means were justified in Sadat's eyes to rid Egypt of their burden, even if that meant unlimited sacrifice on his own part and on the part of his nation. The spirit of defiance which he had developed since his adolescence was further strengthened by this persistent struggle against his country's occupying powers. The impetuous youth of Sadat's generation saw revolution as the only way to restore Egypt to herself and to her past, and to thrust themselves into the forefront of decision-making.

Sadat first heard of the unpalatable reality of British occupation through the ballad of Denshway. In June 1906, when British army officers were marching from Cairo to Alexandria, some of them took off on a pigeon-shooting trip to the village of Denshway. By accident, the wife of the local *Imam* (religious leader) was shot and wounded. Excited and resentful, villagers surrounded the British troops and wounded two of them, one fatally. The British then killed an Egyptian bystander in reprisal and arrested and court-martialled many others. Four Egyptian villagers were sentenced to death, others to imprisonment with hard labour, and the rest to public flogging. These martyrs joined other patriots in the Egyptian national mythology and the incident contributed to the stepping-up of anti-British campaigns of Arab and Islamic nationalists such as Mustafa Kamel and Sheikh Ali Yusuf. The tribunal which sentenced the villagers was presided over by the Egyptian Minister of Justice, Butrus Ghali, who was a Christian, and the sentences were seen as a humiliation of Islam by Westerners and their local Christian proxies (Ghali was assassinated in 1910 by a Muslim nationalist).

Sadat was born twelve years after the incident, only a few miles away from Denshway, in the same district of Manoufiyya. The story, still fresh in the minds of the village elders, reached Sadat in the form of a popular ballad in which Zahran, the first to be executed by hanging, was the hero. The ballad dwelt on Zahran's exemplary courage in the 'battle' against the British and on the way he walked to the scaffold, body erect and head held high. Sadat himself has testified that he listened avidly to the story in his childhood, fascinated by Zahran's audacity and spirit of defiance. Sadat admitted that he often wished he were Zahran and, indeed, on more than one occasion came close to emulating him.

Sadat was at the senior stage of his training in the military academy in 1938 when he first encountered Hassan Kamel, who was to become one of his closest associates and his *chef de bureau* in the presidency. Hassan remembers that, because of academy rules, seniors did not have much contact with juniors and generally snubbed them, but Sadat behaved differently: he was kind to newcomers and never averse to talking to them or socializing with them. In those early days Sadat was a good-humoured, sociable young man who enjoyed singing; he never struck anyone as likely to become a Zahran-like hero. Sometime in 1939 Sadat was transferred to Manqabad, a military base in upper Egypt. There he immersed himself in books about great liberators such as Kemal Atatürk and Mahatma Gandhi, trying to absorb some of their charisma. He began organizing discussion groups where select fellow officers would convene to discuss Egypt's problems. One of those meetings was attended by Gamal Abd al-Nasser, a reserved and awe-inspiring officer, who was to lead Egypt to her modern destiny.

Sadat and his friends attributed most of Egypt's multifaceted problems to the British. When war broke out in 1939, Sadat was in Ma'adi, Cairo, attempting to piece together the bits of ideology he had collected on his way, and to bring together some of his fellow officers who were dedicated, like him, to the cause of liberating Egypt from the British. In 1939 his organization of 'Free Officers' was already in operation, concocting plots to expel the British. In 1940 he met the venerated Sheikh Hassan al-Banna, founder of the Muslim Brotherhood, who also had a vision of a different Egypt, an Egypt governed by *Shari'a* (the Holy Law of Islam). The religious sheikh and the fiery revolutionary understood that they would need each other in their drive to topple the existing system, which had grown abhorrent to both of them. The first opportunity presented itself to Sadat in wartime Egypt, when the British, embroiled in the war effort and under threat from Germany, were perceived as too frail and vulnerable to withstand a domestic upheaval among the Egyptians.

Before the German–British confrontation at Al-Alamein in the Egyptian western desert, German prestige ran high among Egyptian nationalists. This was because of Rommel's gains in North Africa and Germany's victories in Europe, but most of all because of the challenge that the Germans posed to the hated British who had previously seemed unbeatable. In the summer of 1941, when Sadat was posted to Marsa-Matruh with his Egyptian unit – for the British had allotted part of the defence of Alexandria to Egyptian troops – he realized that he had no quarrel with the Germans. What is more, he is reported to have studied the German master of military science, von Clausewitz, to have read and mastered Hitler's *Mein Kampf* and to have greatly admired General Rommel, the invincible Nazi commander of the Afrika Korps. For Sadat the desire to remove the British was paramount, and if he could further his goal by allying himself with his enemies' enemy, so much the better. His task had been made easier because Ali Maher's Government, backed by young King Farouq, had decided to withdraw Egyptian forces from the front line in order to avoid confrontation and defeat at the hands of the inexorably advancing Germans. The fact that the retired Chief of Staff of the Egyptian Army, General al-Masri, had been arrested and court-martialled in May 1941 for attempting to reach the Axis lines in order to defect to the Germans did not deter Sadat. His anti-British stance was further intensified by the serious food shortages in Egypt during the winter of 1941–2, and by sky-rocketing prices on the black market. He concurred with the popular belief that the British were first and foremost to blame for all this: it was alleged that British troops commandeered staple foods which should have gone to Egyptians. By February 1942 crowds were demonstrating in the streets of Cairo, shouting, 'Long live Rommel!' The British sent an ultimatum to King Farouq, asking him to install a new government more to their liking. British armoured troops compelled the King to comply. As a result, Egyptian bitterness at unscrupulous interference in their internal affairs by the British registered an all-time high.

In May 1942, as Rommel's forces renewed their offensive, the Nahhas Government, which lost no opportunity in declaring its loyalty to the British war effort, took strong repressive measures against the former Prime Minister Ali Maher and others who were known for their sympathy to the Axis. Sadat, according to some accounts, convened his Free Officers and decided to draft a pact offering Rommel the collaboration of Egyptian officers when the German troops broke through British lines and captured Cairo, which Sadat had no doubt would happen, in view of the poor performance of the British Eighth Army in the western desert in recent months. So he invented a fantastic plan to drop his draft-pact to German troops from the air. His scheme failed, so he was pleased when two German agents approached him and asked him for help in mending and setting up their broken radio transmitters. He earmarked one of these transmitters for his own future use for communicating with Rommel's troops. However, before he could set it up, the two agents were arrested by British Intelligence. Sadat knew he would be the next target.

What then happened in his house in Kubri al-Kubba is clearly remembered in minute detail by Madame Afifi. She says that she had a premonition that something was going to happen, so she told her husband to lock the front door that night, not something they usually did. When the police came, in the middle of the night, Sadat was paralysed with fear. He stood with his mouth open, unable to move. On her way to open the door, his wife managed to signal to the servant to remove the transmitter to another room. Each room had a door leading into the next room, and then one out to the garden at the back. As the police inspected a room, she would signal to the servant to move the transmitter to the next, until she finally slipped away with him to hide it in the garden. When she came back into the house, she signalled to a mesmerized

Sadat that all was well. It was only then, she recalls, that he came to and began indignantly reprimanding the police for intruding into the peace and privacy of his family in the middle of the night. She had no idea what the machine in question was all about or what her husband intended to use it for.

Although Sadat denied that he had a German radio transmitter, British Intelligence took no chances and ordered that he be arrested and jailed. He thus spent two years of his life (1942–4) in Cairo and Munieh jails for collaborating with Nazi Germany. The transmitter episode has led to considerable controversy about his exact attitude towards the Germans in general and the Nazis in particular. According to one of Sadat's closest associates, who knew him and Germany well, Sadat's view of Germans was stereotyped and highly idealized. He had great admiration for the might that Germany and Hitler represented and great respect for the strength of the German army, but his true adoration was reserved for what he perceived as the typical Teutonic sense of organization, discipline, precision and obedience to superiors. With this image in mind, he often visited Germany during his presidency, refusing to allow personal experience or new information to impinge on his firmly-held preconceptions. If, for example, he saw a rebellious, sloppily dressed youth, he would say, 'But that is not a real German!' Sadat sent at least one of his children to school in Germany, demonstrating his respect for its educational system and discipline. He felt his children deserved, and were bound to benefit from, such an educational experience.

Sadat also had a great admiration for Rommel as an outstanding field commander. He revered Rommel's total self-discipline and admired his strategy and his ingenuity in battle. This interest led him to study the Al-Alamein battles in detail and even to establish a museum in honour of Rommel and his military genius. The museum, which is located in Al-Alamein and includes a collection of the famous General's personal battle gear, has in fact been expanded into a general war museum, where all the great battles of 1956, 1967 and 1973 are commemorated. Moreover, during one of his visits to Germany, Sadat asked to meet Manfred Rommel, the son of the venerated field commander and now the mayor of a German city. Such eagerness to spend what little time he had to spare on a busy visit with an individual who could be of no political interest to him indicates the depth of Sadat's admiration for Rommel.

Sadat's sentiments towards Hitler are much more difficult to understand. There is no question that early on in his life he held Hitler in high esteem, mainly because of the charisma and sense of power he projected and because of what Sadat saw as his unparalleled qualities of leadership. But there is considerable controversy about Sadat's later attitudes. In September 1953, when the leading Cairene magazine *Al-Musawwar* asked a number of Egyptian personalities to assume that Hitler was still alive and to send him a letter,

Sadat, a member of the Egyptian Revolutionary Council, answered thus:

> My Dear Hitler, I admire you from the bottom of my heart. Even if you appear to
> have been defeated, in reality you are the victor. You have succeeded in creating
> dissension between the old man Churchill and his allies, the sons of Satan. Germany
> will triumph because her existence is necessary to preserve the world balance.
> Germany will be reborn in spite of the Western and Eastern powers. There will be no
> peace unless Germany again becomes what she was. Both West and East will pay for
> her rehabilitation, whether they like it or not. Both sides will invest a great deal of
> money and effort in Germany in order to have her on their side. . . . You did some
> mistakes . . . but our faith in your nation has more than compensated for them. You
> must be proud to have become an immortal leader of Germany. We will not be
> surprised if you showed up anew in Germany or if a new Hitler should rise to replace
> you. . . .

The other patriotic Egyptian personalities whose opinions were asked, for the
most part, took a negative stand against Hitler. Ihsan Abd al-Qudus, a noted
Egyptian writer, wrote that Hitler himself deserved to be burned in a gas
chamber and that there was no place in today's world for such a fascist and
totalitarian. Among the statements of abhorrence for Hitler and his regime,
Sadat's letter was the exception. Was his continued anti-British (hence pro-
German) stance fuelled by the continued British occupation of the Suez Canal?

After gaining power in September 1970, all Sadat's references to Hitler
implied criticism and disapproval, while he spoke favourably of the Allies. For
example, in his speeches and press interviews he praised Churchill's war
leadership, the British stand at Dunkirk and in Singapore, and the Russians'
patriotic war-efforts under Stalin, while at the same time reproving Israel,
whose behaviour in occupying Arab lands he likened to that of Nazi Germany.
By implication, just as Great Britain and Russia had not submitted to Nazi
oppression, so Egypt would liberate its occupied lands; as Churchill and Stalin
had led their countries in war, so he would lead Egypt. By the same token,
what he regarded as aggressive Israel was bound to disappear from the world
stage exactly as Nazi Germany had, and the tyrants who ruled the Zionist-
racist entity would eventually pass from the scene precisely as Hitler had.

Perhaps Sadat's ambivalence may be explained by circumstances. Sadat had
always delighted in swimming against the stream. He certainly esteemed the
Germans, but when he was asked to write to Hitler, what better way was there
to cause a stir than by playing devil's advocate? At that time he was not in a
position of power and he could afford the luxury of an eccentric conjecture.
But when he took on the responsibilities of the presidency, he never again
idealized Hitler (although he did keep his own private fantasies about
Germany). When he was preparing for the 1973 war against Israel, his heroes
were the Allied heads of state, not Hitler; the examples of resilience and models
of hope for his country were best offered by the Allies, not Germany. Besides,
Britain had left Egyptian territory by then and no doubt the pragmatic Sadat

felt it was time for a reconciliation.

Germany and the Germans had certainly gripped Sadat's imagination. On the other hand, Israel, whom he accused of being 'Nazi' and 'Hitlerite', must have seemed embarrassingly close to the German model in her military might and efficiency and in her technological superiority. To see Israel achieve in such a short time what he had hoped to achieve for Egypt must have been galling. His love of Germany and his admiration for Rommel and Hitler must have turned a little sour when he witnessed what he perceived as Israel's borrowed Teutonic qualities. Accordingly, he attacked 'aggressive Israel' and likened her to the most destructive invaders in history: the Mongols, the Crusaders and, of course, the Nazis.

Sadat's pro-German inclinations may also have been subconsciously linked with his deep dislike, distrust and contempt for the Jews. Inevitably his attitudes were influenced by derogatory passages in the Holy Quran rejecting Jews and by Islamic political theory which gave them a well-defined subordinate status within the Abode of Islam. He had an unfortunate encounter with a Jew in Cairo which left an indelible mark, reinforcing the anti-Jewish stereotypes he had absorbed in his youth. Sadat made a speech after he became President in which he said that he had purchased a radio from a Jewish businessman in Cairo on his release from prison in 1950, but that the Jew, upon seeing his identity card, naming him as 'Captain Anwar al-Sadat', had refused to allow him to pay in instalments. According to Sadat, the 'Zionist Jew' wished to exact revenge because he thought that the captain had participated in the 1948 war against Israel. In a rare miscalculation of public opinion, Sadat repeated this story to an American audience during a visit to the United States. When he realized his *faux pas*, he protested, with complete candour, that some of his best friends used to be Jewish and that he opposed Zionism, not the Jews.

Following this, Sadat tried to differentiate between Jews, Zionism and Israel, but couldn't help continuing to use the terms interchangeably. Besides his need to dehumanize Jews and Zionists in order to justify his struggle against Israel, his thinking showed residues of European anti-Semitism which could have been drawn from German (probably *Mein Kampf*) and other Western sources. He often invoked standard anti-Semitic arguments about 'international conspiracy', 'world economic domination' and the 'rule of world media'. He also accused Zionism of aligning itself with world imperialism, and attacked some American presidents, notably Lyndon Johnson, for having 'succumbed to Zionist–Jewish pressures'. Not surprisingly, Sadat often expressed his displeasure at the special relationship which developed between Adenauer's Germany and the State of Israel. He fumed over the reparations that the Germans had 'unjustifiably paid to the Jews' either for crimes which they 'did not perpetrate' or for crimes of which the 'alleged victims had nothing to do with Israel'.

Sadat underwent a genuine catharsis during the 1973 war, after which his 'Germanic' and anti-Jewish fervour dwindled. His earlier sense of despair, frustration and bitterness was now transformed into something much more pragmatic, cool-headed and down to earth. He stopped comparing Israel to Nazi Germany (though elements of the Egyptian media, unaware of their leader's metamorphosis, continued to do so), and the Second World War metaphors practically disappeared from his speeches. However, suspicions about his pro-German predilections lingered because he was noticed sporting a Swastika-patterned tie during one of his visits to Israel. Was this insensitivity or a supreme insult to the people who had lost one third of their number in the Nazi Holocaust? We will probably never know. People in Sadat's entourage who were questioned about his tie dismissed it as 'pure Israeli imagination' or 'an unfortunate coincidence'. What is certain is that Sadat seemed deeply shaken when he was taken to the Yad Vashem Holocaust Memorial in Jerusalem in November 1977. It seems unlikely that he would deliberately attack his hosts at their most sensitive spot, but then many unreasonable things have happened in the Middle East.

Sadat's pro-German stance may also have been influenced by his veneration for Gandhi, the great Indian leader, who had also sided with Germany because of his hatred of the British and his desire to oust them from his country. Sadat read many of Gandhi's writings and identified with his struggle against the British, though not to the extent of advocating non-violence. Sadat's sister says that in his boyhood little Anwar delighted in wrapping a white sheet around himself like Gandhi and walking through the village leading a goat. He would then sit under a tree or climb on a roof and pretend he didn't want to eat. Sadat, who acknowledged in his autobiography that he loved Gandhi and tried to emulate him, found comfort in solitude from an early age. Like Gandhi, he spent long sessions in meditation, listening to his 'inner voice'; he tolerated no partners, only disciples; like his model, Sadat preoccupied himself with diet and health problems, was extremely restless and rarely kept silent. Sadat venerated Gandhi for his 'autocratic temperament, unyielding even regarding things he knew nothing about, totally intolerant of all opinions but his own'; he was also to emulate Gandhi's favourite mantra 'Do or die.'[1]

When Germany's armoured divisions were at the pinnacle of their success in Europe, routing all before them, Gandhi reportedly urged the Viceroy of India: 'Stop this manslaughter. You are losing; if you persist, it will only result in greater bloodshed. Hitler is not a bad man. . . .' Gandhi also wrote an open letter to the British urging them to surrender and to accept the fate that Hitler had prepared for them. In late 1941, when Nazi troops stood undefeated in Europe, when Rommel was about to enter Egypt's heartland, when the Americans had suffered defeat at Pearl Harbor and the Japanese were the undisputed rulers of east and south-east Asia, Gandhi addressed a letter to 'Dear Hitler', urging the Führer to embrace all mankind irrespective of colour, race or creed. Later, when the Japanese threatened India from newly conquered Burma, Gandhi launched massive civil disobedience campaigns against the British in India.

If that 'Holy Man' could sustain his pro-German sympathies during the Second World War, why not Sadat? Sadat also borrowed phrases and slogans from the Mahatma's anti-British arsenal. His willingness to sacrifice a million Egyptians to reconquer the Sinai was a close parallel to Gandhi's readiness to 'sacrifice a million Indians' for the sake of his country's independence.

Sadat was in prison for over two years until he escaped from a military hospital in October 1944. He then went underground for about a year, living isolated from his army colleagues in a state of extreme poverty and want. During this time one of his daughters died of starvation. When the war ended and Sadat felt that his pro-German crimes were no longer punishable, he emerged as a political militant, dedicated to expelling the British from Egypt. He then became involved in attempts to murder several Egyptian leaders whom he thought were too accommodating to the hated British occupiers. His first target was Nahhas Pasha, the head of the Wafd Government which had been formed as a result of the British ultimatum of February 1942. When that attempt failed, Sadat's next objective became Amin Osman, who had served as a member of the discredited Nahhas Government and had become, in Sadat's view, too pro-British. Caught red-handed, Sadat was sent back to jail in January 1946, where he remained until August 1948. Some of Sadat's accomplices in those shady days later became his closest associates. One of them, Ibrahim Kamel, was for many years Egypt's Ambassador to Germany and became Minister for Foreign Affairs in late 1977, when Isma'il Fahmi, the experienced foreign affairs expert, bowed out of office in protest at Sadat's 'peace initiative' with Israel.

Although Sadat later tried to hide his involvement with both assassination attempts by giving contradictory statements, he never attempted to conceal the crucial role which 'Cell 54' played in his life. Except for a short daily spell associating with other prisoners, he was left entirely alone in his eight-foot by six-foot cell in the infamous Qurah al-Maydan prison. Sadat had often chosen solitude and contemplation; now isolation was forced upon him. Totally cut off from all distraction, he put his previous experience to good use and spent long hours in soul-searching self-examination. He wrote in his autobiography that there were only two places in the world where a man could not escape from himself: the battlefield and the prison cell. In his brief period of underground activity, he had experienced both. In jail, Sadat was not only forced into total isolation, – no reading, no writing, no radio – but he was also materially deprived, detached from any physical object or presence. Later in life Sadat would always isolate himself whenever he had to make a major decision. Only when he was detached from the material trivia of his surroundings was he capable of elevating himself and inducing the clarity of soul which allowed him his 'visions'.

It seems paradoxical that a man like Sadat, who was thought to have assimilated himself well by the time the Free Officers had attained power in Egypt, should still claim that he could dispense with the material world. But that was characteristic of his dual personality: he could enjoy the trappings of power, the pomp, the attention that the world media granted to him, even displaying a desire to thrust himself into the limelight; but at the same time he knew that not only could he do without all that, but that at times he *needed* to be without all that. His frequent periods of seclusion; his withdrawal into himself; his desire to retire to Mit Abul-kum to write and meditate; his wish to go incognito to the theatre or to walk with his children: all showed his strong need for privacy.

Self-analysis was by no means easy for Sadat. He soon discovered that, even when left alone and without distractions, he could not simply plunge within himself. There were barriers blocking his path into his own subconscious; he himself described the hurdles which barred the way to his inner self and robbed him of its coveted companionship. At times he felt he was standing on the edge of the abyss but was afraid to jump, for he was aware that the 'fall' from himself into himself might destroy the very self-image he had so laboriously built up over the years. In particular, he was tortured by marital worries. Judging from his own memoirs and from some extant letters he sent to Eqbal Afifi from jail, she represented the traditions and conventions of his Mit Abul-kum days. Part of his self-image rested upon acceptance without a second thought of village life and values, wife included. To admit to himself that he actually wanted more out of a marriage than a traditional wife would be to deny part of himself. At first he suppressed thoughts of parting from his wife because he felt ashamed of this disloyalty. But then, detached from his background and isolated in his cell, he longed to discard some aspects of his old life. Could he do this without losing his integrity? After a year and a half of torture and self-flagellation, he knew what he wanted, he became aware of the right thing to do. He would not see Eqbal Afifi during the last eight months of his sentence. He asked her, the loyal and devoted wife, to refrain from visiting him. She was stunned, but she respected his wishes. Divorce ensued soon after his release from prison.

In his total isolation he learned that a distinction had to be made between a man's external image and his inner self-image, the first being ephemeral, the latter the very key to life. He came to realize that for most people the outer success, the image they projected to others, was of primary importance; if that image was disturbed, they were shaken and felt a loss of identity. In prison he was stripped of his outer image and, compelled to look within, discovered his inner, essential self. He turned to Allah as a friend and companion, and found him to be just, merciful, compassionate and loving. Allah provided him with a sense of comfort and solace; he seemed a far cry from the awesome impersonal

God Sadat had been brought up with. Sadat also claims to have discovered love in his prison cell. That Sadat should have experienced this intimacy with his personal Allah as love is quite understandable, but how that love became 'the fountainhead of all his actions and feelings', as he put it, is harder to ascertain. It is true that throughout his life Sadat shunned petty argument and lectured his people on the need to break away from the patrimony of hatred and rancour which had been generated by the deep socio-economic and inter-communal divisions under his predecessors; it is also true that, while the Free Officers under Nasser were feverishly scrambling for power, Sadat stood aside and watched with contempt. However, during his presidency he was involved in many struggles and he was often led to adopt vicious attitudes both on domestic and international issues; one wonders how love squared with this violence and ruthlessness.

In prison he also came to believe that 'suffering crystallizes the soul's intrinsic strength' and that through suffering one can fathom one's own inner depths. He sensed that suffering compelled him to purge himself of evil and then to act righteously. He even felt that it was necessary to suffer in order to achieve anything, hence his later austerity. Before the October War he told the Egyptians that they must suffer in order to emerge victorious. His emphasis on sacrifice smacked of martyrdom, and martyrdom for the sake of Allah and for the sake of Egypt became one of his ideals. His love of Allah became so all-embracing that, like other mystics, he sensed the ultimate happiness which springs from total unity with the Creator; in his words: 'The last eight months in prison were the happiest period of my life. . . . The world of self-abnegation enabled my soul to merge into all other beings, to expand and establish communion with the Lord of all being.'

Once Sadat had reached that stage of detachment and self-liberation it was difficult for him to plunge back into reality. In retrospect, the last eight months in jail must truly have seemed the happiest in his life when they were compared with the vicissitudes of the outside world. Indeed, Sadat felt lost and disoriented when he left prison in August 1948. His metamorphosis in jail had alienated him from his family; his isolation had cost him the leadership of the Free Officers, who had continued with the revolution in his absence. His first impulse was to return, at least temporarily, to the pattern of life of the preceding thirty months, to find some sort of isolation. He retreated to Hilwan, a town south of Cairo, in order to 'decompress' himself, as it were, before returning to real life. Throughout his life Sadat would retreat into isolation when depressed or deflected from his goal. In June 1967, after the terrible Arab defeat, Sadat was totally overwhelmed by his sense of loss and helplessness. He shut himself up in his house for three weeks to concentrate on recent events, trying 'to weather the fierce campaign of denigration launched by both friends and foes against our armed forces'. He again went into isolation in order to meditate before the 1973 war and before he launched his peace initiative in

November 1977. On all these occasions he remembered his experience in Cell 54, which had given him the strength for change. He once remarked that, 'He who cannot change the very fibre of his thought will never be able to change reality and will never, therefore, make any progress.'

3

CONFRONTATION AND DEFIANCE

Reborn after his Cell 54 experience, Sadat was inwardly at peace with himself, yet outwardly he projected an image of restlessness and contentiousness. The eight years of inaction in and out of prison made him feel forgotten and forlorn, incapable of measuring up to the demands of the world about him; he longed to make a fresh start. He wanted to test himself against others, whether individuals, groups or, later, countries. He sized up his rivals, bolstered up his own ego and then launched himself into battle with a zest and dedication which carried him from one success to another.

He developed a new bellicose personality. This does not mean that he would deliberately seek confrontation for its own sake, or that he concocted divisive issues in order to provoke confrontation. Rather, he perceived himself as being engaged in a perpetual struggle with the outside world. By setting himself against accepted conventions, he sharpened his own image. This was analogous to the Chinese idea of Yin and Yang, whereby opposites define each other: the existence of light defines what is darkness, beauty determines the standards of ugliness and strength the contours of weakness. Sadat's opponents did not need to be concrete or verifiable, they could be abstractions: he saw himself engaged in a perpetual 'state of siege', or 'all-out war', or 'psychological warfare'. After he became President, he defined Egypt's 'battle', which was now his:

> I mean the battle which went on before 1967, the battle which came to a climax with the [Israeli] aggression and which continues now. We have been in a state of war since 1967 and this is not new. . . .

Or, on another occasion:

> I am in a state of war with some international factions who have been waging this war against me by means of Arab agents. . . . Thus, the war in Lebanon is my war, and I shall wage it ruthlessly.[2]

One can sense in these words Sadat's fear that 'they are all against me'. But the identity, nature and motives of his adversaries often remained hazy in his mind. His responses, though belligerent, were correspondingly vague: 'I will not forgive them; I alone will fight against them; I will continue to confront them.' Sadat regarded the 'battle' as continuing 'every day and every hour', and projected it into the future, anticipating culmination in a victorious 'battle of destiny'. He was determined to fight this battle, both on the personal and the national level, and the term 'battle of destiny' was one of his favourites. The term connoted something Promethean and unfathomable which had to be expected and prepared for. He wanted to involve everyone, only exonerating the 'feeble and tired who ought to admit their weaknesses without shame'. To Sadat the word 'battle' did not mean a mere military engagement, but rather a continuous display of willpower and readiness to defend one's honour. He would not succumb to enemy pressure:

> The US has been escalating her psychological warfare against the Arabs implying, 'You had better give up and despair! Silence your protests, for there is no hope for you! We supply weapons to Israel despite her superiority and we shall supply her with more!'[3]

America's continuing to supply arms to Israel was interpreted by others as the fulfilment of an obligation to an ally, as continuation of past policy, or as defence of American interests in the Middle East, but for Sadat there was only one interpretation: America and Israel had deliberately launched psychological warfare against Egypt and the Arab world. He perceived US policy as a major, relentless force working against him, and calling for his opposition. Perhaps he reacted in this way because it provided him with an enemy, an opposing force, against which to focus his energies, and with a means to unite the Egyptian and Arab peoples. Throughout his life, when on the point of conflict, Sadat tended to inflate his enemy's image, both in his own mind and publicly, pointing out all the enemy's strengths and advantages. This provided him with an excuse if the enemy emerged victorious; if he triumphed, his victory appeared all the more remarkable. Parallel to this was his tendency to point out how his (or Egypt's) shortcomings would operate to his (or its) disadvantage in the conflict. For example, after the October War he repeatedly emphasized that *his* decisive 'victory' was all the more spectacular because of the heavy odds against him: militarily Egypt 'lagged ten years behind Israel', but his soldiers still triumphed. Moreover, throughout the war he kept repeating that he was facing not only 'invincible Israel' but also the American superpower which stood behind her, and by implication, his defiance of the enemy was all the more remarkable and glorious. In his own words: 'On 19 October 1973 I had been fighting on my own in the field for ten days against the US, which had thrown in all her weight. . . .' Or: 'I was facing both the US and the Jews. . . . The US, using her newest weapons, which had not been used before, and which had never been shipped abroad before. . . .'[4]

Making much of the opposition was a defence mechanism. Sadat also inverted this mechanism, boasting of his own and his country's prowess in the face of attack, while simultaneously belittling the enemy. The magnification of his, or his country's, image could be interpreted as a device to instil self-confidence in himself and his people on the eve of battle. But this mechanism can also be interpreted as a threatening display analogous to a show of teeth in the animal world: mock ferocity hiding a wish to retreat. For example, in 1971, helpless to oppose Israeli occupation, Sadat announced his 'Year of Decision' and promised to teach Israel and her allies a lesson. But that was no more than bombast: praising his own tribe whilst denouncing the enemy in traditional Arab fashion. Often, such intimidating language was as rewarding as a real act of revenge and averted actual confrontation.

Sadat's confrontational behaviour fell into two patterns: one when he was dealing with parties or forces which he deemed less powerful than himself, and the other when he faced his equals or those he perceived as mightier than himself. When the rival was seen as weak or inferior, Sadat would take action in an almost perfunctory manner. For example, when he dealt with the 'foci of power', those who challenged his authority after he had assumed the presidency, he acted with self-confidence: without preamble or hesitation. On domestic issues, when he had to act as the 'father of all Egyptians', he moved rapidly. He did not hesitate to neutralize Muslim or Coptic troublemakers who broke *his* rules. Likewise, he acted decisively against journalists whose writings he did not find to his taste. He dismissed at one stroke 120 newspaper-men; but then granted them amnesty and employed them in his bureaucracy. And he dealt in the same manner with opposition or subversive groups, students, Muslim fundamentalists and others, behaving magnanimously whenever he could afford to do so.

However, if his opponent projected a powerful image, Sadat would be much more cautious, taking time to think out his strategies before moving in to attack. As he himself explained in a press interview:

> Before I make my initiative or take action, I first examine all aspects and implications of what I am going to do until I am satisfied that it meets three criteria:
> a. A clear view. That is to say, I discard all marginal, tangential and minor issues, and I focus on the central problem. Thus, I achieve a clear view of the scope of the struggle. Preoccupation with peripheral issues can impair the clarity of one's view.
> b. The safeguarding of our free will and protection of our interests as Arabs in the light of changing international circumstances and other struggles around us.
> c. Commitment to our objectives. . . .
> In a state of conflict, we ought always to remember who we are and where we stand. What are the objectives, values and aspirations for which we are fighting; who is the enemy and who are the allies . . . what is the enemy like and what are his methods . . . ? Every enemy operates under the assumption that those facing him might forget who they are and where they stand. . . .[5]

In his dealings with Israel and the superpowers, as in his involvement in his youth with the British and his fellow Free Officers, he was much more hesitant and careful to weigh up the consequences of his actions. When he dealt with the superpowers he tried to remain equidistant from them, so as not to become over-dependent upon, or alienate, either one of them. For example when, in July 1972, he felt he had to face a showdown with the Russians, he expelled them from Egypt but tried not to humiliate them publicly. Non-alignment in international politics saved him from involvement in disputes which he was bound to lose. Considered in this light, his relations with Israel after 1973 could be interpreted as a permanent stand-off, brought about by Sadat's realization that even under the best circumstances he could not defeat his enemy.

Sadat did not wait for his rivals or enemies to put his position in jeopardy or to question his authority; it was always he who threw down the gauntlet. His defiance was in part a permanent struggle to initiate change and to retain control over it. He never settled for half-solutions and never tolerated stagnation and complacency. 'If there is a goal to be achieved, work to achieve it; if you must swim against the current, run counter to convention, so much the better; and if confrontation cannot be avoided, plot a course that will lead you to victory.' Consider the reasons he gave for initiating the riskiest conflict of his life, the 1973 war:

> After the Moscow Summit of 1972 (between Nixon and Brezhnev), the communiqué which was issued included a critical phrase which caused us great annoyance. The communiqué said that both parties agreed on military relaxation in our area. Military relaxation meant that the state of no-war-no-peace which prevailed here, and which was the source of all our troubles and dilemmas, would be perpetuated. The next year, at the Washington Summit, it was obvious that the two superpowers had gone one step further. It was quite clear from their communiqué that our problem had been put on ice. So, believe me, when I took the decision to go to war, we had decided that whatever the reaction (of the superpowers), we were not prepared to continue this state of no-war-no-peace.[6]

Similarly, in the aftermath of war:

> I shall not consent to half-solutions. I have not rejected the no-peace-no-war situation in order to bind myself in a condition of half-peace-half-war. Half-solutions carry the potential for destruction of Arab willpower and reflect an inability to face facts.[7]

Sadat was capable of endurance and patience in the face of adversity if circumstances so required; but there would come a point when he would tolerate stalemate no longer: he would take dramatic action to break the deadlock. Milestones, apparent change and movement, and dynamism were of primary importance to him. During his presidency, he obviously delighted in reviewing his achievements and allotting to each year a major feat of specific significance: 1971 was the 'Year of Decision' or the year he eliminated the 'foci of power' in Egypt; 1972 the year he evicted the Soviets from his country; and 1973 the year of the War of Destiny. He did this to demonstrate progress, to give concrete evidence that changes and accomplishments had been achieved in the face of adversity. Unlike his contemporaries who were fatalistically resigned to accepting existing situations as the will of Allah, Sadat looked with faith and hope towards the future, and gave optimistic examples of how events had brought about changes for the better. For example, when he addressed war veterans before the 1973 war, he reminisced over the rout the Egyptians had suffered in 1967:

> The history of great nations does not freeze at any particular moment and its course does not come to a halt as a result of one blow. . . . Great nations absorb blows and endure patiently any unexpected dangers. Then they resume their struggle.[8]

Intolerant of stagnation and an advocate of progress in general, Sadat took particular satisfaction in those changes which he had initiated. By engineering change, he remained master of his environment; inaction deprived him of a dominating role, and thereby undermined his willpower. He would say, 'I shall never be reconciled to this,' or 'I shall take my fate into my own hands,' and then he would act. He ejected the Soviets in 1972; he fought the October War of 1973; he reopened the Suez Canal in 1975; he initiated peace in 1977; all these events were major milestones on his political road.

Sadat behaved as though controlled change under his management could best be accomplished through defiance. By defying convention, he placed his individual stamp on events. Conventional opinions and tactics, even patterns of speech and behaviour, were all seen by Sadat as a current to swim against, so much so that an element of spite may be detected in many of his actions: if no one believed that Egypt could survive without the Soviets, he would evict them; if no one reckoned Egypt capable of launching an offensive against Israel, he would mount one; if no one was willing to receive the exiled Shah of Iran, he would welcome him; if every head of state wore his best suit when making public appearances, he would occasionally don traditional garb.

Sadat's account of his time at secondary school further illustrates this type of defiance. He passed his second-year exams, but his marks were not high enough for admission to the third year. Although he was offered the chance of spending another year improving his grades, he refused and decided to leave that school altogether. He presented his papers to another school, was accepted there for the third year and succeeded in passing his examinations. Then, in that same spirit of defiance, he took his examination papers back to his old school and was readmitted for the fourth year. He failed again at the end of the year, so he went back to the other school, where he was accepted for the fifth year, and where he took his final examination and certificate. Sadat's behaviour in jail similarly bore witness to a desire to vex his captors. All inmates received a monthly ration from the authorities, but Sadat refused to accept his and even convinced one of his friends to act likewise. He escaped from prison with five of his friends, but continued to defy the authorities and was sent back to jail.

Any perceived limitation on his free will or on the sovereignty of Egypt, which he had come to personify, any encroachment on his power or challenge to his authority, was vehemently repudiated:

Our will shall never succumb to coercion or foreign influence. No! No! . . .

Before the Revolution . . . the British were here and capitalism meddled in everything. . . . Today who can give me orders? God forbid! . . . Brezhnev said that withdrawal of Soviet troops from Egypt could affect Soviet status in the world, because it was the Soviet presence that was at stake. That was news to me! Anyone who gets a foothold may also end up sinking in the mud! What does Soviet presence mean? So, I told him: 'Take back your crews, for my own crews are ready to take over immediately. . . .'

I want the American people to listen: they consider that we are a defeated nation, just as General Custer told the leader of the Cheyenne Indians, 'You are a defeated nation, you are a backward nation, you must accept whatever we give you.' Look, I do not agree with all this. We are not a defeated nation, and we are not a backward nation. We must not accept what is offered to us! No! No![9]

Sadat identified with, and held in high esteem, others who acted in defiance. For example, he repeatedly praised the Egyptian people for refusing to capitulate after the defeat of June 1967, for standing fast behind Nasser, who had led them into that disaster and then bowed out of office. The people would not let Nasser depart, thus showing their contempt for Israel, the West and all those who had awaited and hoped for his demise. The drama of 9–10 June 1967, when crowds took to the streets of Cairo and 'forced' Nasser to rescind his resignation, was the pinnacle of defiant self-determination in Sadat's eyes. The tumult in the streets appealed to his well-developed sense of theatre.

After his release from prison in 1948, Sadat wandered around Helwan, then entered into partnership with Hassan Ezzat as a contractor. Through Ezzat he met sixteen-year-old Jihan Raouf, whom he was to marry two years later, when his divorce from Eqbal Afifi had been finalized. At first he did not tell Eqbal that he wished to divorce her, but wrote only to say that he was engaged to Jihan. According to one of his daughters, he said that he never really wanted a divorce; as a Muslim he could marry up to four wives (his father had three) and he wanted to remain married to the bride of his youth, Eqbal. When he came to the house Eqbal was understandably furious and refused to talk to him, whereupon he virtually forced her into an intimate relationship, perhaps to show her that his new bride would not stand in the way of his first marital commitment. But apparently Jihan refused to marry him unless he divorced his first wife. At Jihan's insistence, he sent a second note to Eqbal notifying her that he was divorcing her. Soon after his marriage to Jihan, he renewed contact with Eqbal and continued to look after her and their daughters. He visited the house regularly, talked to the girls, played with Camellia, who was born ten days after the divorce, and shared half of his income with them.

Elegant, young and good looking, Jihan was a fresh start for Sadat after his release from jail. She personified for him the new world to which he aspired, the other half of his torn soul which had never ceased, like Egypt herself, to wander between old tradition and the modern world; she was also strong-willed and ambitious and soon began exerting considerable influence over him. Shortly after the divorce, Madame Afifi underwent an operation, which left her unable to manage the house and raise the children on her own. Anwar Sadat therefore took his two younger daughters into his new household, much to the dislike, one may surmise, of Jihan. Rawiya and Camellia grew up with Jihan's own children, although the large age gap between the two sets of children made the relationship more maternal than sisterly. The two girls did the housework under Jihan's supervision, which created considerable bitterness between them and their stepmother. When Rawiya was fifteen and Camellia twelve and a half, marriages were arranged for them at about the same time. Both of these were to end in divorce. When married, they no longer came to visit their father at the house he shared with Jihan; instead they met him at Mit Abul-kum, or at one of his official resorts, where they could avoid the residue of friction with Jihan.

In January 1950, with the help of Hassan Kamel, his fellow trainee at the military academy who was now an officer in the Department of Personnel, Sadat was reinstated into the armed forces with the rank of captain. In this capacity he served in Rafah, northern Sinai, on the newly formed Israeli border. As he had missed the 1948–9 war, which the Arabs had declared on the day Israel was founded (15 May 1948), his new military assignment was his first opportunity to get to know his enemy.

In 1951 Sadat was contacted by Gamal Abd al-Nasser, who had taken over the leadership of the Free Officers while Sadat was in jail. Nasser had not only used the past eight years to promote the cause of revolution, but had also distinguished himself as a fighter for the Arab cause in Palestine and established himself as the undisputed leader of the young and eager club of Free Officers. Sadat rejoined the club and his comrades helped him to sit the examinations he had missed. He soon earned his promotion to lieutenant-colonel.

There is much controversy among Sadatologists as to whether Sadat rejoined the Free Officers in 1950 or late-1951, and what impact he had on the movement thereafter. One thing is certain: when Sadat relaunched himself into political activity after his military rehabilitation, he had worked out for himself a very concise view of Egyptian history; he had extremely definite views of where Egypt came from and where it should be heading.

His major preoccupation was, as always, with the British occupation and its devastating effect on the socio-economic fibre of the country. He perceived the British occupiers not only as having distorted Egyptian history by teaching that they were the progressive element of the country and that the Khedive, who had ushered them in, was the father of all Egyptians, but also as having corrupted Egyptian society by setting up a network of native 'agents' who worked for them and who were rewarded with jobs, feudal estates and cash. These corrupt notables were imposed on the Egyptian people as their leaders, while the freedom fighters like 'Urabi, Mustafa Kamel, Muhammed Farid and others down to Sadat himself were viewed as terrorists and saboteurs. He also accused the British of having distorted, beyond recognition, the facts concerning the 1919 Revolution, which had been forcefully led by Sa'ad Zaghlul, and of insisting that Egypt was an agricultural land and that the Egyptians were therefore incapable of engaging in industry, trade and banking, so that these functions should be left to foreigners to manage.

Sadat and many of his contemporaries refused to accept the British version of Egypt's recent past, and embarked on a search for what they regarded as the true history of their fatherland. They came to see their country as a victim which had been preyed upon: that since the establishment of modern Egypt at the time of Muhammed Ali, Europe had imposed its will upon it and waged war against it in an effort to stifle the spark of liberation kindled among those who had begun to recognize the nature of their plight. The scramble for Egyptian soil among Europeans had gathered momentum after the digging of the Suez Canal. Under the Khedives the country had deteriorated and had been forced to borrow money, so that all services had been mortgaged to foreign capital. Britain had emerged as the victorious occupier after she had bought the Suez Canal shares, entrenching herself in the country and making Egypt yet another state in her vast empire. Sadat and his colleagues discovered that, in reality, Ahmad 'Urabi had been a national hero who had tried to challenge foreign influence and in so doing had accurately reflected popular sentiment. He had advocated an elected Egyptian parliament, an Egyptian government and a national army free of foreign patronage. They also found out that Mustafa Kamel, though he had not succeeded in expelling the British, had nevertheless fanned the flames of Egyptian patriotism. They discovered that Muhammed Farid had been the first to organize workers' associations and to found schools with the aim of eliminating illiteracy. He had pursued his struggle until overtaken by the advent of the First World War. They ascertained that the 1919 Revolution, far from being an act of sabotage, had on the contrary signalled the first national revolution against the imperialism and the hegemony of the victorious and arrogant allies. Sa'ad Zaghlul, an Egyptian peasant, had been the first to head the constitutional Government; his overthrow had actually been part of another plot by the British and their agents to break Egyptian patriotism.

According to Sadat's analysis, it was the Egyptian people, whose civilization dated back 7,000 years, who were to be credited with Egypt's many achievements in the face of adversity: the expansion of national consciousness, the spread of education, and the growth of an ideological-revolutionary movement, which was to serve as an example to the entire area. The first modern Egyptian institute of higher learning, Cairo University, came into being and a popular movement, led by Tala'at Harb, established the first Egyptian banks and industries, breaking the colonialist monopoly and disproving the disparaging claim that Egyptians were incapable of assimilating modern methods of production and investment. Like all leaders of colonized nations, Sadat blamed Egypt's backwardness on colonial oppression. He advanced the thesis that, had Egypt not been torn apart by eighty years of occupation, the country would today have attained the standards of the occupying power, Great Britain. Sadat credited the modern Egyptian state, under Muhammed Ali, with the development of a strong army, an advanced munitions industry, a navy, military academies, textile factories, faculties for teaching modern sciences, free education at all levels, and even a legislative council which preceded most parliaments in Europe. Following the 'Urabi revolt, however, the British and the Khedives had decided to dismantle the army and to close down armament and other factories. Sadat accused the British and their Egyptian underlings of having dissolved the navy, leaving only the royal yacht, of having reduced the budgets allocated to education, and of having closed down many schools and faculties, including all military colleges and most of the technical schools and institutions.

Far from reckoning that his country's inherent weaknesses had allowed colonization to occur, Sadat attributed the West's scramble for Egypt to its very attractive treasures, human and material. He said that the great powers had not wanted a strong and influential Egypt to emerge in the Middle East, so they had conspired against it to reduce it to submission. In fact, Sadat saw all modern Egyptian history as a succession of plots by foreign powers to subvert and humiliate Egypt. For him that process had begun when Muhammed Ali had been beaten in 1840, had continued through the British occupation of 1882, the establishment of Israel in 1948 and the wars of 1956 and 1967. Sadat felt resentment towards the victorious Allies of the Second World War, because he felt that they had repeated their trickery of the First World War by making empty promises to people during the war in order to win their support. Under British occupation, lamented Sadat, the Egyptian constitution had become a piece of paper that had nothing to do with reality; political parties in Egypt were dissolved and dismembered. After the Second World War, the national struggle had deteriorated into scattered demonstrations and window-breaking. The camps and prisons were filled with political detainees, and the national product of Egypt – cotton – had become an object of speculation, bribery and corruption. To add to the confusion, the 1948 war broke out as a result of the establishment of Israel, which Sadat and his contemporaries regarded as a dagger driven by the imperialist foes into Egypt's heart.

The concerned youth of Sadat's generation turned to overt and covert activities against the regime and against the British. But ideologies ranged from extreme Right to extreme Left and confusion reigned supreme. Fighting broke out in the villages between peasants and feudal landlords, but the shaky regime dragged on until a time came when no government was able to hold out for more than a few weeks. Sadat and others were leading a life of resistance, jail, persecution, humiliation and slavery, until the select group of Free Officers, Sadat a prominent participating member, devised a way to stop the decline and restore honour to their homeland. They would risk death rather than accept failure. The bitter defeat of the Egyptian army during the Palestinian war of 1948–9 aggravated their sense of humiliation and made change all the more urgent.

Those were Sadat's thoughts when, one morning in December 1951, a special session of the Free Officers was held and Nasser was elected chairman for a second term. (He had originally been elected to the same post in January 1951.) Every one of the officers knew that Sadat, as one of the main contacts between the Free Officers and the Muslim Brotherhood in 1939–40, had been pressed by Hassan al-Banna to incorporate the group into the Muslim Brotherhood; but Sadat had rejected the idea because he was loath to tie his fledgling organization to any particular group, party, stratum or individual. He wanted his movement to gain wide popular support when the time for action came and he feared that identification with a particular party line or ideology might limit the movement's appeal. All knew too that while Sadat was in jail Nasser had taken over, organizing lodges throughout the major army units until he had emerged as the undisputed leader. Nasser had maintained a marriage of convenience with the Muslim Brothers, but he too would not let them encroach upon his officers' independence. Sadat accepted without reserve Nasser's leadership and was to remain loyal to him until his last day in September 1970. Sadat, resigned to a secondary role under Nasser, dutifully channelled all his revolutionary zeal and propensity for defiance and confrontation into whatever role Nasser entrusted to him.

At that December 1951 session, the officers decided that their *coup* to seize power in Cairo would take place in November 1955. One month later, in January 1952, Nasser attempted to precipitate the revolution, probably because of British armed attacks against Egyptian police in Isma'iliyya and the mass killings which resulted there (21 January 1952). But the *coup* had to be postponed until November 1952 when the units loyal to the Free Officers could be brought nearer to Cairo. In the meantime, Egyptian underground activity against the British was stepped up in the Suez Canal Zone, and backed up by rioting in the streets of Cairo. British soldiers in the Canal Zone became the targets of Muslim Brotherhood *fedayeen* (fighters prepared to sacrifice themselves for their cause), who were aided by Free Officers. Sadat himself had helped train some of these zealots, who were as fanatically anti-British as himself.

November was selected for the *coup* because King Farouq, the symbol of the *ancien régime* and the main target of the revolution, would then be on holiday in Alexandria and would not be due back in Cairo until the autumn. They also

35

hoped that their sympathizer, General Naguib, would be appointed war minister before then, as this would facilitate their takeover of the Government. However, when the King appointed his brother-in-law, Ismail Shirin, as Minister of War on 20 July 1952, the Free Officers feared that the new appointee might set out to annihilate their movement, so Nasser decided to act without delay on 23 July. Nasser's reasoning was simple and to the point: 'We must wipe out the new War Minister lest he wipe us out.' Sadat later commented, 'If we did not save our one eye, we lost both.' The stakes were high and the enthusiasm great. Some 3,000 soldiers and 200 officers loyal to the Free Officers were to start the revolution at midnight on 22 July.

Sadat's role, as assigned to him by Nasser, was apparently to cut off telephone communications in Cairo that night. But when Sadat arrived in Cairo on 22 July, no one met him at the station. He appears to have thought that some snag had occurred, causing postponement of the *coup*, for he took Jihan to an open-air cinema and watched three movies in a row, unaware of the momentous events which were taking place in his absence. Much scorn was later poured on Sadat, by his opposition critics, for his lack of revolutionary activity, especially as Nasser had been able to take over Cairo without Sadat even knowing, which in his critics' eyes showed how insignificant he was. Be that as it may, the rebel troops occupied military headquarters, airports, telecommunications centres and Cairo's broadcasting station. Sadat found a message from Nasser when he returned home after midnight. He took his personal weapon and rushed to join his command at army headquarters. Sadat watched the army units marching into Cairo and, at 7 a.m. on 23 July, he made the first announcement of the *coup* on Radio Cairo on behalf of the Revolutionary Council, which was now in charge of the country.

On 26 July, Sadat accompanied General Naguib, who had been elected as the figurehead of the revolution because of his personal renown, to Alexandria, where they handed the Prime Minister, Ali Maher, an ultimatum calling on the King to leave the country that same day. The King yielded to military pressure and the *ancien régime* came to an end.

4

A DORMANT VOLCANO

Imagine a young enthusiastic Sadat, fuming over Egypt's problems, openly hating Britain and Israel, prepared to confront the world and defy the universe, suddenly being pushed aside and reduced to political insignificance. His revolutionary dreams had been realized on 23 July 1952, but his own ability to carry things through had been blunted. From now on he would take part in the Revolutionary Council deliberations but all wheeling and dealing, all major decisions, all public admiration, all the limelight, would be Nasser's. Sadat must have thought his political role was as good as finished: Nasser was the same age as him, in good health, popular, the unchallenged leader of the revolution. Sadat's chances of replacing him or sharing power must have seemed so slender as to be non-existent, especially when Abdul Hakim Amer, another Free Officer, became Nasser's choice as his second in command.

Sadat loved and admired Nasser, and was deeply loyal to him. He felt that Nasser's stance against the British and the world, his defiance of Israel and his revolutionizing of Egyptian society, was the only feasible way. After he became President, Sadat often spoke of his 'hundred per cent responsibility' for the revolution and all Nasser's deeds. And this was no mere figure of speech, for every member of the Revolutionary Council, including Sadat, ended up by yielding to Nasser's will. In fact, Sadat told an interesting story about the first days of the revolution, when Nasser wished to resign:

After the King had been dethroned, the first thing Nasser did at a Revolutionary Council meeting was to resign its chairmanship, saying, 'The first phase of the revolution has been successful, so I must resign so that you can elect a new Council chairman.' He did this, although he had been elected unanimously to the chairmanship of the Constituting Committee before the revolution. The seven of us who were present objected, because we thought that he should automatically assume the chairmanship of the Council. But he insisted, a secret ballot was taken and Gamal was unanimously re-elected. But another surprise awaited us: we had thought that with Nasser's unanimous re-election, the problem would be settled, for the King had been removed and overnight we had become responsible for affairs of state. But he said, 'No, there is another issue I wish to bring up, namely what sort of government shall we adopt? A dictatorship or a democracy? Since you have elected me to the chairmanship of the Council, you must tell me whether I am to conduct our affairs in democratic or dictatorial fashion!' The seven of us, including myself, spoke in favour of dictatorship, claiming that the only way to eliminate oppression and corruption was by dictatorial means and that we had to set up gallows in the main squares to execute traitors who had betrayed the people. . . .

But Nasser insisted on democracy and on avoiding bloodshed, for fear that popular sentiment might turn against the revolution. The vote was taken, and Nasser found himself outvoted by the other members of the Revolutionary Council; he resigned and went home, only to return, on his terms, after his colleagues had implored him to come back because they felt lost without him. Sadat told this story in a speech delivered on 28 September 1971, the first anniversary of Nasser's death. It is ironic that Sadat, who boasted about his democratic propensities, was willing to admit to pro-dictatorial leanings at the outbreak of the revolution, while Nasser, who was to rule with a firm grip for eighteen years, was the one to insist on democracy. This story shows how indispensable Nasser was during those early days and how unwilling his fellow officers were – either from diffidence or fear – to take his place, once he had resigned. Sadat too, like all the others, had yielded to Nasser's strong will and had accepted him as leader.

All that Sadat could do now was to restrain his zeal for action, channel his energy into writing, reflect on the revolution and its extraordinary achievements and fulfil whatever role Nasser assigned to him. Sadat always delighted in recalling those early revolutionary days, especially 26 July, when they defied the British Chargé d'Affaires after they had forced the King to abdicate and leave the country.

We were at the Mustafa Pasha military barracks, when we were surprised by the sudden appearance of the British Chargé d'Affaires, the Ambassador being on leave. He came in convoy, as the British did in those days, accompanied by his Military Attaché. He pulled out a document and started reading it. He put forward two demands: first, that we should guarantee the safety of the Muhammed Ali family; secondly, that we should announce a curfew, in order to protect foreigners. . . . He thought that everything would continue as before, when the old politicians had been in charge. He was stunned when we questioned Britain's authority to speak for Muhammed Ali's family. We told him that Muhammed Ali's family had ruled Egypt until 23 July, 9.00 a.m., and that now King Farouq had abdicated in favour of his son. What had that to do with Britain?

We told him that curfews were our concern. We also asked him if his demands were officially submitted by the British Government, as had been the case in the past, or not? The Chargé d'Affaires and the Military Attaché were stunned. After half an hour's argument, they retracted their words and said, 'We just came to give you some friendly advice; it is neither official nor meant as interference. 'So he who had arrived inflated with self-importance departed deflated and stupefied. . . . I think that at that meeting Britain at last learnt that Egypt had turned over a new leaf on 23 July 1952, that the new people in charge in Egypt knew no fear, were aware of their responsibility, proud of the independence of their country, and well able to ignore imperial demands . . . they did not quail when faced with British threats or 'advice'. . . .[10]

In this speech, which was made more than twenty years later, one can still detect Sadat's excitement at his defiance of the British Chargé d'Affaires, showing that a new Egypt had been born. Up until that time, he had used his old village family name of Sadati; he then dropped the final 'i' and began calling himself Sadat. Perhaps he considered himself reborn too.

Sadat's time in jail had taught him acquiescence and endurance, so he was able to accept his existence on the fringes of the new political set-up. When he disagreed with revolutionary policies or became disgusted with the Free Officers' squabbles, he simply stepped aside, watched and waited. In December 1953, he resigned from the Revolutionary Council and founded *Al-Gumhuriyya* (*The Republic*), a daily journal dedicated to becoming the mouthpiece of the revolution. He later served for a year (1954–5) in one of Nasser's cabinets as a minister of state and member of the Council, but then again stepped aside or was dropped by Nasser, being either unable to make his mark on policies or exasperated by continued jealousies among his colleagues. His seemingly passive role in Egyptian politics won him the derogatory nickname 'Bikbashi Sahh' ('Colonel Yes'), as he was supposed to utter an approving '*sahh*' ('correct') for everything and anything he heard. In November 1954, Sadat was appointed a member of the 'People's Tribunal' which tried those Muslim Brothers and their sympathizers who had allegedly plotted to overthrow the regime. Once Sadat had admired the Brotherhood, but now he turned against them.

In 1955, while he was a minister of state without portfolio in Nasser's cabinet, Sadat was also appointed Secretary General of the Islamic Congress, founded by the Egyptian revolutionary regime to advance the cause of Egypt's leadership in the Islamic world, the third circle in Nasser's 'Philosophy of the Revolution'. Sadat travelled extensively during these years and became much more aware, not only of the world in general, but in particular of the immense political potential inherent in the Islamic *Umma* (the congregation of those who follow the Prophet) if it could only be brought together under one unified leadership. Furthermore, he met many international statesmen and took a great interest in their various styles of leadership. This is what he said about meeting Nehru:

> On my way back from Indonesia, I stopped in India, which was headed by Nehru. . . . Nehru gave a party in my honour and when he introduced the guests, a man and a woman who were members of the Indian Congress approached me. Both were members of the House of Representatives, the lower house in the Indian Congress, and I had met both when they had visited Cairo, and had maintained contact with them. They were members of the Communist Party. At that time, the Communists used to attack Nehru vitriolically and never spared his government either. Nehru introduced them to me, but I mentioned that I knew them already. I saw both of them embracing and kissing Nehru, even though he warned me in their

presence: 'I am telling you that they might Bolshevize you and make you a Communist.' Even though those two were in opposition and caused Nehru trouble, they kissed him on his cheek in my presence, as he was the father of India. When I returned to Cairo in 1955, our struggles within the Revolutionary Council were at their peak. So I resigned, but I mentioned Nehru in my letter of resignation. I said that in India there were more than ten languages, more than twenty religions and more than a score of peoples and races, and its population had reached 400 million people. Nevertheless, they all shared the same values, despite their differences in language, religion, faith, race and origin because Nehru was seen to be the father of India, the head of the family. For this reason, the 400 million people of India were a united country, on the lines of a family system. I submitted my resignation in 1955 and the members of the Revolutionary Council engaged me in debate. But I told them that it was natural for young people of the same age and the same rank who were members of the same Revolutionary Council, to squabble among themselves.[11]

Upon his resignation, Sadat returned to *Al-Gumhuriyya*, the revolutionary journal in which he delighted to write. He had apparently relished his brief pre-revolutionary experience as a journalist and now found pride and satisfaction in editing an influential newspaper: he discovered the power of the pen and the great importance of the media in a regime like Nasser's. He learned that in this totalitarian regime which he openly supported, the controlled press was less a reflection of the regime than a tool for shaping public opinion. Control of the media meant control over the minds of the people and a monopoly over their revolutionary indoctrination. In one of his later speeches, he said that only two months after *Al-Gumhuriyya* was first published, an editorial appeared under a pen-name, which dealt with Egypt's affiliation with the Arab world. That editorial had been written by Nasser in person. In 1976 Sadat again talked about his years as head of the *Al-Gumhuriyya* publishing house:

In those days, we were in financial difficulties so we suggested that those contributors who did not write regularly should be paid by the piece. Then, it was decided that salaries would be paid according to each writer's average production. A certain colleague who earned a low average on his production encountered a subsistence problem because he had a big family to provide for, plus the children of his brother who had died. He endured terrible hardship and found fault with the evaluation of his average. As the head of the publishing house, I received a letter from him, full of expletives. . . . It was beautifully written, but was replete with insults, frightening in its provocation. At the end of the letter he wrote, 'This is my address; I assume that I'll be arrested, so have my address.' I inquired into this and learned that the man had been discriminated against. Three days later, during which time the poor journalist could not sleep, fearing arrest after all the insults he'd hurled at me, I sent him a reply. He was surprised to receive my answer instead of being arrested by police. My hand-written answer consisted of two lines: 'Come back to work, but should what you did recur, you will not be permitted to return to your job. . . .' The man was Abd al-Tawab Abd al-Hayy, a journalist who is still around. That was at the beginning of the revolution, when people were scared to speak up. I sympathized with his feelings because I was myself a journalist.[12]

The final evacuation of the British from the Canal Zone in June 1956, the dissolution of the Revolutionary Council, the concentration of the supreme executive power in the hands of the newly-elected President under the new constitution, the confrontation with Secretary of State Dulles, the Suez crisis and then the ensuing Sinai War, all helped to place Nasser firmly on the Egyptian stage as the sole holder of the monopoly of power in the country. Sadat's and other senior revolutionaries' stature inevitably shrank as a result. However, Sadat always expressed admiration for Nasser's handling of the British and other powers and for the swift way in which he had dispossessed foreign firms to return Egypt to the Egyptians. Many years later, Sadat wrote:

As for myself, I sat, followed and listened. For a common peasant like me, to have a good friend of [Nasser's] calibre is something to be proud of. Far from envying him, I felt part of him. He won the battle with his historic decision [to withdraw Egyptian forces from the Sinai] on 31 October 1956. . . .[13]

After Egypt and Syria united early in 1958, Nasser nominated Sadat as the Speaker of the joint Parliament, a fiction that was soon dissipated when, in 1961, the union dissolved. In 1962 Sadat, together with Vice-President Amer, made a fact-finding tour of the Yemen to determine the amount of Egyptian aid required by the rebels who had deposed their feudal *Imam* who had been backed by the Saudi monarchy. Sadat and Amer recommended a limited involvement, but it gradually grew from a 3,000-men brigade to an expedition-ary force of 60,000, including some of Egypt's crack troops. (The disastrous Yemen involvement was only finally brought to an end by Egypt's defeat in the 1967 war against Israel.) In 1966, Sadat was elected Speaker of the Egyptian Parliament, a largely ceremonial position in a House which rubber-stamped Nasser's every whim. But Sadat continued to accumulate expertise in foreign affairs from his missions abroad. He joined a delegation, headed by Nasser, to the USSR in late 1966 which attempted to alleviate Egypt's burden of debt to the Soviet Union for the large quantities of weapons bought during the past decade, both to replenish Egyptian losses in the 1956 war and to sustain Egypt's military effort in the Yemen. Proud Sadat must have found it humiliating to have to admit his country's dismal economic situation, exposing the abysmal gap between what the revolution had promised and what existed in reality. Above all, he must have hated having to publicize the fact that Egypt had merely substituted dependence on Britain for dependence on Russia. Nor can he have found his mission to the US in 1966 any more pleasant. He met President Johnson and Secretary of State Rusk and tried to impress upon them what he saw as the inherent danger in the supply of American arms to Israel. But 'their eyes failed to see and their ears to listen'. Exasperated, he turned his frustrations into a deep dislike of President Johnson which bordered on the irrational. As a shadow-politician, there was little else Sadat could do to give vent to his emotions.

Then came the disaster of June 1967. The Arab armies suffered one of the most shattering defeats in their history in six days. Nasser resigned on 9 June, but was called back by popular demand, although he had nominated the amiable, pro-Western Zakarya Muhyi a-Din as his successor. Nasser survived the disaster, but many of Egypt's top leaders, notably Amer, who had been Nasser's heir for many years, were now tried and convicted for their part in the alleged conspiracy against Nasser's regime.

Sadat had attended cabinet meetings and consultations with President Nasser from the moment it became clear on 1 June 1967 that war was inevitable; he had also, according to his own account, participated in briefings with the top Sinai field commanders. Sadat also heard Amer's self-confident assertions that his troops were ready for combat and witnessed Nasser's approval of the military plan on 2 June.

Therefore, when news reached Sadat on 6 June that Israel had launched her offensive, he was euphoric, certain of a quick and decisive Egyptian victory. He listened to the Egyptian military communiqués which announced that Israeli aeroplanes were being shot down, and heard the number of 'hits' increasing with every communiqué. Sadat later recalled that he remained calm until he entered Field-Marshal Amer's room. There, he found the Commander-in-Chief so stunned that it took him a few moments to notice his uninvited guest's presence. When Sadat asked what had happened, Amer replied that the entire Egyptian air force had been wiped out on the ground and that the air force commander was sitting in his headquarters weeping. Stricken by despair, Sadat shut himself up in his study from 5 June until the 9th, trying to work out the reasons for Egypt's unexpected and unjustified defeat: unexpected, because of the self-confidence that the top army command had radiated about its military plans before the war; unjustified, because the sheer quantities of hardware and manpower in the Egyptian camp did not, could not, provide any rationale for the rout. In fact, as Sadat later remembered, when he met President Podgorny and Defence Minister Zakharov, who had raced to Cairo from the Soviet Union after the defeat to find out what had happened, Zakharov sarcastically remarked that if all Egyptian weapons had fired only once Israel would have collapsed. Sadat knew this was true, for he had read a UN report published in 1967 which gave the Egyptian armed forces the second highest rate of arms *per capita* in the world; only the US army had more.

Sadat stayed at home, avidly read the world press and its accounts of the war, and sank into a depression from which he would take weeks to recover. In the meantime, Jihan visited wounded servicemen, and from her reports he learned that morale was very low. He also learnt that among the wounded at the Ma'adi Hospital lay Kamal Hassan Ali, the commander of an armoured brigade in Sinai; Sadat went to talk to him. On 7 June, Ali had launched a counter-attack at the head of his well-equipped and adequately trained troops. He made the point to Sadat that Israel had no 'secret weapon'; that he lost the battle because of confusion and lack of leadership. He said that he and his hundred tanks had wandered in the Sinai desert for two days, going back and forth; whenever he arrived somewhere, he found an order to move elsewhere. On 7 June he had encountered an Israeli armoured battalion which he had attacked despite having no orders, causing the Israelis casualties and forcing them to retreat. Whereupon, the Israeli air force swept in and destroyed twenty of his tanks, although he had managed to shoot down some of the attacking aeroplanes with his anti-aircraft guns. The Israeli air force had then descended upon Ali's brigade and destroyed all its tanks one by one, until he himself was hit with a missile. Ali's report to Sadat was confirmed by other officers in the hospital, who claimed that they had received no clear orders from their superiors.

Sadat took notice of all that he had learned. When he was preparing for the 1973 October War, he laid great emphasis on the need for planning and clear orders when briefing troops. He also made Kamal Hassan Ali his Minister of Defence and later on his Deputy Prime Minister and Foreign Minister.

But now, on Friday, 9 June 1967, Sadat heard reports that Israeli troops had crossed to the west bank of the Suez Canal. Humiliated by the numbness and resignation that he sensed around him, he decided to act. He went home, packed his personal effects, left orders about how his property was to be distributed among his children should he not return, and headed for Nasser's house. The volcano had erupted; with Nasser at his lowest ebb, Sadat felt that the time had come for action. Egypt should not wait until the Israelis (the Jews, in Sadat's parlance) reached Cairo; Egypt must go out and fight. He found Nasser seated at his desk, writing his letter of resignation:

SADAT: Why are you sitting there so complacently? You must leave for Upper Egypt, where you will continue to be the symbol of our uprising, while we remain here to fight. We shall prepare the people for guerilla warfare, in the Sharqiyah and Suez districts, and fight the Israelis face to face.

NASSER: Why do you want to act in this fashion?

SADAT: Didn't you hear the announcement from the military headquarters that the Jews have crossed to the west bank of the Canal?

NASSER: Did you fall into the same trap as everyone else? Sit down and listen to the truth: when I heard that announcement, I sent someone to check it out. I am told that those at military headquarters, who have lost their nerve, rushed to publish that communiqué because one of our officers, who had fought east of the Canal, has withdrawn westwards. When he realized that the Jews had pursued him to the east bank of the Canal, he got excited and fired his mortar at them. They reacted by sending in an air strike. Within less than one minute, they had bombed the 'Jadid' paint factory that was about to open west of Isma'iliyya. They bombed that factory, but our useless headquarters thought that the Jews had crossed the Canal, and so they issued that communiqué. I heard the announcement but attached no importance to it, because the Jews would not cross the Canal. Their coordinated plan with President Johnson called for my personal elimination, so when they reached the Canal's east bank, the war was won as far as they were concerned. I began reasoning as they themselves probably would. Johnson has achieved what he wanted, therefore they would not cross and venture into the densely populated areas.

When Nasser appeared on national television that Friday to announce his resignation to a stunned nation, he was seen to look to his left; at that moment, a message was handed to him, signed by the top Soviet leadership, the 'Troika', urging him not to resign and assuring him that they would ship anything he wanted to resupply the Egyptian army. Nasser refused to stop speaking or to alter what he had to say; he just continued to the end, to his resignation. The Soviets, however, did mount a huge air and sealift and delivered substantial shipments of hardware between June and July 1967. But it was not enough, for the Egyptians were hard pressed even to hold a new defence line along the Canal. Nasser sent two or three impassioned pleas to the Soviet leadership asking for more, but received no answer: the 'Troika' were enjoying themselves at their holiday *dachas* by the Black Sea.

Sadat, like Nasser, was incensed by the lack of Soviet support at a time of Egyptian suffering. So when, on 10 August, President Tito of Yugoslavia visited Alexandria to offer Nasser his condolences, the latter angrily urged Tito, in Sadat's presence, to go to the Kremlin and tell them that Israeli occupation of his country would be preferable to the treatment that the 'Troika' were meting out. At a later date, during the 1968–70 War of Attrition, the Soviets also refused to replenish Egypt's stocks of ammunition, because, they said, Nasser was involved in a war that they had not approved. He was furious with them and so was Sadat. By July 1972 he had become so exasperated by their condescension that he finally decided to expel them from Egypt.

Sadat, like Nasser, was even more incensed by the US, which was known to be pumping blood into Israel's arteries and was seen by many Egyptians to be an accomplice in the Arabs' humiliating defeat. Sadat was later openly to accuse the US of having actively participated in the 1967 war by lending electronic weaponry to Israel. But he was particularly hurt by insinuations he detected in American statements suggesting that Egypt was incapable of putting up a fight; he saw such comments as attempts to undermine the morale of the Egyptian people in general and their armed forces in particular. President Johnson was seen as the epitome of evil, since he had given his assent to the 1967 war before it broke out and thus failed to honour his May 1967 pledge guaranteeing territorial integrity to all Middle Eastern countries. Sadat comforted himself with the thought that, if the US had failed against the Vietnamese despite their mighty weaponry, then Egyptian resistance, which was no less resilient, would prevail in the end.

What was worse in Sadat's eyes than the individual conduct of the USSR and the US was their mutual agreement to look after their own interests at Egypt's expense. After the 'dark summer of 1967', when Egypt lay injured and exhausted, its pride and honour dashed, Nasser made an official request, to which Sadat agreed, that the USSR should take over responsibility for Egypt's air defence, placing it under the command of a Soviet general. An official meeting was held in Cairo, during the visit of Podgorny and Zakharov in June, at which Sadat was present. Sadat explained that he had agreed to Nasser's request on that occasion because Israel enjoyed a decisive air superiority, while Egypt's air force was practically non-existent. Podgorny agreed to Nasser's plea, and Sadat, like his President, emerged from the meeting sighing with relief; for they both thought that Egypt would now be able to devote time, energy and resources to rebuilding its shattered armed forces under a Soviet air-defence umbrella. This had now become essential because Israel was sending in reconnaissance planes which, because Egypt had no air defences, moved at will across Egyptian skies. But Sadat's sense of relief was not to last. That same evening he received a telephone call from Nasser informing him that he had seen Podgorny again, at the latter's urgent insistence, and been told that the Soviet Union could not possibly take over Egyptian air defence, even if it were to be under Soviet command. Sadat attributed this *volte-face* to the Glasborough meeting between President Johnson and Prime Minister Kosygin which had taken place that morning: the two chief executives had clearly come to some tacit agreement about the Middle East.

As Sadat became increasingly involved in political activity, albeit in Nasser's shadow, he shed his tendency to withdraw and eagerly immersed himself in state affairs. In the face of adversity, his sturdy qualities of defiance, endurance and confrontation surfaced. He felt that although Egypt had been badly beaten militarily, Israel and the US had failed to break the willpower of the people. All that was needed was to rebuild the armed forces with Soviet assistance, for want of a better alternative, reconstruct Egypt's self-confidence and strengthen the nation's will to make sacrifices. In the 1968–70 War of Attrition, Egypt scored some gains, and inflicted some losses on Israel, notably the sinking of the destroyer *Eilat* in October 1967; this boosted Sadat's morale, reinforcing his defiance. Sadat also drew encouragement from the massive demonstrations in Cairo in favour of Nasser's remaining in power, despite the defeat. To him these demonstrations were not acts of despair, nor a desire to hang on to an idol of yesteryear, but the Egyptian people's ultimate rejection of Israel and the US. In Sadat's analysis, the masses were actually telling Nasser, 'Don't worry about one accidental slip, let's start all over again and march forward.'

Nasser now proceeded to reformulate Egypt's two-pronged long-term objectives: to retrieve all lands occupied by Israel, including Jerusalem, the

West Bank, the Syrian Plateau and Sinai; and to stand by the Palestinians until they recovered their lost rights. Palestinian rights were seen by Nasser not only in humanitarian and moral terms, but in terms of Arab nationalism and history; wrong must be redressed. Sadat also firmly believed that nothing could alter Egypt's commitment to these two long-term objectives; they were part of Egypt's destiny. Revolutions in the Sudan in May 1969 and in Libya in September 1969 gave Egypt new allies on her southern and western frontiers, strengthening Sadat's determination. Viewed in retrospect, Sadat looked at the 1967 defeat as the source of a new vitality in the Arab world, the turning-point for a new upsurge.

The 1967 war led to painful soul-searching in all Arab countries. 'What had gone wrong?' Scathing self-condemnatory books, articles and speeches appeared, there were demonstrations and public trials, all of which sought to put the blame for the defeat on someone or something: everyone wallowed in a masochistic orgy of self-deprecation. The result was a remarkable revival of Islam and Islamic values throughout Arab society, including Egypt. An international conference on Islam and the Arab–Israeli conflict was held in Cairo in 1968 under the auspices of Al-Azhar University, where one Muslim scholar after another came to the conclusion that if only Muslims returned to the path of Islam, the 'glorious defeat' of 1967, as one of them bitterly termed it, could be turned into a long-overdue national catharsis. The Muslim Brothers in Egypt took advantage of this mood to reappear, confident that the discredited regime would hardly dare to crack down on them, especially as it now depended on the financial aid of such upright Muslims as the Saudis. Pro-Islamic fervour even gripped Nasser himself: for years he had ordered the Prophet's birthday celebrations to be strictly controlled in case religious fervour got out of hand, but now he appeared before the celebrating crowds in person, joining with them in remembering Muhammed's great feats. Sadat kept to the same pattern in later years, delivering a major speech, playing on the crowds' frenzy to lash out at Israel on purely Islamic grounds, making use of a whole range of Islamic symbols which harped on the people's frustrations today in contrast to the grandeur and glory of the past. This resurgence of faith encouraged Sadat to widen his religious outlook: he became less preoccupied with the personal, friendly Allah he had come to know in jail and more aware of his embodiment in the community as a whole.

Somehow the trauma of the 1967 defeat, coupled with the people's violent demonstrations, made Sadat equate *vox populi* with *vox dei*. Thereafter, he stood in awe of the masses, engaged in dialogue with them, drew inspiration from them and created a mystical link between himself and them. On more than one occasion, he said to his people, 'You are, after Allah, my source of encouragement, stamina, and inspiration.'

This close communion between the people and Allah was to acquire far-reaching implications for Sadat's sense of mission when he became President.

For if he was elected by popular will and popular will was Allah-inspired, then his election to government took on the aura of a divine mission. He repeatedly spoke of his faith in Allah and his mission, and of Destiny which had entrusted him with the sacred duty of leading his community. He frequently voiced his admiration for the faith which was a 'tremendous source of power inherent in our people, guiding them on their way'; the faith of his 'noble people, which was a faith in Allah, his Holy Book and his Messenger'; faith in 'righteousness, justice, peace and forgiveness which drives people to build, not to destroy, to unite not to dismember'. It was this faith which led him to believe that his people could and must 'eliminate the consequences of Israeli aggression' (the 1967 war in Sadat's parlance). Since the willpower of his people came from Allah, it was bound to defeat the 'invaders' despite their technology, weapons and alleged superiority. Egyptian weapons supplemented by faith must ultimately win.

After 1967 Sadat was much more openly pious than before. His Islamic background in Mit Abul-kum had certainly contributed to the make-up of his personality; and his experience in jail had further shaped the image of Allah in his own mind and the relationship between himself and God. Statecraft added yet another dimension to his piety: it marked a transition from passivity and resignation, in the face of Allah's will, to a militant and active striving; a search for manifestations of Allah, something like *Aide-toi, Dieu t'aidera*. He no longer saw faith as an individual belief, a personal way of living, but now perceived it as society's source of strength and cohesion, a potent weapon in war, a tool for national and inter-Arab unity, a rationale to explain historical events:

> Allah has ordained us to believe. I order you to believe. We all need to fill our hearts with faith, in addition to the weapons we are carrying, so that we may enter the battle with faith, so that we may reach the standard of responsibility and of the mission that Allah has ordained. . . . In battle, the Prophet Muhammed has equipped us with the most potent weapon – faith. It has always given us the upper hand. . . . Arab unity (the Federation with Syria and Libya) is part of the campaign we are waging for the sake of Arab honour. We are motivated by faith and the mission that the prophet has destined for us.[14]

In consequence, Allah became omnipresent and immediate, not transcendental and remote. From now on, Sadat uttered the name of Allah more frequently and more noticeably. He hardly ever made a speech without the name of Allah being mentioned somewhere; or without beginning or ending with a quotation from the Holy Quran, the Word of Allah. He thanked Allah that the Saudi mediation between Iraq and Syria had succeeded, called his troops the 'soldiers of Allah', or prayed to Allah during his public addresses:

> Allah forgive us if we have forgotten or been led astray. . . . Allah, do not overburden us the way you did to our predecessors! Allah, do not burden us with

more than we can bear. Forgive us! You are our God! Grant us victory over the unbelievers!

I pray to Allah that He may let our martyrs dwell in the House of the Righteous and that He guard you until you complete your mission. . . . May peace be with you with Allah's compassion. . . .[15]

Later on, during his presidency, Sadat came to see the 1973 conflict with Israel in terms of faith. For Israel was not only perceived as denying the Arabs their rights and territories, but as endeavouring to shatter their faith. In his words:

This is a period of mighty trial, first and foremost for our faith, the faith of the Mission of the Prophet. We find ourselves in the most difficult ordeal of our lives. They want to shatter our faith. Psychological warfare is being waged against us, claiming that we cannot stand up to the Israelis. . . . They all forget that we are the standard bearers of the Mission of Muhammed. They forget that Muhammed did not submit and he remained steadfast. . . . We are carrying on his mission and pursuing its purpose today. We believe that Allah is on our side. . . .[16]

And after the war: 'I was certain that Allah would be on our side, for He supports all devoted believers who seek His help. . . .'[17] No wonder the Egyptian army war-cry during October 1973 was '*Allah Akbar*' (Allah is great); that 'eye-witness' stories abounded in the Egyptian press from those who had 'seen' the Prophet Muhammed riding a white horse, crossing the Suez Canal with the Egyptian troops leading the way before him. Ecstatic Egyptian troops then defied Israeli fire, stormed Israeli defences and, under the cry '*Allah Akbar*', hoisted the Egyptian flag on the shattered Bar-lev Line.★ Sadat had exhorted his troops, as the 'soldiers of Allah', to strive for 'Allah's victory', because 'all victories emanate from Allah'; and they delivered. Sadat, in fact, attested after the war that 'Allah's presence hovered above us on 6 October'. Furthermore, he tended to equate the people's will with Allah's will, not only in the case of Muslims, but also with other people striving for liberation. For example, he viewed the fact that the Americans were taking a beating in Vietnam as an act of God, because 'it is obvious that the will of the people is the will of Allah'.

Sadat saw a link between the intervention of providence and unfolding events. To be sure, Muslim thinking had always attributed all to Allah. Even natural phenomena such as sunrise and sunset, winter and summer, rain and drought, were credited in Islam to Allah's will rather than to the pre-ordained cycle of life. But the Sadat of the post-1967 era went further than that: he directly imputed to Allah's will any happening, good deed, sound policy or turn of events which worked in his, or his people's, favour. Allah came to be perceived as a close overseer of everyday life; Sadat saw his successes and his sheer good fortune as daily evidence of Allah's involvement. For example, he

★The line of defence, built by the Israelis during the War of Attrition along the east bank of the Suez Canal. It was named after the then Israeli Chief of Staff, General Haim Bar-lev.

thanked Allah for having destined one of the superpowers (the Soviet Union) to support the Arab cause, despite the implicit irony (Allah sponsoring a Marxist regime). He attributed to Allah the abundant crops with which Egypt had been blessed from 1968 to 1970, interpreting such a bonanza as a mark of Allah's support for the Arabs and the Egyptians.

However, if 'Allah is free to determine what He wills and one cannot help conforming to His will', as Sadat properly put it, then one has also to accept his trials, tests, demands and sacrifices. Sadat's own predicament before the 1973 war was seen in this light: he had a mission to accomplish, it was God-ordained, therefore he had to endure all the humiliation, denigration and doubt that sceptics voiced against him. He asked his troops, his sons, to undergo the same kind of martyrdom. He constantly urged his people to strive, to struggle, to withstand Allah's test, for 'we are required to sacrifice life in order to deserve life'. The liberation of Egyptian land from Israeli occupation was a 'holy duty' which required sacrifice and Arab unity, both supreme manifestations of faith.

Yet another result of the 1967 defeat and of Nasser's shaken authority was an upsurge of leftist elements within the ruling Arab Socialist Union (ASU), which had been designed to govern the country since 1962 and to implement Nasser's 'Arab Socialism'. It was a one-party system; any competition or political conflict could only be aired within the party. Ali Sabry, who had served as Prime Minister, held the powerful position of Secretary General of the ASU; here he could wheel and deal, and construct his power base, away from the frustrations of his largely ceremonial functions as Vice-President. Nasser was alert to the danger of this new alternative which might challenge his monopoly of power. He removed Ali Sabry from office in 1969 and strengthened his own grip on the apparatus of government, despite his having lingering diabetes and a tough schedule. Abd al-Latif al-Baghdadi, a senior Free Officer, now became Prime Minister, whilst Nasser's choice for the presidency when he resigned in June 1967 was Vice-President Zakarya Muhyi a-Din; these two men were now the top contenders for succession if anything should happen to the ailing Nasser.

On the international level, Nasser, who had launched his War of Attrition against Israel in early 1969, after the artillery duels of late 1968, had trapped himself in an impossible situation: he now longed for some form of diplomatic intervention and signalled the US that he would be willing to accept American mediation. Meanwhile the Israelis escalated their devastating in-depth air strikes into Egypt's heartland, which further undermined Nasser's standing, sank Egypt deeper into economic distress, forced nearly a million Egyptians to evacuate the Canal cities, and demonstrated Soviet impotence to resolve the situation. America eventually took the initiative and produced a cease-fire proposal, persuading Israel to withdraw along the lines of the Security Council's Resolution 242 of November 1967. This American initiative became known as the Rogers Plan (after American Secretary of State William Rogers).

Nasser had capitalized on Nixon's promise of an 'even-handed policy'* in the Middle East when he came to power in January 1969; but increased Israeli air-raids made it essential for him to obtain anti-aircraft missiles to defend his country first.

Despite these problems, Nasser did not abandon the inter-Arab arena. When, in August 1969, the Al-Aqsa Mosque in Jerusalem was burned by an Australian lunatic, and the Arab world decided to use this incident to incite all Muslims against Israel, Egypt responded to Saudi initiative and asked twenty heads of Islamic states to a summit in Rabat. This summit meeting inaugurated a new era in Pan-Islamic politics: it became the first in a series of conferences held annually in one Islamic capital or another, all of which predictably adopted harsh anti-Israeli resolutions, thus contributing to the Islamization of the Arab–Israeli conflict. Sadat, who had acquired experience in this field as Secretary of the Islamic Congress in the 1950s, was dispatched by Nasser to Rabat, in September 1969, to head the Egyptian delegation to the conference. There, his speech gained a thunderous ovation.

Back in Cairo, Sadat felt strong enough and self-confident enough to eye the presidency, although as long as Nasser lived no one would dare try to oust him. Then, in a surprise move, Nasser made Sadat his deputy while he himself was away at the Arab Summit in Rabat in December 1969. So, while Nasser was out of the country, Sadat got his first taste of power as Acting-President, giving him a lead over the other candidates. Why he was given this precedence is unclear. Sadat, of course, saw himself as the natural choice; he was after all one of the most senior of the Free Officers; he felt he had been chosen on merit. According to one of Sadat's top associates, both Zakarya Muhyi a-Din and Baghdadi were too independent, vocal and active to find co-operation easy with the strong-willed Nasser. Moreover, since 1967 Muhyi a-Din had been considered pro-American, almost a mirror-image of the disgraced Ali Sabry, who was recognized as Cairo's Moscow man. Sadat, however, had always seemed neutral and submissive: virtually silent at meetings, he had seldom taken a strong position on any issue, and so appeared to threaten the President's authority least. Leftist opposition claimed that Nasser had originally promised the office of Vice-President to Baghdadi, but that in the hope of pressurizing the Russians into supplying missiles and other weapons he would threaten them with his resignation, thereby leaving the post to Sadat, who would deal with the Americans. The ploy worked, and the Soviets supplied the weapons. The main weakness of this argument is that, had Nasser really wanted to threaten the Soviets, Muhyi a-Din, the 'proven' pro-American, would have been far more effective. It seems more likely that Nasser had heard how successful Sadat had been as leader of the Egyptian delegation to the September Islamic conference, and so decided to reward him

*The term coined by the former Governor of Pennsylvania, William Scranton, who had been dispatched by Nixon on a fact-finding tour of the Middle East.

for his loyalty and for not embroiling himself in Free Officer or ASU power struggles.

Be that as it may, in Nasser's absence Sadat gained first-hand experience of command. He had already witnessed the appalling devastation caused by the Israeli reprisals: in 1968 he had visited Naj-Hamadi in Upper Egypt to assess the extent of damage to a transformer station and a large bridge caused by a daring Israeli commando raid. Now, on 25 December 1969, a major Israeli air strike took place: 264 fighter-bombers (according to Sadat's count) made a series of sorties from 8 a.m. to 4.30 p.m., sunset time. Sadat ordered the anti-aircraft batteries to change their positions before dawn; when the bombings resumed next day, Sadat was delighted to find he had 'outsmarted the Jews', who were forced to alter their plans on finding the previous gun emplacements empty. Despite this, Sadat was deeply shaken by the devastating accuracy of the Israeli bombing. At the end of the two-day raid, he saw the burnt-out guns strewn with the corpses of those who had continued to fire until the end; to Sadat, those who fell, gun in hand, in the defence of Egypt were martyrs who had made the supreme sacrifice. He held the US responsible for these bombings and for the huge number of casualties because, in his words, 'The planes were American and the bombs were American.' When, as President, he had to negotiate with the Americans, he reminded them of the damage their bombs had done to the industrial area of Abu Za'bal.

Sadat was proud of the Egyptian commando counter-attacks across the Canal, which caused considerable damage and casualties to the Israeli troops who were sheltered behind the Bar-lev Line, because they proved that the Egyptians were good fighters given the chance; and he came to the conclusion that, with careful reorganization, it might be possible to turn the Egyptian army into a formidable instrument of war. He also sensed that Israel's deep penetration into Egypt meant that she had neither the men nor the resources to endure endless face-to-face fighting along the Canal: he read it as a good omen, for it showed Israel's inability to sustain casualties for any length of time.

In January 1970, gloom pervaded Egypt: Israel was still making in-depth strikes and the daily losses were huge. As Nasser was in bed with flu, he asked Sadat to call up the Soviet Ambassador and the leading Soviet expert in Cairo and persuade them to come to an urgent meeting. After a frantic search, Sadat discovered that they were at Mahalla al-Kubra, with a Soviet parliamentary delegation which was visiting Egypt. Both of them came to see Nasser the next day, in Sadat's presence. Nasser said that Israeli intentions had become clear: they wanted to shatter Egypt's domestic front. Egypt had no defences against low-flying aircraft, and the attack on Abu Za'bal had been disastrous, so it was essential that he go to Moscow to plead with the Soviet leaders for anti-aircraft missiles; but he wanted his mission to be kept secret. The Russians agreed. Nasser made the trip, concluded a deal with the Soviets for SAM 3 missiles and for crews to man the missile sites until Egyptian teams were trained and ready to take over. Nasser and Sadat were optimistic that the missiles would be a turning-point in Egypt's fortunes, especially as the Soviets had apparently hinted to Nasser that they might send them some MiG 23 fighter-bombers so that Egypt could counter Israel's Phantom jets and strike at her interior. The Soviets also promised to ship electronic equipment.

Forty days after Nasser's return to Cairo, Egypt started frantically to build missile sites along the Suez Canal so that they would be ready for the Soviet missiles and their crews when they arrived. But there was no sign of any aeroplanes or electronic equipment. Nasser was furious; desperate, he called President Nixon, asking him to hurry his cease-fire negotiations. At the end of June, Nasser felt so hard-pressed that he went back to Moscow to plead for the MiG 23s and the promised electronic gear; whilst he was there, he also had medical treatment for his diabetes. For weeks before this meeting took place, Sadat had been planning it in detail with the Soviet Ambassador to Cairo, Vinogradov. They had met each Monday morning in Giza at 11.00 a.m. to iron out Egyptian–Soviet relations, with Sadat reporting all back to Nasser. Despite such meticulous planning, Nasser's USSR visit came to nothing; therefore, Nasser decided that he had no alternative but to tell the stunned Soviet leadership that he had decided to adopt the Rogers Plan and respond positively to the American cease-fire initiative. Meanwhile, in Nasser's absence, Sadat, in his capacity as Acting-President, had convened the politburo of ASU and passed a unanimous resolution rejecting the Rogers Plan. But, when Nasser returned to Cairo and told his colleagues about his icy Soviet reception, Sadat changed his mind and backed Nasser's decision to seek American help. Sadat had been particularly dismayed when Nasser walked off the aeroplane from Moscow and remarked bitterly, 'The Soviets are a hopeless case.' He had then stung Sadat's pride by adding, 'Either all the demands you had worked out with Vinogradov did not reach them, or they intentionally chose to ignore them.'

Dejected by his failure in Moscow, although apparently in better physical shape, and disappointed by his deputy's efforts to pave the way, Nasser lashed out at him at the airport:

SADAT: By Allah! You look well! You seem twenty years younger! What did they do to you?

NASSER: They put me in the oxygen cell where they treat their astronauts . . . but you probably hoped I wouldn't come back so that you could stay in power. . . .

SADAT: By Allah! I have never seen you in such excellent health! What happened? They've made you twenty years younger!

Both men laughed heartily, and the photograph of them laughing hung on the walls of the *Al-Ahram* editorial office for many years. But the aftermath for Sadat was less amusing. In Nasser's absence, Jihan had voiced her desire to acquire a house on the Nile at Giza and, as Acting-President, Sadat had commandeered it from its owner after his offer to buy had been rejected. Nasser was furious when he heard about this and reportedly sent Sadat home 'for a long rest'; so the two men were out of touch for the last three months of Nasser's life. Literally heartbroken, Sadat returned to Mit Abul-kum for a while, imputing his mild heart attack to his master's anger. Finally they made it up, Nasser ordered the house to be made the Vice-President's official residence and came to visit Sadat. However, the visit was not a success. When Sadat ordered his servant to serve tea to President Nasser, the latter asked the servant why he did not serve his master as well. The servant innocently retorted, 'The *Rais* [President] does not drink at this time of day.' (All workers in Sadat's household addressed him as *Rais*, since he was the President of the National Assembly.) At which Nasser caustically inquired, 'How many *Rais* are there in Egypt?'

The rest is rumour, gossip and hearsay. Some people claim that Sadat remained out of favour with Nasser to the end, pointing out that Sadat was the last man to be called to Nasser's death-bed, an obvious sign of his low position on the hierarchical ladder of Egypt in those days. Whatever the truth of the matter, Nasser managed to accomplish two major breakthroughs just before his death, which made his successor's task that much easier: he accepted the cease-fire along the Suez Canal in August 1970, which brought the eighteen-month-old War of Attrition to an end; and he convened the Cairo Arab Summit Conference for September 1970, which stopped the Jordanian slaughter of the Palestinians who had attempted to take over power from King Hussein (Black September). Instead, the Palestinian leadership, under the auspices of an inter-Arab committee, moved to Lebanon where they were to create a future problem.

Nasser died of a heart attack on 28 September 1970, and Sadat, whom many thought an unlikely successor, stepped in as Acting-President. To Sadat it seemed perfectly logical that he should succeed; after all, he had been Nasser's representative at the Islamic conference, he had been Vice-President and had carried out whatever trouble-shooting mission Nasser had delegated to him. He had often been Nasser's confidant, and their friendship, which went back to their first meeting as teenagers in the late 1930s, seemed to have deepened over the years despite the ups and downs resulting from their different temperaments. Furthermore, Sadat had always maintained a good working relationship with the Soviet Ambassador in Cairo, Vinogradov, which gave him crucial contact with Egypt's major source of political, military and economic aid. So, despite Sadat's later declaration that he had never believed he would succeed Nasser; despite the latter's reticence on the subject; and despite the claims of Sadat's detractors that others were more worthy of the presidency, Sadat had probably been grooming himself for this moment for years. At long last, his time had come.

5

ERUPTION

Sadat's hopes were finally realized: all those years of waiting had been worthwhile, for now supreme power was his for the taking. Although previously known to few and not thought much of, he was now to distinguish himself as a supreme ruler, surprising both Egyptians and the world at large with his shrewdness and ruthlessness.

At first Sadat was cautious, as though uncertain of his ability to fill the gap left by Nasser and diffidently determined to prove himself a worthy disciple of the deceased. Again and again, in speech after speech, Sadat promised to carry out Nasser's aims and to be guided by his ideas on socialism, Arab unity, national honour, anti-imperialism, Egyptian leadership in the Arab world, non-alignment in the international scene, the alliance with the Soviet Union, and the perennial anti-Israel and anti-Zionist commitment. But it was soon noticed that Sadat always put greater emphasis on the Islamic faith than his predecessor had done, both in his own behaviour and in response to popular demand for a more Islamic national leadership. That element of Islam was also useful in countering Communists and other leftists in Egyptian politics. Then it gradually became clear that Sadat, whom many considered merely a caretaker until Nasser's true successor emerged, was a totally different kind of leader. He possessed none of Nasser's majestic charisma nor did he have his authority and prestige, but initially he appeared willing to submit to some sort of collective leadership while he slowly built up his power-base and became better known and more experienced. Although other names were mentioned as Nasser's successors, Sadat had the advantage of already being his deputy, and of appearing as a useful compromise candidate who had never antagonized anyone by being too strong-willed or independent. To those who held the reins of power in Egypt, Sadat seemed the least likely to create controversy and the most certain to continue with previous policies. Conveniently, when the constitutional process was applied, Sadat was unanimously confirmed by the National Assembly and was then returned by 90 per cent of the popular vote.

Confident in his popular appeal and in his mission, Sadat set out to make himself *the* authority in the land. His technique was disarmingly simple: he spoke directly to the Egyptian people and to the rest of the world, over the heads of his rivals, using the media for all it was worth. In a hectic six months of public speaking, press and television interviews, and addresses to select gatherings, he managed to talk to most of the influential pressure groups and power lobbies in the Arab world.

In the pre-Islamic Arab world, eloquence had always been extremely important and oral tradition as a whole had been greatly valued; 'the oracle of the tribe, their guide in peace and their champion in war' was the *sha'ir* (the poet). Sadat understood the value of the spoken word and proceeded to combine the oral power of the poet with the authority of the *sheikh* (chieftain).

Modern Arab heads of state, like Sadat, not only led their countries, commanded their armed forces, directed their economies, guided their educational systems, enforced their foreign policies and indoctrinated their subjects, but also glorified themselves, their kin and their tribe-nation; proclaimed their own valour and recounted their brilliant feats in war and peace; castigated or menaced their foes; placated and sometimes flattered their friends or redoubtable rivals. Because Arab audiences are so receptive to what might sound to the Western public sheer bombast and bravado, the impact of Arabic speech on the minds of the Arabic-speaking people is remarkable, and their leaders tend to make generous use of it.

Listening to Sadat's speeches, one was struck by how repetitious, exaggerated and verbose they were, full of unnecessary detail and anecdote. Part of this was due to what an Arab sociologist, E. Shouby, called 'the traditional Arab delight of playing with words, and their tendency to fit the thought to the word or to the combination of words, rather than the word to the thought'. Illustrations and parables were effective means of pleasing the public, and switching from one subject to another was a good way of stopping the audience from becoming bored. Traditionally too, Muslim teachers have always instilled information into their pupils' heads by repetition, so saying things several times over in different words was readily acceptable to Arabs. Sadat became a loquacious and persuasive speaker, adept at making use of every possible nuance and subtlety. He addressed a peasant gathering or a crowd, a military parade or a workmen's rally in the same didactic, patriarchal tone of voice: he sounded like a father organizing his family's education or a teacher instructing a class. When addressing foreign audiences, he liked to challenge universal conventions and shake complacency.

There are few statesmen of Sadat's stature who so readily bared their souls in public, but then he believed in talking directly to the people, and referred to these occasions as 'frank talks' or 'discussions' with audiences, even though he was the only speaker. His speeches were often three or four hours long; packed with *non sequiturs*, they were a far cry from the usual well-planned speech delivered by a head of state. But this was precisely their strength, for they were first-hand, spontaneous, authentic. Sadat would often prepare his texts in impeccable literary Arabic, but then, swept away by his own rhetoric and by his audience's response, he would discard the written text and embark on a peasant-style chat in the Egyptian vernacular. His anecdotes, parables and folk-imagery were drawn from his own peasant experience and from the whole range of Arab literature.

Sadat often gave important press interviews at Mit Abul-kum, sitting on the ground, in order to stress his populist image, in an endeavour to bridge the gap between the ruler and the ruled. He would speak of his real concern, think out loud, bully the people to support his policies, and probably launch a slogan which would dog him and his subordinates ever after. He sensed that when he spoke to the 90 per cent who had voted him into office, he spoke for them. Appearances at public rallies therefore became a tremendous source of comfort to him, reducing his isolation. His addresses reflected not only what he told himself, but what he would write down in his personal diary. Indeed, the stories in his speeches and in his autobiography were almost identical: both were the articulate outpourings of one man's individual vision, candid, artless and amazingly straightforward.

Aware that he lacked credibility when he came to power, he was careful to provide documentary evidence to bolster up his statements. He took great pains to impress his audiences with the authenticity of his information. For example, he would urge them to verify for themselves the truth of what he was saying by consulting a particular personality or certain written evidence; and he would always attempt to be precise, providing his audience with details: 'On 25 December from 8.30 in the morning until 4.10 in the afternoon, 264 Israeli planes bombed Egypt.'

However, he did not always appear logical and consistent, preferring to see-saw between the efficient, scientifically-orientated leader and the simple peasant who lacked expertise; swinging from one to the other according to his mood. Unfortunately he lacked the most elementary knowledge of science and so frequently made mistakes when talking about the role that technology was to play in Egypt's future. However, he was not averse to making a virtue out of his ignorance. For example, he once explained how American-made Phantom jets were superior to the Soviet MiGs and therefore Israel was bound to have the upper hand in air battles: Phantoms, he said, were entirely automatic, worked by the press of a computer button, unlike MiGs which were manually operated. On another occasion he recounted how US Under-Secretary of State, Joseph Sisco, had suggested that the Americans might act as 'a catalyst'. Sadat told his amused audience: 'I did not know what the word meant. You know, I am a peasant, I am not an engineer, and I am not expected to know everything.' Once, when lashing out at the West for having lost its sense of values, Sadat said that Westerners had become so lazy that they could no longer use the simple movement of their hand to clean their teeth and had to resort to electric toothbrushes. When describing what he perceived as the ganging up of the US and Israel against Nasser's regime in the summer of 1970, he said that this had happened when the US consulted her 'computer data and came to the conclusion that Egypt was in distress and was accessible to pressures'.

Peasantry and military life were the two areas that Sadat knew best, perhaps the only ones he had really lived through, sensed and understood. Most of the metaphors and imagery he used in his speeches were taken from those two areas, and the fact that they appealed to the two pillars of his power – the masses and the military – charmed his audience and increased their admiration for his rhetoric. After each of his speeches, people would cluster in the streets of Cairo and in the countryside and discuss his use of language, repeat his metaphors and stories and praise him for his verbal dexterity. Content and substance mattered far less. For example, he frequently used the metaphor of the knife either to describe Israel 'as a dagger in the flank of Egypt', or 'I would never drive a knife in the back of a friend.' Arrows and targets were other simple images easily grasped by his largely illiterate public: for example, Hussein's plan to incorporate the West Bank into his kingdom was scorned by Sadat as an 'arrow which is bound to miss its target, exactly as other arrows aimed at the Arab nation have missed their targets'. Sometimes, the masses and the army would be combined: 'Every village is like a bastion and every plant is like a gun. Every person will be up in arms, and everyone will be under fire . . .'; or, 'Egyptian workers are another victorious army.' At other times, Sadat would harp on his audiences' Islamic souls in order to drive his message home. He invoked the idea of the *Jihad* (holy war) when he said, 'The war we are waging these days is the war we have learned from the Quran'; or he would conjure up great Islamic battles and victories of the past in order to suggest that today's Muslims were bound to win in the end. 'It took Saladin eighty years to regain his land from the Crusader grip,' he said, implying that if he were given the same time he would do as well.

Another large category of images and metaphors were drawn from Sadat's love of nature. For example, the emergence of unity in the Arab world was likened to 'the growth of a tree and the maturation of harvest'. Conspirators against his regime were looked upon by Sadat as 'dropping one after another like autumn leaves', and Arab society was exhorted to 'cultivate itself, to bloom and burgeon and take root in the land'. Those who stood ready to take advantage of a situation were seen by Sadat as 'picking the fruits' without 'burning their fingers in the flames'.

Fire to Sadat was the opposite of stagnation: 'We have to ensure that the flame continues to kindle, until withdrawal has been achieved'; or, speaking about the beginnings of the Lebanese crisis, 'I warned that that fire was being fanned under Assad's and Khaled's noses. . . . Although in those days hostilities had ceased, I warned them that the problems had not been eradicated, because the ashes were still glowing.' Light, as opposed to darkness, was also one of Sadat's favourite images. When reminiscing about the 23 July Revolution, he pledged that 'Its memory shall not wane and its light shall not dim. On that night, before dawn broke, the struggle had been decided in the people's favour.' Or, following the 1973 October War: 'Thank Allah, dawn has come to every inch of Arab land . . . after a long era of obscurity. A new day has dawned on our bastion of freedom. . . .' The 1952 Revolution was remembered as 'a reality that shone bright, rising high and majestic . . . while everything else paled, was pushed into the shadows . . .'. Once, when castigating his critics who were spreading rumours about him, he conjured up light to straighten the record: 'You can ask what you wish, we will shed light on every issue, for light scares away vampires. . . .'

He also used many animal similes. Once he referred to Lafontaine's fable *The Wolf and the Lamb* to describe Israel's 'logic' in the Arab–Israeli conflict; on another occasion, the Arabs were exhorted not to let the world become a 'jungle, because we might not be the strongest beasts there'. Similarly, he warned his people of the dangers inherent in a multi-party system, where 'the big fish indiscriminately swallow the small'. The human body is probably the most simple, immediate and relevant of images, and Sadat used it often, especially the heart – 'Palestine is the heart of the problem' – and the backbone, 'which alone can keep our body firm and upright, regardless of the movement of our limbs'. The heart could evoke pessimistic images, such as 'Israel's dagger in the heart of the Arabs', or optimistic hopes, such as 'the Syrian people, who have always been the beating heart of Arabia', or 'greetings from our hearts which beat at the pulse of victory'. Blood, with its life-enhancing properties, was frequently made use of: 'Our economy was drained, therefore we needed a blood transfusion. . . . When the Chase Manhattan Bank opens branches in Egypt, that will be the beginning of the blood transfusion.' He was fascinated by American know-how and with medical technology; he saw them as the panacea to Egypt's malaise. Talking to his National Security Council on the eve of the 1973 war, he said: 'Our economy is like a drained blood vessel. We are neither dry nor paralysed. All we need is to infuse new blood into our veins.'

While the human body and the illnesses it was heir to may have reflected the uncertainty of the human condition, to Sadat geological objects, such as mountains and rivers, symbolized permanent, immutable continuity in the midst of change. They represented the solidity and stability that he craved. He wished Egypt's domestic front to be as solid as 'the rocks in the village', while his see-saw relations with the Soviet Union were depicted as 'moving sands' from which he must extricate himself in order to move 'to a solid position', presumably a rock. Sadat also drew upon his life experiences. For example, he likened the ruler (presumably himself) to 'a solo performer on the stage, with the spotlight focused on him, so that people can see him clearly but hardly notice anyone else'. An acting metaphor was also resorted to sarcastically when Sadat wanted to castigate his enemies. The Israeli thrust across the Suez Canal during the 1973 October War he called a 'TV-style show', a term he also used for the Entebbe operation launched by Israel in July 1976 to rescue hostages who had been hijacked to Uganda.

Sadat's speeches not only introduced him to his people and to the world, but they were also useful in reassuring everyone that he was only one of a team. In fact, he consulted with the members of Nasser's 'inner circle' about almost every major appointment he made, including his new National Security Council and his cabinet, which was headed by Dr Mahmud Fawzi, a veteran politician from the old school, who had no links with the Free Officers or the 'foci of power'. However, some of his choices for top posts, such as his Prime Minister, were not to the liking of the overlords of Nasser's old entourage, and created friction between Sadat and other contenders for his job. One of them was Ali Sabry, the hard-line socialist whom the Soviets had groomed for the presidency. Immediately upon Nasser's death, Soviet Prime Minister Kosygin and his retinue were among the first guests to arrive in Cairo. Ostensibly they had come for the funeral, but in fact their main concern was the succession. However, they had to reconcile their wants with the reality of the constitutional *fait accompli* by which Sadat had automatically assumed temporary powers until arrangements could be made to elect a successor. As an Interim President, Sadat welcomed the visiting foreign guests, including the Russians, and dealt with them from his *a priori* position of power. The Soviets bowed to reality, especially after Sadat had assured them of his determination to respect Nasser's legacy, to continue in alliance with them, and to nominate Ali Sabry as his Vice-President. Sadat kept his word on all these points. One of the most prominent absentees from the funeral gathering was President Nixon, who sent Elliot Richardson, a member of his cabinet, in his place: Sadat considered this a slur to Egypt's honour, which he never forgave.

After the funeral, Sadat began to tour the country, meeting university professors, students, the top bureaucracy and military units in order to consolidate his power, an essential move before he could embark on his grand schemes for foreign and domestic policy. He called for national unity and astutely pacified those on whom he most depended, the army, the party and the Soviet Union, by invoking the 'will of the people' who had elected him to his post. Gradually, he felt sufficiently self-confident to begin making his own mark; for example, he suggested that it was anachronistic to call the country the 'United Arab Republic'. This name had been created after Egypt's fusion with Syria in 1958, but now that this union had disintegrated Sadat decided it would be more realistic to say the 'Arab Republic of Egypt'. He gave back some of the land that Nasser had seized from the Egyptian middle classes, released thousands of political prisoners and created the position of Socialist Prosecutor to enforce his 'rule by law'. He also promised the army a great battle to wipe out the humiliation of 1967. As a result, he may have considerably enhanced his image in the eyes of some Egyptians but many still believed that he was at the mercy of the 'foci of power'. Sadat felt this latter image of him to be unjust, so he decided to 'take his fate in his own hands', as he was later to repeat so often, and strike at his opponents.

There is some controversy as to whether the 'foci of power' in general, and Ali Sabry in particular, wished to undermine Sadat's authority to the point of ousting him from power altogether. As the opposition to Sadat saw it, the newly installed President wanted sole authority and therefore had become increasingly impatient with the Sabry group who wanted to share power with him. Sadat's critics continued to uphold that view after his death, claiming that Sabry was neither a Communist nor a Soviet agent and that the President had created an artificial crisis in order to rid himself of his potential enemy. What is clear is that, since the beginning of 1971, the 'foci of power' had objected to the way in which Sadat took political decisions without consulting them. Sabry and his clique had pressed for a more militant stance against Israel and for greater power for their own ruling party, the ASU, while Sadat took a more cautious attitude towards the conflict with Israel by agreeing to extend the cease-fire along the Canal; he wished to remain free from the shackles of the party.

Before he was elected to supreme office, while he was still only Acting-President, he was handed a petition signed by former members of the Free Officers, a body that had been disbanded back in 1956 but had reformed themselves into an informal lobby of old comrades-in-arms. The signatories asked to meet Sadat in person, but he refused, saying that it was improper for him to meet pressure groups. Instead, he ordered the petition circulated among the members of ASU. As he read it, the petition amounted to reinstating the Revolutionary Council as the primary legislative power in the country in order that it could work out a new constitution, although it would recognize Sadat's new primacy and offered him the chairmanship of the Council. But Sadat saw this as a retrogressive step, harmful to the very core of the revolution which had taken great constitutional strides since 1956, even if these had not always been to his liking. Sadat rejected the idea out of hand.

Another accusation that Sadat hurled at the 'foci of power' was that they wanted to test his loyalty to Nasser's legacy. He claimed that a few days after Nasser's death, an editorial had been published in a major Cairo daily newspaper depreciating Nasser's stature. At Sadat's first meeting with the leaders of the 'foci of power', one of them had read out the offending article, accused its author of treason, and had expected Sadat to take action. Sadat's version was that his colleagues had expected him to act according to the norms of Nasser's days, and 'chop off the head of the traitor' or send him to a detention camp. But Sadat did not fall into the trap; he reacted calmly, suggesting that the matter be deferred to the next meeting to allow him time to investigate and to invite the accused journalist, who was none other than the renowned Hassanein Haykal, to be present to defend himself. Sadat's cool reaction dissipated the whole issue.

Sadat begged his colleagues in the leadership to 'let our feet remain on the ground even if our dreams shoot sky high'. War against Israel would have to be launched, but only after preparations had been made: it was essential to play for time. According to the terms of the cease-fire agreement that had been worked out under Nasser in August 1970, neither Egypt nor Israel were allowed to improve their positions along the Canal. But almost immediately the Egyptians had moved in new anti-aircraft missiles. This action had been confirmed by the US, who had upheld Israel's demand to redress the *status quo ante bellum*. Joint US–Israeli pressure was brought to bear on Egypt, which Sadat countered not by denial, as Nasser had always done, but by being defiant: 'They made their claim shamelessly, knowing that the territories west and east of the Canal are mine. Even if missiles were moved in, this is still my land.' He further countered the US and Israeli contention that the Soviets had actually occupied Egypt, by reaffirming that 'our lands and skies are ours, and nobody will formulate our policies for us. We do not grant bases to anyone, for we have liberated our will and we have achieved independence after the revolution.'

As early as November 1970, Sadat proudly announced to a meeting of the ASU that his country had gained 'tremendous benefit' from the cease-fire with Israel and that the results would soon become known: his first hint at the war he had in mind, when he was ready. But these promising utterances did not seem to appease the belligerent 'foci of power' who wanted no American cease-fire, no deal with Israel, and were aware that from the beginning of 1971 Sadat had been intimating that he was prepared to accept some kind of settlement with Israel. First, in response to UN emissary Gunnar Jarring's query, he said that he was prepared to make a peace arrangement with Israel; secondly, in a series of interviews to the press, notably *Newsweek* magazine on 16 February, he announced his readiness for peace, if only Israel met his conditions. But what were Sadat's conditions?

Some researchers have consistently advanced the theory that Egypt was indeed ready for peace, and that if Israel had only responded to Sadat's initiative then, the 1973 war might have been averted. The 'evidence' for this kind of wishful thinking comes from Egyptian intellectuals like Ahmed Khamrush, who were beginning to realize the increasing cost of the war. However, this argument can be refuted on the following grounds: first, other intellectuals, more influential than Khamrush, such as the powerful Hassanein Haykal, continued to regard war as the only way to settle the Israeli problem and to regain lost Egyptian territory. Secondly, some intellectual circles, such as the *Siyyasa Dawliyya* (International Politics) led by Butrus Ghali, now the Minister of State for Foreign Affairs, had ostensibly embraced peace in the hopes of bringing Israel into the Arab cultural and political milieu. To make peace with a country that you wish to destroy may be a peaceful way of conquering your enemy, but how about the enemy who does not wish to be 'peacefully' dismembered? And thirdly, intellectuals as such have never counted for much in any regime, least of all in Arab dictatorships. Egypt has always had both established intellectuals who worked for the regime and minor dissidents who mumbled their discontent from the sidelines: neither exerted a decisive voice in Egyptian politics. When intellectuals opposed Nasser or Sadat, they were dismissed, so it is unlikely that they would have been listened to had they suggested peace with Israel. Conversely, when Sadat decided to make peace with Israel in 1977, he did so in the face of an overwhelming boycott by many intellectuals in Egypt, who continued to oppose the peace treaty after it was signed.

Looking carefully at the evidence from Sadat's viewpoint, it is clear that Sadat wanted peace, but that he saw peace not as a contractually binding commitment to reconciliation with Israel, but as a necessity to ensure Israeli withdrawal from all his territories. Recognition of Israel was out of the question. As late as 1975, Sadat dismissed the possibility of engaging in diplomatic relations with Israel or even of participating directly in negotiations with her. In an interview with an Israeli newspaper in August 1980 after the peace treaty had been signed, he said that in May 1971 he had been prepared to sign a cease-fire with Israel but not a peace treaty. He demanded that Israel withdraw from *all* Arab territories occupied in 1967 and restore Palestinian rights. He did not specify what he meant by 'Palestinian rights'. Instead he denounced Israel for failing to respond to his initiative and emphasized that the entire *démarche* had been done through Jarring because 'we do not talk to Israel'. Israel's reply to the Jarring document ruled out total Israeli withdrawal from the occupied Egyptian territories, and her interpretation of Security Council Resolution 242, whose preamble spoke about the inadmissibility of acquisition of territory by war, while its other clauses provided for the evacuation of territories (not *the* territories) occupied in 1967, suggested she wished to retain some of the newly-acquired Arab lands. Sadat therefore concluded that Israel had opted for expansion instead of peace, so he felt that his only answer could be confrontation, both in order to wipe out the 'results of Israeli aggression' and to restore Arab honour which had been humiliated in 1967.

The hard-line 'foci of power' in Egypt could accept this viewpoint but they did not care for Sadat's next move. In April 1971, Sadat travelled to Benghazi, Libya, to sign the Charter of the Federation of Arab Republics, which brought Egypt, Syria, the Sudan and Libya together in a loose federation, more rhetorical and psychological than politically effective. Ali Sabry was opposed to this federation, precisely because of its practical insignificance, and he rallied the ASU secretariat membership against Sadat. The latter gave an impassioned speech, explaining that the new federation was an integral part of the coming battle for Arab power. The Israelis were but the Mongols and Crusaders in modern dress: exactly as it had been necessary for Saladin to unite

Syria and Egypt in order to beat the Crusaders, so it was absolutely imperative to unite with Syria in order to squeeze Israel 'like a walnut in a nutcracker'. Only continued military co-ordination between members of the federation would enable pressure to be kept up against the Zionist enemy. He urged his colleagues to accept the terms of the federation, which had received Nasser's blessing just before his death, because of the enormous advantage of being able to pool resources and the immense strategic value of having Sudan in the south, Libya in the west and Syria in the north all helping each other.

Sabry mounted an acrimonious verbal attack on Sadat, hurling personal insults at him, and then pressed for a vote. Three were for the federation and five against. Sadat then asked to refer the debate to the 150-member Central Committee of ASU, hoping to rally support there. At the meeting, on 25 April, even more recriminations were exchanged between Sadat and Sabry. Sadat therefore decided to 'go to the people' in order to regain the upper hand; having rejected a plea made by an intermediary that Sabry should come to his home and apologize for his outburst at the ASU meeting, Sadat insisted that the 'people would be the only judge'. Disgusted with power politics and what he construed as intrigues against his authority as President, and feeling humiliated that he could not have his way in a matter of supreme political importance, he decided to remove his kid gloves and show his fists.

The opportunity came on 1 May when he was scheduled to meet the workers of the Hilwan steel plant. Sadat began by talking about the Jarring Mission and Israel's belligerency, then thanked the Soviet Union for her help in supplying modern weapons and new electronic warfare devices, which 'Egypt could have developed for herself' but hadn't the time. The Russians were publicly acknowledged for having brought Egypt into the electronics era. He also vowed that, from now on, there would be no more empty talk and that he was going to pursue a new policy of 'an eye for an eye', 'a tooth for a tooth', 'napalm for napalm' and 'deep penetration for deep penetration'. And then, the bombshell: he launched a violent attack against the 'foci of power', accusing them of giving themselves authority 'separate and independent from the people's'; of being dictatorial and of hiding behind slogans and intrigues. The populace, cajoled by Sadat, 'the sole master and teacher', 'the only source of power and inspiration', rewarded Sadat with thunderous applause. The supporters of the 'foci of power', frantically waving Nasser's portrait, were drowned in the uproar.

On 2 May, Sadat dismissed Sabry and held meetings with members of the Assembly, the leaders of ASU, and the military top brass to ensure their loyalty. However, in a surprise counter-move, several senior members of the 'foci of power' resigned, including the powerful Minister of the Interior Sha'rawi Gum'a (whom Sadat said he had deposed), Sami Sharaf, the Chief of the Presidential Cabinet since Nasser's day, and General Muhammed Fawzi, the War Minister. The entire power structure appeared about to collapse and it was hoped that Sadat would have to bow out of office. But they, like others, had misjudged Sadat's determination. He ordered his new loyal Minister of the Interior, Mamduh Salem, an old police chief and governor of Alexandria, to put all those who had resigned and all those he'd dismissed under house arrest, and he secured the backing of the Chief of Staff of the Armed Forces, General Muhammed Sadeq, to all his measures, probably by renewing his pledge to modernize the army and prepare it for the 'battle of destiny'. Sadeq was later promoted to War Minister as a reward for his loyalty, and Mamduh Salem was eventually to be called upon to form a new cabinet after the October War.

Sadat's success was as much the result of his rivals' weakness as of his own shrewdness. Later he charged the 'foci of power', in collusion with the Soviet Union, with plotting to overthrow him. He claimed that when he had sent Sami Sharaf and Ali Sabry to Moscow at the beginning of 1971 they had been told by Brezhnev that 'Sadat is ruining Nasser's revolution', and that Sharaf had then stayed behind for 'medical treatment' after the rest of the delegation had returned to Cairo, in order to co-ordinate the plot with the Soviets. Sadat was able to obtain tape recordings of Ali Sabry allegedly urging his accomplices to 'wipe out' the Sadat regime; when confronted with his own recordings, Sabry 'wept miserably', according to Sadat. Ali Sabry and his clique were also accused of having monitored Sadat's telephone (he said he found a wire-tapping device in his study) and of planning to take over the broadcasting station in order to prevent him from delivering his speech to the people on the night of the ASU debate. Sadat further claimed that when an informer told him about the plot and he began to order arrests, certain officers had attempted to destroy the tapes of the wire-tappings, but the presidential guards had been too quick for them and so the evidence for the plot reached his hands. Sadat ordered that no bugging devices were now to be installed unless permission had been received to do so from a judge, and even then they were only to be used against hostile foreigners. Sadat then publicly burned thousands of wire-tapping tapes collected under the previous rule, to symbolize the birth of a new era. The conspirators were tried and most of them were convicted: but Sadat personally converted some of the death sentences into long periods in prison. As a gesture of goodwill he later arranged for most to be released early, for was he not the forgiving 'father of his family'?

At the time of the crisis, however, many questioned the legitimacy of Sadat's actions. Faced with what he saw as a plot against his life, no one expected him to behave gently, but considering that he had made bombastic statements about upholding the 'rule by law', had liberalized the emergency laws, freed political detainees, created a Socialist Prosecutor and destroyed wire-tappings, one would expect him to respect the principles he preached. Moreover, the procedures he adopted left much to be desired. First, when he put the question of the federation to the vote at the ASU secretariat meeting, and was outvoted, he did not accept the democratic results. Yet presumably, if the vote had gone in his favour, he would have been the first to oppose the losers' demands to reopen the matter in Central Committee. Secondly, his vow to wipe out the 'foci of power' left no room for political pluralism, criticism or opposition to his rule. Thirdly, he condemned Ali Sabry for having divulged 'state secrets' to a meeting of the Central Committee when he mentioned what had been discussed at the Benghazi Conference when the federation had been set up. But Ali Sabry, who had attended the conference with Sadat, was surely entitled to quote from the Benghazi discussions in a closed session of the Central Committee in order to defend himself? To use the argument of 'divulging state secrets' against him sounds more like silencing criticism than concern for state secrets. Fourthly, the 'conspirators' were not brought to justice before an ordinary court, which might have dismissed Sadat's charge, but were submitted to summary trial before a hand-picked secret 'revolutionary court' and were charged with treason, the sentence for which is usually capital punishment. Fifthly, Sadat himself admitted that he had instructed the Socialist Prosecutor not to publish Sami Sharaf's deposition during his interrogation, nor to bring it to the attention of the judiciary, nor to include it in his report about the 'attempted *coup*'. It would appear that Sadat regarded himself as entitled to obstruct the judicial process in the same way as he had interfered with the democratic process.

One must emphasize, however, that Sadat's behaviour was not outside the accepted norm for Egypt. Although Sadat's policies may look undemocratic to Western eyes, they were not regarded by his countrymen as aberrant or particularly heavy-handed. On the contrary, he was widely regarded by the populace as a much more humane, sensible, good-humoured and easy-going father figure than the serious, paranoid Nasser. What is more, Sadat had gained his people's sympathy by telling them his version of the 'plot': they admired him for having moved so swiftly and decisively against the 'enemies of the people'.

Sadat called the events of 14–15 May 1971 the 'Corrective Revolution', because they changed the course of the 1952 July Revolution. The July Revolution had been identified with Nasser. Now, Sadat had *his* revolution, whose dates would henceforth be part of Egyptian history.

The Soviets panicked when Sadat removed their allies in Egypt from office. President Podgorny himself arrived post-haste in order to hold marathon meetings with Sadat. After much arm twisting, Podgorny succeeded in getting Sadat to sign a fifteen-year Treaty of Friendship and Co-operation between Egypt and the USSR on 27 May. Not only had the Rogers Plan failed to produce Israeli withdrawal, but Sadat suspected that the enemies of Egypt, namely the US and Israel, were plotting to 'overwhelm us from within': not on the banks of the Suez Canal but by internal political upheaval. Not a word was uttered, at the time, about Soviet collusion in the 'plot', because Egypt still desperately needed Soviet help, even if the price was a fifteen-year treaty.

Having decided to throw in his lot with the Soviet Union, Sadat went the whole hog. As he said of himself in another context, 'I know no mid-way.'

Once the internal crisis was settled, Sadat turned his attention to the Arab–Israeli conflict. He was afraid that endless three- to six-month extensions to the cease-fire agreements would inevitably mean that the cease-fire lines became a *fait accompli*, which was precisely what he could not accept. He gave as precedent the armistice line for the 1948 Arab–Israeli war, which the world soon accepted as Israel's border. So he wanted *movement*, even if initially he received little back from Israel. If he could just make Israel withdraw a little, so that he could reassert some semblance of Egyptian control over the east bank of the Suez Canal, that would be a start, because it would show that Israel could be made to retreat. Once the principle of withdrawal had been established, then world opinion might pressurize Israel to withdraw a bit further. Recognizing that it was essential to have the United States on his side as they provided Israel with everything from 'Phantom jets to bread and butter', Sadat decided to accept Security Council Resolution 242, despite having first objected to it. He also accepted Jarring's mission and showed eagerness to conclude some deal under UN auspices. He was even prepared to obtain withdrawal under the Rogers Plan, provided it showed quick results, and provided he did not have to negotiate directly with Israel nor sign a comprehensive peace with her. The sort of comprehensive peace he ultimately had in mind was one which would satisfy Arab grievances by total and unconditional Israeli withdrawal from all Arab territories. In return for this, the Arabs might declare a temporary state of non-belligerency if 'Palestinian rights' were requited. That could mean anything from a Palestinian state on the West Bank and in Gaza, to complete fulfilment of the PLO Charter which expressly mentioned a Palestinian state covering the entire territory of Palestine, Israel included. Whenever Sadat was asked what 'Palestinian rights' meant to him, his standard reply was, 'It is up to them to determine their rights.' But supporting the PLO inevitably meant no permanent peace settlement with Israel.

So when Sadat mentioned peace, it was clear he could only mean a temporary or a first-stage agreement. After all, he had absorbed the Nasserite line of thought and was still surrounded by people of that school. It would be expecting too much of Sadat if we were to impute a great vision of peace to him at this early stage. He had to be true to himself, he could not agree to a partial settlement without first removing 'the shame of 1967' and cleansing Egypt's desecrated honour in battle. In a speech he delivered on Nasser's Memorial Day (28 September 1975), he thanked Allah 'that the Jews had rejected my initiative, for we ultimately needed to wage war in 1973 in order to realize the same plan'. Sadat recollected on that occasion that, in return for Israel's partial withdrawal, he had pledged Jarring to accept a six-month cease-fire. But when Israel rejected his initiative, he decided in February 1971 that the Rogers Plan was no longer binding on Egypt.

While the crisis was still brewing, Sadat told the ASU on 10 May 1971, 'As a political leader, I have to follow two courses simultaneously: first, I thoroughly explore all political avenues; secondly, I put my weight behind the military, which in itself may give momentum to diplomacy.' So, in mid-1971, as Sadat became increasingly convinced of the inefficiency of the Americans as mediators (the Rogers Plan had been shelved anyway due to Israeli pressures), and feeling that there was only a 'one per cent hope of a peaceful settlement', he launched his 'Year of Decision', thus signalling to the world that by the end of 1971 he would retaliate. He believed that 'only an act of war would stop the Israelis and their military leaders from boasting'. At various times in 1971, he wanted to reopen hostilities along the Suez Canal so as to force the issue, but the Soviets dissuaded him from doing so.

The chain of events leading up to the decision had been a humiliating one for Sadat. The thirty-day extension of the cease-fire was to expire on 7 March 1971, but Sadat was afraid that, if he resumed the War of Attrition along the Canal, Israel might bomb the Aswan Dam which could cause a disastrous flood. Sadat applied pressure on the USSR and was assured via his War Minister, General Fawzi, that the shipments of Soviet missiles against low-flying aircraft would arrive on 18 and 22 February and that there would be enough of them to defend the High Dam and some vital bridges in Upper Egypt. But neither the shipment, nor an explanation about the delay, arrived. So, on 1 March, Sadat decided to go to Moscow to vent his exasperation on the Soviet leadership. The Soviet leaders assured him that the missiles were ready, but first they lectured him on his hot-headedness and voiced their fears that he would start a war as soon as he had the missiles, and that he ran the risk of being defeated again.

Sadat reported back to the ASU Executive Committee on his mission to Moscow, his first as President. He said that the Soviets were intent on 'keeping him ten steps behind Israel instead of five steps ahead of her', and that he had promised them not to use their advanced weapons, including MiG 23s, unless he was attacked. He explained that before he left Moscow on 2 March, the Soviet leaders had 'played an old trick': they had shown Sadat a list of all the weapons they were prepared to provide. But Sadat said that he could not accept their way of doing business, and angrily left Moscow. As already explained earlier, Podgorny rushed to Cairo after the 14–15 May crisis and forced Sadat to sign the fifteen-year Treaty of Friendship. Sadat had reluctantly signed in the hope that the Soviets would now keep their word and deliver the missiles, and Podgorny had replied that, upon his return home, he would see to it that the shipments were sent within a few days. However, Sadat took a firm line over the Communist rebellion in the Sudan in July, which upset the Soviet Union, and so he received no deliveries and no answers from the Kremlin about the long-overdue shipments.

Sadat felt let down, because it was on the basis of Podgorny's promises of May that he had announced the 'Year of Decision' and finally rejected the Rogers Plan, and now he looked a fool, being unable to deliver. On 12 October, Sadat was invited to Moscow. He accepted, although he was furious about all the delays and disgusted that the Kremlin leaders never answered his monthly letters. He begged them to bail him out of his 'Year of Decision' pledge by giving him the promised arms, but they answered that he should not have been so hot-headed. Angrily, Sadat demanded that the Soviet leadership withdraw their SAM missile experts from Egypt, because the Egyptian military had now learned how to use them. Sadat naïvely suggested that since 'everything relevant to new development in armaments, war and strategy' was written in books and magazines, and since Egyptian officers could read, they could 'follow these developments on their own'. He reminded the Russians that it was his officers who had discovered that the electronic equipment brought by the Soviets and deployed near Cairo at the beginning of 1971 was twenty years out of date. He challenged the way in which the Soviet experts had dealt with their obsolete equipment, monopolizing its use under the pretext that it was 'top secret', and refusing to let Egyptians come near it.

Brezhnev remained firm, arguing that, if the USSR withdrew their missile crews, Soviet stature in the world would be greatly affected, because it was their presence in Egypt that was at stake. Incensed, Sadat asked, 'Presence? What presence? Anyone who gets a foothold may also sink in the mud!' Brezhnev threatened that, if the Soviet crews were evacuated, they would take their missile batteries with them. In a typically defiant move, Sadat attacked again: 'Do you want to keep a Soviet presence in Egypt? All right! Just give me the weapons! I don't fear a Soviet presence.' Brezhnev softened and declared that he would give Sadat 'everything he needed'. The meeting ended as before with Brezhnev pulling a list out of his pocket and reading out what the 'Soviet Government had decided to give Egypt'. Sadat accepted and pressed for an early delivery date, before the 'Year of Decision' was over. The Soviets promised delivery before the end of the year, but by December they had not kept their word.

Sadat needed to save face, for his 'Year of Decision' had made him a laughing stock not only in Egypt but around the world. In desperation he used the Indo–Pakistani war of December 1971 as an excuse, explaining that the Soviet Union had had to divert her war supplies away from Egypt to India, hence the 'unexpected delay'. This justification seemed feeble even to Sadat, so he struggled to give it more weight by linking it to Nasser. He told his people that, on 9 July 1967, Nasser had planned a major strike against the Israelis along the Suez Canal, but just before the Egyptian bombers took off, fog had set in and Nasser had had to call off the attack. The Indo–Pakistani war was Sadat's uncontrollable fog, a *force majeure* to which even a great politician like Nasser must yield.

War broke out between India and Pakistan on 9 December 1971, and on the 10th Sadat called the Soviet Ambassador in Cairo and asked him to convey word to his leaders that he wanted to see them again; he urgently needed to find a way out of the embarrassment occasioned by the delay of the 'Year of Decision.' Sadat wanted to visit Moscow before the end of December so that he could issue a joint communiqué with the Soviets, postponing the 'Year of Decision' until the spring; he hoped that such a move would pull the carpet from under his opponents. The Ambassador did not reply until 28 December: Sadat was invited to Moscow on 1 February 1972. In the meantime, resentment against the Soviet Union increased, compelling Sadat to deliver a broadcast speech to the National Assembly enjoining his people to be patient and to recognize Egypt's great debt to the Soviet Union. Despite mounting discontent and mass student demonstrations in January and February, which condemned Egypt's 'defeatist leadership', Sadat gritted his teeth and waited until he could see Brezhnev. January dragged on endlessly but Sadat stuck it out, challenging those who disagreed with his Soviet policies to endure with him or quit.

On 1 February, Sadat arrived in Moscow and demanded to know why the Soviets were still stalling on their arms deliveries. Why were they treating him in this fashion? Was he friend or foe? Why had he not been warned last October about the coming Indo–Pakistani war? Brezhnev replied that it was not his fault, simply bureaucratic red tape. Then Sadat erupted: 'I cannot accept this kind of treatment; if it continues, it will cause a very serious rift in our relationship.' This time, Prime Minister Kosygin said that he would personally supervise the shipments. At the end of the meeting, the Soviet leader pulled out the list of weapons to be delivered to Egypt yet again, but it did not include what Sadat most wanted, missile batteries for Upper Egypt and MiG 23s. Sadat had no choice but to wait, but his bitterness against the Soviets had nearly reached exploding point.

More snags now cropped up. The 31st of March was the day the Soviet Communist Party Congress began in Moscow and no one in the Soviet leadership could be reached until it was over. In the meantime, the Soviets had invited President Nixon to come to Moscow in May for talks. Sadat was apprehensive that if the missile deliveries were postponed until after Nixon's visit, he might never get them. As he had learned from experience, 'the Soviets were always reluctant to ship weapons when such important visits took place or when they themselves paid visits elsewhere'. At the end of April, Marshal Grechko, the Soviet Defence Minister, came to Cairo, a bare twenty days before Nixon's visit to Moscow. He brought over with him a note from the Central Committee of the Communist Party of the USSR and one sample Sukhoi-17 fighter bomber. But he also read out a prepared joint communiqué to Sadat stating that the USSR would be supplying Egypt with long-range bombers and modern weapons. The communiqué placated Sadat with words and more promises but still no hardware; at the same time, it warned Nixon that the USSR now had a long-standing presence in the Middle East and would henceforth be an indispensable partner in any settlement in the area.

After Grechko left, Sadat was stunned to receive a call from the Soviet Ambassador inviting him to go to Moscow for one day to discuss an extremely urgent and important matter. Sadat thought that the Soviets wanted to impress Nixon by stressing their ties with Egypt. Thinking he had some leverage, Sadat demanded a top-level Soviet visit to Cairo in return, saying he had already been to Moscow three times that year. But the Soviet leaders were not interested. Sadat had to lay pride aside and go. He tried to impress his Soviet hosts by telling them that the US had been made to rejoin the Paris Peace Talks with the Vietnamese because of the latter's large-scale offensive in January 1972. So, reasoned Sadat, if the Egyptians moved first against Israel, the Americans might be made to come to the negotiating table as they had in Paris. In order to move first, however, Egypt needed the long-overdue weapons. Brezhnev seemed to agree with Sadat's analysis, but also thought that since it was a US presidential election year, Nixon was unlikely to do much. Sadat insisted, nevertheless, on the arms deliveries, because 'after Nixon or some other president is elected, we must be able to speak from a position of strength, for neither the Americans nor the Jews will respect us unless they are aware of our strength'.

Sadat left Moscow reassured, for the fourth time, that the arms he needed would arrive at long last. The Soviets had also pledged that they would report the outcome of Nixon's visit to him in detail. Instead, Sadat merely received the joint communiqué concluding Nixon's visit, specifying that the US and the USSR would join hands to produce a relaxation of military tension in the Middle East. Sadat was furious: 'What does relax mean when I am ten to fifteen steps behind Israel? How could the Soviets agree to the term "relaxation"? Such a word could apply only if I were Israel's equal in armaments and if my land were no longer occupied. Under the prevailing circumstances, military relaxation means that my land will remain occupied indefinitely.' Finally, Sadat could endure no more, he lost his temper; the wording of the communiqué was the last straw, it was the epitome of betrayal; all his suffering and humiliation at the hands of the Soviets, all their devious methods of conduct were 'nothing, compared to the military relaxation wording'. Two weeks after the Soviet Ambassador had brought Sadat the text of the communiqué, he sent a reply saying that he felt let down. The Ambassador then left for a month in Moscow, for 'consultations'.

On 8 July, a new two-and-a-half-page message arrived from the Soviet leaders; two and a quarter pages dealt with Soviet efforts to talk the Americans into a peaceful settlement in the Middle East, but there was nothing about arms shipments. The last five lines read: 'As to war, we are concerned about it. Waging wars, preparing for them and training for them is a very dangerous proposition. But it is useful to mention that you are unable at this point to launch a war.' Wounded, Sadat coolly took his revenge. He dictated to the stunned and embarrassed Soviet Ambassador the following reply to the Kremlin leaders:

I reject your message in both content and form. I reject your attitude and behaviour towards me. I reject your methods. Your experts will have to leave within a week. All your installations here will either be handed over to Egypt or you must dismantle them and take them away. Everything you have here must either be sold or withdrawn. I want no Soviet experts. You must do all this within one week. The deadline is set, and our War Minister will be informed in this respect.

The Soviet Ambassador did not believe his ears, but Sadat insisted that it was an official message which must be reported to the Soviet authorities. Hafez Isma'il, Sadat's National Security Adviser, sat at his side and took minutes. The Soviets were packed up within a week, but before the deadline Sadat dispatched his Prime Minister, Aziz Sidqi, to Moscow to assure the Kremlin that his decision that Soviet experts must go was final. Always aware of the need to save face, Sadat suggested that the two parties should publish a joint communiqué stating that both Governments had agreed to terminate Soviet presence (that hated word!) in Egypt. Sadat was even prepared to specify that the Soviets had completed their job and that Egypt was grateful to them. But since the Soviets refused to publish a joint communiqué, it was issued as a one-sided statement from Sadat's presidential office.

The news spread around the world when the communiqué was released at the end of the week. President Assad of Syria, who stopped over in Cairo on 9 July on his way back from Moscow, was informed of the decision. He was told by Sadat, 'You have received modern weapons from them, so you can carry on relations with them. I want no more.' Rumour suggested that Sadat had abandoned the Soviets because of some secret American promise. But Sadat denied such gossip: 'Some people believe that there is no morality in politics, but I wish to tell you my view: morality is indivisible. It would have been immoral to knife the Soviets in the back and then contact the Americans. I would never do that to a friend. I might give my friend an electric shock to wake him up, but I would never knife him because he helped me in time of distress.' Sadat thought that his attitude was vindicated when eight months later, in early 1973, he signed a new agreement with the Soviets for supplies of arms. He was convinced that after the Soviets had understood his motives, they would no longer be loath to provide him with the weapons he needed. His decision to expel their experts from Egypt had been brewing for a long time, for he wanted to wage war in 1973 unencumbered by Soviet presence in Egypt, otherwise he feared that whatever he might accomplish would be credited to the Russians, not to him. And he wanted no partners in his glory. After all, buying protection from someone more powerful was demeaning to one's honour. Sadat made it explicit: 'This is a war for our honour and self-respect. No one will defend my dignity and self-respect for me, for I am the ruler of the land and the bearer of its self-respect.'

6
GEARING UP FOR WAR

After he had settled the challenge to his rule and shrugged off the Soviet bear hug, Sadat had to come to grips with the frightening prospect of leading his country into war with Israel. First he had to overcome his own fears, then to consolidate his home front, and finally to ensure Arab backing. He attacked all these problems simultaneously and succeeded in persuading many sceptics that inertia would be fatal.

Sadat had once said that 'to be gripped by fear was the most degrading of all emotions for a human being. In fear, personality disintegrates, the human will is paralysed and man acts as an automaton. . . . Fear is a most effective tool for destroying the soul of the individual and the soul of a nation.' Sadat realized that fear not only destroys and paralyses but also creates disunity, because in a state of panic human willpower collapses and man thinks only of himself. Paradoxically, we learn most about Sadat's fears from his later utterances made *after* he had overcome them: when fear gripped him, he did not mention it in public at the time. It later became apparent that the 1973 war had had a cathartic effect, so liberating him from fear that he afterwards denied its existence. But he protested too much: his constant denials of fear an admission of its existence. After 1973, Sadat repeatedly announced that he 'feared nothing' or, more specifically, that he 'was not afraid' about what he said or did: 'I do not fear peace, it is Israel who does'; or, 'Egypt is going to Geneva because it has nothing to fear there, it is Israel that has reason for fear'; or, 'I am not afraid that foreigners, imperialism or foreign domination might get me'; or, 'We do not fear the consequences of the abrogation of the Friendship Treaty with the USSR.' It becomes clear that he claimed to be unafraid of precisely those things which he most feared, if we compare the following two statements which he made in 1973:

> When the Soviets threatened in 1970 that they would evacuate the SAM missiles unless Soviet experts were permitted to man them, I said: 'Do you want to keep a Soviet presence in Egypt? All right! Just give me the weapons! I don't fear a Soviet presence!'

But on the same occasion he also said:

> When I accepted the cease-fire in 1970, I took that decision in secret. For while the

US was in front of me, the USSR was at my back [*i.e.* while he was confronting the US, and Israel, on the Suez front, the Soviets were protecting his hinterland], and I fear the USSR exactly as I fear the US.[18]

On another occasion, Sadat claimed that he 'was not afraid' of local demonstrations against him, but it was evident from the oppressive measures he took that he saw them as constituting a very real threat; he felt them to be a sign of disunity, casting doubt on his claim to be the 'head of the family'. Fear and disunity run counter to courage and group cohesion, the two pillars of the Bedouin ethos. Moreover, failure to show courage and group cohesion among your kind may bring shame and disgrace upon you. Hence the need to cultivate values of pride and honour – one's own, the family's, the people's, the nation's. One of the notions of honour in Arab society is, to use Raphael Patai's description, 'to exhibit a strong sense of kin group adherence. It is honourable to behave with dignity and be aware of the imperative of *wajh* (face). That is, under no circumstances must a man allow his face to be blackened; others must always endeavour to "whiten his face" as well as the faces of his kin group. Cost what it may, one must defend one's public image. Any injury done to one's honour must be revenged, or else one becomes permanently dishonoured.'

Sadat, the villager from Mit Abul-kum, was extremely sensitive about matters of pride and honour, and their antitheses, shame and disgrace. He was grateful to the Soviet Union for rushing to his country's help in the 'black days' of 1967, but he refused to give in to the disgrace of totally submitting to her will. Egypt's 'face' has been 'blackened' by the terrible defeat of 1967, therefore only an 'honourable' fight might 'whiten' her face again. For Sadat, pride and honour were possessions to be fiercely guarded and their loss was something to be avoided; if the worst happened and they were lost, then they must be restored at all costs. The disgrace involved in Egypt having 'lost face', in having shown Arab helplessness to the whole world, weighed on Sadat's mind no less than the reality of Egypt's weakness or Arab disunity. His own words in a public speech illustrate this point:

Is it not shameful to the Arab world that we should keep silent in the face of continuing American aggression? Is it not a shame that we should suffer American provocation in silence? All that I have been striving for is to convince the US of the existence of a unified Arab world that is not easy to challenge.[19]

Shame was a source of motivation for Sadat: it made him act not only because action was positive in itself, but because inaction would occasion 'loss of face'. He would strive, he said, to convince the US of Arab unity even though he knew it did not exist. If he could, he would create the right impression that would 'whiten' the Arabs' face. In other words, Sadat was embarrassed that he had lost prestige and wished people to believe that it was not so. Similarly, since Egypt had been shamed by Israel in 1967, he must not only regain his land, but remove the shame by 'putting an end to Israel's arrogant boasting of the past twenty-three years'. For him, 'the way things appear' was supremely important. No wonder that Sadat saw the greatest achievement of the 1973 war as the 'shattering' of Israel's image of invincibility. The 'undoing' of the shame which had been inflicted upon Egypt could be accomplished only when, in Sadat's words, 'the whole world, West and East, could see whether or not we're able to liberate our land, whether or not we're able to fight'.

Sadat was not only concerned about Egypt's loss of face in her struggle against Israel, but he also worried about the poor image her domestic rifts made upon the outside world. Therefore he castigated students who had demonstrated in Cairo at the beginning of 1972, because they had caused Egypt to 'lose face before the whole world', by applying for help from foreign student bodies. Sadat also dismissed Egyptian journalists who had reported these and other disturbances, thus causing damage to Egypt's 'good name'. He was less concerned that his own image might be tarnished as a result of his suppression of the right to demonstrate and to free speech, because these were not considered important in Egypt whereas domestic disunity was. Sadat often spoke on the theme 'We know what honour is and we value it', or, 'We must endure difficult days in order to preserve our honour.' Honour was so important to him and to his people that they were prepared to pay any price to maintain it:

> America gives our enemy weapons to enable him to humiliate our honour and willpower . . . we shall resist at any cost. . . . The battle is costly, but we have to pay the price of honour, whatever it is. We accept this for the sake of honour and justice. . . . The war will be long and bitter, but this is the destiny of free men.[20]

In traditional Arab fashion, Sadat linked 'Arab honour' to the honour of its women, a facet of pride that Arabs must defend, and for which they must be ready to kill. In May 1973, when Israeli commandos landed in West Beirut and killed some Palestinian guerilla leaders in their apartments Sadat was furious. In a public speech he thundered:

> This aggression does not confine itself to apartment houses in Beirut alone but, and I want the entire Arab nation to hear these words, this amounts to aggression against every Arab capital and Arab house, and against Arab dignity, prestige and pride. . . . Yussuf Najjar's wife, who died while defending her husband in their home, is my mother and sister as well as yours. She represents Arab dignity and pride that we must live to defend.[21]

In Sadat's imagery, occupied land sometimes played the role of the desecrated woman. For example, he viewed Israel's crossing to the west side of the Canal, in October 1973, as a personal humiliation; for land, *his* land, which constituted a symbol of honour to him, had been 'raped'. Similarly, the Israeli occupation of the Sinai Peninsula was an encroachment on his honour, on Egypt's collective honour. Removal of the physical symbol of dishonour was the only way to redress the wrong. Sadat could not even envisage talking to

Israel at a negotiating table, as an equal, while Egypt's land was still being 'raped'. Honour had to be restored, at least some of the land must be returned, before he would be prepared to negotiate. And if the enemy was reluctant to return the land peacefully, then the 'battle of destiny' inevitably became a 'battle of honour', and failure to fight would amount to a shameful surrender to the rapist.

Courage and valour in war, which were prerequisites for the recovery of the land, became in themselves indicators of his strength and determination to remove the stigma of humiliation. Sadat impressed upon the Soviets, before the October War, that unless he could speak from a position of strength, 'neither the Americans nor the Jews would respect us'. He had learnt that lesson from the 1967 war, when doubts were cast on Egypt's fighting ability. It was said that Egyptians were unfit for war and would never be able to recover their lands or restore their honour. Sadat was afraid that if this diagnosis were true, it would mean 'death and destruction for our people for thousands of years to come'; he feared that he might end up in the same predicament as the American Red Indians. At stake then was not only the intrinsic loss of territory and freedom, but the humiliation, shame and disgrace before others. The war of 1973 was regarded as essential to prove Egypt's worth in battle and to restore her honour.

Sadat's honour was restored by the war, which enabled him to negotiate and ultimately make peace with Israel. He told his officers in March 1976 that when Kissinger arrived to mediate for a troop disengagement in the Sinai, Kissinger said that the Israelis had openly acknowledged their admiration for the way the Egyptian army had planned and fought during the October War. That, admitted Sadat, made him proud. However, if he had recovered his honour, then Israel must be feeling humiliated, for to Sadat their positions were now reversed and he imagined that Israel was now feeling the shame and dishonour he had suffered when defeated. When Kissinger's mission to mediate for a second disengagement in March 1975 failed, Sadat accused Israel of having intentionally disrupted the peace in order to get rid of Kissinger, because he was the man who had heard their desperate cry for help on the fourth day of the war, and now they did not want the witness of their distress to be present. Sadat reasoned that 'humiliated' Israel wanted no one around who reminded her of her defeat; since Nixon had resigned, only Kissinger remained to attest to her shame. Israel's alleged 'reaction' could then be considered 'shame avoidance', something that Sadat would have resorted to in a similar situation. Sadat also accused Israel of trying to occupy the city of Suez during the war in order to 'regain her honour and hide the magnitude of her defeat and the extent of Arab victory from the world'.

On the domestic front, Sadat had to deal with student disturbances and Nasserite elements who continued to ridicule him for his vain promises of the 'Year of Decision' and 'total confrontation' with Israel; at the same time, he decided to concentrate his efforts on building up the army into a 'state within a state' and to devote to it most of Egypt's dwindling resources, whatever the cost to the civil population and the country's future economic needs. Student demonstrations began on 15 January 1972, when a group supporting the Palestinian revolution gathered in the department of engineering at Cairo University and adopted a resolution, rejecting peaceful solutions and urging the authorities to close down the university in order to allow students to undergo military training. They had threatened to call for picket lines should their demands not be met. Sadat saw this as an affront both to him and his authority. He argued that while 800,000 Egyptian troops and their dependants had been 'swallowing sand' in past years, preparing for the war against Israel, others could not act 'like patrons and impose their views on the people'. He reproved the students for taking two hours to 'start a war amidst impulsiveness, zeal and shouting' without taking into consideration the enmity of the US, the world situation and the balance of power. What particularly hurt Sadat was the students' reaction to Dr Kamal Abd al-Majid, the ASU Secretary for Youth, whom he had delegated to talk to the students. Sadat was enraged that they had hurled insults at his personal delegate, who was also a university lecturer. For, in Sadat's words, 'A youth who does not respect his teacher does not respect his father either.' The implication is clear: a youth who does not stand in awe of his father and his teacher is likely to undermine the authority of the President, the father and teacher of all Egyptians. Sadat took the slight personally.

On 20 January 1972, the students decided to reconvene in the Grand Abd al-Nasser Hall, the largest in Cairo University, and they asked Sadat to appear before them. He felt cornered by their demand, fearing that if he went they might attack him verbally which would be humiliating, so he rejected the students' plea on the grounds that their behaviour towards 'their lecturer, who was like their father, went beyond all accepted norms'. Nevertheless, Sadat decided not to interfere with the conference. At the same time, another gathering was initiated at the Ein Shams University by students who allegedly supported the now defunct 'foci of power'. But Sadat stood firm, refusing to restore Nasser's university guards, which he had earlier abolished. Instead, he publicly attacked the students' conduct. On 25 January 1972, he broadcast his view of the unrest to the nation, sardonically reproving the students for attempting 'to supervise the war and apply a war economy' to Egypt. He said that, when Britain or Russia were at war, no student committees tried to defy the legal rulers of their countries. He defined students as 'people who sought knowledge' (literal translation of the Arabic 'Tullab'), and made it clear that the state invested in their education because it desperately needed every minute of their time, in preparation for the modern 'state of science and faith'. Faith also meant respect for traditional values, and any student who did not honour his seniors at the university did not deserve state-supported free education.

Sadat then warned his listeners that just as the student rebellion in France in May 1968 had brought about the 'collapse' of the French economy, despite the vigour of de Gaulle's political and economic reforms, so the present upheavals among Egyptian students might cause harm to the country. And then he declared: 'We all know that the leader of the student movement in France was Cohen, because de Gaulle had adopted an antagonistic position against world Zionism.' Sadat, not for the first time, wished to stress the Jewish–Zionist connection.

In 1971, and again in 1972, when he accused the US of acting as a 'proxy' for Israel and of seeming unable to control her client, he attributed the weakness, among other factors, to the 'Zionist Arthur Goldberg', head of the US mission to the United Nations, who was the 'first Zionist in American history to occupy that position'. Since then and up until the 1973 war, Sadat would often resort to blaming the Jews and the Zionists for his troubles. In times of stress, when he felt helpless in the face of a great challenge, it was easier for him to lay the blame on some mysterious, uncontrollable and all-pervading 'monster', such as world Zionism or world Jewry, than to incur the shame of admitting his own inability to remedy the situation. Or he would vilify the Jews, by stating their inherent inferiority despite their apparent strength. He would reassure his own people that 'Allah is on our side', 'We are the elected nation of Allah', and at the same time pour scorn on the 'damned Jews' whose history had doomed them to remain inferior and therefore an easy prey to the believers of Allah. On 25 April 1972, on the occasion of the birthday of the Prophet Muhammed, he publicly accused the Jews of having deflected the Prophet from the aim of his mission in Medina, and he pledged to regain Jerusalem 'from those of whom the Quran said: "It was written of them that they shall be demeaned and made wretched." ' He added, in indignation: 'Since when have those people acquired virtue? Only after the forces of imperialism have put themselves behind them. But the forces of imperialism will not be able to challenge Allah's will.' He rejected Israel's plea for direct negotiations, arguing that 'they were the neighbours of the Prophet in Medina and he negotiated with them, but in the end they proved that they were men of deceit and treachery since they concluded a treaty with his enemies so as to strike him in Medina and attack him from within'. He went on: 'They are a nation of traitors and liars, contrivers of plots, a people born to deeds of treachery,' and promised that within a year they would be, as the Quran said of them, 'condemned to humiliation and misery'.

In January 1972, Sadat realized that unless he crushed what he saw as a student conspiracy against his rule, he could not prepare his country for war. He decided to prosecute thirty out of the 900 arrested; in this way he would be able to crush the opposition and also show magnanimity by giving the others a second chance. He said that he understood that the young were the most likely to show impatience in the face of the prevailing political situation, and he saw no wrong in that. His only grievance against the demonstrators was that they had attempted to act outside the framework of government and the established authority of the President. In January 1973, Sadat was trying to prepare for war but he was still having to devote a considerable part of his time to student unrest, although it was only one of many examples of social turbulence in Egypt at the time. In 1973, the winter rains came early, the telephone system in Cairo failed, sewers overflowed, public transport broke down, and everyone blamed Sadat, who felt personally insulted by the implication that he was not looking after his people: it was just that he was determined to postpone economic development until the war was over. Sadat also tried to scotch rumours about a government crisis and to blame the 'adventurist Left' and the 'reactionary Right' for casting doubts on Egypt's capacity to wage war.

Sadat was well aware that he was in the firing-line and being heavily scrutinized by Arab and Western leaders, all of whom doubted Egypt's ability to deal with her internal problems. He publicly announced that he knew the names of Egyptians from the Right and the Left who were discrediting their country by 'selling' stories to the foreign press and spreading rumours against him abroad, but as he moved away from the political oppression of Nasser's period, he was loath to launch massive arrests again. He dismissed 120 journalists, arguing that their irresponsible approach had increased Egypt's suffering instead of helping to bridge internal dissensions. He allowed all of them to resume their posts on 28 September 1973, the anniversary of Nasser's death, and only eight days before the outbreak of war, as he sensed that they had learned their lesson. He also dismissed some writers along with other public figures who had published a petition in the press casting doubts on Sadat's leadership, and who had organized a mass rally against him to ridicule his repeated 'Year of Decision' promises which had come to nothing for the second year running. He felt that even if freedom of expression was sacrosanct, the interests of Egypt were more important.

On the military front, Sadat decided, in October 1972, to dismiss the War Minister, veteran Field-Marshal Muhammed Sadeq, but presented it to the public as a 'resignation'. In his stead he appointed Ahmed Isma'il, and immediately provided him with the necessary funds (EL 20 million) to strengthen Egypt's defences. Sadat then announced that students would be allowed to enrol as volunteers in the Egyptian commando forces, where they would undergo an arduous six months training programme before being sent to the front in Sinai. He felt that this would harness the energies of the young and rebellious and stop them wreaking havoc on the universities and demonstrating in the streets of Cairo against their 'defeatist' President. Sadat also decreed that every province was to have its own military school which must take in sons of fallen Egyptian commandos as top priority and then other able-bodied candidates. Sadat believed that the programme should extend to all universities and high schools, and ultimately to elementary schools too, in order to forge the young generation into a nation of fighters. He reasoned that exactly as Israel was moulding her youth by military training, it became incumbent upon the Arabs to act likewise in order to check 'Zionist designs'.

In March 1973, Sadat made himself Prime Minister, Supreme Commander of the Armed Forces, and Military Governor of Egypt, in addition to being President, and chairman of the ASU Central Committee. He wished the leadership of Egypt to be organized on the lines of a military headquarters, and to launch an all-out national effort in the conduct of the war. His decision to tighten control over the country and the armed forces stemmed from his exasperation at what had happened in 1972. In August of that year Sadat had ordered the War Minister Sadeq to prepare the army for war by November and to inform the Supreme Council of the Armed Forces to that effect. Sadat had been assured at the time that the army would be ready by 1 November, although he had instructed it to be in a state of readiness by 15 November. When Sadat convened the Council at the end of October, in order to finalize the preparations before the November deadline, he was horrified to learn that the War Minister had never informed the Council about the preparations and final deadline. The Quartermaster-General, who was responsible for ensuring that the tanks had their fuel, that food and other supplies were available to the troops, and that all logistic services were ready in case hostilities broke out, did not know what the President was talking about. He said that he had no idea he was supposed to finalize any preparations by 1 or 15 November. Enraged, Sadat turned to the War Minister for an explanation. Sadeq, embarrassed in the presence of his subordinates, whispered to the President's ear that he had informed no one of the deadline because of the secrecy involved. Sadat exploded: 'Secrecy with the Supreme Council of the Armed Forces? This is the authority which approves plans, supplies gasoline and food; this Council is more important than the war itself, and if it defaults I shall dismiss it!' Sadeq was promptly relieved of his job. He, like others, underestimated the seriousness of the President's commitment to go to war; he must have thought that the November deadline was just another of Sadat's fantasies, one more vain promise joining the long line of all those others which had failed to materialize throughout 1971 and most of 1972.

As a result of that mishap, Sadat looked more closely at the famous 'Defence Plan 200' that Nasser had passed on to him before his death, which ordered Egypt's defences along the Canal bank to match or surpass those of Israel. Sadat now discovered that while Israel had piled up a huge, fifty-foot-high earth dyke along the eastern bank of the Canal in the wake of the War of Attrition, the Egyptian troops had remained entrenched behind a six-foot dyke which hardly afforded them any protection. Sadat sent for his two top field commanders, those in charge of the Second and Third Armies, who were to take the brunt of the offensive when the war began. From his interrogation, it transpired that they knew themselves to be in an inferior position along the Canal and realized that their moves were easily detected by the Israelis confronting them. That was not at all what General Fawzi, the father of the 'Plan 200', had envisaged. He had specified that for every foot of dyke the Israelis built, the Egyptians should match it by two, so as to give the Egyptians fire-domination and vantage points for observation.

Sadat received considerable political flak for dismissing Field-Marshal Sadeq: the leftist opposition charged him with thoughtlessness and vindictiveness in his appointment of ministers and top commanders; they also pointed out that it was his disastrous policy-making and decision-taking which had brought about communal unrest, student disturbances and the ousting of the Soviets from Egypt at a time when Egypt most needed a tranquil domestic front and a good working relationship with its major ally. Between October 1972 and February 1973, the Egyptian opposition press preached doom and gloom which Sadat felt undermined the people's morale. But he could not reveal in public the reasons why he had overhauled the Defence Plan, nor why he had reshuffled the top command. General Ahmed Isma'il, the new War Minister, was ordered to rebuild Egypt's defences first – for which he was given the EL 20 million allocated to him by Sadat already mentioned – and then to begin preparations for war. Isma'il personally supervised the building of higher and better earth dykes until they looked like 'real pyramids' to Sadat, and he reinforced the deployment of troops along the Canal. The Egyptians had now regained the initiative and seemed poised for action.

In February 1973, Ahmed Isma'il went to the Soviet Union and returned with a long list of promises for prompt arms deliveries which began to arrive in Alexandria in March. By the end of March 1973, the offensive plan was ready, and a tough training programme had readied the participating units for D-Day. Sadat, who believed in the metaphysical power of symbols, decided to visit High Command headquarters on 5 June 1973, the seventh anniversary of the Six Day War, in order to see the thirty-five-foot sand model of the battleground. Each military commander in turn demonstrated his part of the plan, whilst the President puffed on his pipe and nodded approvingly. Sadat was exhilarated by the pace of events and impressed by the serious and imaginative way each of the commanders had prepared and presented his homework. Sadat was particularly enamoured by the air-force commander, General Husni Mubarak, on whose performance, during the first hours of the offensive, the entire fate of the war would hinge. (Later, he was to appoint Mubarak his deputy, from which position he was eventually able to become President.) Ever since Sadat had discovered that Sadeq had not carried 'Plan 200' out properly, he had not been able to sleep at night for fear the Israelis might strike first. Now he was reassured. He saw the determination in the faces of his field commanders and he knew that, even if the Soviet supplies did not arrive in time, the troops' morale was high and he hoped that the careful planning of the offensive would make up for material shortcomings.

Sadat reckoned that Egypt was in dire need of four major types of weapon: half-tracks for desert warfare and quick deployment of infantry; fighter bombers to counter Israel's Phantoms and allow Egyptian strategists to strike deep into Israel (at one point Sadat considered kamikaze-style attacks by suicide pilots who would crash on Israel's vital installations, but the idea never took off); more torpedoes and/or missile boats especially after the sinking of the *Eilat*, Israel's destroyer, in late 1967; and, finally, advanced electronic equipment, which Sadat believed could be easily operated by his engineers now that they were being augmented by 2,100 new engineering graduates annually.

Sadat was certain that much of this equipment, especially the electronic gear, torpedo-boats and half-tracks, could be manufactured in Egypt. Lines of production had been set up in Hilwan and elsewhere to manufacture military hardware before 1967, but the war had made the matter of rearmament so urgent that it had become necessary to press for speedy Soviet deliveries rather than to depend on their own slow, costly and uncertain processes. Looking back, Sadat thought that Egypt had made the wrong decision, for which he blamed General Fawzi, who had been in charge of updating the army after 1967. Sadat thought that, as a member of the 'foci of power', Fawzi had followed Soviet strategy and sought to perpetuate Egypt's dependence on them for arms and spare parts. Incidentally, Sadat said that he had disagreed with that decision, but as President Nasser had backed it he had been bound to accept it.

Fawzi's successor, Marshal Sadeq, and some of his aides thought that Egypt should not go to war until she had MiG 23s which would deliver in-depth, long-range strikes against Israel. Sadeq was also apprehensive about Israel's array of electronic equipment that was rumoured to be in position behind the Bar-lev Line along the Suez Canal. He strongly opposed confrontation with Israel until Soviet supplies arrived. Sadat refused to submit his war plans to Soviet whim; Egypt would try to rearm as best she could and would enter the war with what she had. In 1968, Sadat had reviewed film footage of the 1967 war, and had come to the conclusion that so-called 'Israeli superiority' could be overcome by creating an Egyptian fighting spirit, by indoctrinating the troops against the Jews, by showing the need to 'purify' the land, by a daring war plan and by imaginative command. He knew that Israel was capitalizing on the assumption that the Egyptians would be unable to handle their missiles efficiently since the Soviets had left, and that the superior Israeli air force would be able to repeat its stunning 1967 victory.

In February 1973, Sadat commissioned research on the best dates for the offensive. The architect of the plan was General Gamasi, Chief of Operations, who was later to become Chief of Staff and War Minister before his power and popularity became too much for Sadat to bear, and he too was demoted. He drew up his plan, handwritten in a small booklet, which he submitted personally to Sadat so as to preserve secrecy. Every date, from February to 31 December 1973, was examined, as well as every hour of the day and night; all natural phenomena likely to have an impact on the planning were also looked at, as were all foreseeable events, weather shifts and astronomical conditions. Gamasi's report won the President's approval for its accuracy, thoroughness and highly scientific approach. Three clusters of dates turned out to be most opportune for D-Day: the second half of May, September or October. Sadat ordered the planning to be finalized before 1 May, so as to keep all options open. He met President Assad of Syria in Bourj al-Arab in April 1973, and showed him the first outlines of the plan. However, the Second Soviet–American Summit in Washington was then announced for May, so the first option was ruled out. As a result of Assad's secret trip to Moscow in early 1973, the Soviets agreed to negotiate new arms deliveries to Egypt and Ahmed Isma'il's visit to the Kremlin in February paved the way for further arms deals, part of which were delivered immediately, the rest withheld.

In August, the Supreme Council of the Egyptian and Syrian Armed Forces held a secret meeting in Alexandria. The discussions between the top field commanders centred around war tactics and co-ordination of the pincer movement between Egypt and Syria. Sadat then went to Syria with his War Minister to meet Assad and General Mustafa Tlas, the Syrian War Minister. At that meeting, D-Day was fixed for 6 October. Sadat left Damascus confident of the outcome. At home, the military preparations went into top gear. Ahmed Isma'il maintained daily contact with the President and consulted him on every minute detail. On 30 September, six days before D-Day, Sadat decided to convene his National Defence Council in order to announce his war plans. Sadat's two Vice-Presidents, his presidential advisers, the Prime Minister's deputies and the head of Intelligence all attended. Sadat's mind had been made up, but he wanted to relieve his inner tension by sharing the secret that had haunted him for months; he also wished to solicit the views of his top advisers to see if they could spot something that had been overlooked or forgotten. Sadat broke the tense atmosphere by stating that war was not an adventure imposed on one's destiny, but was rather a calculated risk, all aspects of which warranted close examination. He emphasized that if Egypt had waited until it was one hundred per cent assured of victory, it might never be able to initiate a war. He was aware, he said, of the million-and-one reasons for postponing the decision: lack of money, shortages of material, insufficient training and lack of food stockpiles, and the disaster that might occur should things go wrong; but, as he pointed out, there would always be reasons for cancelling, avoiding or postponing the war and he mentioned the old Turkish joke about 'No. 17 pretext'. The outbreak of war might drain Egypt's economy to the point where there would be no money available to purchase wheat, but this was largely offset by the probability that the war would cause such wide-range changes in the world that Egypt would somehow be able to endure supply shortages. Sadat dramatically announced that he could have used the 'No. 17' pretext to put the war off until the end of his presidency in order to avert a possible defeat, but had he chosen that easy path he would have considered himself a traitor who tried to escape the verdict of his destiny. Sadat did not tell them the exact date of D-Day, although his naval forces had already begun moving into position, army units had taken up their battle stations and the wheels of war had begun their irreversible roll forwards. Sadat thought that there was a 30 per cent chance that the war plan might fail, but he knew that he and his subordinates had put in every possible effort and not wasted a precious minute. He remained calm because he felt that he had discharged his personal and national duty to the full and that coming generations would recognize this. Egyptians would fall in the battle, but in the process they would cause Israeli casualties and would have defended their honour and their holy land. He considered it much more honourable to die in battle, even if defeated, than to continue in this miserable no-peace-no-war situation, while the world looked on and jeered at them for being so lethargic and incompetent.

Concurrently with his activities on domestic, civilian and military fronts, Sadat conceived a diplomatic campaign that would ensure him Soviet military and diplomatic support until the war broke out, but would also enable him to solicit US mediation and aid once the military operation was successfully completed. To induce the US to make such a shift, he would have to prove first that Israel was not invincible and that Egypt was a military power to reckon with; and secondly, to elicit the united support of the Arab world, including a possible oil embargo, the Achilles heel of the West. Once he had secured a close alliance with Syria and worked out a co-ordinated plan of attack, he set out to widen the circle of his alliances in an attempt to recapture the leadership of the Arab world.

In the ten months before the October War, Sadat travelled to many Arab capitals to deliver appeals on the theme of Arab unity. He urged the Arabs to desist from 'lifting their daggers against each other' and 'rejoicing at their brothers' distress', even if it was impossible for them to be united: unity was the sole counter-measure that the Arabs could put forward to foil imperialism and Zionism, both perceived as outside forces of invasion. Sadat had been depressed by Egypt's abortive union with Syria and with the Federation of Arab Republics (FAR), although he drew three important lessons from these failures. Firstly, that the essence of co-operation was far more important than any constitutional form it might take; in other words, he valued actual assistance from Arab countries far above the lip service provided by some loose, non-binding 'federation'. Secondly, it must be recognized that there were major differences within the Arab world as a result of geographic, economic, social and cultural variations that were 'caused by the history of imperialist occupation'; Sadat, while preserving his sense of the cultural superiority of '7,000-year-old Egypt' over the rest of the Arab world, which he regarded with some disdain, was willing to take into account regional and parochial sensitivities in his bid for unity. Thirdly, it took deeds, based on scientific research, to effect any semblance of unity; enthusiastic speeches and zealous declarations of sentiment and intention were not enough. For Sadat realized full well that while Arab unity potentially held much promise, it could also result in Arab weakness if hurriedly and recklessly executed.

Sadat thought that, since Israel was capitalizing upon Arab disunity, it was a great achievement to have launched the Federation of Arab Republics. A Federal Council of Ministers as well as a joint Parliament were set up, and Sadat knew that even if these institutions did little, the very fact of their creation, which was designed to crystallize the willpower of three or four major Arab countries to undo Israel's strategic assumptions, bore witness to the potentialities of Arab unity. And if unity of action could not be achieved immediately in such a large framework, Sadat was determined to content himself with bilateral agreements with countries within the Federation or outside it. Sadat saw the usefulness of this approach in his close co-operation with Syria as the war drew near. Indeed, a joint command was set up between the two countries and frequent consultations took place between the two in the months before the outbreak of war, on both presidential and technical levels.

Sadat truly believed that an all-pervading world Zionist movement was attempting to undermine Arab unity with a view to beating and humiliating each Arab country separately, in accordance with some alleged master plan that had been adopted at the first Zionist Congress in Basel in 1897. Thus, Arab unity, or at the very least Arab solidarity, would enable all Arabs to come to the help of any Arab country chosen as the next Zionist victim. Therefore, he saw the emergence of new 'progressive' regimes in the Arab world, such as those of Syria, Libya and the Sudan, as beneficial to the long-term ideals of Arab unity and as his potential allies in the war against Israel. He was enthusiastic at first about the Libyan revolution under Qadhafi, in which he detected youth, hope, restlessness, sincerity and loyalty to the Arab cause. He regarded Qadhafi himself as a new type of Arab revolutionary, one who represented freedom and purity, devotion and resolve, so much so that he dubbed him the 'Knight of Revolution'. He also heaped much praise on President Assad of Syria, who had succeeded, despite his continuous 'confrontations with the Zionist enemy', in mobilizing all the resources of his country, human and material, to the service of Arab interests. Together with these two leaders, Sadat had created a large political entity, encompassing half the Arab people and combining the human resources of Egypt, the wealth of Libya and the resourcefulness and fighting spirit of Syria.

Sadat once made the point, during these pre-war years, that mini-states were no longer viable in a setting which was constantly threatened by the superpowers. The USSR, in his mind, had become a world power because it had combined its fifteen 'republics', although they varied in race, culture and wealth. Similarly, China had isolated herself behind her walls long enough to pull herself together and unify her ranks, and had then reappeared as an awesome power. Each of the component states of Western Europe had also realized that they could not stand alone in the face of the two superpowers, and had therefore united. The lesson was clear: the combined forces of the Arabs could constitute the Sixth Power of the world (after the two superpowers, China, Japan and Western Europe), but if they failed to combine they would wither away. It was imperative then to support all Arab regimes which understood that a great destiny awaited the Arabs, particularly his neighbours to the south and the west, the Sudan and Libya.

Ja'far Numeiri, the ruler of the Sudan, who had taken over power at the end of the Nasserite era in Egypt, became one of Sadat's closest associates. Egypt had always valued its relations with the Sudan, the cradle of the Nile, Egypt's life artery, and Sadat came to regard Numeiri as one of his potential allies. When Sadat was troubled by his 'foci of power' crisis in May 1971, Numeiri flew in unannounced to Cairo to stand by his friend. On Friday 13 May at 7 a.m., he landed at Cairo West airport, but remained on board until he saw how the political situation was unfolding. Sadat rushed to the airport to welcome him, but found him still asleep in his aircraft, so he waited for him to wake up. Sadat was escorted by his guest all that day and made his speech announcing the 'conspiracy against him' and the attempted *coup* by Ali Sabry and his clique in front of Numeiri, who did not return to Khartoum until he was sure that Sadat would win. Sadat never forgot his debt to Numeiri. In July 1971, Sadat received some information to the effect that a Communist underground group was plotting a *coup* against Numeiri in the Sudan. He called his friend immediately and asked him to come to Cairo for a meeting. But before Numeiri could come, the Sudanese Communist rebellion broke out, instigated by some Egyptians of the Left. Sadat feared for Numeiri's life and dispatched two prominent Egyptian Marxists who had maintained contacts with Mr Mahjub, the Secretary General of the Sudanese Communist Party, to try to intervene on behalf of the beleaguered Sudanese President. But when the emissaries reported back to Cairo, they told Sadat that the *coup* had succeeded and advised him to recognize the new regime in Khartoum. Sadat was furious. 'Sorry, I did not send you there for that!' he retorted sarcastically. Sadat also rejected a plea by the Soviet Ambassador to Cairo to lend recognition to the new regime, arguing that no Marxist regime could take hold in the Arab world. Ultimately, two exiled members of the Sudanese Communist Party, who were on their way from London to Khartoum to form the new Marxist Government, were intercepted and arrested by Qadhafi of Libya, Numeiri counter-attacked with forces loyal to him, and the *coup* was foiled.

With Libya, the relationship was somewhat more complicated, due to the unpredictability of Qadhafi. Sadat knew right from the beginning of his alliance with Qadhafi, within the FAR, that the young revolutionary from Tripoli reacted erratically to world developments and that he tended to take irresponsible and extremist views on most matters relating to foreign affairs and to the Arab–Israeli conflict, depending on his distance from the area of actual war. But Sadat believed that Libya could contribute enormously to Egypt, especially in the economic field. He thought that if the huge reserves of land that lay waste in Libya, and the vast oil resources which made Libya rich, were combined wtih Egypt's over-population and stifling poverty, a strong country could be created; it would control the longest shore line belonging to one nation in the Mediterranean and would have a hinterland which would render Egypt practically immune to military defeat. What was more, the former American and British sea and air bases in Libya could be turned into a huge military depot beyond the range of Israeli bombers, which would secure Israel's defeat in a prolonged war of attrition which the Jewish state could ill afford. Qadhafi had pushed, from the very outset of FAR in 1970, for a total and immediate 'merger' between the member states. But Nasser, and then Sadat, were wary of a precipitated unification which would divert their resources and attention away from the more pressing issue of the Arab–Israeli conflict, so they tried to dampen Qadhafi's zeal. Qadhafi, who sensed he was the key link in the projected union with Egypt, also made unacceptable demands on Sadat: he wanted Egypt to cut relations with moderate Arab countries, which were not to Libya's liking, to Islamize all aspects of Egyptian society, and to hold a popular referendum in Egypt and Libya which would result, Qadhafi believed, in Egypt adopting the 'Islamic Revolution', Libyan vintage. Sadat baulked. He would rather use Libya for his purposes than let the unstable and unpredictable Qadhafi take command of Egypt. Therefore, he kept repeating to his Egyptian audiences that there was no benefit to be drawn from a hurried union, although he remained committed to its goals.

In July 1973, 50,000 Libyans marched to the Egyptian border in a massive demonstration for immediate merger with Libya. Before the march, Qadhafi announced that if it failed to achieve its objective, he would have to resign from office, since his greatest dream would have proven unrealizable. Up until that moment, Sadat had believed that his rear was safe so he felt able to strike east towards Israel; desperate, he tried to stop the march, then reluctantly received a delegation of the marchers. On 23 July, Qadhafi's Prime Minister, Jallud, landed in Cairo unannounced. He came to demand that union between his country and Egypt be announced instantly. Then, on 29 August, Qadhafi himself arrived in Cairo, without prior notice, when Sadat was away in Syria deciding the final date for D-Day with Assad. Qadhafi demanded that Egypt and Libya pool their resources immediately; Libya was prepared to sign a blank paper on which Egypt could list any conditions she wished for the union. But Sadat saw such moves as empty gestures and tried to calm down his young colleague's unwarranted 'goodwill'. On his seventeen-day visit to Egypt, which caused more embarrassment to Sadat and his Government than comfort, Qadhafi at one point volunteered to contribute to Egypt $1 billion annually, over a period of five years, to help Cairo out of its economic problems. Sadat attempted to temper his guest's enthusiasm and said that $500 million would do. But Qadhafi insisted on his generosity being accepted and a joint committee was set up to formulate the wording of the agreement. Suddenly, Qadhafi made his signature contingent on Sadat's prohibiting the publication of advertisements from Saudi Arabia, Kuwait or Abu Dhabi in Egyptian newspapers. Sadat was exasperated. He rejected Qadhafi's ideas, and in a last effort to salvage something from the visit he suggested that the two adjoining provinces, on either side of the Egyptian–Libyan border, should be unified into one province, as a first step towards the promised union which Qadhafi insisted should be completed by 1 September. Sadat put forward 20 September as the date for declaring the merger of the two provinces, thinking that a joint military parade could be mounted at Tobruk in Libya on that date, together with an air display and a naval show, in the presence of the two Presidents, which would deceive Israel who would not suspect that Egypt, immersed in celebrations and parades, could be preparing for an all-out military offensive. In early September, Sadat attended the conference of the non-aligned in Algeria and got confirmation from the Libyan President that the 20 September parade was on as planned. Immediately upon his return to Cairo, Sadat ordered some naval units to move from Alexandria to Tobruk in anticipation of the parade. But on 11 September, after the navy had sailed off, a Libyan emissary came to see Sadat to tell him that the proposed plan of partial unity 'constituted an obstruction to real unity' and therefore Qadhafi had reneged.

On 17 September, Sadat wrote to Qadhafi again and repeated his plea for an inter-provincial merger as the first step towards total unity. As proof of his intentions, Sadat allocated air, land and sea units to participate in the Tobruk parade although Egypt was due to go to war within twenty days. But when he realized the ephemeral nature of Qadhafi's promises, he ordered the navy back to Alexandria. On 4 October, two days before war was to break out, Sadat invited Prime Minister Jallud of Libya to come to Egypt as he had decided to tell him that he was about to go to war, although he was careful not to divulge the exact date. Sadat pleaded with Jallud to go back to Qadhafi with three requests: first, that the port of Tobruk should serve as a back-up to Alexandria, Egypt's only military port, which was likely to be attacked when the war began; secondly, that Libya deliver immediately by air, spare parts for the Mirage planes that she had stationed in Egypt; thirdly, that Libya be prepared to supply Egypt with oil for the duration of the war, which was expected to last for a long period of time, as Egyptian oil wells would probably have to cease production. Jallud went back to Tripoli that same day and called Sadat on the telephone to confirm Libya's agreement to his three requests. Sadat felt relieved, confident that he could count on his western neighbour when the hostilities began.

Sadat had always felt great sympathy for the destitute Palestinians, who had been trying to find a national solution to their problem for so long. He was well aware that Egypt had joined the abortive war of 1948 against Israel in order to help establish a Palestinian state, and that his country had, as a result, become embroiled in a seemingly unending cycle of violence with Israel, including the disaster of 1967. Now that he was poised to launch an attack to liberate the Egyptian territories occupied by Israel, the Palestinian problem again raised its head. Sadat was well aware of its intricacies and the way in which it had always poisoned inter-Arab relations, but now he wished to unite the Arabs behind him, not to cause any new controversies which might deflect them from facing the main enemy – Israel – so he declared his full support for the Palestinian Resistance, as enshrined in the PLO struggle against Israel, and strongly condemned the Jordanian slaughter of thousands of Palestinians during Black September in 1970. Sadat noted with bitterness that 'history will record with sorrow and shame that the Palestinian Resistance has lost more heroes in her struggle against Arab regimes than in her wars against the Zionist enemy'.

What particularly saddened Sadat was that although he had forged a 'northern front' (Syria) and secured a hinterland behind him (Libya and Sudan), he could not get his eastern front (the Palestinians, Jordan and Iraq) to pull together. As Sadat saw it, the eastern front would never unite because the Arabs disagreed on how to treat the Palestinians. Sadat saw the Fatah, headed by Arafat, as a positive element who ought to be encouraged, while other Palestinian deviationist groups, who were given to foreign influence, should be discarded. Sadat believed that if King Hussein of Jordan gave the Fatah permission to operate from bases in Jordan, the Palestinians could become a factor in the battlefield, and therefore he was interested in mending the Hussein–Arafat rift. But Hussein stalled, for fear that that would mean handing his country over to the PLO. Sadat was infuriated by Hussein, who had 'agreed' to respond positively to the 'moderate' Fatah but did nothing about it, and he bluntly dubbed him a 'cheater and deceiver', vowing never to trust him again.

Sadat came out publicly in support of the establishment of a Palestinian government-in-exile against Golda Meir, the Israeli Prime Minister, who had denied the Palestinians a separate identity of their own. Sadat remembered that during the Algerian War a provisional Algerian government-in-exile had been established, long before Algerian victory was in sight, and although it was only recognized by Arab countries, it was successful in drawing the world's attention to the existence of an Algerian political unit opposed to the slogan 'Algérie Française'. Sadat also hoped that a Palestinian government-in-exile

89

would compel all Palestinian factions to end their internal strife and pose outwardly as a united front, for he feared that internal dissent amongst the resistance movement might do it more harm than Hussein and Israel combined. When an Israeli commando unit attacked some PLO leaders in their apartments in Beirut, killing some of them, in March 1973, Sadat called President Faranjieh of Lebanon and urged him to call a meeting of the UN Security Council to discuss what he viewed as a 'repulsive crime'. However, Sadat later admitted that this *démarche* was part and parcel of his world-wide campaign to discredit Israel diplomatically before the war was launched. In order to attain that goal, he dispatched his Foreign Minister, Dr Zayyat, to attend the UN deliberations; he enlisted support from the African and non-aligned countries in his campaign, but when it came to the vote all members, save the US, cast their vote sanctioning Israel. Sadat did not relent. In his May Day speech in 1973, he condemned Israel for attempting to promote coexistence with the Palestinians in the West Bank and Gaza, and sent an open message of hope to the 'heroes under occupation' to 'stand fast, for the night will not last much longer!' He again pledged never to abandon the Palestinian cause and never to allow it to be 'desecrated' by Arab infighting. He censured Israel for pursuing the Palestinians outside the occupied territories in a 'cruel and criminal manner', alluding to Beirut where 'peaceful houses and civilian apartments were broken into by Israel, a member of the UN, in order to carry out a premeditated act of murder'.

In the summer of 1973, Sadat acknowledged that 'Palestinian commando activities have been continuing' in co-ordination with Egypt. This meant that the acts of terror launched by the PLO and its surrogates against Israel not only had Sadat's blessing, but also his encouragement. When a Japanese terrorist gang, instigated by the PLO, ran amok in the Ben-Gurion airport in Israel and killed dozens of Israeli civilians and Puerto Rican pilgrims in May 1973, Sadat not only refrained from expressing grief or remorse, but censured Israel for protesting and for accusing the PLO, when she herself had committed the Beirut attack. Therefore, although Sadat had accepted Security Council Resolution 242 (on his own interpretation), he declared that he would not pressure the Palestinians to act likewise, because 'Palestine was theirs, both the land occupied in 1948 and the rest of Palestine occupied in 1967 and thereafter'. This remark, coupled with another declaration he made at about the same time that Israel was 'a foreign organ that had been forcibly transplanted into the Arab nation, and our body rejects it', should leave no doubt as to Sadat's belligerent mood in the summer of 1973 and his total rejection of Israel's right to exist.

A few weeks before the war broke out, Sadat met Abu Iyad, the PLO's second-in-command, in Cairo and urged him to go to Beirut and tell chairman Yasser Arafat about the approaching war. True, Sadat refrained from stating the exact date of D-Day, in the same way as he had withheld it from other Arab leaders such as Qadhafi of Libya and King Faisal of Saudi Arabia, but he did counsel the PLO chief to dispatch thirty to forty Palestinian commandos to join the Egyptian troops in crossing the Canal, and insisted that the contingent should arrive in Egypt before 1 October 1973, a good enough hint of D-Day. Sadat's argument was that if the Palestinians participated in the hoped-for victory, they could march with Egypt to impose a settlement on defeated Israel. Sadat must have remembered that one of his heroes, de Gaulle, achieved parity with the Western powers in the post-war settlement of Europe, merely by virtue of his symbolic participation in the Allies' Normandy landings.

For the rest of the Arab countries, Sadat was particularly concerned with the rich oil producers. He once did his soul-searching about them in public, using an inclusive *we* as if the oil states were his vassals or at the very least his assured allies:

> We are now producing 55 per cent of the world oil consumption and we hold 85 per cent of the world reserves. In terms of capital, the Arabs control more than EL 50 billion in bank deposits, which carry crucial weight in the international money markets. If we could use this tremendous potential with wisdom and reason, we could bring our vast Arab power to bear on our national problems. We still welcome co-operation and co-ordination between Arab forces, whatever their geographic position and their political regime, for when it comes to Arab destiny, we must rise above internal wrangles and only think about the dangers menacing us all.

Saudi Arabia had been alienated by Nasser both on ideological grounds (reactionary-monarchical regime versus his own progressive-revolution), and for practical considerations (her support for the Yemenite monarchical loyalists who fought against him, and her reluctance to disburse some of her wealth to provide for Egypt's dire needs), but was now courted vehemently by Sadat. In July 1972 when he decided to evict the Soviet experts but before he announced his decision in public, he contacted Amir Sultan, the Saudi Defence Minister who was in Geneva, and asked him to stop over in Cairo on his way back home to share the momentous news. The Saudis were flattered to have been put in the picture, and Sadat was delighted to be able to involve such a wealthy kingdom more in Arab affairs. This warming of relations between Egypt and Saudi Arabia also tempered Sadat's expectations of Arab oil as a weapon. For Sadat reasoned that, if the oil-producing countries, who in 1972 contributed more than EL 100 million to Egypt, were to cut off their oil revenues, how could they then be expected to continue to support him? He stated that the oil-producing Arab countries should not be burdened with policies they could not bear, especially as oil was their only resource.

In August 1973 Sadat toured some Arab countries in an attempt to bridge the gap between 'Right and Left', 'Progressives and Reactionaries'. Significantly, the tour began with Saudi Arabia. Sadat had long talks with King Faisal and told him he was going to war soon, though again he did not give the exact date. Sadat felt that Faisal was at first receptive to the idea as he said:

FAISAL: Are you ready?

SADAT: Yes.

FAISAL: What are we required to do?

SADAT: Nothing in particular, just take note that I am about to start a war. You will make your decisions in due course, for each of us knows his own domestic affairs best. . . .

FAISAL: I would ask only one thing of you: if you start a war, do not stop it after an hour or a day. Go on, so that we can take a united Arab position at your side. . . .

Proud Sadat, of course, needed financial assistance. But to all the rich Arab leaders whom he met, including King Faisal, he said he needed nothing, only adding, 'Just fulfil your duty as you deem fit.' They understood, and he knew that they did. Sadat promised Saudi Arabia, Kuwait, the United Emirates and Qatar that he was indeed planning a protracted war and that their support was vital to him. He then went to Bludan in Syria to meet Assad and finalize the details of D-Day. Sadat was convinced that, even if they did not have an oil embargo (an idea enthusiastically supported by Syria and Libya but shunned by the Saudis and most of the oil producers), a sophisticated use of Arab monetary reserves and trade pressures could still yield great benefit for the Arab cause in the coming battle, provided they all stood together and were prepared to confront the US.

And then it was necessary to gain support from the non-aligned countries and the members of the Islamic Conference. At the Islamic Conference held in Benghazi, Libya, in early 1973, Hassan al-Tuhami, the Egyptian Deputy Prime Minister, who had been sent by Sadat to gain an Islamic consensus for Egypt, was elected as the organization's Secretary General, and the resolutions adopted at the end of the conference lent, as expected, unconditional support to Egypt and other Arabs in their efforts to liberate their lands from Israeli occupation. Sadat was delighted with the results of the conference:

> This [Islamic] Conference is not founded on fanaticism, obscurantism or one-track-mindedness, the like of which we observe elsewhere, in Israel, which is founded on appalling religious and racist fanaticism. Religious and racist fanaticism are foreign to Islam, for it encompasses peoples from all over the world and from all nationalities.[22]

Islamic backing was particularly important to Sadat in view of his widely publicized arguments with Qadhafi over Islamic problems. Qadhafi had come to Cairo in the summer of 1973 and spent seventeen days talking to public opinion-makers, trying to persuade them to emulate the Libyan Islamic revolution. Sadat, pious Muslim though he was, thought that the Libyan model was incompatible with the Egyptian revolution. To Qadhafi's demand that the *Shari'a* law of Islam should be reintroduced as the basis of Egyptian legislation, Sadat retorted that such a provision was already part of the Egyptian constitution, but for the past fourteen generations Islamic law had been interpreted anew by the scholars of each particular generation. In times of decay, these interpretations were dictated by political rulers, said Sadat, hinting that Qadhafi's fundamentalist interpretation of the *Shari'a* could be seen as a symptom of such decay.

In May 1973, Sadat went to the conference of the Organization of African Unity (OAU) in Addis Ababa, Ethiopia. There he made an impassioned speech in which he tried to explain to the Africans that Israel and South Africa were two racist countries which harboured aggressive desires against the black continent: Israel from the north (against Egyptian territory) and South Africa in the south. Therefore, there was no escape from the need to fight them both. He expressly said that Egypt was gearing up for a war which would help all Africans. Then, in September, Sadat went to the Non-Aligned Conference in Algeria where he repeated the same arguments, and extracted a conference resolution supporting Egypt's right to liberate her lands. There, he enhanced his position still further by violently attacking American policy towards developing countries. He contended that what the Americans called a 'war to conquer deserts' was nothing more than a new scheme to control the resources of developing nations, which amounted to a revival of colonialism (Chile and Zambia were cited as examples of such 'exploitation'). Faced with the double threat of world imperialism and world Zionism, the non-aligned countries should, asserted Sadat, 'effect the transition from words to deeds', and he implied that Egypt was going to lead the way by defying both threats.

China, the new power on the world scene, who had recently occupied her permanent seat on the Security Council of the UN, aligned herself un-reservedly with the Arabs. Sadat sought to secure her support because her veto power in the Security Council might come in handy should that forum have to deal with the war after it broke out, and should the Soviet veto be denied him. Sadat was aware that his close relations with the Chinese might incense the Soviets, but he thought that Egypt's interests came first. So, he dispatched two successive Foreign Ministers, Muhammed Riad in 1972 and Dr Zayyat in early 1973, to Peking to elicit Chinese statements of support, but at the same time he declared that he did not favour anyone at the expense of another. China had not even recognized Israel (unlike the Soviet Union which had, though it ceased diplomatic relations after 1967) and was therefore considered an asset to Egyptian and Arab diplomatic efforts. Dr Zayyat also visited India, Pakistan, Iran and Bangladesh, while Dr Mar'i, another close associate of Sadat's and Chairman of the People's Assembly, was delegated to the Eastern Bloc countries, notably Yugoslavia, Egypt's partner in the founding of the Non-Aligned Group.

The US and Western Europe were a quite different story. Sadat entrusted his National Security Adviser, Hafez Isma'il, with the task of explaining Egyptian attitudes to them, even though he entertained little hope of swaying them towards unequivocal sympathy for the Arab camp. The US had become a 'lost cause' for Sadat, as he felt that she had lent her blessing to Israel, 'slamming all doors' in his face. He therefore concentrated on the major European powers: Britain, France, Italy and Germany. Early in 1973 Sadat remarked that British attitudes towards Egypt had improved. Although he was bitter about the 'propaganda spread by the BBC and the *Guardian*' over student unrest in Egypt, and disappointed that he could not obtain weapons from Britain, he was hopeful that British policy statements would be tempered in his favour. During Isma'il's visit, both the Prime Minister and the Foreign Minister assured him that their position towards Security Council Resolution 242 remained unchanged.

Sadat considered France to be the only country in Western Europe 'whose attitude to the Arabs has been noble and free from ambiguity'. He had come to this conclusion after de Gaulle had distanced himself from his erstwhile 'friend and ally' (Israel) at the outbreak of the Six Day War in 1967 and had then made hostile remarks about the 'domineering character of the Jews'. Such attitudes certainly sounded 'noble' to Sadat, and he was intent on encouraging them under Pompidou's administration. Sadat had some misgivings about Israel's 'illicit' purchases of spare parts for its French-made Mirage jets, but he could do little about it. He even boasted that despite the official French embargo on arms shipments to the Middle East, he too could obtain spare parts not only directly from France but also indirectly via Britain and Belgium. Prime Minister Schumann in particular was praised by Sadat for his clear-cut declarations in favour of the Arabs, and for his influence among the other European Common Market members which had produced some softening in their attitudes. When French-made Mirage jets, purchased by Libya, were transferred to Egypt to aid her air defence, Israel accused Libya of having violated the terms of the sale, which, in order to circumvent the embargo, had prohibited their transfer to countries directly involved in the conflict. Sadat disclaimed the transfer and interpreted Israel's outcry as a propaganda campaign against France. He was delighted to find himself in the same camp as the French, defended the 'French right to sell to anyone she wished', and reproved Israel for trying to dictate to the Arabs what they could buy from whom, and for interfering between the French and the Arabs. In the same breath, he encouraged France and other European countries to safeguard their own interests and to detach themselves from the United States' unjustified support for the Jewish state and for its attempts to become master of the Middle East.

After the March 1973 Beirut incident, France and Britain voted in favour of the Security Council resolution which censured Israel; Sadat regarded that as a direct outcome of his diplomatic success. Italy, who also had economic interests in the Arab world, was encouraged by Sadat to back the Arabs. In February 1973, Prime Minister Andreotti sent his Foreign Minister to Cairo to see Sadat; two months later he put forward some proposals suggesting the Suez

Canal be reopened as it had been closed to navigation since 1967. However, when rumour spread that Andreotti was actually in favour of digging a new canal through Israeli-held territory, Sadat lashed out at the US and Israel for attempting to sow discord between him and the Italians. Sadat claimed that he 'knew' the genesis of that idea: back in 1968, an emissary had arrived in Cairo with an urgent message from the Somali President, which had been handed to Nasser in Sadat's presence. The message said that the US had intimated that the Suez Canal problem could be resolved without a war, simply by digging a new canal through the Sinai desert. The project was to be carried out by a Panamanian company; within eighteen months the new canal would have two-way traffic, unlike the old narrow one, and a free zone to allow international trade. Egypt would be requested to lease the zone to the Panamanian company for a period of ninety-nine years, as had been previously the case with the Suez Canal. Sadat said that Nasser had ordered an investigation into the whole affair, had found out that the idea and the company were American, and that the new canal was intended to separate Egypt from Israel and so remove the reason for further wars. Nasser had rejected the plan out of hand, and Sadat concurred. The new Andreotti proposals revived rumours about the old plan which Sadat was swift to deny, 'crediting' Israel and the US with their fabrication.

Ever since Sadat had broken off contact with the US in 1971, following the shelving of the Rogers Plan, he had become increasingly suspicious of their role in the Arab–Israeli conflict and angered at what he saw as their one-sided interference on Israel's side. In early 1972, the Americans established a naval base in Piraeus, Greece. Sadat saw this move as part of the reinforcement of US power in the east Mediterranean; he felt it had been done to menace the emerging alliance between Egypt and Syria and thus spare Israel the prospect of fighting on two fronts simultaneously when the war broke out. He also interpreted it as America's first move, before establishing another base in Cyprus, after toppling the unfriendly Makarios regime there. In January 1972, Sadat also accused President Nixon of carrying out his predecessor's pledge to update the Israeli air force by delivering all the Phantom and Skyhawk jets that President Johnson had promised to Prime Minister Eshkol in 1968. Under these circumstances, Sadat was infuriated when Secretary of State Rogers visited the Middle East in 1972 and declared at Kuwait airport that the US counted many friends among the Arabs. This encouraged some moderate Arab countries, who had severed their relations with the US in 1967, to resume them again; this did not square with Sadat's desire to punish 'those who harm Arab interests'. Sadat said that he was particularly angry because the Arabs *did* possess the means to pressure the US, and the Americans, in turn, did control the channels of influence upon the Israelis. But since Arab pressure was not exerted, the Americans not only felt free to escape their responsibility to pressure Israel, but they had the nerve to 'take from the Arabs in order to give to Israel'.

Sadat also reproved the Americans for backing Israel's demand for direct negotiations with the Arabs as a prerequisite for settlement. He argued that sitting at the same table with Israel while his territories were occupied meant surrender, not negotiation. He asked the Americans whether they would have been ready to negotiate with the Japanese after Pearl Harbor and the Philippines. Sadat considered that the American stand on direct negotiations reneged on a previous American position stated by Rogers in May 1971, which had ruled out direct talks in favour of indirect negotiations ('proximity talks' in the jargon of the US State Department). Sadat acknowledged that, when he had accepted the Rogers Plan in 1971, he had hoped to drive a wedge between the US and Israel, and as he desperately needed some breathing space in which to prepare his anti-aircraft missile defences, he thought that was an opportune moment to attain both objectives. However, when the Americans explained to him that 'proximity talks' meant that the US would act as a 'catalyst' to bring the parties together, after a preparatory stage of 'go-between', it dawned on Sadat that those were precisely the direct negotiations he was determined to avoid. Thereupon, Sadat walked out of the talks, accusing the Americans of bad faith and 'betrayal'.

Despite this, the Americans again contacted Sadat upon his return from the Soviet Union in October 1971, but he made it clear that he was unwilling to go any further under the circumstances. To change his position he put forward two conditions: that the Americans desist from any kind of direct negotiations in the way of settlement, and that 1971 be considered the 'Year of Decision' – that negotiations (indirect, if any) should be completed by the end of the year. Sadat thought that this time 'proximity talks' would go the way he wanted, and he even nominated his representative for the talks, Minister of State Murad Ghaleb. But that attempt again collapsed when Sadat learned what the Americans understood by 'proximity talks'. In Sadat's mind, Rogers' declaration in January 1972 that Israel would receive more Phantom jets (after an agreement had been concluded in November 1971 between the two countries for the manufacture of American armaments in Israel) amounted to a form of psychological warfare, designed to drive the Arabs to despair and force them into surrender; after that there was no point in discussing the modes of settlement any longer.

Sadat repeatedly expressed anger at the American suggestion that both parties should make concessions. Sadat considered that viewpoint made the aggressor (Israel) equal with the victim (himself). If concessions were to be made, only Israel should make them, because she controlled the territories. He had nothing to give up. Therefore he felt justified in rejecting Israel's conditions for her partial withdrawal from the Canal under the US mediation plan,* and in keeping away from the 'proximity talks' which were designed to discuss his disagreement with Israel's conditions. He did not want to be in a position either to have to give in on the matter of form (direct negotiations) or on the matter of substance (concessions to match Israel's).

Sadat was dismayed at the sight of a small nation like Israel being able to exert such influence on the US, and he remarked sarcastically that it seemed as if Israel were the great power and the US the 'miniature parasite'. He repeatedly asked, 'How could a great power be so acquiescent about such a small country which depended on her for everything from bread to Phantoms?' Sadat concluded that world Zionism did not provide the whole answer, the anomaly was probably due to the US's need for a proxy in the Middle East to check Soviet influence and to isolate and crush Egypt. In his despair, he probably envied Israel's position *vis-à-vis* the US, especially in the light (or obscurity) of his disillusionment with the Soviets. He was infuriated by Israel because she was more successful than he was at taming a superpower; and he fumed at the US because she could not restrain her arrogant client. He seethed with anger at the combination of the two, which allowed Israel not only to hide behind her mighty accomplice and get as much assistance as she wanted, but also, in his words, 'to lie, deceive and provoke the UN and world public opinion'.

In July 1972, when Sadat expelled the Soviets, Henry Kissinger, Nixon's National Security Adviser, asked to meet someone from Egypt to discuss this dénouement. Previously, whenever the Americans had inquired about the permanence of the Soviet presence in Egypt, Sadat had reassured them that if the Israeli partial withdrawal was effected, he would no longer need a Soviet presence. Furthermore, he had always explained that he had granted the Soviets port facilities in Egypt, not bases, which was an indication of the provisional status of their mission in Egypt. Now that the Soviets were ousted, the Americans again evinced interest in Sadat. The meeting did not take place until February 1973 in Paris. On that occasion, Kissinger was understood to have reiterated to Sadat's emissary, Hafez Isma'il, that Egypt was bound to search for a peaceful settlement with Israel because she was unable to beat her enemy militarily, and until the existing military situation altered there was simply no way that Egypt could advance any demands. Sadat was dismayed by the talks which he immediately reported to his Soviet allies.

After Nixon's summit meetings in Moscow and Peking in 1972, Sadat was advised by some European countries, and by moderate Arab states who

---

*Israel had predicated her agreement to withdraw partially from the Canal on the following three conditions:
a That no Egyptian troops should cross the Canal and be positioned in the area to be evacuated by Israel;
b That an unlimited cease-fire be declared;
c That no mention should be made of Israel's ultimate return to the 1967 borders.

maintained a good relationship with the US, not to leave the doors of Washington open to the Israelis alone. So, after initial contacts had proved that America's desire to renew the dialogue with Egypt was genuine, Sadat dispatched Hafez Isma'il to Washington.

Nixon told Isma'il that first he wished to remove or deactivate the 'powder-keg that threatened to blow up in the Middle East', before he engaged in serious talks regarding the future of the region. Nixon also reminded Isma'il that he had visited Egypt back in 1962 and that he harboured a profound respect for that country; he reckoned that, through neglect, differences between the two countries had been allowed to breed hostility, and promised a policy of dialogue and direct encounters in order to remedy the situation. In that two-hour meeting, and at other meetings he attended with Rogers and Kissinger, Isma'il repeated his country's resolve to go to war because it could no longer endure the *status quo* and, according to Sadat, he pledged to do so, come what may, regardless of the sacrifices involved. Isma'il also explained that his country would never give up an inch of land, never let down the Palestinians, and never agree to a partial or separate settlement. Nixon said that he would try a new peace initiative which would strike a compromise between Egypt's sovereignty over Egyptian lands and Israel's security needs. Although Sadat was attentive to any concrete American deeds which might follow Nixon's words, it did not change his mind about the war.

Sadat's disbelief about the new Nixon move stemmed from his perception that the Americans were asking the Egyptians to make one-sided concessions, such as the total demilitarization of the Sinai, which would drive a wedge between Egypt and the rest of the Arab world. The Israeli Foreign Minister Abba Eban, dubbed by Sadat 'the American Secretary of State', who visited Washington at about this time, declared that there was complete agreement between the US and Israel on Middle East policies; no one in Washington refuted this statement. What was more, on the heels of Isma'il's and then Prime Minister Golda Meir's visits to Washington, the US released the details of a new Phantom jet deal with Israel. This increased Sadat's despair about the US. He gave an interview to *Newsweek* magazine in April 1973 in which he assured the US that she was making the gravest mistake in her history if she continued to believe that the Egyptians were crippled and unlikely to take action. He warned:

> Mark my words, the situation here will be much worse than Vietnam, because US interests are at stake. Americans always use computers to solve geo-political equations and they have always been misled. McNamara warned Johnson that by feeding the wrong data to the computers he was getting all the wrong answers. McNamara was right and Johnson was wrong and compelled to abdicate. They simply forgot to feed Vietnamese psychology into the computer. . . . The US has overlooked one factor – Arab psychology. . . .

In his May Day speech of 1973, Sadat disclosed that the new American initiative actually aimed at forcing Egypt to recognize Israel's legitimacy. To Sadat this meant that Israel might retain Arab lands for her own security whilst the Arabs accorded her guarantees to their own detriment; an American solution which he dubbed 'an illusion, a fraud and a mirage'. All Sadat could do was comfort himself that Israel had had no chance to dictate capitulation to the Arabs, and that the Arabs had signed nothing submitting anything to Israel. No, he would not accept the American ploy which was calculated, as he saw it, to secure a partial retreat by Israel in order to reopen the Suez Canal and alleviate the plight of the West Europeans who depended on it for their energy supplies. For if he had acceded to the American plan, Israel would feel safe in the Sinai and would never have any reason to evacuate it completely. Sadat felt that the close American–Israeli relationship prohibited the US from acting as an honest broker.

Further evidence of the 'collusion' between the US and Israel was 'detected' by Sadat in April 1973 when Abba Eban declared that he hoped that when Brezhnev went to Washington for his summit with Nixon, the American position would remain unchanged. Eban was referring to the conclusion of the first summit in Moscow a year earlier, when Nixon had refused Brezhnev's insistence that the Middle East be treated as top priority in their summit discussions. Sadat posed these questions: 'How does Eban know? How could talks between Brezhnev and Nixon, held in the previous year, in privacy, have come to Eban's attention?' Sadat concluded that this high-level presidential information could only have reached Israel because 'Israel is America and America is Israel. This is very sad and shameful, especially as no rebuttal came out of the US. Let our friends in the Kremlin know that their meeting with Nixon had been leaked to Israel while they continued naïvely to believe in the approaching peace settlement.'

That May Day, Sadat attacked the US for yet another 'plot' against the Arabs. He said that America was already suffering from an energy crisis due to the Arabs' effective handling of their oil production and to Qadhafi's nationalization of American oil interests in Libya. Sadat was exhilarated at the news that many gas stations were closing down in the US and that oil companies were going out of business; that was the Arabs' revenge for the exploitation of their oil by American and Western companies over many years. Sadat declared that he 'knew' that the Americans had concocted a plan with Israel to take over Arab oil wells, by force, in order to ensure the flow of energy supplies. If such a plan came to fruition, Israel would eventually come to dominate the region. By using cheap Arab manpower, Israel would control the main industries in the Middle East, distribute jobs and reap the profits and thus hold the entire area under her thumb. Sadat said that Qadhafi's decision to expropriate American assets was only the opening move in an approaching battle, the first manifestation of Arab unity, and a warning to the US that

Israel was unable to watch and defend American interests in the Middle East. If the US truly wanted to secure her vital interests, she must desist from provoking the Arab nations and stop lending outright support to Israel.

Sadat was afraid that if he let the natural course of events unfold he would lose control; nothing could have thrown Sadat more off balance than that, so he decided to seize the initiative. He had endured a long period of humiliation and derision and had explored every avenue to get back his territories and his rights, but all doors had been slammed in his face. He was told that he would not fight, so he would show the entire world that he could. The stage was set for the October War.

7

DRAMA IN OCTOBER

Sadat now set the stage for the great drama that was about to unfold. The actors, the script, the theatre and the date of the première had all been carefully selected, meticulously worked out and conscientiously rehearsed. The Egyptian people, the Arab world, the Islamic and Third Worlds, the Soviets, the US and Europe were the audience before whom the frustrated actor was about to prove that he could not only act, but act big, and direct the greatest show the Arabs had ever seen. After years of working behind the scenes, he was eager to face the footlights and stun the world with what they least expected, at the most unlikely moment, and on a totally unexpected scale.

Sadat's taste for drama must be seen in the context of his penchant for defiance and confrontation. Drama gave him strength and disarmed his foes; dramatic situations enabled him to stem the conventional current, take control of events and channel them in the direction he most desired, especially when drama entailed surprise. Moreover, a dramatic style, whether in dress, speech or action, helped Sadat to define his identity. For Sadat always strove to stand out from the grey, mediocre people around him; he wanted his dress and style to be conspicuous. The knowledge that he was at the centre of attention, watched, admired, talked about, emulated and sought after, bolstered his self-confidence.

There are many examples of Sadat being dramatic to increase his stature. When he decided, against all expectations, to open the Suez Canal to navigation in 1975, he not only did the opposite of what everyone had anticipated, but he did it in style. He sailed up and down the Canal, standing on the deck of his flagship, in full admiral's uniform at the salute: it was reminiscent of the famous painting of George Washington crossing the Delaware River. When Sadat declared in 1980 that he was granting the exiled Shah of Iran asylum in Cairo, he was not only making a friendly gesture towards a deposed head of state, but was making use of the dramatic effect of being seen to offer solace and refuge to a weary leader who had met a tragic and humiliating fate. Such a theatrical gesture would set him apart from other world leaders, especially from those Arabs who had been the Shah's friends, and had visited his court, but had chosen to forget old loyalties once the monarch had lost his power. Another example of Sadat's predilection for stage performances can be seen in his visit to Jerusalem in November 1977: the build-up of tension and expectation surrounding the visit, the audacity of attempting the impossible, and the way in which he captured the stage in face of strong Arab opposition.

Sadat's flair for drama was also illustrated by his concern, some say obsession, with his physical appearance, which was always extraordinary and sometimes 'shocking'. At the opening of the Suez Canal, it was an admiral's uniform; at a press conference in Mit Abul-kum, it might be a traditional *galabiyya*; for an interview with a foreign correspondent, he might don an informal, impeccably fitting safari suit; abroad he always wore custom-made Italian suits; and in his public appearances in Egypt, he often appeared in extravagant military uniforms bedecked with medals. In his autobiography, he repeatedly mentions that his suit was so threadbare that he was unable to wear it on his release from jail. It seems so incongruous that a man who went to jail for his idealism and whilst there learnt detachment from material possessions, should later become so greatly concerned with the minutiae of fashion. Indeed, despite all his protestations of detesting pomp and pretentiousness, and all his claims to prefer the simple life, he admitted that his first purchase after his release from prison was a new suit. Sadat's extravagant dress seemed to have left its mark on many foreign interviewers. One of them said that he seemed to be surrounded by an aura when he appeared sitting under a tree in his village wearing his *galabiyya*. He always seemed to go from one extreme to another, the common denominator being the wish to achieve some kind of dramatic effect. Sadat was very unlikely, under any circumstances, to be found wearing colourless or unobtrusive attire which might, Allah forbid, confuse him with others. He wished to be both unique and charming, although when *he* chose, he would show his contempt for fads and fashions by retiring to his village. Incidentally, if the episode of his wearing a swastika-patterned tie on a visit to Israel was not sheer coincidence, it might very well fit in with the pattern of extravagant and eccentric conduct described here.

Sadat's taste for drama was also widely reflected in his style of speech. We have already seen the richness of his metaphors and his propensity for story-telling which added colour and drama to his talks. He often began his addresses with a rolling, 'I hereby declare to you . . .' or 'I hereby submit to you in front of the entire world . . .'. This mode of speech definitely demands the listeners' attention, indicating that what the speaker is about to say is of great significance. He often used unusual terms, exceptional sentence patterns, or newly-coined phrases in order to make a greater impact on his listeners: 'We do not lack courage to do things; we do not duck our heads in the face of on-coming arrows.'

Sometimes Sadat's speeches attained dramatic effect by skilful use of the same flowery language which Egyptians heard in popular plays or in television soap operas. In his 1974 Revolution Day speech he opened: 'In the name of

Allah, brothers and sisters! Days and nights go by, but the eternal night of twenty-two years ago will continue to dwell in the consciousness of our generation. Its memory shall not wane and its light shall not dim. . . .' During this speech, Sadat heightened the drama in order to arouse strong feelings of patriotism and make a lasting impact. Following 6 October 1973, he said:

> We are meeting today in the aftermath of a glorious event, one of the greatest and most dignified in our history, when our forces, backed by our entire nation, moved forward heroically. The sixth of October was a day that not only altered the history of our country, our nation, and our region, but of the entire world.

The dramatic hyperbole which followed the war could only be matched by Sadat's pre-war 'sweat and blood' Churchillian-style rhetoric:

> Brothers and sisters! The time has come to tell ourselves and others that no obstacle can block our way. No power can frighten us and no enemy shall intimidate us. We shall struggle through both fire and storm. We shall liberate our freedom with sweat and our dignity with blood. We shall hoist our flag, with Allah's will and help, wherever our flags must be hoisted. We shall fight, fight, fight, until Allah, blessed be He, bestow on us victory, victory, victory. . . .

Another device Sadat used to add drama to his speeches was to invoke past events, either from Arab–Islamic or from world history. If de Gaulle, Stalin and Churchill could lead their nations in great battles of destiny in the face of adversity, and ultimately emerge victorious, then he, Sadat, a leader with deep roots in the glorious Arab–Islamic past, could do no worse in his 'momentous' war. He termed his domestic struggles '*ridda* war' ('war of apostasy'), referring to the series of bloody confrontations between the Prophet Muhammed's successors and the Arab tribes who had reneged on the faith after the death of the Prophet. For it seemed to Sadat that it was essential to reassert the values which he treasured but which were threatened by inter-communal strife and 'deviationist' conduct. *Ridda* war was a powerful symbol that Sadat used to dramatize his own crusade against the renegades of his day, just as the Caliph Abu Bakr had done 1,300 years earlier. Similarly, by relating his enemies, the Israelis, to the Jews of Medina of thirteen centuries ago, and equating the 'treacherous conduct' of the one with the 'proven deceit' of the other, he made his crowds relive the drama of the venerated Prophet and by comparison come to appreciate their present predicament.

Hyperbole, over-assertion and repetitiousness have been cited by many an anthropologist as typical traits of Arabic speakers. But Sadat's mastery of them, his need to repeat in order to stress the authenticity of his interpretations and allegations, lent a very dramatic twist even to seemingly banal events. On the seventh anniversary of the Six Day War, in a relatively brief address to his Third Army in the Suez Canal Zone, just before the October campaign, Sadat repeated several times, 'My sons, officers and soldiers. . . '. He addressed them as the father who was going to send them to war again, and his repetition of the familial relations between him and his men was intended to boost their morale, to strengthen their loyalty to him and to increase his credibility in their eyes. In a speech he gave on the fourth Memorial Day for Nasser, he used, no fewer than nine times, the words 'brothers and sisters', with a final 'Brothers and sisters, may Allah make our way successful!'

Like a good stage-performer, Sadat hunted for the right approach for each audience. When he spoke at popular rallies, he drew his inspiration from the crowd, told them stories that cajoled, flattered and excited them, turning his appearance into an entertainment and drawing much applause and laughter. At select meetings he would harp upon the 'common bonds' binding him and his audience, making them feel special. To the Tunisian Parliament, he spoke about 'topics of interest to my country and yours, for both of us belong to one Arab nation, having the same history and past, the same struggle, the same destiny and hope'. To the Palestine National Council, which desperately needed in 1972 to identify with the 'big brother' of the Arab world, he said without restraint, 'You and we are the avant-garde. . . . You and we are incurring the cruelty of the enemy. . . . You and we have been subjected to suffering. . . . You and we are to disengage from these difficult moments. . . . You and we are facing nothing but the battle. . . .'

Once he began, he would sometimes speak for hours: he would probe his audience, circumvent his main topic, touch on it and then retreat, hint at it and then bury it in an avalanche of rhetoric; finally he would drop a bombshell, much to the amazement of his audience. People who listened to him would look at each other in stupefaction, incredulous at what they heard, and then burst into applause, shouting and slogan-crying, admiring their *Rais* for the 'trick' he had played on them and idolizing him for his boldness, bluntness and *savoir faire*.

Sadat's technique for maintaining suspense, an essential part of drama, would vary under different circumstances. We have seen that, before he took his major political decisions, he would quietly vanish from the scene and retreat into seclusion, sometimes for days on end, while his aides, Egypt and the world waited, guessing at what might come next. Paradoxically, the more often he isolated himself and retired from the world, the more attention he gained, for everyone knew that something 'momentous' was in the making. On 1 May 1971, after a lengthy May Day 'socialist' speech, he made his startling declaration about the removal of the 'foci of power'. On 14 March 1976, he made a very lengthy, repetitious and tedious speech in which he recounted in detail all the stages of Egypt's relations with the Soviets, with many asides on domestic, personal and foreign affairs; only towards the end did he break the appalling news: *he* had decided to abrogate the fifteen-year Treaty of Friendship with the Soviet Union. At other times, he would retell of his past encounters with world leaders, citing the dialogues verbatim. The amused audience would be held in suspense until the punchline came, as if it were a skit, with Sadat the hero who outsmarted his interlocutors, taught them a lesson, or castigated them for their failures. Sometimes, the details that he recounted of some incidents were so vivid that he carried the crowds with him, they would take 'his part' in the act, boo the imagined adversary and encourage Sadat to elaborate further on his story.

The drama of October 1973 was so orchestrated that it came as a total surprise to the Israelis, the Arabs and the world. Paradoxically, Sadat had warned of the coming war and its inevitability so often that world attention had become bored by such declarations, dismissing them as 'empty rhetoric'. Indeed, most Arabs, the West, the Soviets and the Israelis remained sceptical of his intentions, and even more so of his ability to act upon them. Sadat, in a masterly ploy that should have made many an intelligence agency suspicious, had desisted from declarations, about war or anything else, from July 1973 onwards, only breaking his reticence once, in September 1973, when he addressed the Conference of the Non-Aligned in Algiers. The paradox is that Sadat should have maintained his pattern of bragging and boasting up until the outbreak of war, if he wanted to achieve total surprise; reversing what was expected of him, he opted to keep silent. Sadat's successful gamble was coupled with a very careful campaign of disinformation and a detailed and well-thought through undermining of what he perceived as Israel's 'security theory'.

First, Sadat believed that Israel's strategy was founded on her power of deterrence which she thought no Arab country would dare to challenge; to launch a powerful, concentrated and surprise attack, when and where the enemy least expected it, was likely to shake that self-confidence. Second, Israel's strength depended upon fighting on only one front at a time. Sadat thought that if this were to happen, Israel would be able to vanquish one Arab army after another, and emerge victorious. Therefore, he ensured a simultaneous attack on the Egyptian and Syrian fronts, forcing Israel to split her might. Also he stocked additional weapons, ammunition and strategic supplies on his flank in Libya and at his rear in the Sudan, ensuring a firm stance in the event of an Israeli counter-thrust. In any case, he believed that the Israeli assumption of Arab disunity, which in the past had worked to her advantage, was not going to recur this time. Third, Israel had always declared that she would rapidly transfer the war to enemy territory to spare destruction of her own lands. But if Egypt and Syria launched a massive, simultaneous surprise offensive, the battle would have to take place in Israeli-held territory. Fourth, Israel always assumed that any war must be brief and devastating, yielding victory before the Great Powers could intervene to stop Israel's advance. This *blitzkrieg*-style of war was essential to Israel because of her shortage of manpower and her reliance on the total mobilization of her able-bodied men and women, which in turn brought about the temporary immobilization of her industrial production. Sadat would counter that by preparing for a long, protracted war which he could endure because of his practically limitless manpower and the support he was to get from his Arab brothers. Fifth, because of her small population, Israel greatly feared high numbers of casualties. Sadat devised a massive attack with deadly weapons that would inflict heavy losses on the enemy. He was prepared to absorb as high, or even higher, a ratio of Egyptian dead and wounded and still continue the offensive. Sixth, Israel's fate hinged largely on a hurried, though admittedly well-organized, mobilization of her reserves. A surprise attack, before Israel could mobilize, would decide her fate. Seventh, Israel's strategy had always depended on taking the initiative. For only if Israel could dictate the moves and force the Arabs onto the defensive, as she had done in the past, would she be able to end the war quickly and emerge victorious. Sadat was not a man to let the initiative fall from his grasp: he would determine the opening move and force the Israelis on to the defensive. Eighth, Israel had always relied on the superiority of her air force to check any surprise Arab attack, allowing time for her reserve forces to mobilize and deploy themselves against Arab land forces; Sadat decided to position a screen of air-defence missiles along the Canal to foil Israel's plans.

To attain most of these strategic goals, Sadat desperately needed to effect total surprise in his offensive. He was able to keep secret within Egypt, and from all Arab leaders save the Syrian, the date of the outbreak of war, which he had agreed with Assad in August. Indeed, no more than a handful of top officers knew the details. He and his general staff chose 6 October because it fell on a Saturday during the Yom Kippur festival in Israel, a time when everyone would be fasting and praying in synagogues and Israeli defences were sure to be lax. By 2 p.m. those Israelis who had fasted would be exhausted; and the sun would be setting in the west, blinding Israeli defenders who were on the east side of the Canal and so facilitating the task of the attacking Egyptians. The fact that October was also the month of Ramadan, when all Muslims fasted, was conversely thought to be beneficial because the Israelis would be unlikely to believe that Egyptians would attack then. Sadat secured special permission for his soldiers to eat before they launched the battle.

Sadat's plan of disinformation actually began on 12 July 1972, when a report was leaked to the effect that Egyptian missiles and sophisticated weaponry had not been used since the Soviet eviction. Such a leak was calculated to indicate to the West and to Israel that Egypt could no longer man and operate her most advanced weapons, therefore she was unlikely to wage war in the foreseeable future. This general leak was later backed up by more detailed 'reports' about insufficiency of arms, the bad maintenance that they were given by the Egyptians, the lack of spare parts and the inability of the Egyptian personnel to operate them. According to Sadat, both Israel and the West 'swallowed' these reports and 'went to sleep', assuming that Egypt was technologically doomed and that all the sophisticated weaponry in her possession had become useless.

As the date for the war drew near, and Sadat heard the conclusions of Gamasi's study, he realized that the 'Jews, who are as good militarily as us, or perhaps better' must have come to the same conclusions about possible dates for crossing the Canal – *i.e.* May, August, September or October. Therefore he decided to play on Israel's nerves by pretending he was preparing for war in May. This would get the Israelis 'used' to Egyptian troop manœuvres, which would come to nothing, and would activate a sufficient number of false alarms to lull Israeli suspicions, before striking for real. In May, the first possible landing date, he ordered the media to print and broadcast morale-boosting slogans, and to quote profusely from the Quran; at the same time he dramatically increased military movements along the Canal. The trick worked: Israel mobilized her armies and reinforced her lines along the Canal. When nothing happened, Israeli forces were called off the alert and eventually demobilized, the Israeli command being convinced that it was yet another of Sadat's exercises in futility. In August, the same exercise was repeated all over again; each one of those partial mobilizations cost Israel some $10 million. So, when Egyptian troops moved for real in October, the Israelis were complacent and decided that the probability of war was slight. It was no doubt just another, by now familiar, abortive exercise. Sadat later said that he had capitalized on the Jewish reluctance to spend money: 'They suffer great pain spending money,' he said. He was 'vindicated' when Israel refrained from that extra spending in October and ended up paying a much higher price.

One side effect of Sadat's campaign of disinformation was the dismissal of the powerful Hassanein Haykal, the editor of the influential *Al-Ahram* since Nasser's time. Because of Haykal's sympathy for the 'foci of power', he fell out of favour with Sadat. Either because of his personal rift with the President, or because he did not believe in Sadat's 'psychological warfare', he refused to print the martial verses from the Quran as directed; he was the only editor to defy the presidential order. After the war, he was relieved of all his functions at the *Al-Ahram* publishing house.

The deceptions worked so well that the Arab heads of state, save Assad, were themselves taken in by Egypt's exercises, despite Sadat's personal assurances to many of them that he was intending to go to war, and soon. The Arabs, like everyone else, had simply lost confidence in what Sadat was saying, and none of them took seriously the actual preparations he was making for war. His deception plan was either ridiculed as *déjà vu* or dismissed in disbelief. They, like the West and Israel, had come to learn that a gap always existed between what Egyptians said and did. This credibility gap was Sadat's greatest asset in his disinformation campaign. He knew that the Americans had approached the Israelis on several occasions inquiring about the significance of the Egyptian troop movements, but each time their suspicions were dispelled by Israel. For once, Sadat could delight in watching Israel unwittingly working as *his* proxy to deceive the US, instead of serving as a tool of American interests in the Middle East.

Other dilemmas posed by the deception plan related to obtaining foreign armaments and materials that had to be imported. One of those suppliers was West Germany. A major engineering problem which challenged Egyptian planners was the high, earth dyke built by Israel along the eastern bank of the Suez Canal. The dyke was impregnable and there was no way Egyptian tanks, artillery, armoured vehicles and large-scale troop transports could break into Sinai unless the dyke was neutralized or removed. Since neither option was feasible, an Egyptian engineer conceived the idea of slashing through the dykes with high-pressure water hoses which would quickly cut wide passages, in sufficient numbers, to allow for the massive Egyptian crossing and landing. The idea was taken from a similar device that had been used during the construction of the Aswan Dam, which had necessitated the removal of huge quantities of earth. The problem was that to obtain high-powered hoses from West Germany they had to pretend that they would be used in fire engines. The Germans ridiculed the Egyptian engineers who had placed the order, assuring them that they would never need such powerful hoses even to extinguish the largest of fires, but they complied, attaching no strategic importance to the order, and it never leaked out. The infantrymen in the Egyptian army were to use rope ladders to climb up the dykes, pull behind them anti-tank missiles and thus take over the high ground before the Israelis woke up, mobilized and counter-attacked. The plan worked almost perfectly.

The Soviet connection posed a much greater dilemma in terms of the deception strategy. For not only had Moscow provided most of the weapons and materials needed for the war, but there were Soviet families still living in Cairo and evacuating them might sound the alarm. Furthermore, if Sadat went to war without consulting, or at least pre-warning, the Soviet Union, how could he expect her military assistance in the case of a protracted conflict, or demand that the Soviets bail him out diplomatically in the case of defeat or deadlock? On the other hand, sharing his secret with them might result in security leaks and other deliberate actions which could undermine his entire strategy of surprise. Then there was the consideration that Syria, ally in the coming war, had been a client of the Soviet Union. Even if Sadat had decided to leave the Soviets in the dark, could Syria afford to follow suit?

Sadat's relations with the Soviet Union began to improve after February 1973, following General Isma'il's visit to Moscow. As a result, Sadat received some shipments of weapons and promises of more. What was more crucial, however, was that the crisis over the MiG 25s, whose genesis had preceded the departure of Soviet experts from Egypt, was finally settled just before the war. At the height of the Soviet presence in Egypt in 1970–72, they had positioned MiG 25s near Cairo. These were high-altitude mach-3 superjets designed for air reconnaissance and intelligence gathering. Some tension had been generated at the time between the Soviets and Sadat, since these planes could not take off for missions unless specifically allowed to do so by Moscow. Sadat had entertained some misgivings about the futile stationing of the planes in

Cairo, because every time his command issued an order for a reconnaissance the Soviets claimed that fog, adverse weather conditions, or mechanical breakdowns impeded the flight mission. Exasperated, Sadat had ordered the Soviets, back in July 1972, either to sell the planes to Egypt or to take them away with the rest of their electronic equipment. They had chosen the latter option, but in February–March 1973 they announced their readiness to re-position them in Cairo, for use in case of hostilities. Sadat, who suspected that Israel had been receiving her intelligence data from American spy satellites, but also knew that they had been 'flying an electronics-equipped Stratocruiser which could overfly Sinai far away from Egyptian missiles and, immune to their fire, gather data at will from the entire Egyptian air space', thought he also needed an aircraft with similar capacities, including night reconnaissance. So, when the Soviets expressed the wish to send back the planes, because it suited their own global interests, Sadat accepted the offer, provided he was given the gathered intelligence data. The planes arrived in Cairo just before the war, but it was all over before they could take off for any mission. However, they provided a much-needed token of military and strategic co-operation between the two countries.

The return of the MiG 25s showed an improvement in Egyptian–Soviet relationships, but this was not to last. After Hafez Isma'il's first meeting with Henry Kissinger in Paris during February 1973, Sadat had the courteous idea of calling on the Soviet Ambassador in Cairo to tell him about the meeting, and to ask if he would let Andropov, who was General Ahmed Isma'il's personal friend, come to Cairo for a more detailed briefing. During General Isma'il's visit to Moscow in February, Andropov had shown a particularly positive attitude towards Egypt and 'volunteered' to help in case of any difficulties between the two countries in the future, so as to avoid any repetition of the episode of the previous year, which had marked the lowest ebb in their relations. Andropov had mentioned, in Moscow, the need to take 'preventive measures' in the future before a crisis set in, and Sadat thought that the Hafez Isma'il–Henry Kissinger talks, whose tone and outcome he deeply disliked, provided a good occasion for relaunching some kind of dialogue between the former allies. Soviet shipments arrived in March and April, according to the agreed schedule, but there was no sign of Andropov; what was worse, the Soviet Ambassador to Egypt did not even bother to produce any excuse. Sadat called the Ambassador again, reprimanded him for his lack of concern for a friend who wanted nothing more than to share with the Soviet leadership his contacts with the US, and waited. When no reply came, Sadat asked the Ambassador to cancel Andropov's invitation to Cairo because Egypt 'needed nothing from him'. It was characteristic of Sadat to have the last word. He could not bear to invite someone and be turned down, so he would rather disinvite them than continue to wait in humility. This incident showed once again Sadat's innate need to be in control of a situation; he would rather initiate a move and bear the consequences than be beholden to the whims of a foreign power.

Soviet support remained crucial for Sadat's war plans. Part of this vital support was supposedly assured by Syria's alliance with the Soviet Union, an alliance which had not suffered any crisis, but it was essential to cultivate relations with Moscow, at least ostensibly, until the war was over. For Sadat made it clear that his strategy relied heavily upon the Egyptian forces, on the potential of Arab backing, and on Soviet political and military aid when the crunch arrived. So he had agreed with Assad that they would break the news about the war in two stages: first, Sadat would call in the Soviet Ambassador to Cairo, on Wednesday 3 October, and give him the following message: 'Egypt and Syria have decided to launch a war in order to put an end to the no-peace-no-war situation. What is the Soviet position in this regard?' The Sadat–Assad agreement had stipulated that, should the Soviet Ambassador ask Sadat about zero hour, he would be told that Assad and Sadat had not yet determined it, but that both were insistent upon knowing beforehand what the Soviet attitude would be when hostilities began. The second stage would happen the next day, Thursday 4 October, when Assad would call in the Soviet Ambassador to Damascus and inform him of the exact date and hour. Indeed, this is what actually happened. But the Soviet Ambassador in Cairo, after having heard Sadat's message and without showing any emotion, asked to see the President again the following morning. Sadat was not convinced that Moscow would reply to his inquiry within twenty-four hours, for in the past he had been used to waiting for months, even years. 'The world could not have changed that fast,' remarked Sadat to himself. On Thursday, Assad informed the Soviet Ambassador in Damascus of the zero hour and Sadat received the Soviet Ambassador in Cairo, not daring to expect an answer from him. The Soviet Ambassador told Sadat that he and his leaders wanted a cease-fire forty-eight hours after the war broke out, presumably fearing that a longer spell of time would have resulted in their allies' total defeat. But Sadat retorted that he would have to consult with Assad first before he could answer, and after a while he declared to the Soviet emissary: 'You can tell your Government that there will be no cease-fire until we have completed our objectives.' The Ambassador did not seem convinced when he left.

Later that day, the Ambassador telephoned Sadat at home and asked to see him urgently. He brought a message to the effect that the Soviet Union would send four large transport aeroplanes to evacuate Soviet nationals from Egypt on Friday 5 October. He asked Sadat for permission for them to land on the Cairo-West military airfield rather than the Cairo International airport where they would attract attention. Sadat concurred and thought that, even if detected by the West and Israel, the aircraft would be mistaken for regular arms delivery aeroplanes so they would not betray the deception strategy. Sadat reverted to his original question about the Soviet attitude after the war broke out, but the Ambassador only reiterated the usual formula about 'the matter being under study'. Ominously for Sadat, however, a Soviet shipment of tanks was due to arrive in Alexandria on Friday 5 October, but when the Soviets learnt that the war was to begin the next day the ship cancelled its arrival date and reported that it was 'lost in the Mediterranean due to a *force majeure*'. Only after the Soviet Union realized the extent of Egyptian advances into the Sinai, during the first few days of the war, was the ship able to overcome the '*force majeure*' and to find her way into Alexandria harbour, after five days of wandering off the Egyptian coast.

After the pro-forma meeting of 30 September with his National Security Council, on 1 October Sadat convened the Supreme Council of the Armed Forces, the body which knew the true details of the coming battle and constituted the expert back-up behind the operation. Satisfied with his final check that everything was on schedule, and after listening throughout the night to reports from all top field commanders and members of the general staff, Sadat signed the strategic order for the war. On 3 October, he signed the battle order, signalling to the Commander-in-Chief, Isma'il, to proceed with the countdown. After that signature, which sealed the political decision-making process, Sadat felt calm, 'like a noble horse who had run a long course and was now taking a rest'. Before that, Sadat had suffered bouts of depression, a result of what he viewed as 'psychological warfare' against him by the US and Israel, the pessimistic mood which prevailed in the Arab world and Egypt, the difficulties with the Soviet Union, the defeatist publications at home and abroad, and the lack of self-confidence which seemed to have pervaded everyone he addressed, except for the top military in Egypt and Syria. But after he signed the battle order, he felt relieved and euphoric, for he had done all that was humanly possible to ensure success.

Sadat chose Al-Tahira palace as his headquarters for the duration of the war. A fully-fledged operations room was constructed in the basement of the palace, so that Sadat could follow the course of events even when he was not in the nearby operations room of the General Headquarters of the Armed Forces. Sadat was aware that concurrently with the military operations it would be necessary for him to conduct diplomatic affairs and meet with foreign emissaries, and therefore he found the proximity of the top military and political headquarters suitable for his purposes. However, he kept secret the fact that he had turned his basement into a full military operations room. He spent Thursday 5 October in prayer at the Kubri-al-Kubba mosque where he had learned to pray fifty years earlier. Field-Marshal Isma'il then contacted Sadat and inquired when he should show up at the military operations room, and the President asked his Commander-in-Chief to report to him the next day, 6 October, at 1.15 p.m., just forty-five minutes before the outbreak of war. Sadat opted to sleep in his palace office that night rather than go home. He slept well, woke up as usual at 8 a.m., read the press as if it were yet another routine day, performed some Swedish gymnastics which he had become accustomed to do since his heart attack, took a bath and dressed. He chose his military uniform for the day of reckoning, and did his daily work as usual, waiting for Isma'il to give him a lift to the main operations room which was a mere ten-minute ride away. At exactly 1.15 p.m., Isma'il stopped by and the two men, in military attire, tight-lipped and grave, rode to their destiny.

At 1.30 p.m. a prepared communiqué was released to the effect that Israel had 'committed an act of aggression' against Egypt, whereupon the Egyptian forces felt justified in 'repelling the aggressors'. That was the euphemism for the unleashing of the 'Badr Operation'. At this point Sadat realized that many of his men, affectionately dubbed 'devils', had disobeyed his orders to eat, although the war made this perfectly acceptable, and had gone into battle whilst still fasting. At headquarters, tension and expectation were further compounded by the formidable presence of the President; no one even smoked, let alone ate; everyone present was embarrassed because the President, too, did neither. To break the fast he asked for a cup of tea; someone fetched his pipe from the car and brought it over to him, and he began smoking. Only then did the others feel relieved and begin smoking too. This rather amusing incident was indicative, nevertheless, of the Islamic mood which had been instilled into the troops, and of the fact that the Islamic symbolism, which Sadat and others had ensured was part and parcel of the preparations for the war, had come to fruition. For, as we have seen, Sadat had compared the 'battle of destiny' to the campaigns of the Prophet Muhammed and had called upon his people to carry the flag of Islam in what he saw as a mammoth clash between Islamic civilization and Zionism. No wonder, then, that the war-cry of 'Allah Akbar' was adopted by the armed forces, and that the code-name of the entire October War was 'Badr', after the name of one of the first battles of the Prophet in Arabia. The Egyptian soldiers were given personal booklets which quoted passages from the Holy Scripture and from subsequent Islamic literature, urging them to 'pursue the Jews and not pity them'.

At exactly 2 p.m., along the hundred-mile stretch of the Canal, from Suez to Port Said, all hell broke loose. Two hundred and forty Egyptian aircraft flew like ferocious beasts low into Sinai, strafing, bombing and destroying everything in sight. The troops, who began crossing the Canal at precisely that moment, were greatly encouraged by this show of force over their heads, and they valiantly thrust forward. Wave after wave crossed the waterway and started, like ants, to battle their way up the dyke and around Israeli strongpoints. The first air strike was very successful and only five aircraft were lost, among them the one piloted by Squadron Commander Atef Sadat, the President's brother; Sadat was not told immediately the identity of the fallen. Fifteen minutes later, when Sadat thought that the air raid had thrown the Israelis off balance, he ordered a second air strike. Again, like a clap of thunder, some 200 aircraft took off, sowing destruction and horror in their wake. Excitement mounted in the HQ when reports came in of the 7th Brigade which, under cover of a terrifying barrage from the Egyptian artillery, had succeeded in planting the Egyptian flag on the summit of the first conquered dyke amidst shouts of '*Allah Akbar*'. At the same time, pontoon bridges were launched on the Canal and the dykes were slashed open by the water hoses, in preparation for the armoured brigades to begin their thrust into Sinai. For the first time, smiles appeared on the faces of the generals who crowded around the President in the command bunker.

At 8 p.m., after six hours of combat, infantry and anti-tank missile teams located atop the dykes were engaged in a daring battle against the counter-attacking Israeli tanks which, unprepared for man-carried missile thrusts on this scale, incurred many casualties. The Israelis began to retreat, closely followed by the Egyptian tanks which began to surge forward to take hold and strengthen the Egyptian bridgehead before dawn of the next day.

In the middle of the battle, Sadat was advised that the Soviet Ambassador wished to see him urgently. Sadat went back to his Tahira palace HQ to meet the Ambassador, who had brought with him a message from the Soviet 'Troika' to the effect that Syria had asked for a cease-fire the next morning. Even though the Syrians denied this vehemently, the Soviets contacted Sadat twice more, each time pleading, 'on Syria's behalf', for a cease-fire. When Foreign Minister Isma'il Fahmi visited the Soviet Union after the war and the controversial question of the cease-fire came up, Brezhnev allegedly showed Fahmi the texts of three Syrian requests for a cease-fire. Moreover, the Soviets had even asked President Tito of Yugoslavia, a close friend of Sadat, to prevail upon him to accept the Syrian request for the cease-fire. There are two possible explanations for this controversy: either the Soviets wanted to drive a wedge between Egypt and Syria, avenging themselves on a rebellious Sadat whilst giving support to a loyal Syria, thus enabling her to retain all her newly-acquired gains; or Assad, realizing that the first day of the war had returned to him most of the Golan Heights, feared that continuation of the war might rob him of those gains, and he therefore asked the Soviets to bail him out of his alliance with Sadat, which obliged both of them not to seek a unilateral end to hostilities.

Sadat himself was inclined to believe that the Soviets were scheming to undermine his alliance with the Syrians, which was at odds with their own arrangements with Damascus. He remembered how on 1 May 1967, when he had represented Nasser at the May Day celebrations in Moscow in his capacity as speaker of the National Assembly, the Soviets had attempted to attract Syria to their orbit by praising the part that the Ba'th Party was playing in inter-Arab politics and by attributing to Syria the major role in Arab attempts to 'liberate Arab lands', thus demeaning Nasser to a secondary role. Sadat also recalled that, in their eagerness to cultivate the Syrian Ba'th, the Soviets had groomed the then chief-of-staff and strong man of the regime, Salah Jedid, and addressed him as '*tovarisch*' (comrade) as if he were one of them, for they were hoping that he might become their chief stooge in the Middle East. In Damascus, in May 1967, the Soviets had told Sadat that the Israelis had concentrated ten brigades on the Syrian border, which was to them a sign of Syria's primacy in the Arab–Israeli conflict. The Soviets had also passed on that information to Nasser in Cairo, prompting him to react with a counter-concentration of troops in Sinai; and it was that, in fact, which had started the downhill drift towards the 1967 war that Nasser had neither wanted, nor been prepared for. In addition, when Sadat had broken from the Soviets in 1972, they had continued to send large amounts of arms and ammunition to Syria, a reward for her loyalty, while he had had to enter the war with a shortage of ammunition. So he was wary of Soviet 'mediation' and of their attempts to interfere on behalf of Syria. In any case, he told the Soviet Ambassador, he rejected the plea for a cease-fire and would pursue the battle until all his war objectives were attained. To be on the safe side, he contacted Assad, who confirmed that he had never asked for, nor agreed to, a cease-fire.

On 7 October in the afternoon, the Soviet Ambassador called again while Sadat, having ascertained that everything was going smoothly on the battlefront, had stayed in his office instead of reporting to military HQ. Half an hour before the arrival of the Ambassador, Assad's belated answer arrived, restating Syria's resolve to reject any cease-fire. Faced with the Syrian response, the Soviet Ambassador turned pale and said, 'Mr President, I'm now bringing you a second application from Syria, via the Soviet leadership, for a cease-fire.' Sadat retorted that for him Assad's word was final and binding, but before the Ambassador departed, Sadat asked him to tell his Government that the war was going to be a long one and that, because of the high tank losses in combat, Egypt would need new tank deliveries soon. Sadat remained suspicious of Soviet conduct, especially as they attempted to pressure him from yet another direction, which left him with the impression that they were behind the machinations of the alleged Syrian request for a cease-fire. On 13 October at dawn, Sadat was woken up by the British Ambassador in order to receive an urgent message inquiring about the cease-fire from the British Prime Minister, Edward Heath. According to the message, Kissinger, now the US Secretary of State, had been contacted by the Soviets and told that the Egyptians had agreed to a cease-fire. Since the Americans had no legation in Cairo, they chose to verify the story via the British. In answer, Sadat reasserted his determination to see the battle through and told the British Ambassador about his two meetings with the Soviet Ambassador in Cairo, insisting that he had rejected the notion of a cease-fire.

At that stage, Sadat did not wish to consider a cease-fire unless he could be sure of retaining the gains in the Sinai that his advancing troops were fighting tooth and nail for. But that would have been unthinkable to the Israelis, who were trying to regroup, mobilize their reserves, deploy their troops and organize counter-attacks. So Sadat was prepared to keep pressing along the entire front and to begin the march of his two armies, the Second in the north and the Third in the south, towards the strategic passes of Sinai. Except for the heavy losses of tanks, on both sides, Sadat saw as yet no reason for worry. The Israelis, on the contrary, seemed to lose their nerve; they were busy pushing back the Syrian attack on the Golan Plateau, which was much closer to their population centres than the Sinai desert, and therefore it was essential for them to defend it first. In fact, during Sadat's frequent visits to the command bunker, he was often heartened by the reports from the battlefield of Israeli units that had been destroyed, Israeli fighters who had been taken prisoner, and the last Israeli strongholds along the Canal which had succumbed to the pressure of the advancing Egyptian troops. Sadat was particularly impressed by the success of the Egyptian air force, which at the height of the battle seemed underemployed. He heard the air-force commander, General Husni Mubarak, informing the army that he could make more air sorties, but they replied that there was no need for them. Sadat felt that the conduct of the Egyptian air force reversed the traditional *status quo*, where demand for air support usually outstrips availability, and land troops who call for air-strike support never obtain the help they need. Sadat's impressions were confirmed when he visited the Second Army on the third day of the war, after it had recaptured Qantara in northern Sinai. The army commander told Sadat that he was full of praise and admiration for the Egyptian pilots who hit the enemy tanks with precision, leaving behind them columns of smoke. Husni Mubarak was to be promoted by Sadat to the vice-presidency, after the war, as a reward for his achievement.

The battle for the skies over the Suez Canal, in which the Egyptians seemed to gain the upper hand in the first few days of the war, was considered by Sadat to be his armed forces' most stunning achievement. Sadat credited his air-defence missiles along the Canal with foiling all Israeli attempts to stop, from the air, both the initial Egyptian offensive and the deployment of the forces set for the attack and, most important of all, averting a recurrence of the carnage of 1967, when the Israeli air force had performed with deadly accuracy against the defenceless Egyptian troops.

Because of the massive losses of Israeli aeroplanes during the first days of the combat, Israel had ordered her pilots not to approach the Canal Zone, and that had allowed the Egyptians to strengthen their foothold and advance into Sinai. Sadat conceded that pre-1973 Israel had had 'air supremacy', by which he meant the technical edge which Phantom and Mirage jets gave Israel over Egypt's MiG 21s. Sadat explained the difference between the aircraft:

> In the MiG 21 the pilot has nothing except the compass. No facilities at all. In the Mirage and the Phantom, as in the Jaguar, everything is computerized for the pilot. If he enters a missile zone, there would be a light to warn him. If anyone is going to attack him from the back, another light will tell him. He just puts a card in the

computer, and it will take him to the place he chooses. It will tell him when to drop the bombs and will bring him back to his air base. In the MiG 21, and all Soviet military gear, all this is done by the pilot, which is very primitive. This is what gave Israel 'air supremacy'.[23]

Moreover, not only was Israel's 'air supremacy' blunted during the October War by the Egyptian missiles, but if you add to it Egyptian 'air superiority', which was reflected in the quality, fighting skills and motivation of the pilots, one could understand, in Sadat's analysis, why Israel lost the air battle and why the Egyptians could finally shatter the image of invincibility attached to Israeli air fighters.

From the fourth day of the war on, and up until the eleventh day (16 October), not much happened on the Suez front to attract Sadat's attention or to warrant any about-turn in his war strategy. The tank battles were bitter, to be sure, losses were heavy on both sides, the wear and tear of military hardware was much higher than expected, and the ammunition began to run low. But the front line was quite stable and it looked as if it was going to become a prolonged 'ditch war', in which Sadat was sure to have the longer breath and ultimately to emerge victorious. He had prepared for that possibility, and he knew that the Israelis could neither sustain a long war nor tolerate the casualties involved. All he needed, he thought, was to replenish his arsenals, dig in and wait until attrition took its toll of the Israelis. A Soviet airlift was mounted to supply some ammunition to Egypt (and Syria), but the more urgent need to replace the hundreds of destroyed tanks was not fulfilled as the war went on. Sadat turned to his allies in the Arab and Third Worlds. President Boumedienne of Algeria made a special trip to Moscow during the war and purchased 150 tanks for Egypt; 140 more tanks were sent in by Tito of Yugoslavia, and erratic Qadhafi committed, for a while, 100 of his own tanks to the battle; he later withdrew them. These were the 400 tanks which had to ward off the Israelis in the second stage of the war after 16 October.

On 16 October, while the war was raging in Sinai, Sadat put on his military uniform and appeared before the People's Assembly to make a dramatic speech in which he outlined his war aims and achievements to date. He was received with resounding applause and was hailed, both in Parliament and by the masses in the streets, as the 'hero of the crossing' and the 'hero of October'. Sure enough, he exalted in his usual flowery language 'the heroes who have emerged from this nation during its dark era when it was immersed in obscurity, brandishing torches of light to illuminate our way, enabling their nation to cross the bridge between despair and hope'. He said that the war was the fulfilment of the pledge he had undertaken before Allah and his people three years earlier, 'not to hand down to the next generation desecrated and humiliated banners' of the past. The climax of his speech was his 'peace programme' which he said he had gone to war to fight for, to wit: to recover the lands lost in 1967 and to restore the legitimate rights of the Palestinians – the very same goals he had inherited from Nasser. If these two objectives were attained, he said, then peace should become possible, not 'peace with aggression' that Israel had always sought to enforce, but 'peace with justice' that he had always strived for. At the same time, however, he voiced some bellicose notes of warning to Israel which did not sound all that conducive to peace. He accused the Zionist state not only of the 'aggression of 1967 to which the Egyptian army had fallen victim', but also of having 'robbed Palestine' since 1948. He challenged the Israelis to show the value of their security doctrine which was now 'shattered in to bits and pieces', together with the Bar-lev Line which was supposed to have provided Israel with an impenetrable shield, and he threatened to use his *Dhafer* (long-range missiles) to hit Israel's hinterland if Israel dared to transfer the war into Egyptian territory. He dubbed his war 'defensive', mindful of the 'values and rules set by the international community in the UN Charter'. He pledged the continuation of 'humanity's war against Fascism and Nazism' for, in his mind, 'Zionism, which teaches Fascist doctrines and advocates expansion through violent means, is nothing but a new and meek version of Fascism and Nazism'. Sadat concluded his condemnation of Israel by proclaiming that 'Zionism evoked contempt, not fear, mockery, not rancour'. He declared that he was committed to peace, but it was unclear from his remarks whether he could, or would, make peace with the Zionist state he despised so deeply, or not.

Sadat thanked all those nations who had expressed sympathy and respect for Egypt's feats of war. He said that it was more important for him to gain respect than sympathy, because for him, respect marked the recovery of his nation's honour while sympathy could simply mean friendship or an expression of interest. All in all it was a brave speech to an eager audience who had been fed by the media with stories of the heroic exploits of the Egyptian troops and who were filled with love and admiration for Sadat. He rode the crest of the wave of his popularity for all it was worth for he suspected that it would be his last chance to indulge in such a euphoric exercise in public relations; he sensed that the tide of war was beginning to turn against him. Whether he knew it, felt it, or assumed it, is hard to assess, but one thing is certain, he understood that Egypt's energies had been stretched to the limit; morale was still high and the troops were still in good shape, but they had been badly mauled and had lost much equipment, and the best Sadat could hope for was a standstill cease-fire which would consolidate his gains, vindicate his war initiative, and allow him to emerge 'victorious'. For the first time in modern Arab history he would not have lost a war against Israel. He could certainly not ask openly for a cease-fire, for that would expose him as a prospective loser, but he could dig in and wait for circumstances to bail him out.

On 16 October, Israeli troops commanded by General Ariel Sharon began to push through between the Egyptian Second and Third Armies, in the central sector of the Suez Canal, an area known as the Deversoir. Such a move, if carried on to completion, would have split the two attacking Egyptian armies and doomed the entire Egyptian war effort to a disastrous rout of untold proportions. On the 16th itself, the Egyptians remained unaware of the scale of the Israeli manœuvre and tended to dismiss it as a small random operation that Israel had launched in desperation. Sadat's first reaction when he heard of the Israeli breakthrough was, 'Well, let us give the Israelis a taste of commando operations in their rear.' He called in ten officers from Egypt's Special Forces who knew Israel ('Palestine' for Sadat) quite well, and shipped them to Jordan aboard a Comet transport with a message to King Hussein, urging him to facilitate the dispatch of the officers, together with some Palestinian volunteers from Jordan, into Israel to wreak havoc. Sadat specified in his message that he was willing to take responsibility for the operation within Israel, since he realized that Hussein might not like to be directly implicated in a hostile act against Israel. According to Sadat's account, King Hussein was reluctant and the Egyptian officers returned home. Sadat was sarcastically 'understanding' of Hussein's situation because he did not want him to 'lose Amman on the second day of fighting', had Israel retaliated against him too.

After Sadat's speech to the People's Assembly on 16 October, he returned to the operations room at the military HQ where War Minister Isma'il sat on his right and Chief-of-Staff Shadhili, a tough and imaginative officer who was credited with much of the planning and leadership of the October War, on his left. Upon hearing the reports of the Israeli landing, Sadat ordered Shadhili to go in person to the city of Isma'iliyya, near the location of the Israeli thrust, and try to ward it off or at least build a *cordon sanitaire* around it so as to prevent its expansion. Sadat said that he had taken such a commando operation into account during the planning stages of the war, and that five days before the outbreak of war, he had issued orders to his field commanders, urging them to keep their cool should Israel launch a dramatic 'TV-style show', such as landing in a remote area of the Red Sea, accompanied by foreign correspondents and cameramen, just in order to prove to the world that she too had occupied a piece of territory. Sadat believed that this kind of operation, which by its very nature is fast, would be designed to cause panic and psychological shock among the Egyptians. He thought that since the 'Jews believed that the Arabs were hot-tempered' and vulnerable to psychological warfare, they had based their strategy on the *blitzkrieg* methods used in the Second World War. However, Sadat said that he knew how to deal with this kind of operation which worked like a clockwork machine: if you dropped a little pebble into the works, the whole system would break down and grind to a halt. So, when the Deversoir operation began, Sadat thought it was something which could easily be contained. Shadhili's dispatch to the scene was calculated to assure the immediate and effective 'dropping of the pebble' into the Israeli war machine.

Sadat returned to his office to deal with other pressing matters, and it was not until 19 October, at 1 a.m., that he was urgently summoned to the military operations room. He found the atmosphere tense with embarrassment, a sharp contrast to the high morale and smiling faces he had seen before 16 October. Shadhili was back from his mission to the front and he seemed upset. He kept mumbling, 'The war is over, disaster has struck, we must withdraw from Sinai!' Questioned by the President, Shadhili confirmed that the situation called for a total retreat of the two armies from Sinai so that they could be redeployed to defend the west bank of the Suez Canal. Because he was the most charismatic, authoritarian and reliable of Sadat's chiefs-of-staff, his words caused consternation. Sadat decided to intervene immediately: he dismissed Shadhili on the spot and nominated General Gamasi, the 'brains behind the operation', in his stead. In counsel with the top command, he determined not to publish the dismissal, so as not to affect the morale of the troops in the middle of the war, and he also decided to avoid retreating from the present positions in Sinai at all costs. It was then that Sadat became desperate for a cease-fire in order to keep his battle gains. He was now convinced that high-level diplomacy would have to enter into the game if disaster was to be averted.

Sadat later protested that he had not really dismissed Shadhili, but had just 'relieved him of his command' because of his mental collapse. As evidence of this Sadat appointed him Egypt's Ambassador to London after the war, in token of his appreciation for the General's contribution to the war effort. But widespread rumours persistently credited the dismissal to Shadhili's charisma and mounting popularity which Sadat had come to perceive as a threat to his own authority. Since Sadat could share neither power nor prestige with anyone, ran this argument, he had to remove his potential rival before the glory of the war was attributed to him. There is no way to ascertain for sure what Sadat's motives were, but it does seem that, had Sadat wished to remove 'competitors' from power, he would perhaps have dismissed General Isma'il first, who was no less popular and who had become one of the heroes of the war. Sadat promoted another war hero, Mubarak, to the vice-presidency, so he could well have repaid Shadhili's loyalty by raising him to ministerial level instead of sending him abroad. It must also be pointed out that had Sadat wished to get Shadhili out of the way, he would have had no compunction about doing so without ceremony, as he was later to show in the case of yet another war hero, General Gamasi, the Operations Chief, who was made War Minister after Isma'il's death from a heart attack and Shadhili's golden exile to London, only to be relieved from command, without explanation, just three years later.

When the Israeli breakthrough began, Prime Minister Kosygin of the Soviet Union had been in Cairo for three days, attempting to convince Sadat to accept a cease-fire, and also trying to impress upon him that the military situation, as the Soviet Union knew from its satellites and other intelligence sources, was not in Egypt's favour. Sadat, suspicious of Russians since the beginning of the war, bluntly rejected the Soviet plea and vowed to continue the battle. Now the Americans entered the arena. Kissinger visited the Kremlin and agreed on a cease-fire with the Soviets, then went to see Sadat and the Israeli Government to probe for similar agreements. Israel agreed provided there was a restoration of the *status quo ante bellum*, which Sadat flatly rejected as he wanted to keep the territories he had conquered east of the Canal. Moreover, when he saw Kissinger for the first time, before 19 October, he could still confidently reject any cease-fire which did not recognize all his gains on the ground. After 19 October, however, Sadat was prepared to accept any standstill cease-fire, and the sooner the better, for the Israelis were making rapid advances on the west side of the Canal and Sharon's troops had begun the encirclement manœuvre which was designed to trap the entire Third Army in a huge pincer movement, first westwards and then southwards, towards the city of Suez on the southern approach to the Canal. So, on 19 October at 2 a.m., Sadat decided to request a standstill cease-fire, guaranteed by the two superpowers, to be followed by the implementation of the famous Security Council Resolution 338, which incorporated 242 as well.

Suddenly roles were reversed on the international scene; in the first week of the war, the US had attempted to arrange for a cease-fire and had tried to convince the Security Council of the UN to deal with this matter, while the Soviets backed their Arab clients' contention that there was no urgency and no need to call for a special meeting of the Council, for it was simply an internal Arab affair involving the retrieval of occupied lands. The Arabs and the Soviets, who were content with the initial steps of the war, obviously had no wish for a hurried settlement that would blunt their advances. However, from 16 October onwards, and especially from the 19th, the Soviets were pressing for a cease-fire which became a matter of supreme urgency once their allies were threatened with the possibility of serious defeat. Conversely, the Americans, who were recognized as the only people who could put pressure on Israel to stem her sweeping advance on the west bank of the Canal, could now afford to take their time, evaluate the situation, and see how they could best benefit in the role of broker between Sadat and Israel. So first of all, in order to show their muscle, their commitment to Israel, and the scope of Israel's dependence upon them, the Americans mounted a huge airlift to resupply Israel with ammunition, aeroplanes, tanks and other items she had lost in the first few days of the war. The greater the US readiness to supply the needed war material, the more she could both convince Israel of her standing obligation to defend the Jewish state and the Arabs of her capacity to exact leverage on Israel. Sadat understood this very well and accepted the US mediation. He realized that the Soviets could bail him out in war, for in war it took only one party to make the decision, but in peace, where both sides were equally indispensable, there was no escaping US mediation.

The Americans promised Sadat the cease-fire he desired, but at the same time they gave Israel enough leeway to attain some of her objectives on the west side of the Canal. In a typical Kissinger-inspired manœuvre, the Americans came to believe that only in a stalemate situation, where both parties made gains but neither party was permitted all it desired, was there any chance for a disengagement of forces as a prelude to settlement. Sadat accepted the rules of the game as he wished the cease-fire to enter into effect as soon as possible after 19 October. The Israelis wished to delay it until they could complete their outflanking of the Third Army. So 22 October was suggested as a date for the cease-fire, sanctioned by both the US and the Soviet Union, at the Security Council. The Egyptians thought that was too late, the Israelis too early, but they both acquiesced in the wishes of the superpowers.

On 19 October, immediately after he took the decision to accept a cease-fire, Sadat notified his ally, President Assad of Syria. Much acrimony followed, which spoiled the close relationship worked out between the two allies before the war. The Ba'th Party discussed the cease-fire, but then decided to reject it, blaming Sadat for abandoning the war and thus losing it, precisely at the moment when the Syrians themselves were preparing a massive counter-attack on the Golan Heights. Sadat countered by claiming that, had it not been for the US who fought on Israel's side during the last stages of the war, he would not have accepted the cease-fire. He maintained that *he* could fight against Israel and win but that *he* had 'fought alone against Israel and the US for ten days' and was not able or willing to expose his people to a military confrontation with a superpower any longer. To his mind, it was the US who had encouraged Israel to launch her 'TV-style' counter-attack across the Canal, and it was the US who provided Israel with new sophisticated weaponry, such as TV-guided bombs and other items which had never been used even by the US military themselves. He found 'evidence' for this conviction in the new tanks provided by the Americans for Israel, some of which were captured by the Egyptians. Sadat asserted that the American transports which brought the tanks had landed directly at Al-Arish in northern Sinai, from where they proceeded to the battlefield on the Suez Canal. The tanks had clocked up just 105 kilometres, the distance between Al-Arish and the front, and the fact that they had been immediately rushed into combat 'proved' that they had been manned by American crews, because the Israelis would have had no time to train in operating them.

While Sadat was busy justifying his acceptance of the cease-fire, the situation at the front went from bad to worse. The Israelis had advanced along the highway to Cairo and were now less than 100 kilometres from the capital. In the south they were near the city of Suez, the Third Army's last link with the Egyptian heartland; if cut off, half of them would be doomed to a humiliating surrender, or even death. Egyptian fighters were giving themselves up to the Israelis in their thousands, while Israel's stranglehold tightened every hour. The cease-fire, which was eagerly sought by the Egyptians and reluctantly agreed upon by the Israelis, did not hold. Six hours after its enforcement, the fighting was renewed, with the Israelis eyeing the city of Suez as their objective, in order to complete the encirclement of the Third Army. Sadat thought that Israel had aimed at the city, in the first place because of its 'world reputation' and in order to cover up the 'Israeli defeat all along the other front lines'. Thus Sadat was determined to put up a fight, for he was loath to let the Israelis reap the prestige of having broken into the city. For him, it was a kind of 'Stalingrad' where he would have the Israelis tire themselves out. So when Israeli elite troops, supported by tanks, reached the outskirts of what looked like a 'ghost city', all hell broke loose: the Egyptian military defenders, together with the local police and militia, put up a harsh and sustained battle, finally repelling the Israelis who lost many men and much military hardware.

Sadat regarded Suez's 'heroic stand' as the pinnacle of his achievement against the Israeli occupation of Sinai. The city, which was once the pride of the Canal Zone, had been thoroughly destroyed by Israeli artillery fire and ceaseless bombing, and all its major industrial plants, including the large oil refineries, had been reduced to rubble. Since fighting could not cause any further damage to the already levelled city, it had become a symbol for Sadat. He said that when the Egyptian leadership had decided to evacuate the city in 1969–70, at the height of the War of Attrition, the meaning of that decision had been confrontation, not surrender. For Nasser had determined that the Suez Canal cities would become the battlefield and that the Egyptians would persist in the fighting come what may. Sadat was determined not to break with that 'tradition of sacrifice', and he issued strict orders to prevent an enemy take-over at any cost.

Sadat saw in the Suez battle a true reflection of the actual balance of forces between the Israelis and the 'noble Egyptians'. The outskirts of Suez had become a 'graveyard for Israeli tanks and soldiers', who were for the first time fighting away from the barren desert and had to prove themselves in a 'real battle' against Egyptian soldiers and civilians. It was the civilians in particular who 'gave birth to sublime acts of heroism'. Sadat also stated that the battle of Suez would go down in the history books and the heroism displayed that day told from generation to generation, to be used as a symbol of courage for all Egypt. Thereafter, 24 October became National Suez Day which was to be observed by all state institutions, and celebrated throughout the country as a national festival. That was Sadat's way not only of commemorating a supreme act of military and civilian sacrifice, but also of establishing his own equivalent of the 'Port Said Day' that Nasser had declared following the 1956 war, when that city had played a role in repulsing the Anglo-French attack.

Ultimately, the Israelis decided to circumvent Suez, which was proving a hard nut to crack, and in a rapid sweep completed the encirclement of the Third Army, which would give them a major trump card in the post-war settlement. It was the ideal state of deadlock that Kissinger was seeking: a double sandwich of Israeli and Egyptian forces engaged one behind the other, consisting of remnants of the Egyptian troops on the Suez–Cairo road, then the

Israeli bridgehead, then the Egyptian Third Army, then the bulk of Israeli troops in Sinai. Only a mediator could unravel this complex situation; the US was the only power around who could provide such a service. Kissinger's first meeting with Sadat during the war had inspired some understanding between the two, and Sadat delighted thereafter in meeting 'brother Henry', a fellow strategist, and exchanging views with him on world affairs. For a few days, Sadat insisted that Israel should withdraw to the 22 October cease-fire lines, which would have lifted the siege around the Third Army and robbed Israel of her trump card in the coming negotiations. However, despite Soviet support, Sadat was pragmatic enough to accept the situation that existed and begin to negotiate from there. He was assured by Kissinger that the US would guarantee, pending the forthcoming disengagement talks, that the Third Army would continue to be supplied through Israeli lines. For Sadat, it was a humiliating admission that he depended upon the goodwill of both Israel and the US to avert total disaster for his troops, and he never forgot that General Sharon had been the architect of the bridgehead which had brought Egypt to the verge of catastrophe. While Sadat often bragged, after the war, of having deceived and then outmanœuvred General Dayan, the Israeli Defence Minister, during the war, he regarded Sharon with both bitterness and awe. When he came to Jerusalem in November 1977, Sadat's first request at the airport was to see Sharon. The two men embraced and Sadat, with a glow of admiration in his eyes, said, 'I almost trapped you at the Deversoir.' That was his way of admitting, 'You almost trapped me!'

What embarrassed Sadat most was that news about the difficulties his troops were in started filtering through to Egypt, despite stringent censorship measures. Rumours abounded: that 10,000 Egyptian soldiers had surrendered to the Israelis; that the Israelis had gained a large enclave on the west bank of the Suez Canal, just sixty miles away from Cairo; and that Sadat was reluctant to initiate diplomatic moves in order to extricate himself from the dangerous situation he was in. All this stood in sharp contrast to the bombast of the preceding three weeks, the reports of victory upon victory, the advance of the 'heroic soldiers of Allah' towards the Sinai passes, the parades of the few Israeli POWs and war spoils in the streets of Cairo, and the pictures of the shattered Bar-lev Line, which all attested to Israel's 'defeat'. In fact, the good-humoured Egyptians began fabricating custom-made jokes to describe Sadat's plight, whilst rumours began spreading in Cairo about the true state of affairs. One joke said that the Israeli enclave was no longer a pocket (*gayb*) in Egyptian territory, as the authorities claimed, but had become an entire pair of trousers (*sārat bantalōn*). Another joke had Golda Meir, the Israeli Prime Minister, talking to Sadat. She said, '*Bonjour*', and he unwittingly answered '*Al-Ubour*' (the crossing). And then he wished her, '*Bonsoir*', and she retorted, '*Deversoir*'. These and other self-deprecating jokes, which signified that the people in Cairo did know the true situation and took it seriously, could not have escaped

Sadat's attention. Therefore he spent much of his time, in the immediate aftermath of the war, in apologetic and explanatory speeches and interviews. Most of the blame he put on Israel, the US, the Soviet Union and some Arabs, like the Libyans, who had not lived up to their promises; some of the praise he imparted to other Arabs, like the Saudis, the Kuwaitis and the Algerians who had assisted Egyptian efforts during the war; and all the laudatory remarks he could muster he poured on the Egyptian armed forces and their leadership. In the end, however, Sadat sensed that the war was *his* war; that unlike Nasser, who had led the Arabs from defeat to defeat, he had reversed the trend; that he had made the Israelis retreat for the first time since Israel was established; that he had broken the 'barrier of fear' by showing that Israel was no longer invincible and her defences were not impregnable; and that he was a worthy leader of the Arab–Islamic world now that he had acquired the aura of victor.

It is interesting to note how Sadat succeeded in reliving, and repeating to himself and his audiences, the first few days of the war from which he had gained so much inspiration, and at the same time shutting his mind off to the events of 16 October and after. It was as if the first part of the reel, which recorded the unfolding of the war, was played and replayed by Sadat in slow motion and its delight savoured again and again to perpetuate the sweet taste of victory, but the rest of the tape was simply wiped clean, or jammed beyond recognition, so as to escape the bad memories of the war's last stages. To replace the missing record, which he had to account for, Sadat simply made up his own, which must have sounded so convincing to him that he kept repeating it and thus ended up believing in it. It is fascinating to look at one of Sadat's accounts of the unpleasant phase of the war:

On 19 October, I was invited to the operations room where Shadhili had just returned from the front in a mood of confusion. He said that the Americans were landing equipment in Al-Arish, just behind the Israeli lines, from where it was immediately shipped to the front. I have to admit that the Israelis are very capable militarily both in planning and performance, but as of 16 October it became evident to me that what we were facing was not Israeli planning, for in the preceding four days we had drained Israel's main military force. . . . How could I, therefore, face the fresh armoured brigades which were pouring on the front like rain? Nonetheless, we stood up to all that and we engaged in some of the most famous and ruthless armoured battles in military history. . . . New planning had come into action, fresh blood had begun flowing, as the US officially declared her airlift to Israel. As a matter of fact, it was not an airlift but a virtual American intervention. . . .

For the historical record I must repeat that before we struck at the 400 Israeli tanks on the front I told the Soviet Ambassador, 'We are going to engage in armoured battles. Be sure to send us more armour, for the party in possession of more armour stands the chance of sustaining the combat for a longer period of time.' However, the armour I asked the Soviet Union for was not delivered to me until one week subsequent to the cease-fire. The tanks I did receive during the war originated from Algeria, Yugoslavia and Libya. In short, my consent to the cease-fire was prompted by my reluctance to fight the US although I was prepared to fight Israel.[24]

Apart from Sadat's perceptions of the final stages of the war, he was realistic and shrewd enough to ride the crest of victory and to embark on a domestic and external information crusade aimed at convincing the Arab world and the West that a new era had dawned on the Middle East in which he would play a decisive role. The fact that he was courted by the US Government and the world media only added to his aura of glory and led him to believe that he had a universal mission to accomplish. He felt confident enough to settle accounts with Qadhafi, who had not lived up to Egypt's expectations; to lecture the world about the strategic importance that the new Arab nation had assumed as a result of the war; and to tread new ground in international politics in general and towards the Arab and Israeli conflict in particular.

A few months after the war, Sadat published a message that he had sent to the Libyan Revolutionary Council detailing what he regarded as Libya's misconduct during the war, which had seriously undermined the relations between the two countries. It transpired from that message that on 27 February 1973 Sadat had sent a cable to Qadhafi announcing that the plans for the war had been outlined, in conjunction with Syria. In that cable, Sadat had also rejected Qadhafi's bid that Egypt and Libya should mount a joint reprisal against Israel for the Libyan airline shot down over Sinai earlier that year. Qadhafi's suggestion for a retaliatory raid against Israel had been coupled with a personal attack on Sadat for having led Egypt into isolation, while at her 'two gates' stood Israel on the one hand and the 'reactionary forces' on the other. Sadat's reply was brief: 'May Allah forgive you!' Sadat sent another cable on 15 March 1973, repeating his pledge to launch the war in due course, in response to another of Qadhafi's threats that if Sadat did not join him in his quest to mount a raid against Israel, he might initiate a retaliatory operation on his own, and if he should fail he would have to conclude that 'Allah is on the Jews' side'. Later in the same month, Sadat told Qadhafi, in good collegiate spirit, about the many changes he was planning in his domestic affairs as part of his preparations for war, including his decision to take over the prime ministership. Just a few weeks before the war began, Sadat sent yet another secret cable to Qadhafi announcing that the countdown for the war had begun. Qadhafi, instead of taking such classified information seriously, used it in one of his public addresses, ridiculing the planned Egyptian and Syrian attack against Israel and forecasting disaster.

Qadhafi's speech, which had been monitored in Egypt, caused considerable consternation and bitterness among the top military officers who were making the preparations for war, and saw Qadhafi's public disclosures of their best-kept secret as a betrayal of their cause. What was worse, when the attack began on 6 October, Qadhafi made another fiery speech, voicing his doubts about the war and its chances of success. At the time, that speech gained little attention because of the momentous events that were taking place along the Bar-lev Line and the Golan Heights, but for Sadat it reconfirmed Qadhafi's lunacy. During the initial days of the war, Radio Tripoli kept quoting Israeli official communiqués which belittled the Arab attack and played up the Israeli attempt to ward off the offensive. Then Libya announced officially that she would only support the war financially and would not commit any of her troops to the battlefield. Sadat was enraged, not only because the Libyan broadcast had reached some front-line troops during the battle, but also because Sadat regarded such comments as 'stone-throwing' at a sister state while she was struggling for her life. What was more, Qadhafi had demanded that his speech be broadcast from Cairo by *Sawt al-Arab* Radio, and Sadat had had to agree because he needed Qadhafi's co-operation during the war: Sadat was probably ignorant of the contents of the speech until it was pronounced and the Egyptian public was shocked by it. When the cease-fire was declared, Qadhafi broadcast an appeal that fighting should be pursued at all costs, without even consulting with Sadat about the reasons for the cease-fire and its hoped-for objectives. Instead, Qadhafi showed up in Cairo, in his paratrooper's uniform, vowing to lead troops to liberate the Israeli-occupied enclave from the invaders.

Before the war broke out, Sadat had specified to Qadhafi three areas where Libya could be of assistance: one, by making the harbour of Tobruk available as a back-up to Alexandria; two, by signing an arms deal with a Western country (presumably France) for spare parts to be provided during the war for the Mirage planes stationed in Egypt; three, by ensuring the supply of four million tons of oil during the year following the outbreak of fighting, as Egypt's oil wells would have to stop production. The Libyans never refused any of these requests specifically and therefore Sadat was led to believe that they would be honoured, but only the use of Tobruk materialized during the war. As for the arrangements to help with the supply of spare parts, Qadhafi was to pay for the deliveries six months in advance – he was to make the first payment in January 1973 in order to get the deliveries in June; but since he delayed the payment until June, under the pretext that Egypt was not in earnest in her preparations for war, it was too late to get the spare parts via Libya. Sadat had to rush to the Saudis for help, who paid for the equipment and arranged for emergency deliveries to Egypt. Ultimately, Libya got part of the equipment that Saudi Arabia had paid for, but it was too late to help in the war effort. The supplying of oil went smoothly until the cease-fire was declared; then, further to humiliate Sadat, the Libyans simply sent back the Egyptian tankers empty, claiming that, since the war had stopped, there was no longer a need for oil shipments to Egypt. All in all, only 800,000 tons out of the promised four million were shipped to Egypt before the cease-fire. This was a deadly blow for Sadat because it occurred while Israel still occupied the west bank of the Canal, before the disengagement negotiations had begun, and there was a very serious threat that fighting might resume. Sadat felt betrayed and had to ask other Arab countries – Algeria and Saudi Arabia – for emergency supplies. Libya also discontinued the payments of financial aid that had been agreed upon at the Khartoum Conference in August 1967, and reneged on a special emergency grant of $60 million she had pledged to pay to Egypt just before the war began. These funds were to finance contracts with foreign countries for the purchase of basic foodstuffs for the population of Egypt during the war, and only when Qadhafi realized that he might lose the remnants of his popularity in some Egyptian circles did he agree to pay half the money so that some of the contracts could be carried out.

Compared with the shameful role that Libya had played in the war, Sadat was gratified by the conduct of the other Arab countries, especially Saudi Arabia, Kuwait and Abu Dhabi, all of whom sent him money and stopped the flow of oil to the US once American involvement in the war became 'evident'. Sadat had shown all Arabs the validity of his pre-war slogan: 'Demonstrate your might and then talk; show your muscle and then negotiate'; and they were satisfied that this was precisely what had happened. The war enabled all Arabs to hold their heads up high, for not only had the joint armies of Egypt and Syria emerged 'victorious', at least during the early stages of the war, but the Arabs had emerged self-confident in their collective powers: militarily, economically and morally. Sadat saw in the Arab offensive the undoing of Israel's defence strategy: not only was total surprise achieved, but the Israelis were compelled to fight on two fronts simultaneously, and they faced a united Arab world which did not hesitate either to come to Egypt's aid or to activate the oil weapon for the first time. Sadat boasted that, as a result of the war, the prestigious London-based Institute of Strategic Studies had come to the conclusion that the Arabs had indeed become the world's Sixth Power. Moreover, the war had taken eighteen days, not the one week prescribed by Israel, and had demonstrated Arab capacity for a protracted war. Sadat said that his promise to King Faisal before the war, that he would not ask for a cease-fire immediately, actually constituted one of the pillars of his strategy. Sadat's penchant for historical analogies led him to declare that *his* war had been more formidable in some respects than even the Second World War. During the latter, he said, the greatest armour battle in history had taken place in Kursk, in Russia, with 500 tanks participating, while during the war *he* initiated 3,000 tanks were destroyed on all sides, which meant that at least 5,000 tanks (tenfold the figures of Kursk!) had taken part in the battle. Incidentally, he compared the Israeli breakthrough to the west bank of the Canal to the battle of the Ardennes during the Second World War. Sadat said that the Israelis, who had adopted the 'Nazi militaristic mentality', had mounted a Nazi-style suicide attack and then used Goebbels-like propaganda to turn it into a virtue. He also made the point that the Bar-lev Line was analogous to the German Atlantic Wall.

When summing up the war, Sadat heaped praise upon both the Egyptian air-defence system and the Egyptian air force, commanded by Husni Mubarak, whom *he* had appointed to the job briefly before the war and who had emerged from it as a national hero. Sadat said that these two powerful arms of the Egyptian armed services had thrown Israel off balance and accounted for the success of the 'Six Hour War' which was compared to Israel's victory in the Six Day War of 1967. Although the Soviet Union was to blame for sending deficient equipment, such as inferior planes, compared to Israel's, the Egyptian pilots performed 'ten times better than their weapons allowed them' and scored a victory over the redoubtable Israeli air force. The Soviet Union was also condemned for providing Egypt with Second World War vintage crossing bridges which took six hours to assemble, and also for delivering faulty ammunition dating back to 1969, which Sadat suspected had been left over from ammunition purchased by Nasser that year, but which the Soviets had held back because he had refused to desist from the War of Attrition. In 1973, they finally 'remembered', claimed Sadat, to ship it, when it could no longer be of effective use. Sadat also censored the Soviets for allotting to him only two to three 'portions' of ammunition for his artillery during the war, while they delivered to their obedient Syrian clients eight to eleven 'portions'. Furthermore, while Syrian arsenals and stockpiles of ammunition were replenished by the Soviets, and they were compensated for all the aircraft and tanks they lost in battle before the 22 October cease-fire, Sadat did not receive any immediate deliveries, which in some measure curtailed his bargaining position when he came to negotiate disengagement with the Israelis, and ultimately forced him to turn to the United States. The Soviets only renewed the shipments of arms at the beginning of 1975, after the first disengagement agreement in Sinai and on the eve of the second. So, while Sadat said that he had modelled his war plans on three assumptions – Egyptian might, the Arab world and Soviet support – he ended up praising the first, holding reserved esteem for the second (the withdrawal of 100 Libyan tanks from the battle had marred the impression of Arab unity), and deprecating the third. Sadat knew that he needed to emerge from the war with the greater part of his armies and weapons intact lest he be exposed to pressure by the Soviets. It was thanks to the fact that 85 per cent of the weapons survived that war that, Sadat said, he was able to survive the post-war sixteen-month embargo imposed by the Soviets.

Three years after the war, Sadat was disappointed that his conception of the glory of the war was not shared by other Egyptians. He said in a public address in October 1976 that Egyptian literature had fallen short of reflecting the war adequately, and of treating it as a major event of world import, 'since the post-October world is different from the pre-October one'. Sadat thought that Egypt's literature's lag behind events might be attributable to the 'vestiges of defeatism which are still extant in some writers'. Sadat was not prepared to put up with the fact that the war had not inspired any great work of art or literature and he was determined to act. He summoned Omar Sharif, the famous film star who was of Egyptian origin, to get him interested in producing a movie like *The*

Longest Day, which had portrayed the Allies landing in Normandy in the Second World War. Sadat also organized a symposium at the Nasser Military College where commanders at all levels were encouraged to draw their own conclusions about the war. There, the Israeli westward crossing occupied the minds of the participants, and they concluded that a breakdown in communications had resulted in Egyptian military commanders being unaware of the size and increasing scope of the Israeli breakthrough. In the beginning, they believed, local commanders had reported 'Israeli infiltration', but the high command had decided to concentrate their attention on what they thought were more pressing issues. By the time the Commander-in-Chief understood the picture, the 'pocket' had indeed become 'trousers'.

The symposium also drew the conclusion that the Israeli idea of substituting well-trained small armies for massive armed troops had failed, and with it the doctrine of 'quality at the expense of quantity'. Sadat stated at the symposium that the October War had proved that numerical superiority of troops was of strategic importance. Moreover, General Dayan had counted on his air superiority to compensate for his numerical inferiority; he had boasted, according to Sadat: 'My arms are long, I can strike anywhere I want and however I wish.' Sadat retorted: 'I struck him in his soft underbelly, attacking the morale of his men: my superior man-power drove him out of the battle. We have yet to see an Israeli government who will dare to declare general mobilization again. . . . Therefore, I foresee no problem over the Israeli retreat from Sinai. They are bound to retreat, either under Dayan or anyone else.' One of the lessons Sadat learnt from the war was that, due to the unpopularity of general mobilization in Israel, the latter was bound to withdraw if he kept up his military pressure, forcing her to maintain a high level of mobilization.

Another major lesson that Sadat drew from the war was that the close alliance of Israel with the US meant that success could only be achieved by driving a wedge between them. He was convinced that the Israeli breakthrough had only been gained by active American help, including intelligence obtained from American military satellites and made available to Israel, and the supply of 'Maverick' missiles, the like of which Sadat saw later in Iran.

In contrast with what he regarded as total American commitment to Israel, he recalled Kosygin's visit to him before 16 October. Sadat, desperate to sustain the war effort, had tried to persuade his guest to forget the July 1972 crisis between the two countries and resume friendly relations on a new basis. Kosygin began to enumerate all the hardware the Soviets had already delivered to Egypt, but Sadat shut him up by complaining about being sent Second World War bridges which took six hours to assemble, while there were others, available in the Soviet Union, which could be assembled in half an hour, but which the Soviets had refused to deliver. And so, complained Sadat, *he* had been forced to cross the 'largest water obstacle in history' by primitive means.

He went on: 'So, *I* crossed and removed the seventeen-metre high dyke obstacle, within less than six hours. All *my* forces marched in. The bridges were set up and the tanks broke through. A miracle. Despite your six-hour bridges, *I* pursued *my* operation and emerged almost without casualties.'[25] Sadat also confronted Kosygin with pre-war Soviet estimates that the crossing of the Canal would cost forty to sixty thousand dead, while actually the crossing took only a toll of 400. Sadat now pressed for a new relationship, to reach a new understanding and forget the past. At the same time, however, Sadat refused to accept Kosygin's plea for a cease-fire and to let the Soviet Union speak for him in requesting one. Sadat said that 'only Egypt could speak for Egypt', not the USSR. Kosygin left angry, and Sadat took the decision to probe for a new relationship with the US. It stands to reason that had the USSR acceded to all of Sadat's demands, he would have stayed loyally in their camp as did his ally President Assad of Syria. Ironically, every time the Soviets received a blow from Sadat, they learned their lesson and hastened to pour on Assad all the bounties they had refused to Sadat. So they lost Sadat not because he was pro-American but because they made him anti-Soviet; they were not sensitive to his national pride, to his style of leadership, to the sovereignty of Egypt and to his desperate need to accomplish the liberation of his land.

On the strategic level too, Sadat drew several lessons from the war: first, that the Arabs were capable of organization, keeping a secret and improvisation. He thought that in all direct confrontations with Israel, given equal circumstances, the Arabs would emerge with the upper hand, be they infantry, tank or air battles. This had been demonstrated by the collapse of the Israeli army during the first days of war. His evidence: 'We saw their soldiers running away and surrendering, and their Prime Minister asking on the telephone for help from the US. We saw, and the entire world saw, what we could do.' Sadat said that Israel had been allowed to boast of her invincibility simply because of Arab disunity, not because of her intrinsic qualities. Gone with the myth of Israel's invincibility was the image of Arab lethargy and recklessness.

Second, the Arabs had wielded the oil weapon effectively, with wisdom and courage, and in so doing had broken through the barrier of fear which had previously paralysed them, fear of retaliation by Western consumers. The Arabs never lacked the courage to act, asserted Sadat, but they needed an Arab party to initiate necessary surveys, draw plans and commit acts of daring in order to rise and throw their weight into the battle. That leadership had been provided by Egypt. Sadat said that he was confident that, if he took the lead, an electric shock would jolt the entire Arab nation.

Third, the war had proved that strategic disinformation was still possible. The world and the superpowers were confident that they had mastered the scientific means of obtaining intelligence data by means of satellites, high-altitude photos and electronic gear. October had proved that knowing about troop movements was one thing but scrutinizing their intentions was quite another. The US and Israel had monitored Egyptian moves but they had failed to comprehend them.

Fourth, military schools the world over believed that physical obstacles like Suez could eliminate the factor of surprise, and that these obstacles could only be broken by limited breaches. But the October War proved, according to Sadat, that such obstacles could be overcome in a matter of hours.

Fifth, all armies were trained on the assumption that planes and tanks were the decisive weapons of war. Egypt had proved that missiles and infantry could still reverse these theories, if afforded new weapons and if the fighting men showed the daring of the Egyptian troops. Young soldiers had stood fast, waiting to blow up heavily armoured, firing tanks at point-blank range.

Sixth, it became evident to Sadat that small and medium-sized countries were still able, once they made up their minds, to recover their rights, to break conventional international relationships and superpower agreements with regard to 'military relaxation' and non-confrontation, to take their destiny into their own hands and to make their own decisions to fight. Therefore, peace should only be established after justice has been achieved. Peace cannot be established by the strong; it is the outcome of a settlement of disputed rights.

Seventh, the Arab world had emerged as a new factor in international relations: it had a strategic position commanding the link between three continents (Europe, Asia and Africa); it had waterways and vital communication lines, such as the Suez Canal, the Red Sea, Bab al-Mandab, the Arab (Persian) Gulf and the approaches to the Indian Ocean; it owned the most important national resource on which modern civilization was founded – oil; it possessed vast expanses of arable lands in a world which faced starvation and where wheat was about to become a more potent weapon than navies and armies; and it had acquired a new-found harmony between its component people, unparalleled in other areas of the world such as Europe. One thing was missing: the engine that could turn this huge skeleton into an efficient, awesome machine. The October War had provided the 'means to start the engine', in Sadat's words. Now, contended Sadat, the world could no longer dismiss the Arabs, who had become a force to be reckoned with. Moreover, the world had had to learn to adopt a new style of diplomacy if it wanted to deal with the Arab nation, even though its peoples may be small or poor. 'Just watch America and Europe', said Sadat, 'complying to the rise of oil prices and to the decrease in oil production! The era of foreign commissioners has gone, when a lift of their finger was enough to impress local rulers. The era has gone when terror and gun diplomacy prevailed. We have become equal to others in this world, not satellites of others. We have finally implemented what we had set out to do on 23 July 1952 and on 6 October 1973.' Sadat accused 'Zionist circles' of trying to put the blame on Arab capital for all the political, economic and social problems facing the world today. He said that 'those who have invented the rules of marketing, supply and demand cannot now complain once these rules no longer work in their favour. Those who have let the gap between them and the developing nations widen cannot now cry for help.'

Sadat also came to believe that the Palestinian problem which lay at the 'heart and the core of the Middle Eastern conflict' had taken a new turn, thanks to the October War, when 'thousands of Palestinian casualties were endured by the Palestinian people who fought alongside Arab nations'. For the first time, claimed Sadat, the world has recognized the reality of the Palestinian people and their legitimate rights. Israel has remained the only exception to this recognition, but even there voices were raised urging her to recognize the new reality. Since the Palestinian problem would continue to 'poison world peace', there would be no peaceful solution until a solution was found for the Palestinian people. Therefore, concluded Sadat, the return of Sinai and the Golan, occupied by Israel, would not resolve the issue. The PLO, which had become the new embodiment of the Palestinian people, was the party to be negotiated with, and the fact that the UN had come to recognize this reality was in itself a new phenomenon, which would have been impossible as long as the Arabs provided nothing but memoranda and speeches. The October War changed all that. As a result of the October War, the Arab problem had risen, in Sadat's mind, to the top of the world agenda and it demanded an urgent solution, namely a full withdrawal of Israel from all occupied territories and the recognition of the legitimate rights of the Palestinian people. He made it clear that the Arabs would not rely on any country to gain this solution, or depend on the rise or fall of any particular ruler to press for it. Henceforth, pledged Sadat, the Arabs were capable of weighing their friendships and enmities towards other countries in terms of the support they could elicit for their cause. The patience that the Arabs had shown before 1973 had been exhausted and therefore it was time for the world to wake up and not sleep under misapprehensions about Arab tolerance.

All the lessons that Sadat drew from the war, on domestic, inter-Arab and international levels, seemed to him feats which the world had deemed impossible, but which had nevertheless been accomplished. Furthermore, Arab honour had been retrieved, although the world had been led to believe that the Arabs could not be trusted to behave honourably. Therefore, the way was now open for an about-turn: for vigorous diplomacy, supported by changed world public opinion, resting on Arab unity, to enforce the Arab point of view as of right. So, when Sadat spoke at the end of the war about the 'new dawn that was rising on Arab land after 500 years of obscurity', he truly believed that it was time for diplomacy to stand out as the 'continuation of war by other means'. He also believed that he had been reborn as a new world leader, his record of accomplishments now enriched with the 'miraculous' implications of a victory that no one had deemed attainable.

8

THE REBORN LEADER

In his speech before the People's Assembly on 16 October 1972, Sadat said that nations revealed their true colours only when engaged in struggle; only when rising to meet a great challenge did they reveal their full potential. The same could be said of Sadat himself, and one may suspect that when he delivered this speech, he was thinking of Egypt as a reflection of himself, just as he often thought of himself as the personification of Egypt. Indeed, the October War, and more precisely the initial victorious offensive, marked a major watershed not only for Egypt but also for Sadat. Thereafter, his personality, his style of leadership and the authority he brought to it, his thinking, his imagery, the degree of his self-confidence and his world view all changed. He shed the last vestiges of servility to Nasser – the man, his ideas and his heritage – and set out to forge a path of his own, both ideologically and politically, both on the domestic and on the international fronts. Capitalizing on his 'victory' in the war, he claimed the authority to change Egypt's internal political system, to overhaul his policies towards the Arab world and to alter his relations with the superpowers and the rest of the world. He sensed that the 'shame' of 1967 had been removed; he could again expose his face to the world.

One of the most striking developments was the almost total disappearance from Sadat's speeches of bellicosity and vengeful condemnation of Israel and the US, and the substitution of a more rational and pragmatic approach to state affairs in general and to the Arab–Israeli conflict in particular. So while before the war he spoke in religious terms, of his 'holy duty' to liberate the land, exhorting his audiences to struggle and to be ready for sacrifice, after the war he repeatedly called upon the Arabs to desist from emotionalism and to begin 'to use their brains and to think', to recognize that Israel, satanic as it might be, was a *fait accompli*. He condemned those among the Arabs who fought 'with words instead of deeds', and urged them to espouse 'analysis and rationality in accordance with the era in which we are living'. On the domestic front, he said that the handling of Egypt's interests should be governed by 'realism and not by emotional considerations'. He advocated a 'state of institutions' which would rationalize Egypt's affairs and remove them from 'emotionalism and chaos'. On the international front, he decided that he had to co-operate with the US, regardless of the identity of the President, and to 'ignore friendships, enmities, sentiments and emotions'.

In response to Syrian charges that his completion of the disengagement agreement with Israel in 1975 was not in Arab interests, he said:

> This does not justify calling me a traitor to the Arab cause. . . . If we [Egypt and Syria] have a disagreement, we ought to sit down and talk. If they [the Syrians] can get something from the USSR that I cannot obtain from the US, then our arsenals could complement each other. This is the way thoughtful and wise people ought to behave.[26]

And regarding his relations with the Soviet Union after the war:

> There is no need for resentment or emotionalism. The times when we were frustrated have been done away with since 6 October. Now we are calm and in control; we have a clear view of our objectives and see no reason for resentment or emotionalism. . . . In due course, we shall quietly approach the Soviet Union, ask them for the reasons for their behaviour, and then we will be able to exchange our views.[27]

These statements are a stark contrast to the outbursts of anger, bitterness, vengefulness and self-justification of pre-war Sadat. Before the war he had frequently roused the people and communicated to them his sense of frustration; he now told them that, 'We do not use the methods of the rabble. . . . We use our brains, hold firm to our cause, our way of thinking and to the people who fight alongside us. . . .'[28] Before the war, Sadat was concerned to combine faith and science, religion and technology, emotion and reason, words and deeds, heart and brain; following the October 'victory', there seems to have developed a clear shift to the latter components of these dichotomies. It seemed as though bitterness and vindictiveness had run the course of their usefulness and it was now time to change if things were to be kept moving. Revolution could only be perpetuated if new strategies were developed once the old had become routine and ineffective.

The second major development concerning Sadat's personality and his conduct of state affairs was his evolution into a mature and accomplished leader of world stature. He simply took on a charisma that he had not had before, proving in his defiant way that charisma is not necessarily innate and can be acquired through hard work and daring action. Sadat regarded the personal authority of the head of state as the key to good government; this consideration determined for him the nature of the regime he wanted, the nature of his relationship with the people and with other factions in Egypt, and the division of labour between himself, as the super-father of the country, and the 'state institutions' he was proud to have created. Strong leadership would ensure that his policies were implemented, as he wished, by his subordinates. Sadat liked to credit himself with having established 'democracy' in Egypt. But what did that 'democracy' mean? Where would his authority have been if a true Western-style liberal democracy had been introduced in Egypt? Sadat had dubbed Nasser a 'democrat' too and had insisted that, unlike the other Free

Officers, including himself, who had opted for dictatorship, Nasser had foreseen no future for the Egyptian revolution unless it embraced democracy. But now things seemed to be turning around: by claiming to have brought democracy to Egypt, he implied that the previous regime, in which Nasser's towering authority had stood undisputed, had not been democratic. Could Sadat preserve the leader's authority while abandoning Nasser's style of dictatorial rule?

Sadat was convinced that he was cultivating democracy and that sovereignty was vested in him. While he was conscious of the need to adopt a less stringent form of governmental control than had been in force under Nasser, he remained jealous of his power, and was reluctant to share it with anyone or any institution. As a result, he increasingly paid lip service to social and political liberties, to freedom of enterprise, association and expression, while at the same time making clear that 'democratic' steps were taken at *his* instruction and that it was in *his* power to withdraw liberties at any time in the event of abuse. The name of the game was: caution, tentative reform and a close watch lest things got out of hand.

Since ascending to power, Sadat had boasted about his 'liberal' policies and had contrasted himself with the more doctrinaire and militant 'foci of power', but before the 1973 war little had been done truly to democratize the political system in Egypt. One might attribute this to Sadat's own insecurity at the helm of power and to his urgent need to concentrate on the coming war. After the war, however, Sadat increasingly turned his attention to the question of democracy and to defining his views on the subject more clearly. He asserted that:

> for the first time in forty years, we are undertaking the work of laying the foundations for a genuinely democratic society in this land. . . . Our people will become a model for the entire Arab nation and for all peoples of the Third World who have been striving for a regime similar to ours. . . . Our people, who developed the first civilization in history, are also the first to produce the right form of democracy, whereby the individual can live safely and honourably.

At the same time, however, he spoke of 'my free press', 'my parliament', 'my judicial system' and 'my military', and stated that the office of the President was over and above political controversy and that the President's role was to oversee the other branches of government in Egypt. No word of the President's being limited by any branch of government, no mention of checks and balances, no accountability to any state institution.

At times, Sadat admitted that his brand of democracy fell somewhat short of the ideal regime he had envisaged, but he promised that he would eventually embark on the final stage of his democratization programme, which would allow a plurality of views instead of the one-party system. Even then, however, a coalition would have to be maintained in the interests of 'national unity' and in order to ensure that 'no single stratum of society could impose its will on the others' and that the 'socialist approach' to the solution of Egypt's problems was retained. He also pledged that, in place of autocracy or oligarchy, he would install a 'rule by institutions'; but when he specified the role of those institutions, it was evident that they would have to submit to his supreme authority. Democracy for him meant 'direct rule by the people', which was achieved via the office of the President, who was elected by popular vote (the kind of elections where 95 per cent of the votes go to a single candidate), or via local and regional 'popular councils', which were supposed to reflect grass-roots opinion. Egypt, the great family, embodied the 'popular will' for Sadat. This was an Egypt where 'imprisonment and detention have ended forever, law has become sovereign, and even the opposition can speak up without incurring arrest'. In other words, as long as people behaved like brothers, aired their concerns within the family, and recognized and accepted the supreme authority of the head of the family, all was for the best. The debate within the family, of which discussions among local councils and parliamentary com-mittees were a part, amounted for Sadat to a broad popular participation in the decision-making process, which for him was the essence of democracy. (In the same way, the planning and carrying out of the 'glorious October war' had involved the participation of members of the military at all levels.) When the constitution was to be amended or a new political programme drafted, Sadat would 'humbly' announce that he would merely prepare the text and present it to state institutions for their 'consideration' and then for a plebiscite of the entire people, but he and everyone else knew that although he took the trouble to go through the motions of playing the democratic game, political decision-making remained virtually a one-man show. Sadat did take cognizance of the views of those around him who occupied positions of leadership – generals, cabinet ministers, top bureaucrats, distinguished journalists and others – but for him these people constituted a horde of helpers and underlings who were expected to carry out the orders of the leader. A string of excerpts from Sadat's own utterances on democracy and leadership will illustrate some of the above generalizations:

> I do not mind anyone saying what he wants, provided he does not harm the country's reputation. I have dismissed 120 newsmen, but instead of wasting their talents . . . I have re-employed them in government information services. Despite the sentences they have received, I have granted them amnesty. . . . I shall never abolish the freedom of the press or impose limitations on it, but we must replace some of the boards of directors of the newspapers and inject new blood into the papers. Anyone in this country may be exposed to criticism, as long as criticism is to the point and does not drift towards defamation. I shall allow no one, either within the press or outside it, to create 'foci of power' or to spread rumours. Free competition is legitimate and healthy, as long as it is guided by the public interest. We welcome open debate on the problems and dilemmas facing us, hoping thereby to find

desirable solutions. As long as our political programmes remain faithful to the principles of the 23 July Revolution, we have nothing to fear; but any deviation from these principles will deny the new political programmes their legitimacy. . . . I suggest that there should be no struggle over the presidency, as some people would have it. Some people want an election campaign to be conducted, but we have our own tradition. . . . Our upbringing was founded on respect for the family and for the father of the family. If we should deviate from that, we would be betraying our values and we may end up with undesirable results.[29]

Sadat regarded free elections and competition from other candidates, freedom of expression and freedom to criticize, and all the trappings that we tend to associate with democracy, as challenging his authority and potentially setting limits to his rule. He wanted to remain master of the situation and to encounter no surprises. To those critics who wished to see a different kind of democracy, he simply replied that democracy in Egypt did not necessarily have to be in the exact form adopted elsewhere. It was plausible for Sadat to claim that he was bound to oppose free elections if traditional upbringing, values and identity were not to be betrayed, and if the country's peculiar needs were to be met. Sadat saw no internal contradiction in his announcement, 'I have eliminated the "foci of power" in order to start the implementation of democracy in its broadest sense.'

As 'head of the Egyptian family', Sadat claimed for himself an authority not quite like that of other heads of state. First, a father's authority is immutable, permanent and not given to political fluctuations. As a father need not be elected, let alone re-elected or approved in his power by the family, so Sadat's authority had to be taken as a fact of life and not subject to question or qualification. Secondly, the family relationship is a close one and entails mutual obligation between father and sons. As the sons ought to obey the father and accept his authority and judgement without reservation, so the father is obliged to provide for his sons' needs and oversee their welfare. The concept of the greater family, though of particular significance for Sadat, is common to Arabs in general: all Arabs speak of themselves as 'brothers' and the Arab countries, when they are not at each other's throats, are 'sister states'.

Sadat cited the family in his numerous public addresses, in order to impress upon his audiences his expectations of them as subordinate members of the family. He would talk to students 'with the frankness proper among members of the same family, proper to the relationship between father and sons', and would indicate that he had asked the university president to do away with all formal ceremonies so that 'we can convene in a family atmosphere'. In making repeated reference to the 'family of Egypt', Sadat was implicitly justifying his authority and his right to redress grievances within the family. Sadat demanded of his people that they 'consider themselves members of one family which knows its values and believes in Allah', 'one family where all are bound to one another by feelings of brotherhood and all acknowledge as brothers and sons those who crossed the Canal on 6 October'. 'As one family,' he said, 'we can be superb':

> We marvel at this united family which has no failings, where each member fulfils his role, and whose head assigns to everyone his just portion. We are one family that must stand united and ready for war. . . . The President is the defender of his people and the homeland. He is also the father of the entire family: he arbitrates between the state institutions and the various authorities; he is the symbol and the protector of national unity.[30]

Sadat also used the image of the family to allay feelings of bitterness and quell internal strife in the Arab world. A conflict between unrelated parties may create a lasting rift; but members of a family are held together by obligation and are bound to strive to resolve their conflicts. Thus, for example, when Sadat signed the first disengagement agreement with Israel in 1974 and drew criticism from the Arab world, he pointed out that it was 'only natural that within a family brothers should differ. These differences will be resolved as conflicts between brothers are normally resolved.' Even his deteriorating relations with Qadhafi of Libya, Sadat explained in family terms. 'Qadhafi', he said, 'was one of my sons . . . but sometimes a child in the family may go astray or get sick.' Disowning a child or ostracizing a deviant member of the family was a sign of the basic soundness of the family as a whole. Sadat insisted that the divisions which emerged in the Arab world after the 1973 war amounted to no more than 'conflict within the family'.

As the father of Egypt, and occasionally of all Arabs, Sadat regarded himself not only as protector and provider, but also as teacher. He felt it incumbent upon him to reassure his 'sons' of his protection and to instruct them. Before the war, he told his soldiers that he would not throw them into battle unprepared just 'to show off in front of the world'. He often felt obliged not only to deliver his message but to make a long-winded speech explaining the historical background. On one occasion, he gave publicly a very detailed blow-by-blow account of the October War, describing his strategy, events behind the scenes in the Arab world and contacts he had had with the superpowers. He supported his narrative by statements such as 'I'll tell you the whole story.' When he decided to reopen the Suez Canal after the war, he said of his critics in the Arab world, 'I wish to teach them a lesson: in diplomacy the use of a bargaining card can be reversed . . . when world interests hinge upon you. The reopening of the Canal will bring us better results than its closure.'

Sadat also considered responsibility an important element of leadership. There were many instances when, in paternal fashion, he took full responsibility for his people and for what had occurred to them. However, he would not admit responsibility for particular mistakes or mishaps. He would say, 'I am responsible for everything,' or 'I shared responsibility with Nasser for all his deeds,' but when a specific accusation was laid at his door, he would defiantly reject it and go into an elaborate defence of his personal integrity and exemption from blame. On occasion, he attributed to Allah responsibility for his decisions or actions. He would say, 'Allah has decreed that I . . .', or 'Destiny has so willed it that I should . . .'. When he took the credit for successful actions, he would acknowledge the support he had received from Allah and from the people.

Sadat identified his interests and will with those of the Egyptians and regarded himself as a personification of Egypt. An interview that Sadat gave to Walter Cronkite illustrates this point:

> I have Soviet advisers here. They are helping *me* to rebuild *my* army. But as *I* told you, the battle is *my* battle, it is not the Soviets' battle. . . . It is *my* battle and *I* shall fight *my* battle here, with *my* soldiers, and *my* officers, not with Soviet advisers. . . . I am not asking the Soviet Union to bring its forces, and face the battle with *me*. . . . This would be humiliating for *me*. *I* am fighting *my* battle with my own people, because, as *I* told you, the land is *my* land . . . this is *my* battle.[31]

Sadat's identification of 'I' with 'Egypt' carried him beyond consideration of himself as shepherd of his flock, father and patron of his people: he saw Egypt as a projection, or perhaps an appendage, of himself. Hence his boundless devotion to it and his incapacity to distance himself from it or to judge it as a separate entity. An injury suffered by Egypt was a personal injury to him; its humiliation was his; the people were his sons; the country's prosperity he relished as his own. Any failure on Egypt's part was a failure on his; any tarnishing of its image reflected poorly on him and was a blow to his ego. Hence his sensitivity to criticism, opposition, competition, anything which implied that things could have been done better or differently; but hence also his commitment to accepting responsibility, in general terms, for all happenings, good or bad.

Sadat's identification with Egypt can be traced back to his early childhood: the anti-British climate, the stirrings of nationalism, the tales of the Denshway heroes, and later his views on suffering and sacrifice for one's country; all these served to encourage Sadat in his identification of his own struggle with Egypt's. Interestingly, at times he described Egypt's aspirations, character and obligations in such anthropomorphic terms that he seemed to be speaking of a person or of himself as a personification of the country:

> Egypt's destiny has been to bear responsibility for herself and for this part of the world. Egypt has never revolted against her lot, for her responsibility is inherent in her character. Whatever the circumstances, the attempts to deny her role among movements of national liberation, or to deny her Arab identity, she will remain firm in her basic character and will not deviate from her destiny. . . . Egypt never goes back on her word. Egypt will not be frightened by demonstrations, resolutions, oneupmanship and slogans. Egypt works quietly and in accordance with principles and ethics before anything else.[32]

Conspiracies, plots, subversion directed against Egypt Sadat considered as directed against him; similarly, threats to his power were threats to Egypt. When he spoke about the great powers concluding alliances against Egypt 'in order to humiliate me', or when he voiced his concern about *his* economic problems, or when he insisted that *he* had bought with *his* own money an early-warning system because *he* felt free to spend *his* money as *he* wished, he was signalling that Egypt and himself were one. Any persecution of Egypt would humiliate him; *his* choice was Egypt's choice. He once told Yasser Arafat: 'If someone wants to attack Egypt, he need not resort to Palestinian slogans: let him attack me directly. . . . If the Soviet Union wants to attack me, she need not use the Palestinians. . . .' Sadat sometimes referred in the same breath to himself and to Egypt as though the two were interchangeable: 'I am saying that without *Egypt* there can be no Arab war, for it was *I* who refused to cease fire for seventeen days,' or 'Some people have claimed that *Egypt* has actually been defeated and that *I* did not have the courage to admit that *I* was defeated.'

Sadat's propensity for initiative and movement, his constant striving to fulfil his vision for the future even if the means to that end had to be tried, abandoned and tried again, his permanent search for new paths and his pragmatic and flexible approach made him willing to try schemes that had been rejected by his predecessors; the economic open door was a revolutionary experiment after the austere years of Nasser's stringent socialism; reopening the Suez Canal was heretical after Nasser's vow that it would remain closed until Israel's withdrawal; negotiating directly with Israel was anathema to Egypt and to all Arabs. But Sadat implemented these controversial policies. He believed that an open-door policy would achieve for Egypt what the Marshall Plan had achieved for Germany. He turned to the Americans and accepted their mediation because he recognized that their role in the conflict in the Middle East was a major one. In discharging his responsibility towards his country, Sadat was realistic, reasonable and logical, even if – or perhaps because – this approach entailed political iconoclasm. The more surprising his measures, the more he would be viewed as an innovator and liberator.

Sadat realized that he would have to break the moulds of pre-1973 policy if he was to escape the limitations of dependence on the Soviet Union. He said that Egypt had to open up to the world in order to catch up technologically with other nations. It made no sense to remain cut off from the West while the USSR, through the process of détente, was trading more freely with the West and obtaining all the technology she needed. Sadat needed to diversify his sources of weapons; he was compelled to recognize that the West was the only alternative to the USSR as a supplier of arms. Sadat once formulated his pragmatism thus: 'We have to cling rigidly to our principles, but be flexible in our actions.' As long as Egypt was strong, developing and acquiring new technologies, it mattered little that instead of continuing the sterile two-decade partnership with the Soviet Union, he now opened his doors to entrepreneurs from the West and to the flow of Western capital, weapons and technology. Sadat recognized that the policies of the revolution had been dictated by force of circumstance, but felt that it was now time to adapt to the inter-Arab and international changes of the era of détente.

The Egyptian–Israeli disengagement agreements of 1974 and 1975 marked for Sadat both the adoption by the US of a more even-handed approach in the Middle East and an end to stagnation, an end to the strains of no-war-no-peace. Reaching these agreements required flexibility on Egypt's part and some hitherto unthinkable recognition of hard facts, but Sadat met these difficulties head-on. For example, after he signed the second agreement with Israel on 1 September 1975, he announced in response to charges against him by hard-line Arab rejectionists:

> I said and I repeat again that Israel is a fact. An Arab President [presumably Qadhafi] said that he had a plan to wipe Israel out within three hours, but three years or more have elapsed and he has failed to eliminate it. Moreover, twenty years have elapsed and Israel, far from being exterminated, remains a reality and stands firm. We will have nothing to do with anyone who wishes to hide his head in the sand in this regard. Israel is a fact, and anyone who wishes to wipe her out – please go ahead and do it! I assure you that you will have my acclaim. But tricky formulae and declarations about throwing Israel into the sea are groundless talk.[33]

A revolutionary statement of this sort would have been unthinkable before the October War and continued to be seen as aberrant in the Arab world. But Sadat was no longer willing to fool himself that he had signed an agreement with a 'country that did not exist', or to continue to entertain the illusion that he could wipe her out, although he made it clear that he would shed no tears if she were somehow eliminated. He had launched a surprise attack on her under the circumstances most favourable to Egypt, but he had not accomplished what he had set for himself as a goal. It was wise to come to terms with reality, to recognize how things stood in the Middle East and to try to make the best of the situation. He did not concede Israel's right to exist, but he had awakened to her invincibility and had apparently decided to reconcile himself to her existence rather than persist in an attitude of confrontation, which was pointless.

The process which led to the agreements with Israel began on 15 October 1973, when the US moved into the picture. On that day, in response to Henry Kissinger's repeated requests for a cease-fire, Sadat instructed his National Security Adviser, Hafez Isma'il, to pass on to Kissinger a message inviting him to Egypt to discuss proposals for a settlement. Sadat stipulated, as a precondition, Egyptian sovereignty over the Israeli-occupied lands in the Sinai. Kissinger did not arrive in the Middle East until 22 October, after his visit to Moscow and the conclusion of an agreement with the Kremlin, which was to become Security Council Resolution 338, and which established a cease-fire and sought a settlement along the lines of Resolution 242. Kissinger first visited Israel, where he received a hero's welcome, thanks to the American airlift which had preceded him and which had helped turn the tide in the war in favour of Israel; having obtained Israeli consent to an immediate cease-fire, he flew on to Cairo, arriving at 5 p.m. Sadat, realizing that his Third Army was almost totally surrounded, also accepted the cease-fire and even suggested an American military presence to enforce it. The next day, 23 October, the cease-fire collapsed and the Israelis completed the encirclement of the Third Army south of Suez. Sadat sent an urgent message to President Nixon. It was the first time since 1971 that Sadat had personally addressed a message to the American President; this signalled to the American administration both Sadat's desperate need to maintain the cease-fire, and his resolution to reorientate himself politically, now that he realized the Soviets would not bail him out militarily, while the Americans could shore him up diplomatically. On 24 October, Sadat and Isma'il sent two more messages to the Americans asking for the immediate enforcement of the cease-fire and dropping their previous 'suggestion' that Soviet observers should enter Egypt to supervise the cessation of hostilities. Originally, Sadat had suggested that the two superpowers should intervene militarily to control the advancing Israelis, but he soon reconciled himself to the idea that the US should act alone diplomatically. At America's insistence, he also accepted that an international force, which would exclude the permanent members of the Security Council (*i.e.* the US and the USSR), should be entrusted with overseeing the cease-fire. The two superpowers were heading for confrontation over Moscow's insistence that she bring in 'observers' unilaterally; however, on 26 October, the crisis was defused and the superpowers called off their high state of alert.

Sadat sent a second personal message to President Nixon complaining that the Israelis were attempting to force the Third Army to surrender and were obstructing the deployment of the UN observers who were sent instead of superpower observers. He threatened that if the Third Army were cut off, he would have to take unilateral action to reach supply lines in order to avert disaster. Kissinger supported Sadat's plea and conveyed it to Israel with his own endorsement, correctly sensing that for Sadat the fate of the Third Army had become symbolic and was closely tied to his own: the surrender or further humiliation of the encircled army would mean Sadat's own surrender and humiliation, and that had to be avoided at any price if American mediation was to bear fruit. On 27 October, bowing to American pressure, Israel allowed non-military supplies to cross its lines and reach the beleaguered Third Army, in return for which Sadat accepted a proposal that he had previously rejected regarding direct negotiations with the Israelis. Sadat had repeatedly pledged in the past not to negotiate with Israel; he sought an honourable way out of this bind by dubbing the talks as 'technical' and emphasizing that they dealt with 'the military aspects of implementing Security Council Resolutions 338 and 339' (339 was a later reconfirmation of the cease-fire by the Security Council of the UN). Thus began the 'Km 101 talks', named after the place on the Cairo–

Suez road where a military encampment had been set up marking the encirclement of the Third Army and the extent of Israel's advance towards Cairo. Sadat agreed to the meeting provided the cease-fire held, the passage of non-military supplies to the Third Army went unhindered, and the UN and the Red Cross supervision of both was assured. Kissinger endorsed all these stipulations. After some last-minute snags, the first negotiations took place on 28 October, with Egypt represented by General Gamasi.

With the cease-fire stabilized, Sadat was now hoping for a rapid removal of the Israeli presence from the west side of the Canal, which bore witness to Israel's success in the war and cast doubts on Sadat's own claims of 'victory'. He sent his new acting Foreign Minister, Isma'il Fahmi, to Washington on 29 October to prepare the ground for Kissinger's next visit to the Middle East, during which he was to launch the first disengagement talks, and inaugurate what came to be known as 'shuttle diplomacy'. Kissinger arrived in Cairo on 6 November. He immediately established with Sadat a working rapport which very quickly grew into a warm, close personal relationship and which was nurtured by the respect and trust the two men felt for each other. Indeed, Sadat's amiability and Kissinger's bent for analysis and wit somehow combined into an instant chemistry that was to outlast Kissinger's ability to fulfil Sadat's expectations of him. During their protracted meeting of 7 November, Sadat voiced concern over Israel's advance beyond the 22 October cease-fire lines. He maintained that if Egypt regained her position, the Third Army would no longer be besieged and the Israelis would be in a trap. Kissinger presented Sadat with two choices: either he continued to press for the re-establishment of the now defunct 22 October lines, and to invest much time and energy in regaining a relatively insignificant stretch of territory, or he worked for a large-scale disengagement of forces, which would take into account the present *status quo*, but which brought with it the strong possibility of Israeli withdrawal from their position west of the Canal and the securing for Sadat of territorial gains in Sinai. Kissinger hinted that he preferred the second option. Sadat, according to Kissinger,

> sat brooding, saying nothing for many minutes and then he astonished me. He did not haggle or argue. He did not dispute my analysis. He did not offer an alternative, violating the normal method of diplomacy – which is to see what one can extract in return for concessions – he said simply that he agreed with both my analysis and my proposed procedure.[34]

Accordingly, Kissinger advanced his proposal and broke the deadlock at 'Km 101'. To satisfy Israeli demands, negotiations were ostensibly held at 'Km 101'; in fact, the actual negotiation was held indirectly through Kissinger, in accordance with Sadat's desire. Kissinger put forward six points: these provided for the maintenance of the current cease-fire, the discussion of a return to the 22 October lines within the framework of a comprehensive agreement over the disengagement of forces, the provision of supplies of a non-military nature to the Third Army, the replacement of Israelis by UN personnel in the roadblocks along the Suez–Cairo roads, and an eventual exchange of POWs. These provisions were acceptable to both parties as a starting-point, and discussion over disengagement began.

On 29 November, Sadat decided to break off the 'Km 101' meetings, which to his mind were leading nowhere, but in early December he agreed to send a delegation to Geneva with a view to continuing the military talks. There were recurrent last-minute hitches regarding the formula of the letters of invitation to the parties concerned and Sadat repeatedly threatened that he would have to wipe out the Israeli enclave militarily, if Israel did not retreat eastwards. Sadat said he could hardly contain the grudge of his armed forces over the many 'concessions' he had already made to Israel at Kissinger's prompting; and he needed to resort to force to remove the humiliation of Israel's continued presence in the heart of Egypt and the imminent threat that Israel might retighten the siege around the Third Army. But threatened by Israel and placated by Kissinger in turn, Sadat agreed both to desist from his war-like rhetoric and to participate in Geneva, even if the Syrians refrained from showing up. However, by mid-December, Sadat realized that Geneva did not serve any purpose and he recalled his delegation. On 24 December, he convened the Supreme Council of the Armed Forces and, after eight hours of deliberation, plans to launch a military operation against the Israeli 'pocket' west of the Canal were drawn up and approved by Sadat.

On 26 December, Sadat went to his winter resort in Aswan to take a rest after the stress of the past twelve months and to ponder upon the diplomatic strains of the coming year. He had decided that if everything else failed, he would order his Chief-of-Staff to act along the lines of the new military plan. Kissinger called Sadat and asked for a meeting with a view to defusing the dangerous situation and starting indirect negotiations over disengagement. Sadat agreed to see Kissinger. In a series of shuttles from Aswan to Jerusalem and back during January 1974, Kissinger produced Israeli proposals, with maps, showing the suggested areas where deployment of arms should be limited and indicating the reopening of the Suez Canal and the redeployment of forces on either side of the waterway. For Israel it was essential that no Egyptian heavy weapons, notably tanks, remained on the east side of the Canal and that the surface-to-air missiles, which had proved their devastating effect during the war, should not be repositioned anywhere within thirty kilometres of the Canal on either side. Sadat said at first that it was *his* right to position in *his* territory any sort of weapon *he* wished, but then agreed that Kissinger should put forward his own proposal to break the *impasse*. For Sadat it was humiliating to seem to yield to any Israeli proposal, but it looked judicious and magnanimous of him to deal with a superpower and accept its suggestions. On 13–14 January, the final obstacles were removed, and Sadat overruled his disgruntled Chief-of-Staff, Gamasi, and Foreign Minister, Fahmi, and ordered the former to sign the agreement at 'Km 101'. Sadat was later harshly criticized by some hard-line Egyptians and rejectionist Arabs for his deal with Israel, and especially for renouncing the positioning of Egyptian tanks in Suez and for agreeing that the Israelis could retain, under the terms of the agreement, important passes in Sinai, the Giddi and the Mitla, which Sadat had desperately but unsuccessfully sought to take over during the war. Sadat thought that as long as the Israelis were prepared to accept *in principle* the right of Egyptian tanks to cross the Canal, he was prepared not to exercise that right. He must have felt that it would be more degrading for him to fight for the positioning, with Israeli consent, of a mere thirty tanks in Sinai than to put on a show of largesse by offering to put no tanks there at all. That was Sadat. On the last day of the disengagement talks, 18 January, Kissinger carried to Sadat a letter from Prime Minister Golda Meir stating her hopes for a permanent settlement. Someone whispered to Sadat that the disengagement agreement had just been signed at 'Km 101'. In an outburst of relief and gratitude, Sadat rushed to Kissinger and kissed him on both cheeks, and dramatically announced that he was taking off his military uniform 'never to wear it again except for ceremonial occasions'. That, he said, was his response to Golda's letter. That too was Sadat.

The interim political settlement with Israel relieved the urgency of the past months and allowed Sadat to turn to the domestic front, which was crying out for reform. But first Sadat had to remove the blemishes which had begun to tarnish the glamour of victory. At home, the army was blamed for having performed poorly in the face of Israeli encirclement; within the Arab world, a rift developed between Sadat, on the one hand, and his war ally Assad and other rejectionist Arabs, on the other. At home, Sadat attempted to suppress mention of the siege of the Third Army and the facts surrounding the capture of 10,000 Egyptians (a full army division). However, the street rumours, popular jokes about the Egyptian 'pocket', and sardonic criticism in opposition circles, for a while proved stronger than the authorities' desperate attempts to deny or dismiss them. Shortly after the war, Sadat, himself sporting a field-marshal's uniform, called in the high command of the army to a special session of the People's Assembly, and in a nationally televised ceremony decorated the heroes of the war and questioned General Badawi, the commander of the besieged Third Army, who affirmed that his soldiers had stood fast in the face of the enemy. Sadat also vehemently denied that he had signed any secret agreements with Israel, or that he had covertly agreed to reopen the Suez Canal or to resettle the populations of the Canal Zone cities, or that he had betrayed the Arab cause, all of which accusations were hurled at him by the leftist opposition and by other Arabs. Sadat felt extremely hurt that his rivals, at home and abroad, failed to perceive the great achievements of the war, political if not military, and were capitalizing on marginal issues to denigrate Egypt and her President.

Disengagement with Israel was completed in March 1974, but Sadat knew that the danger of war had not been totally eliminated. He had to press for the next round of talks if he was to push Israel further into Sinai and to work towards a permanent settlement. The military build-up had created much deprivation among the populace, as had the War of Attrition of 1969–70, which had caused the fatal devastation of the Canal Zone cities and the flocking of some million refugees to temporary sites in over-burdened Cairo and elsewhere. Sadat's aim was now dual: to maintain a strong military force in order to 'complete the battle', ensuring the total evacuation of Israel from Arab lands and the restoration of the rights of the Palestinian people; and to encourage a national effort to rebuild Egypt and to bring relief to its deprived population. Once again, to achieve either goal, Sadat would have to rely heavily on the superpowers.

If Sadat wanted to maintain a strong military arm, he needed weapons from the outside. However strong his desire to diversify his sources of military supply by turning to the West, he knew that the process of cultivating the West would take years and that in the meantime he needed to maintain a good working relationship with the Soviet Union as a provider of spare parts for his still predominantly Soviet-made hardware. Therefore, in early 1974, he cajoled the USSR with the promise that, despite the 'misunderstandings that have affected our relationship', he would follow the traditional path of friendship with the Soviet Union. He did point out that the Soviets had failed to supply him with several vital items of weaponry, but he also acknowledged that they had made a considerable contribution to the rebuilding of the armed forces and to their restoration to pre-war strength. However, Sadat was annoyed, and felt a sense of *déjà vu*, when the four messages he sent to Brezhnev between October 1973 and April 1974 urging delivery of advanced aircraft and electronics were answered only by a message in February assuring him that his requests were 'under consideration'. When the Soviet Foreign Minister visited Cairo in March, he repeated the same 'under consideration' refrain. This did not satisfy Sadat. He thought and said that there was nothing extraordinary about his requests to the Soviets and that there was no justification for this six-month-long period of 'consideration'. He added the delay to his already long list of 'misunderstandings' with the Kremlin.

At that point Sadat was very sensitive to insinuations that he had abandoned the Soviets and embraced the Americans instead. His image of himself as a loyal friend to whomever had helped him in time of distress simply did not allow him to switch sides without first finding a plausible justification for so doing. At first, he was apologetic. He denied Soviet contentions that he had relinquished socialism, and stressed that just as Egypt had chosen the path of socialism for her own sake, and not in order to please anyone, so today he needed no comment from the outside on his regime and on the brand of socialism he chose to implement. Sadat attributed the Soviet interpretation of events to 'their misapprehension of the improvements and openness we have introduced and their misconstruction of our ties with the US and the West'. Soviet allegations required no answer because the matters of which they spoke concerned Egypt and Egypt alone. Sadat stressed that since both superpowers were guarantors of the cease-fire, he had no interest in antagonizing either of them; on the contrary, he was interested in maintaining good relations with both. Sadat also publicly reiterated his commitment to 'positive neutrality' in a position between the two world camps, although he admitted that he was 'in the process of reorienting our foreign relations', because international trends 'entail that course of action'. He made it clear that, after the European Security Conference, at which the spirit of détente had prevailed and where the contending ideologies – capitalism and communism – had come together to seek a formula for coexistence and an end to the Cold War, it was unthinkable on his part to ignore the rapid changes in the world or to promote conflict or friction with either of the superpowers. In accordance with this line of thought, and exasperated by the long and vain wait of six months for a response from the Soviets, Sadat announced on 18 April 1974 that he had begun to implement his new policy of diversifying his sources of arms supply. He said that he had hoped for a frank and friendly reappraisal of his relations with the Soviets after the July 1972 experience, which should have proved to them that he had acted on his own and not in collusion with the US; instead, he felt that the Soviets had reverted to the 'tactics of procrastination and hesitation'.

Sadat also stated publicly, as early as April 1974, that although he was reluctant to build a new relationship with the US at the expense of his old alliance with the USSR, he perceived a shift in the American attitude towards him and therefore, in the best interests of Egypt, was modifying his attitude. He said that he had first detected the change in American policy when Kissinger played the intermediary role in November 1973 and proved that the US could be fair, honest and even-handed. Compared to the times of the Johnson administration, which were, in Sadat's words, 'a dark age in American and Arab history', the Nixon–Kissinger era held promise for him and for the Arabs in general. He felt justified in resuming diplomatic relations with the US, broken off since 1967, and in maintaining a high level of diplomatic contact with the Americans. Sadat was highly flattered by the accessibility of the American administration and by its responsiveness and frank reactions. On the day the disengagement agreement was signed with Israel, President Nixon called Sadat on the telephone and complimented him on his achievement. Sadat graciously returned the compliment by saying that it had all come about thanks to the wise policies of the Nixon–Kissinger administration, for if Kissinger had not bridged the gap between the Israeli and Egyptian positions, the agreement would never have been formulated. He credited Kissinger with 'more guts than any previous American Secretary of State' because, instead of insisting on direct negotiations with Israel (an oblique reference to Rogers–Sisco in 1971), he prevailed on both parties to accept an American proposal. For Sadat this had been a tremendous relief: firstly, he had been taken off the hook of direct negotiations and, secondly, he could always say that he had responded to American proposals, not to Israeli dictates. Moreover, since the Americans did not occupy any part of Egypt, it was far less humiliating for him to talk to them than it would have been to talk directly to the Israelis, whose trump card was their occupation of Egyptian territory. Sadat indeed reiterated on many an occasion during this period that his agreement and signature constituted a commitment to the US, not to Israel, even though the cease-fire agreement, the six points and the disengagement agreement had actually been signed by Egypt and Israel. This, together with his repeated insistence that the disengagement agreement was a 'purely military matter without any political ramifications', and his clinging to mediation lest, Allah forbid!, he had to confront 'the Jews' in negotiations, were indicative of Sadat's unpreparedness at that stage to seek a lasting peace with Israel.

Sadat entertained the idea that owing to the new American even-handedness in the Middle East and to the fact that the two superpowers were co-chairmen of the Geneva Conference, where the Syrians, Lebanese, Jordanians and Palestinians were to come together with Israel and Egypt, the Israelis would be outnumbered, outvoted, outmanœuvred and pressured to make concessions on both the Arab territories and the Palestinian question, without the Arabs having to concede anything significant in return. He was convinced that if the Arabs showed the same enthusiasm and united front in Geneva that they had during the war, they could achieve the brand of peace they wanted, that is to say, a peace without Israel or with Israel on the sidelines, and no one would be able to impose on them the peace Israel wished for, namely a contractual peace with diplomatic ties and normalization of relations.

As a result, upon completion in May 1974 of a disengagement agreement between Israel and Syria under Kissinger's auspices, Sadat immediately began to press for the convening of the Geneva Conference, where he was sure he would bring off his next masterstroke. It was essential for him to keep things on the move, lest they decline once again into the no-peace-no-war situation which he most abhorred. At this point, Sadat rejected the idea of separate settlements between individual Arab countries and Israel, for he believed that only a united Arab effort would ensure 'a full Israeli withdrawal from all Arab lands and Israeli recognition of the rights of the Palestinian people'. He said that he would try the diplomatic approach like Nasser, who had vowed 'to retrieve by force what had been taken by force' but at the same time had accepted Security Council Resolution 242, the Rogers Plan and the cease-fire arranged by the Americans in August 1970. Sadat quoted Clausewitz's maxim: 'Diplomacy is the continuation of war by other means.' However, Sadat believed that just as Egypt's peaceful policies had given way to war in October 1973 so he believed today the pendulum might swing back to war if Geneva came to a standstill. Sadat remained convinced that what had produced the shift in American policy was not 'diplomatic measures, legal documents, articles or UN resolutions', but the Arabs' resolve to launch war, to use the oil weapon, and to set things in motion. He wanted to keep open both diplomatic and military options and to preserve a united Arab front in case the need arose to go to war once again. It should be recognized that Sadat was not at all optimistic that the Arab–Israeli conflict was nearing a solution, militarily or diplomatically. In mid-1974, he kept repeating to his audiences that the October War had only been a 'spark', a 'beginning', and that the disengagement of forces would be followed by more difficult stages in the conflict. Sadat declared that the struggle would be a protracted one and might take generations to settle. His generation was 'merely fulfilling its obligation to extricate the Arabs from the shame of defeat and opening the gates for a leap forward'; the coming generations would have to pick up where he left off and carry the struggle on to victory.

In June 1974, President Nixon paid a visit to Cairo, which not only made amends for his absence from Nasser's funeral in 1970, but instilled a new sense of hope in Sadat and the enthusiastic Egyptians. Who would have believed that the man, who only eight months before was perceived as the arch-enemy of the Arabs, would receive a hero's welcome overshadowing any received by a Soviet leader during the long Moscow–Cairo alliance? Sadat was exhilarated at the sight of the huge crowds which turned up to greet the honoured guest, and he saw their enthusiasm as a popular endorsement of his new and, among hardliners, harshly criticized policy towards the US. Sadat had lashed out at his leftist critics in his May Day speech of 1974, just before Nixon's visit:

Those who have not yet matured politically and those who talk much but harbour weakness in their hearts still hesitate to give credence to the newly awakened Arab power. These people are blind to changes in the Middle East and throughout the world and fail to realize that our nation is now entitled to stand up confidently, just like other nations. When Kissinger goes to Moscow and Peking, all is well; but when he comes to Cairo, Damascus or Algiers, that is betrayal. When Kissinger mediates in Vietnam and conducts talks with North Vietnam, that is considered to be a victory for Vietnam and to have no bearing on the Soviet Union; but when he mediates in the Middle East and talks to us, that is a defeat for us and a sign of anti-Sovietism. When the American Chase Manhattan Bank opens a branch in Moscow, that is good; but a branch of the same bank in Cairo is dangerous to us! When American, German and Japanese capital is invested in Russian plants and in oil exploitation in Siberia, that is acceptable; but to use the same capital to rebuild the Canal cities is unacceptable. The least I can say about this lack of political maturity and this empty clamouring is that they betray illness and a lack of self-confidence. Those who are trying to block our activities by shouting irresponsibly shall not make any headway, for if we care to examine their outcries, we will find that they are attempting to deprecate our victories and to return us to a state of immobility, when we have spilled blood to set things in motion.

During his talks with Nixon, Sadat brought up the Palestinian problem, describing it as the 'core of the Middle Eastern issue' and, predictably, blaming Israel for causing the problem through her 'aggression'. Without a national solution to the Palestinian problem, he said, there would be no permanent settlement in the Middle East. It is interesting to note, however, that in his welcoming address to Nixon he said that the solution to the Palestinian problem would not necessarily mean the elimination of Israel, and implicitly upheld the official PLO policy of replacing Israel by a 'secular democratic state where Jews, Muslims and Christians live peacefully side by side'. He invoked 'history, which bears witness to the fact that Jews have lived under the same roof with Palestinians, both Christian and Muslim, and which shows beyond any doubt that Jews have lived for centuries under Arab rule without suffering discrimination or oppression'. Whether he meant that the Israelis should melt into a Palestinian-dominated state or that the Jews as individuals should submit again to benevolent Arab rule is not clear; but he mentioned nothing of the right of Israel to exist as a separate state, side by side with Palestine or otherwise. One may surmise that, in Sadat's thinking, Jewish existence remained assured (that was a 'lesson of history') whether a Palestinian state was established side by side with Israel or in its place.

Sadat also announced to Nixon that Egypt was intent on retrieving her lost territories 'whether by peaceful means or by force'. He blamed Israel for 'refusing to obey common sense and logic', and insisted that, since 1967, Egypt had merely been trying to secure Israel's peaceful withdrawal from Egyptian territory. He never specified what he was prepared to give Israel in return for her withdrawal; for him, it was sufficient to condemn her 'illusions, her false sense of superiority, and her failure to comprehend that conquests by force can not last indefinitely'.

Sadat also extracted from Nixon a pledge for some economic help in the coming months, even though he realized that he could not pin much hope on a President who was tottering to his political death. Nixon was exhilarated by the warm welcome he received in Cairo and by the large inscriptions on the balconies of the Egyptian capital, 'Nixon, we trust you!' and 'Nixon, you have our confidence!'; he must have thought that he stood a better chance of eliciting trust in Cairo than in Washington, where the Watergate affair was closing in on his career. Buoyed up, he was apparently very forthcoming in his response to Sadat's requests. In a CBS interview, on 21 June 1974, Sadat remarked that he would be sad to see Nixon removed from office after all the policy-advances he had made towards the Arabs. It was evident to Sadat that Nixon had personally intervened during the October War to save Israel from disaster; however, he thought that he could make Nixon realize that while guaranteeing Israel's security was one thing, helping her maintain her occupation of Arab territory was quite another.

Another development which loomed on Sadat's horizon during the summer of 1974 were the persistent reports in the world press that Israel had accumulated a stockpile of nuclear weapons, and that she would have been ready to use them during the October War if her fortunes had not taken a turn for the better after 16 October. The story, which was first carried in the British *Daily Telegraph*, was later confirmed by Egyptian intelligence and caused serious alarm in Arab circles. Not that Sadat had been unaware of Israel's nuclear capabilities, but these concrete reports confirmed how close Israel was to becoming a nuclear power. The previous vague reports about potential capacity now took on ominous substance, and Sadat had to take them into consideration. He reckoned that if Israel did announce that she possessed a nuclear capability, this would start an uncontrollable spiral of threats and counter-threats, blackmail and psychological pressure, which would diminish the chances of controlling Israel diplomatically via her American patron. Sadat pointed out to the media that while Egypt had signed the non-proliferation treaty, Israel had dragged her feet, offering all kinds of excuses, and that this was indicative of her intentions. Sadat's gloom was compounded when the new Israeli Government, under Rabin, was sworn in after Golda Meir's resignation. On the one hand, Sadat could savour the fact that his October War had generated the domestic turmoil in Israel which had brought down one of the most popular governments in the country's history and one of the most charismatic and widely respected of world leaders. At the same time, however, Sadat was worried because he now had to face an unknown quantity. He was particularly concerned that a weak government in Israel would be unable to make the difficult decisions which he saw in prospect. He regarded Rabin's slim majority, and the fact that a strong and militant opposition – 'fifty hawks in the Israeli parliament', as Sadat put it – was breathing down Rabin's neck, as a forewarning of future inflexibility from Israel.

It soon became apparent that, contrary to Sadat's earlier hopes, the Geneva Conference was not going to be convened as soon as the Israeli–Syrian disengagement agreement was finalized. First, there was disagreement among the Arabs over the terms of its convening, notably over whether the Palestinians should be represented by the PLO or by Jordan. Secondly, whatever Arab feeling on the matter, Israel would not negotiate with the PLO. Thirdly, the US, one of the co-chairmen of the Conference, was distracted by the Watergate affair: the impending impeachment of President Nixon, his removal from office and the ascent of the inexperienced Gerald Ford to the presidency. Fourthly, following the success of the first disengagement, Kissinger had come to believe, and convinced Sadat, that a step-by-step policy would be much more beneficial and feasible than the overall settlement sought in Geneva. Sadat, who wanted to sustain the momentum of the Israeli withdrawal and recover Sinai, did not want to achieve this end by squabbling in Geneva, where he would have to align himself with hard-line Syria and the PLO, with the possibility of again reaching stalemate. What was more, Sadat felt that he could best continue to court world attention, the interest of the media, and favourable public opinion in the West by acting as a soloist under Kissinger's conductorship (itself a glamorous affair). He would gain little by performing as a member of a large orchestra in the sagging routine of an international conference, where the two superpowers would at best play the major parts and at worst neutralize each other. At first, Sadat was keen on mending his relations with the USSR and continued to push for the holding of the Conference since the Soviets were to play a major part; but as his hopes of reconciliation with the USSR dwindled, Sadat was only too happy to oust the Soviets from the peace progress and to 'punish' them again for their 'misconduct' towards him. The Conference was postponed several times during 1974, and then, in early 1975, the talks for a second disengagement with Israel pushed it to the sidelines. Sadat elected to follow two courses simultaneously: to work out, via Kissinger, a second disengagement with Israel, and, at the same time, to launch an international campaign for the recognition of the PLO as the only representative of the Palestinians, a proposition that had been adopted by the Arab Summit of 1974. In this way, Sadat hoped both to maintain his position as the leading patron of the Palestinian cause, a prerequisite for retaining leadership of the Arab world, and also to prevent a return to the no-peace-no-war impasse with Israel.

Sadat saw the second disengagement as the means of paving the road to Geneva. He said that such a disengagement, which was in effect a euphemism for a further Israeli withdrawal from Sinai, would give Israel the opportunity to prove that she meant peace and would lend her credibility when the peace conference convened. What Sadat really thought was that, if he could get a major concession from Israel before Geneva convened, he would go to the Conference in a strong position to negotiate and therefore would be able to extract more concessions from Israel. At the end of 1974, President Ford sent a message to Sadat announcing Kissinger's two trips to the Middle East, in February and March 1975. Sadat thought that one trip would suffice but, at Ford's insistence, two dates were agreed upon. In February, Kissinger made a quick exploratory trip to Israel and Egypt, and in March he spent seventeen days shuttling back and forth in an effort to pull the new agreement together. Sadat insisted that Israel should withdraw beyond the strategic passes of Sinai and evacuate the oil fields in Sinai that she now operated. Israel agreed on condition that Sadat gave a commitment to 'non-belligerency'. Sadat refused to give this undertaking, arguing that signing a pledge of that sort would amount to submitting to the perpetuation of Israeli occupation of the rest of Sinai; if Israel baulked at final withdrawal, he would be bound by the agreement and would be unable to make Israel retreat further. For Sadat, Israel's reluctance to retreat meant that she was 'neither ready to conclude peace nor capable of doing so'. He ridiculed the Rabin Government as 'weak and shaky' and declared that the frustration that had afflicted the Arabs before

1973 had now been 'exported' to Israel. He said that Israel's doctrine of imposing peace and reconciliation on the Arabs by force of arms would never succeed, and that the Arabs would never submit to Israel's *diktat*. As a reminder to Israel that she had suffered more casualties in the October War than was tolerable, he ordered his armed forces, when the negotiations were under way, to deliver to Israel the corpses of thirty-nine of her missing soldiers, who had been buried in Sinai in the heat of battle. Even though Israel treated this as a humanitarian gesture, Sadat defiantly insisted that he acted not out of good will but in 'order to expose Israel in public'.

Sadat wished to view the new agreement as another 'military agreement with no political implications', and to reserve the political solution, if there was to be one, for Geneva. He rejected the Israeli approach, which was to seek a political settlement in return for withdrawal and which was epitomized by the slogan: 'Territory in exchange for peace.' The Israelis were prepared to compromise with Sadat, on their formula of 'non-belligerency', by substituting wording such as 'ruling out hostility', 'desisting from the use of force', etc. Sadat agreed, provided the non-use of force be made contingent upon progress towards peace and provided his pledge of non-hostility be considered void if Israel were to launch an attack on Syria. As the formula of non-belligerency was being worked out, a new difficulty emerged. The Israeli map of their proposed withdrawal looked to Sadat like 'a crooked line full of meanders', and he saw a plot or an intrigue in every curve of the line. He said that the Israelis wished in fact to hold on to some of the key positions in the Sinai to compensate for those which they were to evacuate. Sadat insisted on Israeli evacuation of the passes and wanted nothing but a 'clear, straight line'. Kissinger seemed to back Sadat's demands, and Sadat hoped that he might drive a wedge, or at least create a rift, between the Americans and the Israelis. Besides, Sadat thought, if the Israelis rejected Kissinger's proposals, the convening of the Geneva Conference would become inevitable; Israel would unwittingly promote the favoured approach of the Soviet Union. If neither disengagement talks nor Geneva were successful, either Israel and the US or the Soviets would be to blame. Sadat believed that he should let the superpowers fight over which approach to adopt, while he waited on the side-lines, taking advantage of their rivalry and taking care not to become a 'pawn in the game'. Kissinger, the wizard who had until now succeeded in his mediation efforts in the Middle East, left the area heartbroken and pessimistic, his mission incomplete.

Following the failure of Kissinger's mission, President Ford announced a reassessment of his Middle Eastern policy, which meant, in effect, renewed pressure on Israel to yield to Sadat's demands and to sign the second disengagement on his terms. Sadat was encouraged by the apparent success of his strategy, but was soon disillusioned when seventy-six US senators signed a petition to the President discouraging him from taking any step likely to weaken Israel, and urging him not to cease arms supplies to Israel. Sadat accused Israel of 'taking advantage of the differences between the White House and Congress' to put off settlement during 1975, in the knowledge that 1976 was an election year and Israel could expect a relaxation of American pressure on her. Exasperated by what he saw as further Israeli procrastination, Sadat vowed to produce a new plan of his own to counter Israel's disruption of Kissinger's mission. In May 1975, President Ford invited Sadat to attend talks in June, in Salzburg, Austria, to seek a way out of the stalemate. To those who ridiculed Sadat for attending that meeting following the failure of America's step-by-step policy, he retorted that he would 'turn to the US, the Soviet Union, or the devil himself' if this would resolve the problem of securing Israeli withdrawal from the Sinai. He also stated that '90 per cent of the cards of the Middle Eastern game were in American hands', therefore he had no choice but to consider anything President Ford might suggest to him.

The Sadat–Ford meeting on 1 June rekindled hope in Sadat. He found the new US President 'an honest and open man, truly devoted to peace', and felt pleased with the relationship they established. Both men agreed that the situation in the Middle East was explosive and that progress, which to Sadat meant Israeli withdrawal from the Sinai, was essential if a further outbreak of hostilities was to be avoided. They also agreed that rhetoric was not enough and that some practical measures had to be taken if momentum was to be regained and if the Arabs and the Israelis were to be shown that peace was not merely an aspiration, but an attainable objective. Sadat bluntly asked Ford whether the US was committed to defend Israel's borders only, or whether she would also support Israel's continued occupation of Arab land. A newsreel of the American Congress welcoming Ford upon his assumption of the presidency had given Sadat the impression that the new President was a straightforward man who would give him a clear and decent answer about American objectives in the Middle East. He regarded as 'unfortunate and sad' the US Senate's support of Israel and bluntly commented that he would have preferred to see the senators 'display more courage' and say openly that they wanted Israel to continue her occupation of Arab land, while receiving more economic and military aid from the US. He came up with the idea that the senators' message to the White House 'did not represent American public opinion', but was rather a manifestation of the 'horrifying Zionist influence' which had undermined Kissinger's mission and which was now trying to bring pressure to bear in the forthcoming US elections.

The practical outcome of the Salzburg Summit was twofold: an Egyptian decision to reopen the Suez Canal for navigation, and a resumption of the Kissinger mission to work out a new disengagement. Reopening the Canal was an implicit concession to Israel's demand for 'non-belligerency': the reopening of the Canal and the rebuilding and repopulation of the Canal cities constituted *de facto* non-belligerency, because Sadat would not want to jeopardize these 'gains' of the October War. Proud Sadat, however, would not confess that he had conceded anything to Israel, and he gave an elaborate explanation of his motives for opening the Canal: first, he said, the entire world expected him to leave the Canal closed, so *he* was opening it in order to signal to the American people and Congress that 'he was not afraid of peace'; secondly, keeping the Canal closed would amount to punishment of Egypt's friends in Western Europe, Asia and Africa, who depended on the Canal for their trade and welfare. He seriously believed, or so he said, that the reopening of the Canal was the panacea to end the world's economic difficulties. He also insisted that the reopening of the waterway was one of the fruits of the October victory because it resulted from the removal by the 'glorious Egyptian armed forces' of the 'Jews, who had taken their positions on the east bank of the Canal'. And finally, the revenue from the Canal was considered of major importance for the domestic reconstruction that Sadat was envisaging.

On 5 June 1975, the Canal was re-inaugurated with great pomp and amid much celebration. The clearing work had started a year earlier and had ended several months before the day chosen by Sadat to open the Canal. Sadat himself wore his navy uniform and sailed down the Canal on the Egyptian flagship. It was eight years to the day since the June 1967 war had broken out and the Canal had been closed by the Egyptians. Now it was reopened, following the 'October victory', by the man who had presided over that victory. To those critics in the Arab world who claimed that Sadat had submitted to US and Israeli extortion, he responded that he had a lesson to teach them in the 'science of diplomacy', namely, the reversal of a bargaining chip: the closed Canal had served in the past as a lever to make the world more responsive to Arab interests, now world interests hinged on the reopened Canal. Sadat would benefit much more from the reopening of the Canal than from its continued closure. To sceptics, he pledged that 'under no circumstances will I allow Israeli ships to navigate through the Canal'. But he conceded that, if Israel made the right concessions in Geneva, he would consider whether this justified granting her use of the Canal as part of a permanent settlement. With the Canal open, Sadat again pinned his hopes on the US and especially on President Ford. In an interview given to a Lebanese newspaper, he characterized the US President thus:

President Ford . . . is not a cowboy like Johnson. He is from the Mid-West where most of the population are farmers. In a peasant population you always find stability of character, respect for promises made, simplicity, straightforwardness and honesty. It was a pleasure to detect in him all these qualities, because we are tired of the cowboy policy that the Americans conducted before the October War. . . . I can tell you that Ford wants to solve the problem and he is determined to do so. During the two banquets that we offered to each other, he reiterated his commitment to avoiding a return to stagnation or ambiguity. He was very frank during our talks and he explained his view more clearly and in more depth than he had done in his public speeches. His attitude is quite clear.[35]

Sadat had understood from Ford that the US would neither abandon Israel nor forsake her special relationship with her, but he kept pressing the US to make clear her views on a peace settlement in the area; he wished to ascertain whether he would still be able to count on the Americans after the present negotiations had run their course. He thought that the US should discipline Israel, who had undermined Kissinger's mission in February, thus 'dealing a blow to American policy in the Middle East', while continuing to receive sustenance from the Americans. With this in mind, Sadat asked the Americans to adopt a policy that would 'make sense to the Arabs'. As he read it, if the Americans committed themselves publicly to going to Geneva after a second disengagement, he was assured of the implementation of Resolutions 242 and 338, which called first of all, he believed, for total Israeli withdrawal from all occupied Arab territories. He felt he was bound by the resolutions of the Arab Summit in Rabat in October 1974, which had pledged not to surrender one inch of Arab land to Israel and not to strike any compromise over the rights of the Palestinians. In Salzburg, Sadat also agreed to an American suggestion that the US should establish and operate an early-warning system in the strategic Mitla and Gaddi passes, which Israel had agreed to relinquish on condition that the American system was installed. Sadat also agreed that the second disengagement should be extended annually and the role of the peace-keeping forces in the Sinai buffer zones reviewed periodically. Sadat felt he was making a great concession in agreeing to an extension every year instead of every three to six months. Israel had actually demanded an extension every three to five years so the annual extension was a compromise. Sadat wished to ensure that the second disengagement did not petrify into a new *status quo*.

On 1 September 1975, the second disengagement was finalized and signed by both parties. Sadat was elated at the Israeli evacuation of the passes and major oil fields in the Sinai, but he felt obliged to answer his critics in the Arab world, who accused him of selling out to the US and of offering to the Americans 'military bases' under the guise of early-warning systems. He vigorously pointed out to his critics that, when Russians had manned Egyptian warning stations in the past, no one had claimed that this presence amounted to occupation of Egyptian territory. He insisted that the new stations were Egyptian, and that the Americans were merely 'witnesses positioned between *me* and the Israelis'. He lashed back: 'The new station is Egyptian and I have paid for it with *my* own money. *I* am free to spend my money as I wish. The station is Egyptian, the crew is Egyptian and it was *I* who equipped it.'

When, at the end of October 1975, Sadat left for his first presidential visit to the US, France and Britain, he had come to the conclusion that the step-by-step policy had run its course and that it was now time to make preparations for Geneva. Convinced the US was solidly behind him, he had invited the flagship of the US Sixth Fleet in the Mediterranean to attend the ceremonies at the reopening of the Suez Canal. Ford and Kissinger agreed that no more step-by-step moves were possible, and Sadat was certain that the Americans would now push for an overall settlement, whether at Geneva or elsewhere. At the same time, however, he remained reluctant to conclude any peace arrangement with Israel which entailed diplomatic relations. He repeatedly declared, in various press interviews, that after so many years of enmity, bloodshed and bitterness, complete normalization of relations with Israel was too much to expect of him; in his generation, he said, the most that could be hoped for was a state of non-belligerency, which could be achieved once Israel had withdrawn from occupied territories and restored Palestinian rights; the rest would be decided by coming generations. He said in one of those interviews that he distinguished between a 'peace treaty' and a 'peace agreement', expressing his readiness to sign the latter, but not the former, and even the latter only on condition that Israel responded to the double prescription of the Rabat Conference regarding Arab lands and Palestinian rights. However, Sadat was by now deeply sunk in renewed controversy with the Soviet Union and in the Lebanese Civil War, neither of which did anything to speed up movement towards the overall settlement he was envisaging.

The more firmly established Sadat became in his relationship with the US and Western Europe, the more he was courted by the Western media, and the more important he felt he had become. By extension, he felt that Egypt had attained a new stature in the world. He believed that he had outgrown the regional strait-jacket, which the Soviet Union had carefully tightened around him, and that his capacities as a world leader were now fully developed. He was enamoured of his new status, undertook much travelling, interviewing and speaking, and everywhere concluded that 'everyone now seeks Egypt's friendship and is attentive to her word and decision'. Of course, Egypt meant him; recognition for Egypt was recognition for him. He said to his proud audiences in Cairo that 'Egyptian policies are the ones that ultimately prevail, determine the course of events and serve as the focus for all inter-Arab initiatives'. He came to credit himself not only with the 'glorious victory of October', but also, in his own words, with:

> overcoming the dangers of the Cold War, the easing of international tension, the promotion of peaceful coexistence (between the two blocs), the elimination of colonialism, furtherance of the war against racial discrimination, and the promotion of a democratic conception of international relations whereby all countries can take part in the achievement and maintenance of a balance of power in all parts of the world.

With these achievements, he felt he had transcended the parochial bickerings of the Middle East and had risen to a position of world leadership. He felt self-confident enough to lash out at both 'the hostile tongues and mercenary pens in the Arab world' and the Soviets, who had aligned themselves with the Syrians and the Palestinians in total opposition to his peace moves.

During the uncertain months which followed the October War Sadat was still willing, as we have seen, to try to mend his relationship with the Soviet Union; at that time, he had no guarantee of an American turn-about in his favour. Improved relations with the Soviet Union seemingly foundered on a question of prestige: Sadat insisted that since he had already gone to Moscow four times during his presidency, he would not go again unless Brezhnev came to Cairo. In fact, a Brezhnev visit would signal the importance that the USSR still attached to Egypt and would encourage the Soviet Union to come forward with the undelivered items of military hardware that Sadat had been waiting for since 1971. Sadat said that if Brezhnev did come to Cairo, he was prepared for a soul-searching review of all aspects of their relationship, for mutual explanation of their past actions and mutual admission of error in their dealings with one another; he was prepared to turn over a new leaf, to establish a new relationship founded on understanding and straightforwardness. At first, Brezhnev was supposed to go to Cairo in January 1974, but the trip was postponed. Anxious not to alienate a superpower, Sadat dispatched his Foreign and War Ministers to the Soviet Union to discuss the establishment of the new relationship. His rationale for courting the US whilst trying to restore his links with Moscow, was that the Kremlin too was reverting to détente, trade and co-operation with the Americans after fifty-five years of isolation. If they were doing so, why not he? Sadat knew that the Russians were resentful of his deals with the US and of his decision to diversify his sources of weapons (they had channelled their grievances via the Algerian President, Boumedienne, who had paid for some Egyptian-ordered weapons), but he said that he had had to turn to the West because the Soviets had turned their back on him. It was not too late to redress the wrongs they had done one another, he thought. Sadat also concurred with the Soviet view that time was not working in the Arabs' favour, and that it would therefore be to their advantage to go to Geneva to press for a settlement. So, in the summer of 1974, a preliminary agreement was reached between Sadat and the Soviets to the effect that Brezhnev would come to Cairo, but that before this summit took place a high-level Egyptian delegation would visit Moscow on 15 July. In Cairo, the preparations to dispatch a delegation of top diplomats and army officers were already completed when the Soviets backed down and asked for a postponement until October or later. In June, Sadat visited Bulgaria and met President Zhivkov, one of the closest associates of the Soviet leadership. Sadat questioned Zhivkov on the reasons for the Soviet reluctance to come forward and restore relations with Egypt, and assured Zhivkov that he had no intention of withdrawing the facilities in Alexandria that he had made available to the Soviets on an annual basis, even after the crisis of July 1972.

At the American–Soviet summit in Vladivostok in late 1974, Brezhnev continued to press for the holding of a conference in Geneva, while Ford wished to continue with the step-by-step approach before reverting to the

Geneva option. Sadat decided to opt for the American approach, but still did not want to lose the Soviets. On 25 December 1974, Sadat received a message from Brezhnev about the Soviet leader's forthcoming visit and an invitation for an Egyptian delegation to go to Moscow for talks. Foreign Minister Gromyko came to Cairo on 3 February 1975. Talks got under way to restore a sound relationship between the two countries, and a renewed pledge was made by the Soviets concerning Brezhnev's visit to Cairo at some later date. The talks with Gromyko covered Geneva and the American mediation plan, economic relations, especially the huge Egyptian debts that Cairo was no longer able to repay to Moscow, and the resumption of military supplies, especially spare parts, without which all the Soviet material still in operation in Egypt would become useless. Some understanding was reached, but the major issues were left until Brezhnev's visit to Egypt. In the meantime, Sadat dispatched to Moscow, on 17 February, a ministerial delegation, which attempted to settle the question of a moratorium on Egyptian debts. He was also hopeful that the Soviets would speed up the deliveries of weapons which had been contracted in the years 1973–4, but which had failed to arrive during the fourteen months before February 1975. Sadat thought that he urgently needed what he called 'weapons in compensation for those he had lost in the October War', especially as he saw that Israel and Syria were replenishing their arsenals with military supplies rushed to them by the US and the Soviet Union respectively.

Sadat wanted to send a large delegation to Moscow comprising the Ministers of Planning, Economic Co-operation and Industry, as well as top bureaucrats and military officers, with a view to discussing and settling all outstanding issues, but the Soviets insisted that it be cut down to two ministers only. When they came back they reported to Sadat that the Soviets would deliver some arms provided they were not termed 'compensation'. Not much more came out of that trip, and both the question of the moratorium on debts and that of new military equipment remained unsettled. The Soviets argued that rearming the Egyptians might inflame their border, but the Soviets did not specify whether they meant the Egyptian–Israeli border or the Egyptian–Libyan border, where a new controversy was brewing between their discarded ally, Sadat, and their new client, Qadhafi. Sadat pleaded that the October War had proved that there was no justification for Soviet fears of irresponsible adventurism on his part, for he was 'beyond the stage of mistaken evaluations and ill-conceived schemes'. In his May Day speech of 1975, after the failure of Kissinger's mission and before the renewal of hope at the Salzburg Summit, he reverted to publicly expressing his gratitude to the Soviet Union for her aid in building the Aswan Dam and for her help during the 'bleak hours of 1967'. He said that no human being could do more than Allah enabled him to do, and, from the rostrum, he asked the Soviets to postpone repayment of the debts he was unable to meet. He said that he was not reneging on his debts; he just wanted a rescheduling of the payments so that he could make them in full in the coming years and would not have to ask his 'people and family to tighten their belts even further'. Sadat also said that during Foreign Minister Fahmi's visit to Moscow in April, the Soviets had interpreted Egypt's plea for a moratorium as an attempt to impose on them 'conditions' for the repayment of the debts. Sadat chose the festive occasion of May Day literally to beg the Soviets to 'understand our difficulties . . . we are not imposing conditions on anyone; we just want everyone to assess the situation and appreciate our difficulties . . . we do not dictate conditions to anyone. . . . Our Soviet friends should take our situation into consideration: we cannot arrest the momentum of construction, social progress and the rebuilding of our armed forces.'

On 5 June 1975, just back from the Salzburg meeting with Ford, Sadat posed a few harsh questions to the Soviet Union, during the celebrations for the reopening of the Canal, about her armament policy in the Middle East. He said that he understood that the Soviets wished to build a new defence network for Libya. Why, he asked, should Libya take precedence in receiving this kind of advanced weaponry over Egypt and Syria, who had been strong allies of the Soviets? Secondly, complained Sadat, Libya's population was a mere 1.5 million; the weapons that she was acquiring from the Soviet Union would necessitate training by thousands of Soviet experts over decades. The Soviet Union, whilst heaping bounty on Libya, small and backward as she was, refrained from 'compensating' him, the fighter of October, the loyal ally of yesteryear, who stood in the front line among the confrontation states.

In the meantime, the Soviets remained reticent about Brezhnev's visit to Cairo and continued to procrastinate on granting a moratorium on Egyptian debts. Knowing Sadat's proclivity for sudden and dramatic action, they feared that he might abrogate the Treaty of Friendship that they had imposed on him in May 1971, and even gave credence to rumours that the abrogation would be announced on 20 July 1975. Accordingly, on 20 July, they asked the Finance Minister of Egypt to go to Moscow for new negotiations; Sadat responded, dispatching him on the 23rd. Sadat delivered his Revolution Day speech on that day, without saying anything about the treaty, much to Soviet relief and to others' disappointment. However, the Finance Minister came back from Moscow empty-handed (in Sadat's figure of speech 'hung by the heels'). Moreover, the renewed pledge that a Soviet delegation would go to Cairo for negotiations and that Brezhnev would carry out his long overdue visit to Sadat, remained unfulfilled. By September 1975, Sadat had come to the conclusion that 'no respectable man could approve of the methods used by the Soviets in their dealings'. He felt able to state this publicly once the second disengagement had been sealed under the auspices of the US and once its implementation was under way.

Worst of all, from Sadat's viewpoint, was the Soviet cancellation of the MiG engine plant which they had promised to set up in Egypt and which was to make the country self-sufficient in this vital area of defence. Sadat was facing the possibility that all his Soviet-made aircraft would be grounded in a matter of months if he could not get spare parts for them. As it became clear that the Soviets would not relent in their demands that Sadat pay his debts to them, he accused them publicly of having themselves reneged on paying their Second World War debts to the US, and said that it was a regular procedure for debts occasioned by war to be waived altogether or paid only in token. In early 1976, Sadat was heading for a new collision with the Soviets. He hurled his past grievances at them in public. He said that he would never forget that on 23 September 1973, only two weeks before he launched his war, the Soviets began harassing him for 22.1 million roubles in overdue debt and demanded that he should pay interest on the outstanding sum. He also declared that unless he moved to counter the Soviet embargo on spare parts, all his military hardware was doomed for the junk yard. What was more, the Soviets refused even to do the expert technical work necessary for the maintenance of Egypt's jet fighters, thus disregarding the agreement they had signed ten years earlier to provide continuing maintenance for Cairo's MiG 21s. Sadat applied for help to India – a close friend of Egypt in the non-aligned world since the Nasser–Nehru alliance – because she herself manufactured and did maintenance work on MiGs. He waited four months, and then India announced that she could not respond because the Soviets refused to allow her to deliver the requested help. Sadat regarded the Soviets' negative attitude as an economic and military sanction against his country, designed to undermine his drive for economic growth and to turn his weapons into useless toys within a matter of months. Only now did Sadat realize how the Soviets had schemed to maintain Egypt's dependence on them. Back in 1971–2, during his various trips to the Soviet Union, he had asked the Soviets to build, in Hilwan, facilities for the maintenance of his aircraft engines: in time of war, he did not want to depend on maintenance facilities 5,000 kilometres away. In 1975–6, they refused even to continue their long-distance logistic assistance, and Sadat was left without facilities of his own.

Rounding off his list of complaints about Soviet conduct, Sadat castigated the Kremlin for turning down his request for air reconnaissance by the Soviet MiG 25s positioned in Cairo. After the first disengagement had been signed, Sadat told his air-force commander, General Mubarak, to ask for Soviet air photography and data gathering on Israeli troops as a response to Israel's own reconnaissance. The Soviets said that they could not overfly Sinai, which was occupied by Israel. Sadat was infuriated because, he said, 'Sinai is an integral part of my land.' Mubarak told them that they could carry out the spying missions without overflying the Sinai simply by taking air photos from Egyptian-held territory. But when the Soviets continued to stall, under the pretext that they could not fly without orders from Moscow, Sadat burst out: 'Sorry, then those planes cannot fly from here at all; if they are to serve objectives other than ours, they ought not to take off at all.' In 1975, the Soviets decided to remove their aircraft and Sadat wished them well.

This list of grievances against the Soviets, coupled with India's negative reply to Sadat's plea for maintenance, made Sadat decide that he had had enough. He thought that the Soviets were now expecting him to come to them on his knees, but he vowed that he would 'kneel only before Allah'. On 14 March 1976, he addressed the People's Assembly, which had approved the Treaty of Friendship with the Soviets five years earlier, and asked it to abrogate that treaty forthwith; he received thunderous applause and a standing ovation. Even then, Sadat was still reluctant to break totally with the Soviets, for he needed their good offices in the forthcoming talks in Geneva. In his May Day speech of 1976 he was careful not to widen the rift with Moscow and called upon the Soviets to accept him as he was and not as they wanted him to be. He dispatched his Minister of Commerce to the Soviet Union, and then delegated his War Minister to represent him at the funeral of Marshal Grechko, the Soviet War Minister who died in Moscow later that year. But the Soviet presence in Egypt had ended, the port facilities in Alexandria were discontinued, and a new era had begun in Soviet–Egyptian relations.

Sadat's final extrication from the Soviet bear hug was compensated for by solidifying his alignment with the US, following the second Sinai disengagement, and by strengthening his relations with the Third World, Western Europe and Communist countries who were independent of the Soviets, such as Romania and China. He needed China not only as a permanent member of the Security Council who would, when necessary, cast a veto on Egypt's behalf despite, or rather because of, Cairo's rift with the Soviets, but also as a source of Soviet-made and Chinese-made spare parts for his military hardware. The more his relations with the Soviets worsened, the more he could afford to approach the Chinese; and the worse his position became among Arab rejectionists, the more he sought solace in the Third World.

On 22 February 1974, Sadat appeared at the Second Islamic Summit Conference in Lahore, Pakistan, where he was hailed as the 'hero of October'. He was gratified to hear the 'voice of 500 million Muslims' again, as he had at the first Islamic Summit in Rabat, in December 1969, when he had represented Nasser. And when all those Muslim representatives acclaimed him, he felt that he was indeed the unofficial leader of the Islamic world, that downtrodden world which had known little glory or military victory in modern times. The members of the gathering were elated at the presence of Sadat, Assad, Qadhafi and other 'war heroes', who heralded, so it seemed to many, a new Islamic leadership which would stir the world of Islam from its lethargy. Sadat advocated support for the Palestinians, strong resolve in the battle against Israel, a renewed vow to liberate Jerusalem, and the provision of financial support by the rich countries in the rear to the poor on the front line. These were all old items of business, but to listen to a united Muslim front of some forty countries committing themselves to all these causes was an elevating experience for Sadat, and for all the other participants. What was more, Sadat realized full well that the sheer size of the Islamic movement, compounded by the wealth of some members and their consequent political influence, would of necessity vastly improve Arab–Muslim standing in any world forum and would almost automatically ensure the adoption of any motion, anti-Israeli or otherwise, that the Arabs/Muslims cared to table.

At the end of June 1974, after the departure of President Nixon from Cairo, Sadat embarked on his tour of Bulgaria and Romania. He went in search of alternative sources of weapon supplies, spare parts for his Soviet-made arms and support for the Palestinian cause, of which he was determined to remain champion. In Romania, personified by the charismatic, strong-willed and hard-nosed realist, President Ceaucescu, he saw not only a country which had escaped the orbit of the Soviet Union and which pursued its independent ways, at times in outright defiance of Moscow, but also a country which offered the means to comprehend Israel, her leaders and motives. The Romanians were the only Eastern Bloc nation to maintain relations with Israel after the 1967 war, and their ties with the Jewish state allowed them to provide Sadat with an insightful, yet unbiased, view of the Jerusalem Government, something he could not hope to get from the US.

In 1975–6, China was only too glad to provide MiG 21 engines and a wide variety of spare parts to the, by now, desperate Sadat. For the Chinese, this was a good way to reward Egypt for having been the first Arab country to establish diplomatic relations with them, back in April 1956, when the People's Republic was still ostracized by other nations. It was also a good opportunity to demonstrate solidarity with a leading co-member of the Third World which was in dire need owing to Soviet machinations, and a chance to try to supplant, if only symbolically, the Soviet Union, which the Chinese were happy to see squeezed out of the Middle East peace process. What was particularly gratifying for Sadat was the Chinese refusal to accept any payment for their emergency supplies; this prompted him to remark: 'They do not act like the other superpowers, they are not arms dealers.' It is interesting to note that as Sadat edged towards China, possibly seeing her as a model of a developing country which had shrugged off Soviet patronage, but had nevertheless become a nuclear power capable of manufacturing her own armaments, he read some of the writings of Mao, whom he had always admired as a great liberator of his country. He never acknowledged borrowing from Mao, but judging from the vocabulary he began using in 1975–6 – references to 'self-reliance' and a 'great leap' in economic development – and considering his own disposition towards permanent revolution, one is tempted to assume that he found in Egypt, and in himself, affinities with China and with Mao in his heyday.

In July 1975, Sadat participated in the OAU Conference in Kampala, Uganda, and in August 1976, he took a major part in the Non-Aligned

Conference in Colombo, Sri Lanka. In both instances, Sadat used his audiences, as he had at the Lahore Conference, to rally support for the Arab cause in general, and for that of the Palestinians in particular, and to explain from his viewpoint his rift with the radical Arab states. He was particularly grateful to the Africans because, during the October War, they had broken off relations with Israel *en bloc*, in support of their sister state, Egypt. Most of them continued to declare that although Israel had painstakingly cultivated them over the past two decades, they would not resume relations until Israel withdrew from the occupied Arab lands. He also thanked the Africans for their efforts, dating back to 1971, to mediate between Israel and the Arabs, and he particularly thanked the commission of the ten African heads of state who had led a study mission to the Middle East in November 1971, and had concluded that the Africans were directly interested in the Middle Eastern conflict and had a stake in resolving it, in what Sadat saw as the Arabs' favour. Having secured from the Conference an unconditional demand that Israel retreat from Arab territories and an insistence upon the right of the Palestinians to self-determination, Sadat went on to Colombo. There he accused the superpowers of pursuing their own egotistic interests to the detriment of the Third World. He justified his October War as a withdrawal from the superpower game in which they had tried to impose, on a selective basis, 'détente' and 'relaxation' in some areas of the world to cover up their scramble for spheres of influence. He pledged his renewed faith in the Third World and in the politics of 'non-alignment' and exhorted all member states to stand united behind those 'sisters' who confronted the superpowers or asserted their rights. If imperialism and racism were to be condemned, he said, the Conference should stand unanimously in its support of Arab rights and of Zionist withdrawal from Arab lands. There too he got full support for the Palestinian right of self-determination.

Sadat truly believed that the intimacy he had achieved with many Third World leaders, and the primacy Egypt had assumed in the non-aligned movement since Nasser's day, in conjunction with Tito's Yugoslavia and Nehru's India, entitled him to show the way to, and to lay demands before, the Afro–Asian countries. He told his non-aligned audiences that since he had succeeded in handling the mightiest powers, he would not, as they should not, hesitate to take on the 'tails' of those powers, such as the 'racist Tel Aviv–Pretoria Axis' which sought to 'intimidate the African and Arab peoples' by means of the 'nuclear weapons they were developing together' and through 'theatrical moves' such as the hostage-rescuing commando operation launched by Israel in Entebbe, Uganda. Sadat pledged his support to the people of Asia in their struggle against the superpowers, who 'were extending their domain over the lands and oceans of that continent'. He demanded of the members of the Conference that they all stand by Lebanon, a 'non-aligned sister state', and condemn the foreign intervention which 'harmed peaceful coexistence between the Palestinians and the Lebanese people'. He demanded that the Conference call upon the Israelis and the Syrians to take their hands off Lebanon so that it could revert to independence and regain its national integrity. About the Palestinians, who were wreaking havoc on that country, he dared say nothing, lest his appeal to the Conference to support their national aspirations sounded ridiculous. In Africa, said Sadat, Egypt was the 'elder sister', in as much as all movements of national liberation in the continent 'looked up to Cairo'. Before many African countries had become independent, Egypt had been the home of their movements of national liberation, and Sadat vowed that it would remain a friendly asylum for members of these movements in the future. In 1976, he condemned the Soviets and their Cuban surrogates for their role in Angola and he played an active part, as the head of an African Committee, in aiding the national liberation movements in Rhodesia and South Africa. He invited Joshua Nkomo, one of the freedom fighters in Rhodesia, to Cairo and promised him that he would work for majority rule, in other words black rule, in that country.

In Europe, Sadat was particularly gratified with the favourable response that he received in France. First under Pompidou and then under Giscard d'Estaing, the French administration was willing to provide economic support to Egypt and to open up a new channel for the arms he so desperately needed. Sadat was convinced that the October War had caused the turn-about in West European attitudes towards him, for the Europeans had discovered that the Arabs were not 'defeated people who could not fight' or 'backward people who could not make progress'. Sadat said that Europeans had also come to understand the significance of the oil weapon following the October War and had therefore rushed to establish European–Arab dialogue. France, who had lifted her embargo on deliveries of weapons to the Middle East, became a bridgehead in Europe for Sadat. Through France, he hoped to gain the understanding of the entire European community, and to secure from it the advanced science and technology that his country needed. In January 1975, he visited France, held talks with President d'Estaing, and inspected the famous Thomson arms factories. Shortly before his trip to France, Sadat had received the Shah of Iran in Cairo and had heard from him about the 'stunning military advances in technology which take place hourly'; in the Thomson plants he posed all the questions that had occurred to him during his meeting with the Shah. He received both oral answers and practical demonstrations to satisfy his queries about electronics, which most fascinated him, and about other advanced weaponry. During his visit to France, he heaped praise on the country; it had been 'the first to establish cultural and industrial relations with modern Egypt' more than a century earlier; it had provided the first foreign language that the Egyptians learnt; during the rule of Muhammed Ali, it had assisted in the manufacture of heavy weapons; and it had built Egypt's first dam, the first modern irrigation system and the Abadin Palace, where Sadat had his own office. Sadat went so far as to declare that he himself would not be alive if it were not for the French-trained Egyptian lawyer who 'saved his neck' when he was convicted by the British in the Second World War. That, he said, was why he was proud of the French legal system which still functioned in Egypt. Now, of course, he wanted to revive the old relationship and forget the 'nightmare' of the French–Israeli alliance of the 1950s and 1960s. He implored the historically-minded French to let history repeat itself, asking them to help Egypt set up a new arms industry and suggesting that French support for total Israeli withdrawal from all occupied Arab lands and for the recognition of Arab rights would be the 'best possible expression' of France's position in the Arab–Israeli conflict. Sadat concluded his visit by signing an arms deal with the French, the most prominent item of which was the delivery of 120 Mirage jets in the years to come.

In April 1976, Sadat visited Europe again. In France, where he was now a familiar figure, he was acclaimed by the local media and thoroughly pampered by his French hosts. In a moment of exhilaration at the attention he was getting on all sides, he declared to the surprised French press that he regarded the 'Cairo Declaration' that he had signed a year earlier with President d'Estaing in Egypt as a 'Treaty of Friendship' between the two countries. This came merely three weeks after he had abrogated his 'Treaty of Friendship' with the Soviets; his eagerness to enter into a new treaty with France showed his disgust with his former 'allies', who had been thrust upon him, and his preference for treaties and alliances which he personally initiated and which gave power to his country and grandeur to himself. He said that he was prepared to sign with France 'anything she wanted', and intimated that his relations with France had grown so close and warm that he no longer even found it necessary to discuss arms deals with the French President. That question, he said, had been settled during the visit of his War Minister, Gamasi, to Paris. He then proceeded to West Germany, where he was delighted to see the culture he most venerated in action. He met Chancellor Schmidt and then took some time off to visit the mountainous countryside which he loved. His talks in Germany centred on economic aid, since the Germans remained reluctant to send weapons to areas of controversy. And then he went on to Austria, to see his old friend, Chancellor Kreisky, with whom Sadat had established a close rapport during his previous visit a year earlier. Sadat was most impressed by Kreisky's successful socialist republic, which he wished to study carefully in order to emulate certain aspects. In fact, Sadat felt so close to Kreisky that he did not wait for an invitation from him to visit Austria again; he simply sent a message to the Chancellor, informing him that he would be staying overnight on his way home from Germany.

Sadat's remarkable growth as an international statesman, and ease with which he criss-crossed countries and met with their leaders, were marred by his relations with the Arabs. Ever since he had elected to go over to the

American sphere of influence, and specifically since he had concluded his two American-sponsored disengagement agreements with Israel, he had alienated the hard-core rejectionists such as Syria, Iraq and the PLO; and had even compelled some moderates, who were reluctant to take sides in the dispute, to distance themselves somewhat from him. What made things worse was the outbreak of the civil war in Lebanon in the summer of 1975. The Syrians and the PLO became embroiled and Sadat was pushed to the sidelines, where he felt helpless, most embarrassed and restless. His manœuvres within the Arab world in the years 1974–6 were largely a product of this situation.

The inter-Arab post-war euphoria was short-lived, although Sadat made every effort to prolong it in order to keep the Arabs together under his leadership. Indeed, in the early months of 1974, Sadat still publicly acknowledged the active roles of Syria, Libya, Iraq and other Arabs in the 'victory', and credited the 'success' of the war to the united Arab front. For example, he recalled with enthusiasm how he had personally gone to one of his air bases in the Nile Delta just before the war, to welcome an Iraqi air squadron which had been sent to Egypt to participate in the war. Despite the fact that in the last crucial days of the war the Iraqi Government had ordered its pilots to discontinue fighting, and despite the eventual withdrawal of their squadron from Egypt, Sadat placed on record his gratitude to those Iraqis who had successfully participated in the first air strike in Sinai on the afternoon of 6 October. He said that even when Libya decided, in the middle of the war, to renege on her obligation to supply oil to Egypt, other Arab countries, like Saudi Arabia and Algeria, had stepped in to supply her needs, and more. This meant, for Sadat, that Arab unity had suffered only 'slight scratches', not deep wounds that could seriously handicap the Arab body. He believed that misconduct by one Arab country did not disrupt the larger picture of Arab unity, and that attempts to revive inter-Arab rivalries were doomed to failure. He was convinced that the Arabs would not inflict self-defeat upon themselves by sinking into internal strife when they had seen for themselves, and proved to the world, the power of the oil weapon to affect the balance of power in the world, global strategies and superpower politics: it was a weapon they could use only when unified.

Sadat pinned his hopes on the Arab Summit in Rabat, due to convene in April 1974, but later rescheduled for October. The major topic on the agenda was the Arab position at the forthcoming Geneva Conference; Sadat hoped that the compelling importance of unity would force the Arabs to pull themselves together and close ranks as they had done during the war. More precisely, the summit was to put an end to the Jordanian–Palestinian controversy, dating back to 1970, over who would represent the Palestinians of the West Bank and Gaza at the negotiating table. Jordan maintained that since those territories had been taken from her by force during the 1967 war, it was her right and duty to negotiate their retrieval; the PLO, which was ejected from Jordan in Black

September 1970, claimed the right to represent the Palestinians everywhere. Sadat clearly sided with the view that the PLO was the only representative of the Palestinians, and he specified that the question of representation in Geneva should be left to the Palestinians to determine. Sadat also announced that he was at odds with King Hussein's view that if the PLO claimed the right to represent the West Bank and Gaza, it should also be entrusted with the task of liberating them from Israel. He encouraged Hussein and the PLO to sort out between them whose duty it was to represent the Palestinians and whose to liberate the West Bank and Gaza. If they failed to agree, then the Arab Summit would have to decide, for it was unthinkable to him that the Arabs should present themselves in Geneva while in disagreement over this major issue. To underline his unqualified support for the PLO, Sadat invited Yasser Arafat and the participants in the Palestinian National Council, held in Cairo in June 1974, to visit the front lines of the Third Army and see for themselves how determined he was to resume war if the Geneva Conference failed to resolve their problem. Sadat also reminded the Palestinians that, back in 1972, he and the Saudis had attempted to mediate between the PLO and King Hussein; when he had realized that Jordan was taking an unacceptable position, he had not hesitated to condemn her and to break off relations. Relations had not been resumed until the eve of the war, when Sadat had considered Arab unity of supreme importance. Before the convening of the Rabat Summit, Sadat invited King Hussein to Alexandria and persuaded him to accept the formula suggested at the previous Arab Summit in Algeria: that the PLO be regarded as the Palestinian representative. On 9 October 1974, he met with Arafat in Cairo, and conveyed to him the essence of his talks with the Jordanian monarch.

Sadat rejected the notion, current in the Arab world, that an 'Egyptian – Saudi Axis' had emerged after the October War. Such an axis would, of course, be detrimental to the idea of Arab unity, for it implied preferential treatment for one Arab country over another. Sadat was desperate to give the impression that as the new leader-father of all Arabs he treated them all equally. He said that it was ordained that Egypt would be the main base of Arab power and that Saudi Arabia would own 60 per cent of the Arab oil reserves. When Egyptian military might was combined with Saudi oil power, each of them became more effective, he said. He was careful to mention that, despite the implied primacy of the two 'superpowers' of the Arab world, the October victory was achieved by all Arabs. Giving marks for good behaviour to the Arabs was Sadat's way of distributing patronage and calming, so he hoped, fermenting disputes which threatened to erupt. Sadat took pride in the fact that when Kissinger had come to Aswan to discuss the first disengagement with Israel, he had mentioned the severe damage that the Arab oil embargo was inflicting on the US; of course, thought Sadat, Egypt having no oil to speak of, Kissinger had talked to him about Saudi oil because he was aware of the weight Egypt carried in the Arab world. Sadat had then talked to King Faisal about the oil embargo and they had co-ordinated their policy on how to use the energy weapon.

The Egyptian–Saudi alliance became a fact of life, nevertheless, and Sadat was careful to cultivate it without giving to it too much prominence in his speeches. King Faisal was instrumental in obtaining for Egypt various types of Western weapons and ammunition, which the Egyptians were not yet able to purchase directly. Sadat came to enjoy a very close relationship with the Saudi monarch. He was persuaded that Egypt and Saudi Arabia should merge their policies, in order to strengthen their combined resources and political clout. Before the war, Faisal had been one of the few Arab leaders to have faith in the war's successful outcome and to pledge his help; during the war, he had called Sadat twice every day and every night offering to help rebuild the Suez Canal cities, and was Sadat's major ally in political debates within the Arab world. Faisal approved of the disengagement agreements, and was of help to Egypt in taming political rivals such as the Syrians, the PLO and the Jordanians. When King Faisal was murdered in early 1975, Sadat was very apprehensive in case there was an about-turn in Saudi policy. When he heard the news of Faisal's death, he ordered his armed forces on alert and sent some naval units to the Red Sea to assist the royal house in case of need. Only when he was assured by Prince Sultan, the Saudi Defence Minister, that all was well did Sadat call off the alert. Thereafter, he maintained good relations with the new king, Khaled.

Before long, however, Sadat's vision of a unified Arab world started to evaporate, despite the agreement reached in Rabat that the PLO should act as the only legitimate representative of the Palestinians, and that the Arabs should unite in pledging not to yield any Arab territory to Israel. The upheaval in inter-Arab relations after 1975 was partly caused by Sadat's second disengagement. He learned the hard way that there was simply no possibility of satisfying everyone. He once reflected that wider international politics were easy for him, because when he dealt with the superpowers, Europe, Asia or Africa, all the facts were clear and he had no difficulty in choosing his course; but in the Arab world there was so much debate, insinuation and accusation, and all was pursued with so much emotion and over-excitement, that he could not chart his way through the cross-currents. He said that, during the past twenty-five years, Arab policy had been confined to reacting to others or moving haphazardly in one direction and then another. But when he tried to introduce some long-term planning and rational thinking into Arab policy, he found himself thwarted, losing the support of his fellow Arabs and being violently attacked by short-sighted rulers who thought of themselves as leaders.

A case in point was his second disengagement with Israel, which was branded by the Syrians and the PLO as a 'sell-out to the US', or a 'surrender to Israel', or a 'betrayal of the Arab cause'. Sadat felt increasingly hurt by these flurries of accusations because he thought of himself as the champion of the

Palestinian cause and he still considered the Syrians as the comrades-in-arms of October. He had made great efforts, during his negotiations with Kissinger, to bring about a second disengagement on the Israeli–Syrian front too and had, on many occasions, tried to prevail on the US to open a dialogue with the PLO. Sadat defended his strategy, saying that since 1973 he had sought to attain Arab goals gradually and to maintain a momentum that would carry him forward to an eventual solution of all Arab problems. He vowed to continue that course until all Arab territories were liberated and the rights of the Palestinians restored. He rejected the accusation that he was now under US influence, saying he had always been wary of foreign patronage; he had accepted the American-initiated disengagement only because it was beneficial to Egypt and enhanced the Arabs' stature in the world. He accused the Soviets of having incited their clients, the Syrians and the PLO, with whom he had been on the best of terms, to oppose his disengagement policies. He dated the radical Arab rebellion against him from the day the second disengagement was signed in Geneva. The Soviets, in their capacity as co-chairmen of that gathering, should have attended the signing ceremony, but instead they chose to stay away. When the Soviet Ambassador to Damascus went to announce his country's decision to the Syrian Foreign Minister, the latter pulled out a copy of the decision adopted by the Ba'th Party Command on 4 September 1975, which stated that the 'agreement was a serious defeat to the Arab cause', and handed it over to the Ambassador. At the same time, Assad sent special emissaries to all Arab capitals to explain his view of the Egyptian–Israeli Agreement; violent anti-Egyptian demonstrations were also mounted in Damascus.

Sadat was particularly incensed by the parallel declaration made by the Ba'th Party of Iraq to the effect that Sadat had expressed his 'readiness to conclude peace with the enemy', an 'accusation' that was immediately echoed by Syria. Sadat burst out: 'When have I made such a commitment?' Sadat was astonished at the Iraqi communiqué because, despite his differences with Iraq after the October cease-fire and the withdrawal of the Iraqi air squadron from Egypt before the war had finished, Sadat had visited Iraq in May 1975, and ever since the Arab Summit in Rabat had maintained a close relationship with Iraq's strong man, Saddam Hussein. As a result of that relationship, Sadat had mediated between Iraq and Iran, and Iraq and Kuwait, and he had even envisaged a mediatory role, such as befitted an all-Arab leader, between Iraq and Syria. In a dramatic move, which symbolized his desire for reconciliation, Sadat decorated the commander of the Iraqi air squadron in Baghdad with the highest Egyptian medal of honour and thanked him publicly for his role in the air strike at the war's opening on 6 October. He said that if he had wanted to achieve peace with the enemy, he would have had the courage to say so and to seek it openly. But that was not the case, for he had rejected Israel's offer to withdraw from most of Sinai if he would end the state of belligerency; he had done so out of consideration for the Syrians and the Palestinians.

Sadat also reiterated that the second disengagement had been signed by the Egyptian Chief-of-Staff; this was a mark of the military and temporary nature of the agreement, and demonstrated that it was a far cry from the 'peace' he was accused of having signed. He reminded his rivals and critics in the Arab world that, following the first disengagement agreement, the Syrians had sounded the same alarms and had hurled the same accusations at him, so much so that the worried Saudis and Kuwaitis had dispatched emissaries to inquire whether he had truly disavowed the rest of the Arab world, but then everything had quietened down when Syria too had achieved her disengagement with Israel. Sadat felt that Assad was replaying the same farce all over again. Sadat had dispatched his Vice-President to Syria to explain the nature of the new disengagement in an attempt to pre-empt another outburst of acrimony against him, but his precaution now proved vain. Sadat determined to avoid emotionalism, and to continue to regard Assad as his 'brother', but also to respect and implement what he had signed and not to yield or be intimidated by 'demonstrations, resolutions, one-upmanship and slogans'. Egypt should keep to her 'quiet and ethical way' of pursuing her policies, he thought.

Similar accusations were made by Yasser Arafat, who added that the 'Egyptian army will not stand idly by if the Palestinian revolution is harmed'. This constituted, for Sadat, a PLO attempt to pit the Egyptian armed forces against the authority of their President. He could not understand how Arafat could utter these words after all the respect that Sadat had shown him, when Egypt had done no more than recover fifty kilometres of her territory and obtain Israeli withdrawal from the Sinai oil wells and strategic passes. Without actually naming the Soviet Union, Sadat said that the same 'furtive devil' who had attempted to disrupt the first disengagement was now trying to undo the second by claiming that the agreement included 'secret clauses' which were detrimental to the Arab cause. He vowed that despite this 'devil's' efforts, he would continue to seek the friendship, comradeship and brotherhood of the Arabs, even if they continued to reject him. He said that Egypt could never turn her back on those with whom she had joined hands, or on those who had stood by her in times of hardship. He counselled those who cursed the US for having taken advantage of the disengagement agreement to 'post her electronic stations in the Sinai' that their cursing would not affect the course of events. He said, 'Let them curse America as long as they wish! We cursed America for fifty years and nothing happened; Israel stayed where it was. Curse America for another fifty years, and we shall see!'

Sadat reproved the Arabs for their failure to realize that '90 per cent of the cards are in American hands', and that without the US they stood simply no chance of achieving any of their national goals. He said that he would have been perfectly prepared to buy electronic warning stations from the Soviets if they had agreed to sell him some. But since the Soviets had elected to remove their electronic equipment from Egypt rather than sell it to him, he had no other recourse but to apply to the US. If the US could be useful to the Arabs, why not take advantage of her services? He said that unless the Arabs understood the realities of the new era, and undertook a critical and rational analysis of world affairs, they would remain bogged down in their trivial bickerings and internecine hatreds, which would certainly not help them regain lost territories nor resolve the painful and long-standing Palestinian problem. Egypt, for her part, Sadat assured the Arabs, would continue to shoulder her national responsibilities, without compromise, on both scores. He would not consent to isolating Egypt from the Arab world, because Egypt had an Arab role to play and without Egypt neither Syria nor the Palestinians could attain anything. He declared that those who attempted to isolate Egypt would end up isolating themselves.

Rhetoric apart, Sadat slowly came to adopt a more 'realistic approach' as it dawned on him that the rift between him and the radicals had become unbridgeable. He came to the conclusion, sometime in late 1975 or early 1976, that he had to go his own way in defining the Arab cause and the means of attaining it, leaning when he could on the moderate Arabs. There was no longer any point in trying to smother very real issues with words of conciliation. He pledged, nonetheless, that he would remain loyal to both principles decided upon at Rabat. He informed the Arab leaders who wished to listen to him that he would remain within the agreed parameters of Arab strategy, but that he reserved the right to act freely and expected the Arabs to trust his judgement. He formulated and announced his 'triangular strategy'. The base of the triangle, which consisted of his commitment to the agreed double strategy of the Arabs, remained fixed, while the apex of the triangle, explained Sadat, was movable and corresponded to the shifting tactics he adopted in his day-by-day conduct of politics. As long as the base was firm, as long as he did not lose sight of the ultimate goals, the tactics he adopted mattered very little.

Confident of his newly-formulated strategy, Sadat was ready to counter-attack. He strongly denounced his radical Arab critics, whose accusations 'sank to the level of meanness and irresponsibility', and he was confident that these 'artificial storms' would soon recede as people realized that they were 'peripheral struggles' engendered by 'narrow-minded' leaders whose 'petty attempts' to score points were based upon a 'poor understanding' of the world and the Arab nation. He said that most Arab public opinion stood firmly behind him and that the accusations of the 'storm raisers' would ultimately arouse only 'pity and ridicule'. His arsenal of imagery was never exhausted: his Arab critics were 'sharp-shooters who witnessed the quick depletion of their faulty ammunition', and whose 'ammunition was mere talk, while ours, of which we have plenty, is step-by-step action'. He explained to sceptics that he supported without reserve the Palestinians and the PLO, despite their mischief-making, but that the struggle for the recovery of Palestine would take generations – hence the need to 'take what you can, and then ask for more', and the need for perseverance and farsightedness in following a long-term strategy. At the same time, he bluntly told the Arab radicals: 'All issues relating to the Egyptian homeland are the business of the Egyptian people only.' He explained that while doing what he thought was beneficial for Egypt, he did not undertake anything that could 'inhibit the Arab march forward'; and while his mind and heart were open to dialogue, and his hands remained extended in brotherhood, he would not tolerate any interference in his country's affairs, for that was strictly his area of jurisdiction. This was a far cry indeed from the 'Arab solidarity' and unity, the 'communality of fate' and the 'unity of action' which he thought he had achieved during the October War.

In February 1975, while Kissinger was working on the initial, abortive plans for a second disengagement, a Palestinian gang landed with two rubber-boats on a Tel Aviv beach, took over one of the Israeli tourist hotels and held several hostages before they were overpowered by an elite Israeli counter-terrorist unit. The problem for Sadat was that this daring act by the PLO was not merely another routine attack against Israel, which he would normally have welcomed; the two rubber-boats bore the names *Port Said* and *Egypt*, and their arrested occupants claimed that they had sailed to the Israeli shore from the Canal city of Port Said. Sadat thought that this was a calculated ploy by the Palestinians to implicate the Egyptians in the attack, just as Kissinger's diplomatic efforts were getting under way, in order to 'convince' the Israelis of Egypt's aggressive intentions and to undermine the second disengagement. Sadat believed that it was owing to that incident, in which he had no involvement, that the Israelis demanded that Egypt should consent to the termination of the state of belligerency as a test of her goodwill and intent. This demand, which Sadat had understood to be 'taboo' in his talks with Kissinger as long as Israel occupied Arab territories, drove the negotiations to an impasse and they were discontinued in March 1975. Then, the Palestinians, under the instructions of the Syrians and the Soviets, continued to attack Sadat personally, his Prime Minister Mamduh Salem and Egypt's policies, over the Voice of Palestine Radio from both Baghdad and Cairo. Sadat thought that it was the height of discourtesy and ingratitude on the part of the PLO to take advantage of the hospitality and the broadcasting facilities offered to them by Egypt, and at the same time to level against their hosts such an intense barrage of abuse and slander. Sadat sent a message to Arafat, urging him not to abuse Egypt's tolerance and sense of solidarity; but the station continued its cursing unabated. Sadat then ordered his Prime Minister to close down the station and dispatched another message to Arafat explaining that he had had to take this step to put an end to the PLO's campaign of libel. The Palestinians and their allies, the Syrians and the Soviets, claimed that Sadat had closed the station in accordance with one of his secret commitments to Israel, but Sadat vehemently denied the charge.

Sadat, King Hussein of Jordan, King Hassan of Morocco, Assad and Arafat had been elected to form a 'Committee of Five' at the Rabat Conference; they were to try to mediate between the Palestinians and Jordanians. Sadat thought that he would continue to have a say in Palestinian affairs and congratulated himself on more than one occasion for his stand on their behalf. But when, in 1975, Jordan and Syria announced their plan for co-operation, which included a 'Joint Command' for their combined armed forces, Sadat saw his influence slipping and Syrian hegemony on the ascendant; Assad was able to revive his scheme for a 'greater Syria', which was to encompass Syria, Lebanon, Jordan and Palestine. Sadat, who was loath publicly to condemn a new union between Arabs, wished to secure, at the very least, Lebanon's independence from Syrian domination and he repeated his 'hands-off Lebanon' slogan. In February 1975, the PLO published a manifesto in which they charged Sadat with making 'secret agreements with Israel', and with 'trading principles for territory'. Sadat saw this as a manifestation of the total domination of the PLO by Syria and the Soviet Union. He said that instead of attacking him directly, the Soviets and the Syrians whispered the story of Sadat's 'treason' to the Palestinians and urged them to break the story to the world.

In late 1975, Sadat invited Kamal Jumblatt, the Lebanese Druze leader, to Cairo to discuss the Lebanese crisis. Jumblatt pleaded with Sadat to accept Syrian mediation in Lebanon and Sadat responded that he would agree to mediation by 'the Devil himself' if that would stop the bloodshed. However, Sadat learned that the Syrian-dominated Sa'iqah group of Palestinians, under Zuheir Muhsin, whom the Syrians had been grooming as the successor to Arafat, were (presumably as a proxy for their Syrian masters) exacerbating the civil war in Lebanon because renewed stability in Lebanon might be detrimental, they believed, to the Palestinian revolution and might make Syrian intervention unnecessary. Earlier that summer, when Sadat was at his seaside residence near Alexandria, a prominent Lebanese businessman had come to see him to complain that the Sa'iqah had robbed his company of ten cars. Before that, the man had taken his grievance to Jumblatt, who had retorted that he had perhaps been punished by the Sa'iqah for his collaboration with the Christian Phalange. But when the plaintiff had insisted that he was a car distributor and minded only his own business, Jumblatt had agreed to send one of his aides to see Zuheir Muhsin and had prevailed upon him to return the stolen cars. Muhsin consented to return nine of the cars (the tenth had been burnt) provided the dealer paid £10,000 for their release. Sadat thought that if that was the way the PLO behaved in Lebanon, on behalf of the Syrians, whose mediation he was now asked to back, that was too much. Nevertheless, he was willing to agree if that could avert a full Syrian take-over of Lebanon.

In April and May 1976, when disturbances erupted on the West Bank and in Gaza supporting the 'Day of the Land' demonstrations mounted by Arabs in

Israel proper, Sadat voiced his support for the 'Palestinian uprising against the terror and oppression' of Israeli rule and enjoined the Palestinians to sustain their pressure against Israel. Sadat credited the PLO's success in the mayoral elections held on the West Bank at that time to the 'impact of the October victory'. He could not explain how, 'under Israeli terror', free elections were held, allowing a pro-PLO take-over of most of the local councils on the West Bank; but he advanced the theory that the PLO leadership had seized the opportunity provided by the municipal elections on the West Bank to 'force their national representatives on to the local councils', and to signal to the Syrians, King Hussein and Israel that the PLO would not bend to Israeli wishes. With the Syrian military intervention in Lebanon in May 1976, during which many Palestinians were massacred, Sadat hoped to capitalize on anti-Syrian feeling amongst the Palestinians and to regain his position as their patron. But shrewdly, Assad quickly offered his support to the PLO in their battle against the Lebanese Christians, thus nipping in the bud Sadat's renewed claims to the title of champion of the Palestinian cause. Sadat charged that Assad had 'collaborated with the Israelis in Lebanon', since he dared not cross the 'red line' that they had set for him there, and in desperation he even insinuated that the Americans had actually encouraged Syria to invade Lebanon.

On 15 September 1975, the Egyptian Embassy in Madrid was attacked by a Palestinian gang headed by an Iraqi Arab. The Palestinians were said to be members of the Fatah group, which Sadat had previously praised as representing the 'moderate' trend within the PLO. The demands of the terrorists, who had taken hostage the ambassador and two of his aides, were clear: they wanted Egypt to declare that the second disengagement was a 'betrayal of the Arab cause', and they wanted the Egyptian delegation to the talks with Israel in Geneva to quit the negotiations immediately. The hostages were not released until various Arab ambassadors, including the Algerian, the Iraqi and the Kuwaiti, signed a statement condemning the agreement. In order not to drive the PLO into the arms of Syria, and not to jeopardize his position among the Arabs, all of whom supported the Palestinians, Sadat muted his criticism of the PLO. He continued to lash out at the Syrian Ba'th Party, which he labelled as 'constituting only a small non-representative minority of the Syrian people', and accused them of having pleaded with the Soviet Union, on three occasions during the October War, to arrange for a cease-fire, when he himself had been busy fighting in earnest. At the same time, he announced that 1976 would be the 'year of Palestine', which meant that during his visits that year to the US, Europe, Saudi Arabia and the Gulf States, he would reiterate the need to provide a national solution for the Palestinians, hoping thereby to remain spokesman on the only issue likely to rally the entire Arab world to united action. In 1976, Sadat mentioned that he had told Arafat: 'Your problem is in good hands with Egypt, because it does not concern you only. My future, here in Egypt, hinges on that issue.'

On 19 February 1976 Sadat watched the movie *The Longest Day*, which featured the landing of the Allies in Normandy during the Second World War. He saw the Americans, the British, the French, the Canadians and the Dutch fighting together, which reminded him of his October War and the large degree of co-operation he had secured among the Arabs. But he observed that while the Western Allies had strengthened their ties of friendship after the war, the Arabs had slid back into controversy and outright enmity. He was saddened by his own observation and asked himself, 'What kind of curse has descended upon us Arabs?' After the war, rival camps had emerged in the Arab world, instead of the unity he had been hoping for: the Arabs were accusing each other of 'treason' rather than conducting a civilized debate among themselves about their difficulties. Sadat's relations with the Shah of Iran were a case in point.

Sadat, unlike Nasser, had developed a very close working relationship with the Shah, who supported the Arab consensus regarding Israeli withdrawal from the occupied territories and Palestinian rights despite his good relations with Israel. The Shah had given generous aid to Egypt and pledged to help further with her economic development. Sadat had even achieved an unprecedented feat: he had arranged for the Shah to meet Iraq's Saddam Hussein in 1975, and the two had agreed to end their mutual antagonism by determining their border along the Shatt-al-Arab River and putting an end to the Kurdish rebellion. So Sadat saw no reason why he should not visit Teheran during his sweep through the Gulf countries in July 1976. But Arab radicals, who were enraged over the Shah's policy towards Israel, and over Iran's continued reference to the 'Arab Gulf' as the 'Persian Gulf', saw Sadat's co-operation with him as yet another sign of 'treason', as another 'sell-out'. Sadat upheld his right to do business with anyone who could further his cause, just as he respected the right of other Arabs to conclude their own alliances and to determine their partners in accordance with their own interests. Another example of Arab rivalry had occurred after April 1975, when King Khaled of Saudi Arabia had invited Sadat and Assad to Riyadh in an effort to bridge the widening rift between them. After many hours of discussion, which had culminated in the 'Riyadh Communiqué', Sadat had been hopeful that his conflict with Assad was settled, only to discover a short time later that the Ba'th Party was still clinging to its uncompromising and nationalistic view, which made real reconciliation between the two countries impossible, as the September 1975 outburst of recriminations proved. After the Riyadh meeting, and before he went to Salzburg to meet with President Ford, Sadat again made a tour of Kuwait, Iraq, Syria and Jordan, and met with Arafat in Damascus, in an attempt to explain to them in person his views and to elicit their support. But his efforts were in vain.

Sadat came to the realization that while he could trust Assad himself, he could not rely on the Syrian Ba'th, whose hot-headed and erratic decisions were inspired by the Soviet Union. He accused the Ba'th of having initiated, at Soviet instigation, the thrice-rejected cease-fire at the opening of the war, of having torpedoed the Geneva Conference despite their commitment to joining, and of having initiated a compaign of defamation against Egypt after the first and second disengagement agreements had been signed with Israel. But the Ba'th did not relent and continued to brand Sadat as an 'American agent' and a 'traitor'. Sadat decided that there was no way he could placate the Syrians unless he subscribed to Ba'th ideology; this he had no intention of doing. Instead, he pointed out that while the Syrians were talking, threatening, cajoling and promising, he was achieving through diplomacy, through his contacts with the US, and through the strengthening of his reputation for credibility and reasonableness, results which they could not hope to achieve. He credited the acceptance of the PLO in the world to his visit to the United States and to his speech at the General Assembly of the UN. He felt that the blame heaped on him was nothing but jealousy on the part of his Arab opponents, who were pushed by the Soviets towards 'blackmail and demagoguery' instead of towards 'reasonable and logical argument'.

Sadat ascribed the worsening situation in Lebanon to the Ba'th Party policy, instituted in May 1976, of massive Syrian intervention. He accused the Ba'th of having supplied weapons to both warring parties: the Muslims, who were supported by the PLO, and the Christians. Sadat said that he had a list of all the supplies that the Ba'th had sent to the Muslims for them to kill the Christians and vice versa, and charged Syria with responsibility for the carnage. Sadat contrasted the outlandish conduct of the Syrians with the moderation of Egyptian society, 'whose culture and civilization had endowed her with a willingness to forgive, a tendency to reject extremism in her customs, religion and faith, and with the instinct to shun arrogance and boasting'. He thought that Egypt would remain tolerant of different races, cultures and faiths, and that the Egyptian people would continue to be imbued with a deep faith in Arab unity. Unlike other Arabs, who ostensibly stood for unity, but in fact nurtured parochialism and separatism, the Egyptians, thought Sadat, stood for a genuine Arab unity which would grow and eventually blossom. Sadat compared Lebanon, where the chaos was being exacerbated by Syria and the PLO, and Egypt, which was a stronghold of sanity, stability, predictability and reason. He firmly believed that the Arabs would look to Egypt for guidance once again, when they matured sufficiently to abandon their vain exercises in power politics.

Sadat thought that the major problem of the Arab countries he most strongly criticized – Syria and Libya – was their internal regime. He believed that any leader, no matter what his personal qualities, could only come to full bloom in a democratic society founded on freedom, respect for the rights of groups and individuals, and popular participation. Where a national government was weakly constituted, he said, it could not expect other nations to look to it for leadership. He was implying, of course, that while his regime was well constituted, the other Arab countries, where minority parties ruled, exhibited such impotence in their internal affairs that they could not claim the leadership of the Arab movement as a whole. He hinted that rulers such as Assad and Qadhafi, who now had the Arab leadership in their sights after their challenge to Sadat's authority, were not fit to embrace the members of the Arab movement because of their suppression of minority groups in their own countries. If an idea was to take hold and sweep through the Arab populace, he said, it would have to emanate from a country and a leader who could serve as an example to all Arabs; it also had to be associated with an open regime which avoided isolation. The Arab leaders he criticized had cut themselves off from their own people and from the people of other nations, including other Arab nations; they had nothing to offer but empty slogans. By contrast, Egypt, which was encouraging free dialogue at home and opening up to the outside world, was the natural home for struggling peoples throughout the Arab world. The implication was that Sadat, the father of Egypt and creator of this 'open and free society', was also the undisputed claimant to the title of leader of all Arabs; his model regime made him a model leader too.

Sadat also believed he had a strong moral claim to the leadership of the Arab world. He contended that while some Arab countries – meaning Syria and Libya – meddled in the internal affairs of other Arab states, hiring agents and pen-mercenaries who purchased newspapers and bribed anyone who was prepared to act upon their whims, Egypt had shunned that easy and cheap way of conducting inter-Arab business. He said that Egypt, that is himself, as the responsible leader of all Arabs, preferred long-term strategies to short-term 'flashes of action' which left no mark on history. Being a historically-minded man, Sadat was confident that when the story of the modern Arab world was written, the empty words of others would go unrecorded, as would their plots and intrigues against other peoples and countries, while his own deeds, which were genuine achievements and marked real progress, would be recorded and studied. History, he said, skipped over petty acts and childish dramas, but dwelt upon focal events which influenced the fate of nations. Sadat enumerated his great works on behalf of the Arab nation: the war with Israel in October, and the consequent uniting of the Arabs; the elimination, for a while, of past hatreds within the Arab world; an end to the categorization of Arabs as 'progressives' and 'reactionaries'; and the mobilization of Arab resources for the sake of the Arab nation as a whole. This was rational and proper conduct which would not escape the attention of historians in the generations to come. Sadat reckoned that he had worked for many years to 'turn all Arabs into one family', as he had done in Egypt, and he had faith that if he adhered to his course and ignored the libels hurled against him, then on some future day, the recalcitrant rejectionists would come to realize that they were wrong and he was right. He viewed 'sick people', such as Qadhafi, as representing a small minority of only 10 per cent in the Arab world, and believed that the remaining 90 per cent were basically sound. He warned that anyone leaving the ranks of the majority, which he believed he represented, was 'likely to sink', while Egypt would hold the balance of power in the Middle East whether his opponents liked it or not.

Sadat exercised his claim to leadership in the Arab world not only by apportioning blame or credit to Arab countries, but also by taking action which showed his mettle. Lebanon offered no direct threat to him, and he was content to do no more than reprimand the Syrians for their interference; the Sudan, on the other hand, was a vital neighbour, and Sadat believed that he had to take serious action if he was to uphold his credibility in the face of Qadhafi's meddling. In fact, 'Libya's madman', as Sadat came to label Qadhafi, posed a new threat to Egypt: from without, by accumulating huge stockpiles of Soviet weapons; and, from within, by orchestrating subversive activity against Sadat's regime. Sadat was careful to absolve the Libyan people from the crimes of their 'lunatic ruler', and sympathized with them for incurring the tyranny of this 'criminal'. In July 1976, Sadat concluded a mutual defence pact with President Numeiri, who had supported him in his agreements with Israel. The pact was intended to give greater depth and significance to the co-operation which the two countries already enjoyed as members of the Arab League. This was Sadat's way of signalling to Libya and the Soviets that he was prepared to fight them both in the Sudan because they were encroaching on his backyard. Sadat and Numeiri established a Joint Defence Council and a Joint General Staff to implement the close co-operation on defence envisaged in the pact. The joint defence plan was backed by the Saudis, who had as much to fear from the Libyans and their patrons as from the Sudanese. To Sadat's great satisfaction, Saudi generals participated in the strategic co-operation, lending it a solid inter-Arab character.

Sadat's resolute step in defence of the Sudan followed a new attempt by Qadhafi, this time, Sadat believed, on behalf of the Soviets, to launch a *coup* against Numeiri and so complete the encirclement of Egypt from the west and the south. In May 1976, Sadat received information that the Ma'adi supporters, together with the Communists and the Muslim Brothers, were joining together in a strange coalition of convenience to take over power in Khartoum. The *coup* was planned for 24 May 1976, Revolution Day in the Sudan. Sadat rushed the information by special envoy to Numeiri, who, upon receiving it, said that the evidence pointed to Qadhafi as the chief instigator. Just before the *coup*, Qadhafi had announced that he wished to meet Sadat in order to turn over a new leaf in their relationship, but when the information about the plot became known, Sadat interpreted Qadhafi's overtures as a calculated ploy to deceive him. He said that Qadhafi always used to 'numb his victims when he was plotting something against them'. Sadat himself had experienced this before: in early 1974, at a time when the Libyan leader was giving the impression that he still stood for unity with Egypt, a number of his anti-Egyptian propaganda tracts and books, some of them distributed by the Libyan Ambassador himself, were seized in Egypt. The attempt against Sadat's life by a Military Technical College student was also widely believed to be a result of Qadhafi's accusations that Sadat had forsaken Palestinian rights by concluding his disengagement with Israel. The *coup* in the Sudan was launched on 26 May, but it was rapidly quelled by Numeiri's armed forces. At one point, the Sudanese Minister of Information conveyed to Sadat a request from Numeiri asking for the repatriation of the Sudanese contingent which had been stationed along the Suez Canal as a symbol of Khartoum's support for Egypt. Since Egypt's War Minister, Gamasi, was on a trip to London, Sadat personally called General Ali Fahmi, the Chief-of-Staff, who had commanded the missile units during the October War, and ordered him to set up an airlift in order to dispatch the Sudanese troops home immediately. The pilots of the first Egyptian transports to land in Khartoum reported that they could still hear the Government's artillery firing against the rapidly disbanding rebels. That airlift, carried out by heavy Antonov 22s, transported the entire contingent of 1,500 soldiers and officers, with their equipment and ammunition, within a matter of hours. Sadat was quick to make the most of the airlift, which made him look like a superpower rushing to the aid of a client state. He served notice to his opponents in the Arab world that, when necessary, he was both willing and able to flex his muscles, and to protect his allies, as befitted a great leader.

After the *coup* had been foiled, Sadat disclosed that he had known all along about Qadhafi's involvement in the plot. He said that his air force had taken photos of the triangle between the borders of Egypt, Libya and the Sudan, where the Libyans had been gathering mercenaries and equipment ready to intervene after the success of the *coup*. Sadat accused Qadhafi, whom he described as 'miserable, mentally sick, megalomaniac, narrow-minded and poorly educated', of having given asylum in Libya to the international terrorist Carlos, and he said that he was personally aware of all Qadhafi's plots against the Sudan. Sadat said that he was even aware that Qadhafi had bought special vehicles in the US for the transport of his mercenaries through the Libyan–Sudanese desert, and that hundreds of Libyan agents were hiding in Khartoum in civilian dress waiting for Qadhafi's orders to wreak havoc on the Sudanese capital and to take advantage of the chaos to topple Numeiri. Sadat also claimed that Qadhafi's embassies around the world had become arsenals, filled with weapons which had been smuggled in diplomatic bags; he vowed that he would shadow him and foil his conspiracies against other countries.

In 1975, when the Lebanese civil war broke out, Sadat was confident that President Faranjieh would be able to handle the situation and he praised the President's great qualities as an Arab patriot. But in 1976 when massive Syrian intervention threatened that both the Lebanese national movement under

Jumblatt and the PLO would become dominated by the Syrians, who could then wrest from Sadat the title of leader of the Arabs, he reversed his position. He made attempts to persuade the Arab League to intercede in Lebanon and asked the Saudis to prevail upon Syria to pull out. On 28 March 1976, he discussed the Lebanese situation with his National Security Council and decided upon a triple initiative: to seek a declaration of cease-fire; to ask the Arab League to position Arab troops in Lebanon to supervise the cease-fire and separate the belligerent parties; and to start a collective Arab programme that would put an end to hostilities. Sadat's initiative was calculated to deny Syria control over the Lebanese and the Palestinians who were involved in the civil war. President Faranjieh, however, sold out to the Syrians and justified their presence in Lebanon on constitutional grounds, claiming that his Government had asked the Syrians to intervene. Sadat dismissed that argument by saying that there was no point in speaking of constitutional legitimacy when Lebanon lay in ruins. The Lebanese leaders were concentrating on peripheral issues while their country was being devastated; and Sadat described them as 'rotten'. Then, in the summer of 1976, the Arab League adopted the solution Sadat had been advocating. At the same time, a new President, Sarkis, was voted into power in Beirut. Sadat pledged to assist Sarkis and the Arab peace-keeping force, which was to be sent to Lebanon, with all the weaponry and logistics he had. He said that Syrians who battled with the PLO did Israel's work, and he was afraid that the Iraelis might step in and bring about the partition of Lebanon. Sadat published a warning to Israel that he would continue to support the 'Palestinian resistance' in the face of Syrian interference and possible Israeli intervention. Sadat implored the Palestinians on the West Bank and in Gaza to continue to resist Israel so as to relieve some of the pressure on their brethren in Lebanon.

Though the prospect of Arab unity receded, Sadat continued to insist that the Arabs had to revitalize their policy and find positive solutions if they were to end the ineffectiveness of recent years. He said that in one of his meetings with King Faisal of Saudi Arabia, they had reminisced about the time when the Arabs had been asked to consent to the immigration of up to a hundred thousand Jews into Palestine in return for independent Arab rule over the country. The Arabs had refused. Now all Palestinian territory was lost to Israel and even more land had been occupied by the Jewish state during subsequent wars. He thought that further refusals and hostility would be counter-productive and would lead to more losses. If the Arabs wanted their territories back, they had to be pragmatic. Sadat observed that the Arabs tended to ignore facts which rendered their position untenable. When the European Common Market signed a new agreement with Israel in 1976 and many Arab factions clamoured for a boycott of Western Europe, Sadat again introduced a note of reason. He pointed out that over-excitement, a boycott of Europe and abuse hurled at the Europeans would not change the situation. Instead he counselled the Arabs to face up to the Israeli challenge, to sign their own agreement with the Common Market and to take on Israel there as everywhere else. He enjoined the Arabs to desist from shirking issues, boycotting and acting as they had in the past; such behaviour had caused them to lose Palestine, and then Sinai and Golan. Now, he said, the Arabs should appear in international forums where Israel was present and face up to her. This was Sadat's way of defending himself against the accusations of 'treason' which were hurled at him by the Syrians, the Libyans and the PLO for having negotiated and signed agreements with the Israelis. He could show that his techniques worked and that he had to his credit a long list of Israeli withdrawals and concessions, while the rejectionists could only deplore the past and decry the outrages inflicted upon them by the Zionist state. As to reconciliation with Israel, which he was accused of promoting in collaboration with the US, he declared again, publicly, during his visit to Rome in April 1976, that he was in favour of the Palestinian notion of a 'secular state where Jews, Christians and Muslims could live together'. He said that he did not seek to eliminate Israel; what the Palestinians desired was an ideal, and if it was unattainable they should content themselves with a Palestinian state on the West Bank and in Gaza. That was why he urged PLO participation in the Geneva talks: he thought it better to overlook the question of Palestine, and to confront Israel and pressure her into making concessions. In an interview given to the Austrian *Kronen Zeitung* (11 April 1976), he reiterated that he was willing to sign a 'peace agreement' (he did not say with whom) that would 'terminate the state of war', so long as it provided for 'total Israeli withdrawal from all Arab territory occupied in 1967'. The rest, he said, implying trade and diplomatic relations, should be left to the 'coming generations', after he had stepped down from office and after the 'other party' (he avoided mention of 'Israel') had proved her goodwill by behaving properly. But he observed that the process might take five, ten or maybe twenty years.

9
TURNING INWARDS

From the moment Sadat had become President, he had been confronted with the daunting task of tackling Egypt's domestic affairs: a crumbling economy, a population explosion, pressure for political change, inter-communal tensions, Muslim extremism, widespread poverty, an overblown and corrupt bureaucracy, overburdened and inefficient services, food shortages and any number of internal problems which usually affect authoritarian regimes in Third World developing countries. Before the war, he had had to devote much of his time to enhancing the dwindling authority of his leadership and to settling pressing domestic issues such as student disturbances, power struggles, Coptic–Muslim clashes and food supplies, all of which had had to be done in an *ad hoc* manner in order to be able to concentrate on the even more urgent issue of preparing for war with Israel. It was not until after the 'October crossing', which Sadat later considered to be a major political and military breakthrough, that he was prepared to launch the socio-economic 'great leap forward', which was to follow up the October War. And if prospects for success did not seem to tally with Sadat's great visions of enlightenment, democracy, prosperity and liberalization, at least at the level of rhetoric and symbolism he could claim a new *ubur* (crossing).

The war had brought world recognition and an imposing new self-image to Sadat so that he could now turn resolutely to domestic affairs. He sensed that he had at last established himself not only as a patriarchal figure who cared for his country, but as one who showed his mettle in combat and 'defeated' his enemies, a *sine qua non* virtue of leadership in his culture. Just as the October War had needed a complex, well-rehearsed and imaginative plan to succeed, and a reliable and resolute commander to carry it through, so would the domestic 'crossing'.

Sadat personally worked out the framework for his new domestic policies: he reshuffled his Government, capitalized on his newly-won prestige, and set himself up as the supervisor, arbitrator and judge of the plan's execution. The plan was spelt out in detail in what came to be known as the 'October Paper', the most systematic, well-thought through and comprehensive policy Sadat had ever produced. While borrowing the extraneous symbolism of October for its title, his paper was essentially an introspective blueprint.

The 'October Paper', published on 18 April 1974, was meant, on the symbolic level, to be a counterpart to Nasser's '30 March Announcement' of 1968, which followed the 1967 *débâcle*, and it was no coincidence that it followed that previous document in form and rhetoric. There was one difference: Sadat's paper was promulgated in an atmosphere of public euphoria, which the Egyptian media called the 'Ramadan spirit', and amidst great enthusiasm for the 'Hero of October'. The 'October Paper', which was first revealed to the public in Sadat's speech to a joint session of the People's Assembly and the Central Committee of ASU, was essentially an attempt to capitalize on that public euphoria in order to mobilize the people to carry out the President's new ideas. The public was encouraged to rally round Sadat, their undisputed leader, and transfer their enthusiasm for the military victory to other sectors of human endeavour in Egyptian society. Hence, the symbolism of the 'crossing', the 'Ramadan spirit', the 'October Paper' and the new mouthpiece of the regime, the *October Magazine*, founded and supervised by one of Sadat's confidants, Anis Mansur. Sadat's thesis was that since Egyptian society had proven its worth in battle, it could now do as well in other pursuits. Sadat told his people that their self-deprecating image was a thing of the past, and that if their new self-confidence, won in battle, could be applied to socio-economic development, there was practically no limit to their potential. Sadat's blueprint for overhauling Egyptian society encompassed the ideological, political, social, economic and scientific visions that he had held since he came to the presidency. Now all was brought together in one comprehensive plan, sandwiched between generalities on Egypt's role in the Arab world and with the world powers.

In order to give warning of, and to justify, the transformations he was planning, Sadat needed to show that his country had always been able to adapt to changes without great difficulty; modern Egyptians would have to accept his reforms without extremism or fanaticism, just as their ancestors had done. At the same time, Sadat pledged to fulfil his country's commitment to help to protect all Arabs, although he did not see Egypt as a domineering master who would categorize them into 'reactionaries' and 'progressives' as Nasser had done. Instead, Egypt would act as a co-ordinator or big brother who would try to bring all of them together and create some common ground among them, as the October experience had done.

Sadat's paper also struck a delicate balance: his commitment to Nasser's heritage and to the July 1952 Revolution (of which he himself had been one of the instigators) was upheld; on the other hand, his own reforms had already taken him some distance from Nasser and were to make an even more substantial departure in the coming years. His own master-stroke against the 'foci of power' was considered the pivotal point towards democratization and liberalization. The rule of law now replaced the haphazard emergency measures which had predominated in Nasser's day. Shimon Shamir, one of the foremost experts on contemporary Egypt, detected new connotations in the use of the word 'revolution' in Sadat's glossary. Instead of the fiery, radical, almost metaphysical term of Nasser's day, it had become, in Sadat's mind, an expression for profound and momentous change in Egyptian society. Sadat said in his paper that Egypt should undergo 'revolutions' in technology, communications and other domains, an indication of the loose meaning that the word 'revolution' had come to have for him. Shamir also pointed out that even Sadat's style was no longer 'revolutionary' in the Nasserite sense; instead of the rhetoric of radicalism and messianism characteristic of the previous era, Sadat's pragmatic, down-to-earth approach used a much more modern vocabulary. Such expressions as 'open society', 'projections towards the year 2000', 'high expectations' are words that can be found in the professional jargon of any Western society. The word 'ideology', which evoked an emotionalism, a blind obligation, and a link to the recent past that Sadat could no longer abide by, was not used; instead, he spoke in terms of a 'Civilizatory Strategy', which meant a master-plan for the future of Egypt based on long-term thinking, but to be carried out pragmatically from day to day.

In the realm of politics, the 'October Paper' can be regarded as a follow-up to Sadat's 15 May 1971 Corrective Revolution, which had put an end to the 'foci of power'. With the benefit of hindsight and the self-confidence of a victor in war, Sadat felt free to lash out at the 'foci of power' again. He blamed them for the 'rule of terror' that had prevailed in Nasser's day, which he contrasted with 'rule by law', 'civil liberties' and 'democratic principles' that he was offering to his fellow Egyptians. Without directly criticizing Nasser, Sadat nevertheless obliquely referred to the many shortcomings of his predecessor's rule, defects which had belied the promise of 'political freedom' (democracy) and 'social freedom' (socialism) made in Nasser's 'National Covenant' of 1962. At the same time, however, Sadat remained adamant about the monolithic character of his regime. He rejected, as he had in Nasser's day, the idea of a pluralistic society where a multi-party system should prevail, for in Sadat's mind that would bring about the deterioration of 'national unity'. The Arab Socialist Union which had ruled under Nasser would continue to be the pillar of Sadat's political government, although in a somewhat more human and liberal form. And he made it quite clear that all political decisions, reforms and even U-turns had to emanate from him in order to be legitimate.

'Socialism' remained Sadat's catchword for his internal social policies, and he went to great lengths to restate his commitment to it in his 'October Paper'. However, Sadat's socialism, which was the 'only solution to Egypt's problems', was a far cry from the rigidity of Nasser's doctrinaire and austere 'Arab socialism'; although the 'alliance of the toiling popular forces', the Nasserite slogan for the coalition of the working forces which had displaced the 'feudalists and the capitalists' of pre-revolutionary Egypt, continued to be a force in Sadat's world view, as he regarded it as the framework of unity which had saved Egypt from the calamity of an all-out civil war or a bitter class struggle. However, Sadat, as a pragmatist, was keener to advance social development than to indulge in ideological bickering.

His 'October Paper' emphasized the need to expand the education system so as to eradicate illiteracy and keep children at school rather than have them run away to join the unemployed. Massive efforts would be made to increase employment, to improve health services, housing and social benefits, and to advance the educational and employment opportunities for women and youth. A start would be made on reversing the steady trend of deterioration in Cairo, with a view to turning it into a habitable and viable city which should attract international financial and cultural interests. Finally, the rural areas would be turned over to modern farming methods. He had begun to give his native Mit Abul-kum a taste of this before his assassination in October 1981. For Sadat, social development was a *sine qua non* for the grand economic programmes he envisaged for post-war Egypt and which he knew were prerequisites for building a new, strong, modern Egypt that would become a model to other Arabs and to the rest of the developing world.

Economic development under Nasser had been governed by the doctrine that social and economic justice could only be attained through the near-monopolization by the state of the means of production. Indeed, shortly after the revolution, most of the heavy industry and public services were transferred to the ownership of 'the people', that is they were nationalized in what came to be known as the 'public sector' of the economy, which was state-owned, state-managed, state-supervised and state-controlled. Although the public sector could claim credit for the economic development in Egypt in the 1960s – the Aswan Dam, the Hilwan steel complex, the military industries and more came into being and provided jobs for the new proletariat – the private sector had nevertheless retained a considerable, if apologetic, place in the economy in the form of housing contractors, small factory owners, tradesmen, financial agencies and other entrepreneurs.

Sadat viewed the public sector as a powerful tool for the development of the economy since, unlike the private sector, it did not seek profit at the expense of development. It could be used to create cadres of professionals and managers, boost investments and generally strengthen the infrastructure on a long-term basis. Thus, for Sadat the public sector was not charged with an ideological 'mission' as is usual in the case of socialist regimes, having instead a utilitarian role to fill in Egyptian society. Centralized planning of the economy did not involve ideological commitment to any particular brand of political philosophy, because Sadat was aware that state intervention in economic planning and development had also come to be an accepted norm in Western regimes such as Austria, Sweden, and England under the Labour Party. For that reason, Sadat accepted in his 'October Paper' the need to bolster the existence of the private sector, and to recognize its contribution to the economy. There was much to be gained from involving private enterprise in the economic impetus he was planning for Egypt. In other words, Sadat not only legitimized the private sector but seemed to lend it preferential treatment over the public sector, although he never said so openly. Sadat awoke to the fact that the public sector had stifled initiative and had bred in its place an enormous, and often corrupt, bureaucracy which had no incentive. Sadat believed that the private sector, coupled with foreign investment, was capable of efficient and diversified economic development and was Egypt's best chance of overcoming the growing imbalance between demographic growth and static productivity.

The 'October Paper' expressed the concern that Sadat had voiced before the war, about the priority he attached to economic development once the fighting was over. He had viewed Egypt's economy on the eve of the war as so hopelessly backward that he had revealed to his National Security Council that the economic situation was 'under zero'. His foreign currency reserves had been completely depleted, and Egypt could not even have purchased the most basic foodstuffs for its population. He had been confident that if he launched the war and showed his 'Arab brothers' his resolve in battle, they would certainly respond by showering part of their wealth on him. Now, it was time to reap the fruit of victory. The wording of the 'October Paper' was designed to awaken all Egyptians to the urgency of the economic situation; sacrifices equivalent to those endured during the war would be required. Sadat had declared, before the outbreak of the war, that he was aiming at an economic 'open-door' policy which would facilitate foreign investments and bring about the economic 'miracle' of his dreams. The 'October Paper' was geared to provide the precise ideological and contextual framework for such an undertaking. The U-turn in Egypt's loyalties, away from the Soviets and towards the West, held much promise for the realization of these dreams. Sadat was well aware that his proposed 'open-door' policy, which was essentially orientated towards private enterprise and foreign capital, smacked of the 'capitalism' and 'imperialism' that Nasser had all but eliminated in his stringent socialist years. However, beyond paying due lip service to 'social-ism', Sadat did not seem unduly disturbed by the boldness of his own proposals. He was determined to open up new lands for agriculture and, with foreign aid and private enterprise, to turn the fertile parts of Egypt into a vast agro-industrial park with tourist and free-trading facilities on its periphery.

The October War inspired Sadat's economic vision not only by its daring and imagination in the face of unfavourable odds, but also by the 'scientific planning' that Sadat now viewed as the new panacea of Egypt's ills. Just as in the months before October the emphasis had been on turning the Egyptian army into an exalted and self-sufficient body, so now Sadat cultivated his *idée fixe* of the necessity to concentrate his and his nation's efforts on building an 'economic bridgehead'. Then an elite of committed officers had been the leaders, now it was to be men of great managerial ability. Then the army had taken priority at the expense of the needs of the population and at the risk of building a state within a state, now the concentration on the economic programme threatened quick profits, temporarily widening the social gap between the rich and poor, and nurturing corruption. He sensed that if his *laissez-faire* policy were applied to encourage the formation of an infrastructure in communications, banking, marketing and transportation, the net profit of rapid economic recovery would by far offset the disadvantages he foresaw. He would not shrink from turning the 'private sector' into a state within a state, encouraging scientific research and personally involving himself in setting the pace of economic development.

Sadat was not quite sure which model to follow in economic development. He knew that striving for the Western pattern would be a hopeless aspiration; he also knew that the Russian centralized five-year-plan model adopted under Nasser, with its emphasis on heavy industry and grandiose schemes to develop a military industrial complex, had ended in failure. He wanted to chart a new course for his country but, being poorly educated in economic matters, he could only voice pipe dreams on the basis of the impressions that he had gleaned from his readings and his travels abroad. He left it to his advisers and economists to translate his desires into viable plans. He was deeply impressed during his visit to Iran by the great success with which the Shah seemed to conduct his economic, technological and military build-up. Although he did not have the funds to match such dynamism, Sadat was hopeful that his improved relations with the Arab world and his newly-won position as leader and co-ordinator of the rival Arab states would enable him to get loans or outright grants to launch his great scheme. Technology fascinated him and he sought to adapt to his needs the most advanced and sophisticated discoveries and inventions of his day. His travels abroad, notably to France and Germany, convinced him that he could and should get technology from the West, especially if he could rely on Western European and American banks and economic concerns to assist on the financial side. There were times when he marvelled at the People's Republic of China who, despite her over-population, under-development and poverty, had succeeded in becoming a world power and had even entered the nuclear age on her own. Sadat held China in great respect and noted her principle of 'self-reliance', which had been activated after her break with the Russians in 1959 – something he hoped to emulate after his own rift with Moscow. On the other hand, he was probably unaware of the significance of the other economic slogan that he borrowed from the Chinese: the 'great leap forward', which in the case of China had ended in disaster. Sadat's repeated visits to Austria and his close association with its socialist Chancellor Kreisky led him to believe that the Austrian pattern of economic recovery might well be worth following. Sadat was particularly impressed by the agricultural technology he saw in Austria and, acting on impulse, he ordered Austrian cattle to be flown to Egypt to start his own programme of cattle-breeding.

Sadat believed that Egypt had a sound basis on which to launch the economic growth he envisaged. He acknowledged the poverty, the low productivity and the lack of an advanced infrastructure, all of which had been occasioned by the waste and corruption of Nasser's socialism, but he was certain that Egypt could pull through the crisis. The Suez Canal was reopened in 1975 and the Canal cities resettled. Egypt became an oil-exporting country for the first time, following Israel's retreat from the Sinai oil fields. The remittances from Egyptians abroad were growing, American aid increasing, and the prospects of Arab and foreign investment were good. All this held promise for Sadat that enough capital could be amassed to fund the great schemes that he entertained for his country. He was confident that within a few years Egypt could overcome her economic problems if he could achieve, as he put it, a 'triangular co-operation' whereby the West would provide technology and know-how, Egypt manpower and skilled labour, and the Arabs capital and finance.

Sadat understood that economic development could not be divorced from the political system in Egypt: if he wished to liberalize one, he had to reform the other. He sensed that giving leeway to private entrepreneurs, whether Egyptian or foreign, would also entail a measure of political liberty. Moreover, Sadat had pledged his people to institute 'democracy', 'rule by law' and 'state of institutions', and his *infitah* (post-war economic open-door policy) seemed a good moment to advance some reform in the political arena as well. Sadat was aware of the pressure for some liberalization of the system which had been building up, not only among his opponents (some of whom, ironically, were hard-line Nasserites), but also within his circle of supporters. Back in 1972, just before the crisis with the Soviets in July, ten major personalities in the Government and the ASU, among them the moderate Mustafa Khalil, who was to become Prime Minister after Sadat's peace initiative was launched, had submitted a letter to the President detailing their grievances against the prevailing regime. They urged him to establish a true democracy at all levels, beginning with three *manabir* (political platforms) within the ASU, which would ultimately be allowed to develop into fully-fledged political parties. They also asked that there should be freedom of speech and expression, that Egypt should disengage herself from the 'shackles' of the Soviets, and that a more favourable stance towards the West should be adopted. That petition had also made the connection between the political and economic liberalizations and had specifically emphasized that the private sector should be given top priority. At the time, Sadat had violently denounced the 'ten', perhaps not so much because of their programme, which he was ultimately to adopt in full, but because of the corporate nature of their protest. It was only a year since he had liquidated the leftist elements of Ali Sabry and company, and here, apparently, was a new focus of power, emerging this time on the Right which might pose a threat to his rule. Sadat, preoccupied by the Soviet crisis and then by preparations for war, did not take any measures against the group, save for Madkur Abu al-Izza, whom he personally interrogated for hours in order to ensure that no political plot was being concocted against him.

After the war, the time was ripe for change, but it was to emanate from Sadat himself, not to be imposed on him or demanded by any group or individual. First, however, he had to rid himself of Nasser's long shadow and to graduate from what psychologists call an 'Oedipal son' to an 'Oedipal father' status. Before 1973, Sadat had always seen Nasser as the 'irreplaceable leader', the 'great hero of the revolution', the 'loyal son of his nation' and the 'champion of the Arabs'. Sadat had always spoken of his predecessor in laudatory tones out of 'love, respect and gratitude to the memory of that illustrious leader', in almost total submission to his 'genius, charisma and *savoir faire*'. It was only after the war that things began to change. During the student disturbances of January 1973, when Sadat was being criticized for his indecisive policies, he went as far as to claim that there had been 'no limitation on liberty in Nasser's time, when I served as his partner. . . . I feel I am responsible for every decision Nasser made and for everything that took place during his lifetime. I am historically responsible because I was his deputy.' But as Sadat's self-confidence grew as a result of the war, his praise for Nasser declined. First, he spoke of himself and Nasser as equal links in the chain of Egypt's leaders. His association with Nasser permitted him, he thought, to mend the mistakes of his predecessor and forge ahead on his own as an innovative reformer, without appearing to be a spiteful iconoclast. In fact, he said that if Nasser had lived he would be pursuing exactly the same road as he himself was. Instead of presenting Nasser's leadership as unimpeachable, Sadat's new image of his predecessor was open to controversy and debate. He shifted responsibility for the revolution from Nasser to the people of Egypt, although at the same time he kept praising the extraordinary qualities of the founder of revolutionary Egypt. He realized that if under his newly-established system of a 'free press' criticism of Nasser should be pushed to the extreme, the Nasserites would in turn criticize not only Nasser's detractors but also the whole regime which permitted them freedom of expression. It was not until 1974–5 that Sadat began to speak of himself not only as the best and the most logical successor to Nasser, but also as one of the men who had engineered the revolution. Since he was as revolutionary as Nasser had been, it seemed to him nonsensical that his critics should say he was 'betraying Nasserism'. He agreed that the issue was not 'Nasserism' versus 'Sadatism' but the fate of the Egyptian revolution. Nasser, he asserted, had been a human being, and his stature was not diminished if one admitted that he had both virtues and shortcomings and that whilst he had implemented some of the revolution's objectives he had failed to realize others. From his stance as Nasser's equal and critic, Sadat could also ensure that he had control over what was remembered of Nasser's heritage, relegating him to the status of a historical figure. The past was past, and all that the present generation could do was to remember it and learn from its errors.

In his Revolution Day speech in 1975, Sadat was ready to assert that his May 1971 struggle against the 'foci of power' had actually constituted a 'Corrective Revolution' bringing the July Revolution back on course. He implied that Nasser had driven Egypt into isolation, that his mistaken policies had won only the support of the now redundant 'foci of power' and of the infamous Ba'th Party of Syria, which was no true representative of its people. Sadat also implied that all that Nasser and the Nasserites had tried and failed to accomplish in the fifteen years of their rule had been achieved in a mere five years of his own regime. In his argument with the leftists of the ASU, who were headed by Khaled Muhyi-a-Din, Sadat was now ready to admit that he had indeed departed from Nasser's socialist ideology. He had done so in order to open up the country which could no longer survive, let alone develop, on her own resources. Nasser was great, admitted Sadat, and had left his mark on everything in Egypt; it was Nasserism that was the subject of interpretation and controversy. On that occasion, Sadat also claimed that he, not Nasser, had been the father of the revolution on the grounds that he had, in the years 1939–42, been the leader of the Free Officers, a post that was taken over by Nasser when he himself was incarcerated in 1942 for his anti-British activities. Having taken a solid grip on the past, Sadat thought that he had established himself as the uncontested patron of Nasser's heritage and as the legitimate successor of his predecessor's grandeur and prestige. He was the only authorized critic of Nasser's faults, and was the leader whose own achievements had come to overshadow Nasser's. He believed that his own record was impressive enough to challenge Nasser's hovering presence. Just as Nasser had made dramatic decisions – the revolution, the internationalization of the Canal – so had Sadat – the 15 May Revolution, the expulsion of the Soviets, the 1973 war, the open-door policy, the reopening of the Canal, and later the peace initiative of 1977.

No wonder that one of the signs of Sadat's growth and disengagement from Nasser's ghost was his constant reminder to his people and to the world of his long series of achievements; his great annual feats were carefully calculated to make a dramatic impact upon the world scene. Nasser had written his 'Philosophy of the Revolution', Sadat could boast the production of the 'October Paper'. Nasser's reign had abounded with dates which symbolized momentous events (July 1952, July 1956, December 1956, May 1962, March 1968, 9–10 June 1967); Sadat had enriched the Egyptian revolutionary calendar with many more dates (15 May 1971, July 1972, 5 June 1975, 6 October 1973, November 1977, September 1978, March 1979). He lived to celebrate the return of most of Sinai which Nasser's reckless policies had lost to Israel, and he made 28 September, the day of Nasser's death, one of the new national days. By delivering the keynote speech on that date, Sadat made sure that he retained control both of the ceremonies and of the 'correct' interpretation of Nasser's heritage. Sadat also kept Nasser's diaries in his custody for the 'sake of history', continued to impose limitations upon the cult of Nasser's memory, and finally relegated his great predecessor to the glass showcase where he could safely pass from 'history in the making' into past history. This allowed Sadat to raise the tone of his own criticism of Nasser's regime and to label it as a 'Godless rule', much to the delight of some Muslim fundamentalists who had been quelled and persecuted under Nasser and were now raising their heads again, taking advantage of Sadat's declared liberalization.

Liberalization and democratization, which from his ascent to power were repeatedly claimed by Sadat as the avowed goals of his domestic policy, should not be taken in their Western sense. Sadat's regime, which cultivated the myth of rule 'by the people', developed over the years into what could be termed a 'limited and controlled democracy'. He had inherited the strictly socialist and monolithic hegemony of the ASU, which he wished to convert gradually, first into a multi-platform system within the same ruling party, and then into a fully-fledged multi-party system. He realized that the democratic game could not be played without an opposition to government; but, on the other hand, he would not consider eroding the almost absolute power of the President. He therefore devised a novel formula: he, as head of state and sovereign authority of the people, stood above and outside the state institutions. So, although opposition was essential to the mechanics of the system, it should be directed against the Government, not against the sovereign. Sadat believed that since he was vested with the authority of the people, who elected him almost unanimously, he knew what was in Egypt's best interest, he could judge between views, political parties and factions, and could praise or discipline them in accordance with their behaviour. His unique place outside and above them also gave him a position of control. He was against allowing democracy in the Western sense, for fear that Egypt might fall back into the chaos which had preceded the revolution. He made it clear that, as the 'head of the family', he would make sure that the various political contenders would use 'common sense'. It was his prerogative to discipline any troublemaker. He said that the US-style election campaign made evident the corruption of democracy, as the parties there squandered public money on their publicity and media broadcasts and looked after their own interests rather than the public's. He suspected that the American system gave various pressure groups the opportunity to help finance the campaign of their candidate and then exercise some influence on policies after their candidates were elected into office. A case in point was, from Sadat's perspective, the 'Zionist Lobby' which exerted a 'horrifying impact' on American politics.

Back in 1971 and 1972, Sadat's rhetoric regarding democracy sounded like a mixture of eighteenth-century European liberalism (man at the centre, the state at the service of man) and the modern welfare state (people's welfare and rights safeguarded by institutional means). But in reality Sadat had neither the need nor the intention of carrying out the 'liberal democracy' that he so often talked about. For even in that early period of his rule, he never considered the 'People's Assembly' as representative of the people, and therefore never viewed it as the reflection of the people's sovereignty. Instead, he saw legislative and executive branches of government as carrying equal weight, recognizing that there should be 'free debate' among them. If there was free debate, then the President, as the head of the family and the direct personification of the people's will, could always arbitrate between Parliament and government. Sadat's submission to the supremacy of the legislative branch would have implied his own subordination to the ostensibly supreme constitutional power of the land. He once explained his reluctance to serve as Prime Minister, except for times of emergency, on the grounds that the Prime Minister was the head of the executive branch, and he wanted to stay above that.

Sadat also spoke at length about the freedom of speech, expression and organization which he regarded as part of the new 'democratic' Egypt he had in mind. He made clear, however, that imposed limitations on freedom were the only way to avert social and political chaos. Every group had the right to organize and express itself, provided that this was done as a recognized part of the state institutions and the state-accepted frames of reference. Otherwise, the separate growth of an organization and an unlicensed liberty to speak its mind might amount to subversion of state authority and illicit opposition to the elected leader. Sadat put his theory about freedom into practice during the student disturbances of January and February 1973, which he labelled as being 'calculated to encroach upon national unity'. He said that there could never be 'absolute rights' and 'absolute freedom', for both would always have to submit to the 'sovereignty of law'. Sadat admitted that every individual was entitled to a passive freedom of thought, but the expression of that thought was strictly limited to what *he* viewed as being 'constructive' and 'conforming to the value of society'. Arguing within the regime and the set rules was acceptable, but questioning the very validity of the system was anathema. By March 1973, Sadat had come to admit that the high hopes he had entertained with regard to the 'state of institutions' and the 'rule by law' had been frustrated by the unrest in his country. He thought that by allowing a measure of freedom he could channel and control 'democratic' energies, but he soon learned that, once restrictions are partly lifted, developments acquire a life of their own and tend to get out of hand.

With the October War behind him, Sadat thought that he could again venture into some institutional reforms. After he had formulated and published his 'October Paper', it became evident that he was interested in watering down the Marxist rhetoric of the ASU ideology and in eroding any real ruling power it possessed. Theoretically, the ASU was to be the supreme organ of power, which embodied the people's sovereignty, provided the ideological underpinning of the regime and directed domestic and foreign policy. In fact, even under Nasser, these functions had been gradually overtaken by the leadership of Egypt and by its fledgling institutions. When Sadat came to power, he left the ASU ostensibly intact but he replaced the leadership and reformed some of its procedures and functions. By placing his man, Sayyid Mar'i, at the helm of the ASU in 1972, he signalled that he would no longer allow it to become an arena of power struggles or permit its encroachment upon state institutions. He made it clear that, as a party machine, the ASU should serve the political establishment, not rule it. Sadat had also determined that the ASU should continue to 'supervise' the media without interfering in their daily affairs, and that it should become an open and universal body, representative of all the 'toiling national forces' of Egypt, not only of the proletariat. In other words, as early as 1972 Sadat was determined to turn from the model of the Eastern Bloc countries, who maintained their doctrinal and political grip on governments, towards a more pluralistic and pragmatic organization which could be moulded according to his own needs.

In August 1974, Sadat published 'The Development of the Arab Socialist Union', in which he widened the basis of his new concept of the ASU. Sadat's own dissatisfaction with the ASU, which could be construed as rivalry, was now, after the October War, coupled with the growing public demand for a less monolithic regime and more freedom of organization and expression. Sadat still insisted that any liberalization ought to emanate from him and he tried to avoid appearing to be giving in under pressure. Therefore, when in October 1974 some journalists demanded more freedom for the press, he scolded them publicly, asserting that he was not opposed to freedom of expression but that he wished the journalists to guide the masses and criticize 'constructively'. He said that he was willing to increase the freedom of the press if the press made sure that it did not become 'an arena for settling old accounts'.

At the end of 1974, Sadat outlined the institutions he wished to see growing in the light of his revised experience. He envisaged the body politic as consisting of four authorities: firstly, a government, headed by a prime minister (he himself had relinquished the post after the war in order to remain above the state authorities); secondly, a legislative council, or Parliament; thirdly, the ASU, which was to provide, in Sadat's words, an 'umbrella for all political activities'; and fourthly the press, to be supervised jointly by the ASU and the employees of each communications medium. The judiciary is noticeably absent from this scheme, for Sadat regarded it as an arm of the executive designed to enforce policy. However, the political party and the media figured in Sadat's blueprint as 'branches' of government, indicating the sort of controlled democracy he had in mind. At the apex of this organization would stand the President. His role was to oversee the entire system in order to ensure a harmonious interaction between the authorities and the preservation of stability and unity. Sadat particularly elaborated in his public addresses upon the role of the press, which he said could not be the private property of any individual or group. At the same time, he vehemently asserted that he would guarantee the freedom of the press and non-interference in its activities. He made no secret, however, of his view that the role of the press in society was to educate and to guide. It had a duty to mould public opinion and to supervise it, and was for that purpose a tool of the government and not an expression of the public mind. Sadat had also envisaged a change within the ASU so as to allow a diversity of political views. He reached the conclusion that the 'majority of the people were basically in favour of the ASU' but, at the same time, he was wary of 'divisions and rifts between various party machineries' at a time when Egypt needed national unity. He therefore promised to allow a multi-party system to develop in the future, but in the meantime all he would yield was limited scope for the expression of different ideas within a single organization. Hence the *manabir* (political platforms, schematically split between Left, Centre and Right) were formed, around which the whole spectrum of political ideas could cluster and yet remain within the framework of the ASU, the only legal political organization. Sadat intended that the Centre would represent the majority, under his own guidance, while the Left and Right wings would be kept politically insignificant. Nevertheless they would illustrate on the one hand the national balance of power within the party, and on the other the democracy-by-opposition that he wished to show to the world as evidence of his 'liberal' intentions. The furthest he went towards democracy was to say, in response to student and inter-communal unrest in early 1975, that instead of smashing store windows, anyone who entertained grievances ought to present them via the People's Council, 'exactly as people in America apply to the congress of the US'.

Sadat was extremely sensitive to foreign criticism of his 'democracy', which, in the light of his bombastic statements, was said to be not quite what the world and his people in Egypt had expected. He went to great lengths to show that the 'model state' he was trying to build in Egypt did not fall short of his own visionary statements and promises. He claimed that, compared to 1971, there was no longer a single political detainee in Egypt and stressed that his opposition to a multi-party system was simply generated by his reluctance to see 'counter-organizations' emerge in the country. He asserted that the one organization which prevailed (the ASU) was able to handle, within its framework, all of Egypt's problems, and therefore any separate grouping must be considered as an anti-organization, namely a subversive and divisive faction which had to be banned and punished 'by law'. He said that he intended the Centre platform in the ASU to represent Egypt, that is the national consensus around him, and to serve as a bridge behind Right and Left. He warned, however, that if anyone went as far as establishing an anti-Egypt, Left or

Right, he would have to consider it as having stepped outside the 'pale of the law'. Sadat was adamant that the democracy he had introduced into Egypt was 'more genuine than anywhere else', in as much as he intended to make, by 1976, membership in the ASU voluntary and individual, without any regard to membership in any other union or association. Even members of the People's Council, insisted Sadat, would be free not to adhere to the ASU if they so chose. He explained his constant wavering between freedom and liberalism on the one hand and restrictions and limitations on the other, in terms of the logic of his duty as a 'responsible patriarchal ruler'. He said that the village had taught him tolerance and generosity, but also that 'only truthful things had the right to exist'.

By mid-1975, Sadat felt that he had achieved the political neutralization of the ASU which he had been seeking since he came to power in 1970. He was satisfied that while the platforms within the party could be seen to be performing the mechanics of democracy in Egypt, their activity remained solidly under his control and patronage. Other partisan organizations, such as the Communists, who did not fit into the ASU pattern, were accused of subversion and factionalism, and prohibited accordingly. Sadat exhorted the students, who had caused unrest in the past, to rally to the ASU as part of the national consensus. He promised the students freedom to express their views, but only so long as that did not interfere with their studies. He suggested that student organizations should draw up, at the beginning of each school year, a full schedule of their planned activities and political debates, so that some representative of the Government might be present at all of them and 'share with the students his information and knowledge'. He said that the state had invested very heavily in the students' education and therefore it had the right to expect that they attend to their studies first. He encouraged the universities, like other professional associations in the land (doctors, lawyers, journalists), to draw up their own rules of ethics so that the rules of the game were clear and known. On the one hand, these unions and institutions could be said to be 'independent', since they were 'free' to devise their own ground rules of behaviour, but on the other, unless these rules were 'right', they could expect none of the state support on which they depended. If they deviated, they risked a government crackdown.

In March 1976, Sadat reshuffled his Government. He took the new ministers to Qantara West, to swear them in. This had been one of the first places to be stormed and taken by the Second Army during the October War, and Sadat wanted his ministry to learn from the 'collective spirit' of the military. He announced that he had transferred much of his authority to his Prime Minister, Mamduh Salem, as a step towards the 'state of institutions' he was so keen to establish, and explained that 'concentration of power is harmful and inhibits full implementation of policies'. He pledged that the platforms within the ASU were only the first step towards a multi-party system. At the same time, however, he warned that one should heed the examples of other countries, notably Portugal, where an abrupt transition from dictatorship to democracy had resulted in national disunity and social chaos. Eventually, said Sadat, he would establish a socialist regime, modelled on Kreisky's Austria, where total freedom was guaranteed within the framework of a strong central government with socialist principles, state controls and a planned economy. He explained that while the Right was conservative and stood for slow progress, the Left advocated rapid and broad changes. He, however, opted for the Centre, which professed progress without 'leaping into the dark'. He likened the ASU to a 'father who has three children', and therefore any Egyptian who adhered to one of the ASU's three platforms would remain a son of the ASU and of Egypt. He emphasized that unless specifically authorized by the ASU secretariat, over which he had full control, none of the platforms could become affiliated with foreign parties or organizations. He insisted that the idea was not to prohibit but to permit; the process of affiliation, however, would be orderly and controlled, so that international movements such as Communism, Socialism or Islamic fundamentalism would not be allowed to subvert the ASU from within. He also laid down that youth and women's organizations as well as the press should remain under the aegis of the ASU. The new experiment was worthwhile, thought Sadat, because he believed that the office of the presidency would act as a 'safety valve' which could regulate the pressures that were bound to emerge from the Right and the Left. If the experiment succeeded, then the way towards a fully-fledged three-party political system would be open.

All the while, however, Sadat continued to remind his people that it was he who had granted the 'October Paper' and the document on the development of the ASU, and that once Parliament completed its legal term in September, he would launch new elections to the three platforms of the ASU which would then make up the new People's Assembly. At the same time, however, he warned against undue competition and divisive debates during the coming election campaign. He made it clear, for example, that if a platform demanded the right to strike 'just because this right is upheld in other countries', he would have to interfere. He explained that strikes existed only in long-established capitalist countries 'whose conditions were different from ours'; in Egypt, he asserted, strikes would be superfluous and wasteful, because 50 per cent of the parliamentary seats were earmarked for peasants and workers, laws prohibited arbitrary lay-offs, and workers participated in the management and the profits of the state-owned public sector of the economy. Under these conditions, which did not prevail in other countries, strikes would be 'criminal' because they would hamper production; they were a 'luxury' that Egypt could ill afford. He declared that 'deviating minorities ought not be allowed to tarnish the reputation of thousands of respectable citizens', a clear warning that democracy could only go so far.

Sadat's obvious pride in the 'democracy' he had brought to his country should be judged against the shortcomings of his predecessors and the failure of pre-revolutionary Egypt to establish a reasonably free democratic polity under parliamentary rule and with a multi-party system. Sadat was obsessed by the fear that Egypt might easily slip back into chaos, and that the noble goals of July 1952 would be lost in the corruption and inefficiency that had made the revolution necessary in the first place. Thus the 'platforms', and any step towards democratization for that matter, would never be more than an experiment unless they were gradually digested by Egyptian society and became an organic part of its being. Therefore, it would be too simplistic to argue that Sadat's 'limited democracy' was no more than a necessary compromise between his own personal power and the pressure for democratization in Egypt. Sadat was indeed an authoritarian, even autocratic, ruler and had a patriarchal view of his country and society. Moreover, like many of his counterparts in the Arab and Third World countries, he was aware of the realities of power politics and of the frequently cruel necessity of oppressing his countrymen to ensure his own survival. However, one should not discount Sadat's belief in his mission to grant his people the liberties that they had never known, and to thrust upon them a democracy that they had never experienced or understood. He wished to leave his mark on Egypt for generations to come, by handing on an iron-clad legacy of institutions which could not be reversed once he departed. He was therefore always one step ahead of his people in vision and rhetoric, but was at the same time groping for a sure way to introduce his changes slowly and to let them seep into the fabric of his society until they became an integral part of it. He was aiming high, but advanced slowly towards his goals, sometimes seemingly zigzagging his way, sometimes retracing his steps, only to set himself back on a solid base and start again.

Two elections claimed Sadat's attention as the year of 1976 drew to its close: he was to conclude his first six-year term in office in October, and at the same time the five-year term of the People's Assembly would be up. It was now a foregone conclusion that the new People's Assembly would be elected along the lines of the three-platform ASU instead of the forty different groups who had applied for permission to establish their own platforms. The election of the President, however, was for a while a less predictable affair. Sadat had on several occasions voiced his craving for peace and tranquillity, and for a return to the privacy that he so cherished but that was denied him by his public obligations. He was particularly looking forward to retirement in a setting that would allow him to write his memoirs. He wanted to go back to Mit Abul-kum and had even begun to build a new house there. It was a good time to retire: the October War was won and a new course was charted for Egyptian domestic policy. On the other hand, the job was far from complete, the temptation to stay in power was overwhelming, and pressure had built up around Sadat to sustain the momentum of his recent political and economic achievements. It is conceivable that had Sadat felt that he was unpopular, or that his policies were a total failure, or that his mission had run its course, the weight of his longing for retirement would have tipped the balance in that direction. But nothing of that sort seemed to be the case: his international reputation was at its highest, he was riding the tide of reform at home and his belief that he was heading in the right direction was unshakeable. The arguments were so finely balanced that it was only 'pressure' exerted by his associates and 'public opinion' that made him decide to remain in power – albeit on his own terms. He thought it would be demeaning for him, at this point in his career, to run for election, let alone struggle for it. He demanded that no other candidates should be allowed to challenge him, and made it clear that he would feel insulted if someone contested his 'right' to continue to rule, or questioned his ability to do so. He urged the various factions to avoid an election campaign for the presidency and to reach a consensus around the candidacy of a single man, who would symbolize the new Egypt and the unity of his people. Sure enough, he was returned by 99 per cent of the votes, compared with the 'mere' 90 per cent he got six years earlier when he was still relatively unknown. Similarly, the parliamentary elections were swept by a landslide of Sadat's central platform candidates, who won over 330 of the 350-seat assembly while the Right and the Left obtained only fourteen and two seats respectively. Emboldened by his double success, Sadat announced in November 1976 his decision to turn the platforms into fully-fledged political parties. He had obviously calculated that it would make no substantial difference if, once elected, the minority platforms were dubbed 'parties', while on the public relations level he could claim that he had attained a 'fully democratic' regime with the institution of a formal political opposition in his Parliament. This change, which Sadat had not dared to introduce before the elections, for fear that the minority parties might multiply and carve themselves a large slice of the political pie, was also announced as a 'presidential decision', implying that it could be retracted if circumstances so warranted. It was not until June 1977 that a new law was adopted in the Assembly, regulating the structure of the three-party system, which followed in many details the limitations that Sadat had imposed on the three platforms on the eve of the 1976 elections.

In one of his speeches in early 1974, Sadat likened the reconstruction of Egypt to erecting a building. He said:

> After we have completed the foundations and got to the second and third floors, we can then allow our door to remain wide open to argument and we can debate with whoever so desires, the shape of our balconies. We can let in more sunshine and air, we shall listen to alternative suggestions as to the form of our windows, as to whether or not we should preserve the Egyptian style, etc. . . . After twenty years of self-imposed isolation, we cannot expect our administrative machinery to respond instantly to the openness we are striving for, we cannot avoid some confusion and

mistakes. However, the state machinery is bound to respond to the requirements of the new era. We shall review our legislation item by item and correct the defects that we have detected. There are national councils in operation which have begun to harness local talent for our benefit in this new era. We have also started to adopt foreign scientific institutions. For example, in our Port Said projects, there are four institutions participating in the planning of the free zone. We are also drawing from the many talents that exist in our midst as well as from the large technological know-how to be found in the world. We are determined to launch ourselves from the springboard of the 1970s, not the 1950s.

This was the essence of the grand plan of *infitah* (open door) that Sadat announced after the October War and elaborated upon in his 'October Paper'. Sadat's stated goal was to return to the rapid annual rates of economic development which had been achieved in 1965 and even to surpass them. He stated that economic development was a question of life or death for Egypt, for upon economic growth depended the beginnings of the solution of the other staggering socio-economic problems which plagued the country: poverty, illiteracy, demographic explosion, unemployment, scarcity and inadequacy of housing, the horrifying growth of Cairo and the pathetic backwardness of the countryside. The need for economic recovery, which was an end in itself now that the 'October victory' had restored Sadat's ability to function domestically, had been coupled with the rising expectations of the masses who hoped that the economy would be advanced to top priority on the national agenda, as indeed Sadat had promised it would. But where was he to begin? Sadat himself knew nothing about economics and had to rely on his technocrats and economists, but he bore the political responsibility and sensed that, unless he effected a rapid economic recovery, something that would be obvious to the Egyptian public at large, his very political future would be in doubt. He began with a series of small steps designed to prepare the ground for the development of an infrastructure that could exploit the investments he was hoping to attract to Egypt. For investments meant industrialization and new jobs, and that was the only hope for Egypt's future.

In 1974 it became legal for Egyptians to act as agents for foreign companies. Law 43, adopted in June of that year, provided that any new enterprise, even if totally foreign-owned, was entitled to a five-year tax exemption period. Sadat and his advisers were confident that the influx of foreign capital, if encouraged by local legislation, would bring about the expansion of the private sector, create jobs and widen the base of Egypt's economy. Sadat thought that his accompanying removal of the emergency rules and his steps to enhance democratic liberties would also create a positive ambience for free enterprise and would encourage an entrepreneurial attitude among Egyptian business-men. 'Free zones' for industrial development and international investment were devised along the Suez Canal, where foreign employers would pay no taxes and be exempt from the mandatory 25 per cent profit-sharing requirements that Egyptian concerns were subject to. Foreign currency exchanges were to be free and unlimited in these zones. Egyptian labour laws were eased with regard to such privileged areas and guarantees were issued against nationalization of foreign business.

Once Sadat had decided to relieve himself of the duties of Prime Minister, following the first disengagement of forces in 1974, he appointed Higazi, a technocrat, to fill the post and to take charge of the economic programme. When it transpired that Higazi was too weak and indecisive, Sadat appointed Mamduh Salem, his trusted Minister of the Interior, to replace him and to oversee the new economic breakthrough. However, much to Sadat's displeasure, things just did not seem to be moving rapidly enough. For one thing, a new elite of *munfatihun* (those who directly benefited from the *infitah*) emerged and took advantage of the liberalized economic policies and of the lax government controls to import luxury consumer goods instead of investing in the infrastructure and in production. In the process they amassed great personal fortunes and indulged in a high level of exhibitionist consumerism. This only widened the gap between the extremely privileged, who constituted a small minority, and the abysmally deprived who were, and still are, the vast majority.

Sadat attracted much personal criticism from the opposition for his open-door policy and all the apparent economic, social and moral ills it had generated. Dissent increased after Sadat's assassination in 1981, culminating in a campaign to discredit the entire concept of *infitah* in the *Al-Ahaly* daily, the mouthpiece of the opposition National Progressive Union Party. The editions issued on 9 and 11 August 1982 called for the complete abandonment of the open-door policy as a solution to Egypt's economic malaise. Former ministers of Sadat's own Government have also joined the chorus of criticism of his policy, which is now widely held to have been disastrous for Egyptian development. However, while Sadat's economic policy was, at best, marking time, and at worst wreaking havoc on the ill-prepared Egyptian infrastructure, he himself felt able, as early as late 1974, to argue that it was both 'successful' and 'miraculous'. He frequently claimed that his 'economic miracle' had given each individual the main necessities of life in food, clothing, housing and public services. Whether Sadat was out of touch with reality, or being poorly advised and informed by his technocrats, is hard to judge. In any case, when workers and the 'lumpen-proletariat' took to the streets in January 1975 to tell the President that the promised miracle had not happened, he could no longer turn his back on reality. He was deeply disturbed, not only by the violence that accompanied the immense manifestation of discontent (huge marching crowds, smashed commuter trains), but also by the telling sarcasm that was directed against him by the demonstrators. Many embarrassing slogans were coined during these demonstrations, taunting and ridiculing Sadat, the 'hero of the crossing', for the scarcity of basic food supplies and for the heavy-handedness of state rule. In fact, one of the chants which jerked Sadat out of his 'October euphoria' was '*Ya-batal al-ubur, feen el-futúr?*' ('O, hero of the crossing, where is our breakfast?') The bitterness and the rhetorical power of the rhyme brought the message home to Sadat more directly than any of the long-winded reports of his ministers. He had never liked having to study detailed memoranda and charts. He was not a meticulous worker, he simply envisaged a goal and wished it to come true instantly; the 'details' he left for the cabinet to work out. But as he sat impatiently on the sidelines, waiting for results, or dreaming up the next 'miracle', he lost contact with the reality of the domestic position. His forays into world politics and into the international limelight, where he felt he was accorded more respect and recognition, only divorced him further from the internal situation.

Sadat could not simply take the blame for the upheaval and change course. He regarded the demonstrations as a vile and derogatory campaign aimed at him in person, which indeed they were. Fearing the loss of his heroic image, which he was eager to maintain, he decided to act. However, instead of tackling the issues which had created the unrest in the first place, Sadat organized a violent campaign against the Communists and the 'leftist adventurers' for wantonly inciting the masses against him and his Government. Only one major newspaper, *Rooz al-Youssef*, urged Sadat to face the problems honestly instead of seeking scapegoats. The other media obediently carried out the anti-Communist campaign. However, in March 1975, there was more trouble: 40,000 textile workers in Mahalla al-Kubra went on strike; clashes with the police resulted in some casualties and several arrests. Sadat's answer was again an 'implied responsibilty reaction': he removed Prime Minister Higazi from office in April and appointed Mamduh Salem in his stead. Salem had once been chief of police and was renowned for his iron-fisted methods of law enforcement. The Mahalla riots, however, had disclosed to the public yet another hidden aspect of the *infitah* 'miracle': the easy profiteering achieved by a small group of managers and bureaucrats at the expense of the populace. Some demonstrators, armed with clubs and rocks, stormed the houses of their bosses and seized expensive imported goods, foodstuffs and liquor which, according to some crowd leaders, showed 'how those thieves lived while the people went hungry'.

March 1975 also saw the failure of Kissinger's first attempt to achieve the second disengagement between Egypt and Israel. Thus, Sadat urgently needed to make some dramatic move to distract attention from the embarrassing riots which were damaging his reputation. He went to Salzburg to meet President Ford, reopened the Suez Canal amid great pomp and embarked on the next round of the second disengagement talks which bore their fruit in August. When the agreement was signed with Israel on 1 September 1975, Sadat could at least claim to have retrieved parts of Sinai, including some oil-producing wells from the Israelis along with some international prestige for Egypt.

Thanks to these achievements, which were widely praised by the media in Egypt, Sadat could buy a breathing space for himself and make new pledges for economic recovery now that the conflict with Israel seemed to be coming to an end. No one remembered or reminded the public that Sadat had vowed never to reopen the Canal unless Israel withdrew completely from the Sinai. The economic benefits of Israel's withdrawal from the Sinai (the oil wells) and of reopening the Canal (passage fees) seemed promising enough to allow the people to entertain new hopes that Sadat might well be able to deliver on his hitherto unfulfilled promises.

Shaken by the 1975 disturbances, Sadat devoted much of 1976 to the economy. Not that he showed any more inclination than before to ponder upon the everyday details of economic recovery, but he was willing, indeed eager, to undertake the more glamorous task of fund-raising on a grand scale, and he felt compelled to explain to the angry crowds what had gone wrong. He negotiated and obtained a vast American aid programme, totalling $1 billion in outright grants and food surplus supplies. In February, during his sweep through the oil-rich Gulf States, he succeeded in eliciting pledges for another $10 billion in aid. The American contribution was intended for the short term, in order to appease the hungry crowds in the streets of Cairo, while the Gulf States' grants, which ultimately dwindled to $2 billion over the next five years, were primarily earmarked for rebuilding the Canal cities, for new housing development and for long-term investment in the economic infrastructure. But the Egyptians were exhausted: they had expected economic improvement only to suffer continued deterioration. They had heard promises which had never been fulfilled. Their Government was expending much time and effort, working patiently to bring about the economic boom, but the crowds wanted results immediately and viewed the Government's 'much ado' with scepticism, believing that it had ended in nothing. The economic problems spread as impoverished small-town and rural populations flocked to the chaotic environment of overburdened Cairo. This caused growing discontent among the urban masses, which coupled with the unrest among students and university graduates, whose employment prospects looked bleak, increased hatred for the drive for modernization which was producing little relief. Against this background, the teachings of the Muslim fundamentalists spread rapidly. These movements, which stressed individual morality as well as social justice, regarded secular rule and modernization as having corrupted the Islamic principles which alone could restore Islam to its old glory and bring economic well-being to the down-trodden masses. The fundamentalist Repentance and Hijra group struck in 1976, kidnapping the Minister of *Awqāf* (religious endowments) in Egypt. This venerated sheikh from the state-controlled Islamic establishment of the country was a symbol of corruption in the eyes of the Muslim fundamentalists. His abductors demanded that the Government declare in public that Egypt had not in the past been governed by

Islamic principles and pledge that in future it would be. When Sadat stalled, the Minister was executed, an ominous portent of what was to come.

Sadat was re-elected in October 1976 against a backdrop of continuing unrest, both political and socio-economic. There was increasing demand from various quarters for more freedom of organization and expression, and strikers continued to riot in the streets. In November, left-wing students demonstrated in Cairo against the political system. Sadat again responded by appointing a respected liberal-economist, Qaisuni, to head the economic recovery programme, hoping to stem the tide of discontent. Mamduh Salem, the blood-and-iron Prime Minister, would continue to quell the unrest and attempt to re-establish order, the precondition of any economic breakthrough; whilst, it was hoped, the bourgeois-minded Qaisuni, favouring the free market, would capitalize on the new stability to effect the much-needed breakthrough. Sadat felt he had to appear before the people and defend in person what he had been doing. In a series of speeches he explained that the economic malaise and the price rises were attributable to the high inflation rate in the world which was affecting Egypt directly, because she had to import her foodstuffs and raw materials. He emphasized that, as the 'father of the family', he had to take into account all the needs of its members and spend his income with an eye to the future. It was for this reason, he claimed, that he had elected to continue to carry the heavy burden of subsidies on basic staple foods. These subsidies would alleviate the distress of the populace, even if they did so at the expense of long-term investment. On the other hand, he exhorted his people to show patience until the long-term results of his policy could take effect. He reinforced his case by pointing out that, of the twenty-two cents that each loaf of bread cost the Government, the consumers paid only five while the rest was underwritten by the state. Sadat said that at a time when many thousands of Egyptians were waiting for the Government to rebuild the Canal cities in order to restore their destroyed homes and businesses, the demands were daunting and income was limited; therefore, there was no escape from ordering priorities as he, the head of the family, saw fit. He warned that the 1970s would be difficult, for those were to be the years of heavy investment in order to create employment. The 1980s, however, would mark an upturn in Egypt's economy, as the construction of new plans would be advanced, the oil fields in the Sinai would begin to function, and the broadened Suez Canal would bring in users' fees. He also announced the rise of the minimum wage from $18 to $24 monthly and the widening of the brackets of tax exemption so as to relieve anyone who earned less than $60 a month from the burden of income tax. Pensions would be increased, public services would be overhauled with major financial injections, bank loans would be extended and emergency relief was promised to the needy. Some of these pledges were met, but they did little to comfort the masses or to meet their rising expectations. What was worse, the new mood of conspicuous consumption among the privileged few only exacerbated jealousies, competition and a general feeling of hopelessness amidst the underprivileged many. What good does it do to a wretched city-worker to receive a 25 per cent rise in his salary (assuming he has a job) and a promise of a 'decent' retirement pension (about half the minimum wage), if he cannot be sure that there will be even basic foodstuffs in the shops for his family tomorrow?

Sadat tried to plead for understanding from his deprived nation. He explained that income could not be increased beyond the rate of productivity growth, because that would necessitate 'giving with one hand and snatching the same money back in taxes with the other', a 'fraudulent procedure' that he was reluctant to adopt. He assured his people that if they worked harder and produced more, they would live to see the major economic changes he knew were in store for them. He claimed that he faced two alternatives: either to spend the scarce resources to buy more basic foodstuffs, 'which would please us for a moment and then disappear, leaving behind them a burden of debt'; or use a large proportion of these resources to import spare parts for machinery, raw materials, primary goods and agricultural implements, fertilizer and insecticides, all of which would contribute to self-sufficiency in the production of textiles, meat, sugar and other basic products. He said that he chose to follow the second alternative, despite all the short-term difficulties. To the fundamentalists, who questioned the Islamic base of his rule, he repeated the slogan of 'Science and Faith' which he said was the foundation of his modernization programme. He argued that while science was the *sine qua non* without which Egypt could not emerge into the modern era and build a society based on prosperity and justice, faith was the source of power and the driving force behind his people's endeavour to attain entrance into the modern world. He went on to assert that his faith was a 'belief in Allah, in his Holy Book and his Messenger; a faith in the right, in justice, in peace and well-being; a faith in forgiveness, which drives people to build, not to destroy, to unite, not to dismember; a faith that hoists the flag of serenity and love, not of evil'. He explained that he carried the banner of faith in order to educate Egypt's young people in the way of truth; at the same time he warned against any abuse or deviation from this faith, 'which might destroy its essence, dim its light and distort its beauty'. Referring to the abortive *coup* against him at the Military Technical College, he said that 'that frivolous attempt only serves to illustrate the possible danger of confusion inherent in deviating from the essence of religion and from the realities of its relation to life'. He commended the '*Ulama* (the doctors of the Holy Law of Islam, who were the tame element in the priestly establishment), for their 'burden of responsibility, their part in the network of religious teaching in the country and their endeavour to enlighten our youth and to stimulate them with supreme human values'. In an oblique reference to the young officers who plotted against him and to other fundamentalists who were creating trouble, he recognized that 'abnormal phenomena occur in every society where certain sub-human strata exist which need treatment more than they do punishment'. He warned that 'those who teach false religion to our youth' would be exposed, isolated and prosecuted whenever 'they voiced their twisted slogans'.

In previous years, Sadat had spoken of the terrible burden of military expenditure. This had totalled $10 billion in the years 1967–73, over and above which Egypt was losing a matching figure in damages, and in income withheld, because of the Israeli occupation of Sinai. He claimed that military spending had lowered the rate of economic growth in Egypt from 6.7 per cent during the years 1956–65 to 5 per cent annually thereafter. He said that damage and destruction to the Canal cities alone amounted to some $5 billion. Therefore his interim settlements with Israel, which were attracting criticism from other Arabs and from some opposition leaders, could be explained by implication as a desire on his part to scale down the conflict in order to divert resources to internal economic development. Moreover, the Sinai oil fields and the reopened Suez Canal, both achievements of these interim arrangements, could now be harnessed to the task of reconstruction. On the other hand, Sadat repeatedly insisted that military expenditure had been necessary in the past in order to prepare for October, which in turn had born economic fruits for Egypt. He argued that the massive rise in the price of oil which had followed the October War had allowed Arab oil-producing countries to accumulate financial resources, part of which they were now intending to invest in Egypt. Sadat could thus claim that both his economic and military strategies had shown great sophistication, foresight, and long-term thinking: because of the war, Egypt now stood to gain economically, and because of his economic foresight the war could be justified, even if the other gains of that war had never been made. Sadat also believed that heavy economic investment by the Arabs in Egypt would further strengthen his grip on the leadership of the Arab world, because of the interwoven interests that would be built up between him and the investors. Moreover, the strong military presence his country would be able to sustain, once economic growth provided the funds for higher levels of military expenditure, would further enhance his international position. Sadat was convinced, especially before the 1975 rift with Syria and the PLO, that inter-Arab economic co-operation, which effectively meant grants by the rich to Egypt and other poor Arab countries, would ultimately provide firm foundations for the growing political and military strength of the Arab world.

Once Sadat had accepted American economic aid and adopted the 'capitalist' road of the open-door policy he had to face accusations of 'selling out' to the US. He retorted that although there were now great opportunities in Egypt for private entrepreneurs, the public sector, in which all Egyptians had a share, would remain the dominant factor in the economy for years to come. He asserted that he was taking advantage of 'prevailing conditions in the world' to obtain resources, which might not be available tomorrow, to strengthen Egypt's economy. Sadat also protested that he only accepted foreign capital, whether grants or loans, provided there were no strings attached. He said that Egypt badly needed the high standards of technology of the West, and that it ought to adopt them 'without fears or complexes'. He justified his open-door policy on the grounds that it was not directed exclusively towards the West; in fact, he said, his country was open to anyone and everyone, to 'the whole world' in his words. Moreover, he said that it was in his interest to diversify his international economic relations, because it was the only way he could ensure his freedom to manœuvre politically. To balance the coming revolution in the Egyptian economy, Sadat also announced the 'necessity to revolutionize methods of education and culture at all levels, beginning with the eradication of illiteracy, and the promotion of high standards of academic education and of scientific and technological research'. He said that Egypt must 'free herself from the strait-jacket of uniform and centralized educational curriculi and adapt different levels of education to suit their varying environmental conditions'. He also thought it was necessary to stress long-term educational programmes, drawing from experience available the world over. Egypt's libraries would be renewed, innovative educational programmes launched, and special attention given to scientific and techno-logical training. He hoped that the establishment of new scientific centres would help adapt imported technology to Egyptian needs, with a view to providing 'daring solutions to our problems, just as our armed forces adapted new weapon systems and new fighting methods to the special requirements of our battle'. Sadat thought that there was no reason for the Arabs to feel inferior *vis-à-vis* the West, even though they were now in need of its technology. He reminded the nation that until the seventeenth century it was Europe who learnt from the Arabs, proving that the Arabs were creative if afforded the proper opportunities.

Social development in the fields of education, culture, creativity, health, housing, the emancipation of women and the cultivation of youth seemed unattainable in the over-crowded cities which, rather than allowing human growth according to Sadat's vision, made for deterioration and despair. The cities of the Delta area and of the narrow strip of the Nile Valley were over-populated, while the vast expanses of the western and eastern deserts were empty and awaiting development. Sadat thought that the confinement of thirty-five million Egyptians to 3 per cent of Egyptian territory could only increase the impoverishment of the population and held no prospect for accommodating them in satisfactory living conditions. The situation was worst of all in the capital city, Cairo, where between one fifth and one quarter of all Egyptians found shelter, and which continued to grow to a monstrously out-of-hand metropolis as thousands more flocked in from the countryside. Many of them camped in cemeteries and made tombstones into tables and beds. Necropolis (the city of the dead, where the living dwelt) stood as a reminder that the rate of urbanization could no longer be contained. When questioned by this author about living among tombs, one of those unfortunate yet good-humoured Upper Egyptian villagers, now turned urban, said, 'Blessed by Allah, we lack nothing.' From the bottom of his pit he could see one little patch of blue sky and he thought that was the entire universe. He had no ambition except for a daily loaf of bread and he accepted what Allah had ordained for him without protest. He made the comment that he had simply 'got to the cemetery slightly before all the rest, but everyone would end up there anyway'. But this attitude of resignation changed where the slums were penetrated by Muslim fundamentalists or leftist opposition militants, who thought that the wretched of the earth had nothing to lose by opposing the regime, and who introduced a new element of hope for a better life if the present regime could be wiped out. Sadat became acutely aware of this during the street riots in the capital, and therefore regarded the building of new cities away from the congested population belt as a matter of the highest priority. The aim was not merely to ease the human misery of the slums, but also to eliminate the potential nests of revolution which were being set up in these extremely deprived areas. Sadat hoped that the new areas of settlement would be modern and accommodating enough to attract large numbers of citizens, who would then be offered a productive and stable life, public services and jobs. The Canal Zone, the Red Sea strip and the Nasser Lake in the south seemed likely areas for such development. Sadat vowed that together with the redistribution of the population, he would reorganize the administration of the country by redefining the borders of provinces, with the aim of turning them into larger units of settlement, and economic and administrative activity. Anything that could be done locally, said Sadat, ought to be delegated to the provinces.

Elimination of *hiqd* (rancour) was one of Sadat's major themes in his post-war domestic policy. For him, political struggles, the challenge posed to his authority, economic criticism, street rioting and even sarcastic jokes about him or his regime were all symptoms of rancour. He had envisaged an Egypt under his own aegis, based on national unity, where everybody knew his place and held the 'father of the family' in respect. He viewed disregard for these rules not as dissent, disagreement, competition or debate, but as rancour among the members of the Egyptian family, occasioned by jealousy, pettiness, bickering and other unworthy clashes between personalities. Hence his repeated appeals to Egyptians to look beyond their individual pursuits, forget their personal quarrels and strive for the common goal of Egypt. He said that opposing ideas could be settled from within if dialogue within the political organization were pursued so as to allow the 'trends representative of the broad popular base to emerge'. He stressed that rather than the Egyptians perpetuating the trivial conflicts of yesteryear, they should all face the struggles of the future, of construction and progress. He set the 'Year 2000' as the national challenge for development and initiated a series of symposia and intellectual gatherings to discuss and plan for the quarter-century ahead, all in the 'spirit of Ramadan', that is of the October War. By focusing on the period from October 1973 onwards, he signalled to his people that the new era, which he had ushered in, would become a new golden age in Egypt's fortunes. Fearing that his people would look back in anger, he endeavoured to make them face the future with hope.

In an address to a delegation from the American Congress which visited Egypt in August 1975, Sadat for the first time publicly linked the vision of economic development in Egypt with the necessity for peace, although his ideas about how such a settlement would work remained vague and ill-defined. He made it plain that he saw no point in rebuilding his country as long as a new threat of war might jeopardize the entire effort of reconstruction; therefore, he longed for peace. He acknowledged, at the same time, that the process would be long, due to the 'old differences which separate us from Israel'. He said that after peace set in 'everything would be easy', because all the unexploited resources of the country would then be harnessed to the cause of economic advancement. It is likely that it was in 1975, around the time the second disengagement with Israel was signed, and criticism at home was mounting, that Sadat began to reflect seriously on a fundamental change of course which would extricate his country from economic disaster. It was also around that time that Sadat came to realize that, in order to control the future, he had to take a firm hold of both past and present. He established a History Commission, headed by his deputy, Husni Mubarak, and entrusted it with investigating modern Egyptian history since the 1919 Revolution, with a sub-committee detailed to look into the defeat of June 1967, and another into the origins of the 1919 Revolution. In many of his speeches and press interviews, Sadat gave a preview of the major issues that he wished to be tackled and brought to an acceptable conclusion by the commission. For example, he discussed the comparisons which were made by some opposition elements between his rule and the old capitalist Egypt of the pre-revolutionary period, where *laissez-faire* was carried to its extreme without much government say. He protested that this was not the case and that he personally set the pace of the new policy:

All *I* am granting to the open door today are safeguards. *I* shall not confiscate foreign investments. The investors would be able to take their money out, after *I* had received half of it. But if they want to take out part of their half, they are free to do so. To *my* mind, the complexes relating to foreigners and foreign occupation are, since 1952, no longer valid. The foreigners now come to work for *me* and bring *me* technology. As long as they work effectively, all is well; otherwise, *I* shall repay them their money and show them the way out. Before the revolution the British were here and capitalism meddled in everything. Our government obeyed the orders of capitalism, of the king and of the British. Today, who can give *me* orders? Allah forbid! . . . So, the open door is simply a transfusion of new blood which will help us back to our feet.[36]

Sadat also wanted it on record that he had not acquiesced in the corruption and easy money that had allegedly been rampant in Egypt under the shield of his open-door policy. He said that he had no objection to anyone making money; however, taxes must be duly levied on all gains. He directed his Prime Minister to make an announcement to this effect, and he himself declared that he would collect the full amount of taxes due and use it to create a package of social security for the handicapped, the aged, the sick and the families of the deceased. He explained that having himself come from the countryside he had always understood that the values of the village, and the noble human virtues which existed amidst the misery there, had always prevailed over the transient material amenities of the big cities. He said that Egypt's hope lay with the *fellah* in the village, not with the rich of the city. He recalled that while going to school in Cairo he had always been confident that he was superior to the rich who had cars. At that time, he contended, the rich got richer and the poor poorer, while under his own rule the state 'controlled everything' and would not allow such disparities to develop. He asserted that *he* afforded everyone in Egypt the opportunity to make as much money as they wanted or could, but only so long as they met their obligations to the state. He said that this new system was an improvement upon the one which had prevailed under his predecessor, where 'everyone waited for one's salary, queued up for promotion, and had no other opportunity to build one's life'. He said that this was what his open-door policy was all about. He felt confident that he had freed himself from the old xenophobia and that he was no longer afraid of foreign or imperialist domination. He also assured the Egyptian public that although he was encouraging the private sector, the public sector would remain, under state control and ownership, the backbone of the economy. In his words, 'I want the private sector to grow and match the assets of the public sector, for when the former has risen to $7 billion the latter will have leaped to $100 billion.'

Sadat also refuted charges made against Nasser and his policies by the other extreme of the political spectrum in Egypt. Sadat must have reckoned that an uncontrolled anti-Nasserite campaign would not only arouse emotions among those who valued Nasser's legacy, but might get out of hand and hamper the attempts made by the History Commission to assign, under Sadat's guidance, a proper place in history to each one of his major predecessors since 1919. First, in response to persistent rumours spread in early 1976, which cast doubt on Nasser's personal integrity, Sadat set out to defend him by assuring the people that 'Nasser had never embezzled public money', and he got the Prosecutor General to back these assurances. Secondly, he vehemently refuted allegations from various quarters that the Aswan Dam, Nasser's showpiece of the 1960s, had become a liability for Egypt. The dam's critics were producing all manner of statistics to prove that the environmental side-effects of the dam were detrimental to Egypt's agriculture and well-being. Sadat, without being himself an expert in the field, nevertheless sang the praise of the dam as one of the 'most glorious battles, both political and economic' that modern Egypt had ever waged. He invited the critics to go and see for themselves the old dam, 'a simple wall, supported by some pillars and a 180-metre pool of water behind it'. The slightest explosion, he said, could cause the water to burst out, flood the countryside and leave Egypt starving. He asserted that the new dam was 'like a mountain' by comparison, one which could even resist nuclear bombs. The base of the dam was built of huge rocks, laid in the Nile river-bed, and its top was as wide as a city street. He said that, back in 1913, the old dam had not been strong enough to ward off the huge floods which had cost the lives of many, and that in 1972 similar floods could have wreaked havoc on Egypt's population and agricultural land had it not been for the new dam. He also enumerated the huge quantities of hydro-electric power and the annual three-crop yield, afforded by regulated irrigation from the new dam's water system, to justify the project which had been undertaken with massive Soviet aid. He asserted that the critics of the dam were simply jealous, frustrated or angry, and took advantage of the political freedom that he had instituted in Egypt to lash out. Sadat contended that the side-effects had been known even before the dam was erected, and the disaster that was averted in 1972 alone paid for the cost of the project many times over.

On the other hand, Sadat began to admit that 'many things had been done incorrectly', and he rationalized that 'no human being was infallible, and I am a human being'. He recognized that his economic and social policies were 'faulty at times and did not produce the desired results', but he attributed that to the heavy burden of debt to the Soviet Union, and to the red tape in Egypt itself which hampered his decisions for reform. He said that his new laws, which 'were designed to shatter the iron curtain that we had erected around us in the past', had produced results in the upper levels of government, but the lower echelons of the bureaucracy had remained impregnable to change. He admitted that Egypt was not 'good enough yet' and that he could no longer assure his people that 'within a year the whole matter will be mended'. He said that more time was required to restore Egypt's blood to full strength, and only then would she be able to provide the 'best opportunities for investors'. Sadat blamed the price rises in consumer commodities on the world markets for the creation of the huge deficits in Egypt's budgets, as he was reluctant to eliminate or cut the state subsidies for imported basic consumer foods. Cheap imported foods encouraged consumption and forced Egypt to dip into her hard currency reserves or take more loans to finance the imports. Hence the difficulty in the balance of payments. He said that because of this series of economic mishaps, he had to revamp the economy and adopt a new five-year plan that would keep Egypt afloat until income from current investments, from the Suez Canal and from the oil wells, allowed him to reverse the present trend. In March 1976, he dramatically revealed that he had been kept in the dark as to the real economic situation until Mamduh Salem became Prime Minister in 1975. Sadat gave an example of the 'misinformation' of which he was the victim. He said that he had been told that Egypt's deficit was $4 billion a year and he thought that an amount such as this could be covered by foreign loans and grants from abroad and by the domestic economic progress that he was assured was being made. But then it turned out that the deficit was £4 billion, *i.e.* two and a half times the amount he was told, according to the exchange rate of 1975. Such a gap had seemed insurmountable; it was only because Saudi Arabia and Kuwait had sent emergency aid of $500 million each that he had made it through that year. In other words, Sadat admitted that all through the euphoric years of 1973–5, whilst he was indulging in his dreams of a quick recovery, he had been unaware of the near-disastrous plunge the economy had taken.

Exasperated by local incompetence and frustrated by his inability to realize his much-vaunted 'economic crossing', Sadat called in foreign experts to examine the situation, to authenticate the disastrous forecasts of his own experts and to recommend a way out. He suddenly realized that 'since 1962 we have been papering over our problems and drawing up ambitious plans that could not be implemented'. He also said that before the 1973 war he had not been able to ask for 'one single dollar from any Arab', although Egypt's economy 'had reached the zero level', because Egypt's credibility with regard to her struggle with Israel was at an all-time low. He said that if he had asked for help then, in the state of despair and defeatism that had prevailed in the Arab world, he would have been told that he had already received enough assistance for the weapons he had, which he had made no use of anyway. He explained that Egypt's economy in 1973 was comparable to a person who 'looked healthy, but had actually no blood in his veins and needed a transfusion to function again, lest he became paralysed and died'. Now he came to the conclusion, with the foreign experts' help, that 'my economy has not collapsed, but is only undergoing a very serious crisis, which can be remedied by a five-year plan'. Sadat bluntly admitted that the plan in question would have to be devised in co-operation with foreign experts, because 'only then could I be sure that the right policy would be followed'. Encouraged by his foreign advisers, Sadat set out for his fund-raising trip to the Arab Gulf States in 1976. Pledges worth billions of dollars were made to Sadat by the Arab oil-producing countries and he gained fresh confidence in the future, a confidence that was tempered by his new realistic view of his country's economy, and by his realization that ultimately it was *he* who was responsible, not the economists and the technocrats that he had counted on in the past. He warned his people that the newly-raised Arab money would not increase the flow of cash within his country, so they should not build up new hopes. On the contrary, he said that he had ordered his trusted Prime Minister, Mamduh

Salem, to inaugurate an era of austerity for the coming five years until the new plan bore fruit. In other words, the abundance and prosperity were now put off for a decade, from the 1970s to the 1980s. He warned his nation, and all Arabs for that matter, that unless development prevailed in his country and in the Arab world in general, the Arabs would again isolate themselves and lag behind. And if the Arabs were doomed to backwardness, they would end up 'like the Indians of America; we would lose our lands and houses and Israel would treat us the way America treats its Indians'. This was a far cry from the boasting optimism on the morrow of the October War, when every goal – economic, political and military – seemed attainable and Israel was deemed to be in decline.

Sadat's mood of pessimism also brought him to accept the debilitated state of the capital city of Cairo, which he had dreamt, in the euphoria of 1974, of making beautiful, and in which he had pledged to erect the infrastructure necessary for foreign investment and for the multi-national corporations that he believed would flock to his country. Now it seemed to him that there was a process almost of 'Indianization' of Egyptian cities, for Cairo and Alexandria were looking more and more like Bombay and Calcutta. He understood that in an impoverished country like Egypt, where 1.2 million were born every year, population growth meant the constant provision of new housing, education, health services and job opportunities which threw a heavy burden on the state. Under these conditions, Egypt's resources were not sufficient even to keep the country afloat. The destitute masses who streamed to Cairo, a city planned for two million and now having to support eight or ten million, added to this impossibly burdensome situation. The sewer system, the water supply, the roads, public transport, electricity and telephone exchange were all crumbling under the weight of the uncontrollable masses who were suffocating Cairo's services to death. There was simply no way that these shortcomings, which had accumulated over the years, could be resolved in the foreseeable future. In this context, one can understand why Sadat had given serious thought in 1976, before his re-election, to retiring to the serenity of Mit Abul-kum. On the other hand, if he did not try to rescue Egypt and relaunch her on the right course, he might be judged by history as having run away from the call of duty. Had he quit, his October glory might have been forgotten and his economic failures remembered. Instead, he chose to fight back. In blood-and-sweat speeches reminiscent of the pre-1973 years, he exhorted his nation to adopt austerity as a way of life and to ignore local and foreign agitators, notably Qadhafi of Libya, who were exploiting the situation by clamouring that 'Egypt under Sadat was starving' and therefore that it was necessary to get rid of her ruler. He admitted that the economic situation was difficult, but Egyptians counted too much on the Government for their supplies, instead of taking the initiative and raising chickens, vegetables and other staple foods that they needed themselves. He recognized that it was a 'great shame' for Egypt, the most ancient agricultural civilization on earth, to be dependent on imports for its food supply, and urged the Egyptians to follow the model of post-war Germany, which rose from the ashes of the Second World War to become one of the richest nations on earth, all thanks to its own citizenry and private initiative, not to its Government. He said that when the Marshall Plan came to Germany, all Germans devoted themselves to intensive activity until their country had recovered. They had done it through the revival of their agricultural system and through an open-door policy, exactly the same projects that he was himself pursuing.

As part of his open-door policy, Sadat invited foreign banks to establish their branches in Cairo and to help finance Egypt's economic plans. In response to a current complaint among the leftist opposition that Sadat was going 'capitalist' and totally abandoning Socialism, he explained that he had indeed brought the foreign banks to Egypt, but they did not enjoy the privileged position of foreign banks in Egypt before the 1952 Revolution. Sadat submitted that under the socialist regime of his predecessor only the Bank of Egypt had been allowed to operate, while all the others, which had held government deposits and were trying to influence the Egyptian economy in their own interests, had been nationalized. Sadat said that, like so many other aspects of Egypt's economic life, banking had also come under governmental control and this was a mistake. Again, the example of Germany after the Second World War showed that the banks were an important factor in using private enterprise to rebuild the economy, since they gave out loans to individuals who invested, made profits, repaid their debts and in the meantime developed the country. According to Sadat's own reckoning, for every dollar brought in by the Marshall Plan, ten had been loaned out by German banks, and this formed the bulk of post-war German investment. That was the reason why he had invited the banks to assist in Egypt's development. He said that Egypt would hold 50 per cent of the shares of foreign banks operating in his country in order to ensure that they would operate in the public's interest; and if they did not, he reserved the right to oust them. He said that before he ascended to power, he had noticed that Egyptian banks had no talent for business. For example, he recalled that Nasser used to draw his salary from the Bank of Egypt, but whenever he needed an overdraft the bank would not give him a loan, from which it could make a profit. Instead, they would let the Prime Minister's personal cheque bounce and so embarrass a man whose salary was regularly deposited in the bank; at the same time they lost business. The trouble with Egypt's National Bank, asserted Sadat, was that it had become like just another government office; he could find no spirit of co-operation or innovation there when he introduced his open-door policy. He had no choice, then, but to invite foreign banks to fill the gap.

So, while he continued to stress his commitment to Socialism, Sadat distinguished between aspects of social welfare and of business. He was prepared to maintain the benefits made available by the previous regime in the fields of education, health and housing, and even to increase them. However, he believed that the management of, and investment in, business ought to be left to private initiative and open-market competition, even if he should incur charges of being a 'capitalist roader'. Free-market economy had been relinquished in 1952 in favour of state planning, but it turned out that planning was so clumsy, corrupt and swaddled in red tape that it was preferable to abandon it and to revert to entrepreneurship, although not always necessarily to foreign investors. For example, Sadat established a special ministry within his Government to plan land reclamation from the desert in an attempt to create desperately needed arable land. At the same time he invited an American corporation from California to develop a new farm on 300,000 acres of land, but when he thought that the terms offered by the company were not advantageous to Egypt, he decided to break up that project into three small, locally directed ones. Sadat recalled that, under Nasser, the Minister of Agriculture had suggested using private investors to develop land for agriculture. The 'foci of power', however, had insisted on collective farming. The result was that land was reclaimed by the Government but did not produce any food. By the end of 1976, Sadat declared that he had taken personal charge of the economy and that he would himself supervise the building of the agro-industrial complexes, the reconstruction of the Suez Canal cities and the implementation of the five-year plan. He frequently flew by helicopter to the construction sites, asked for updates and gave instructions. He boasted that David and Nelson Rockefeller, the magnates of the Chase Manhattan Bank, as well as Robert McNamara, the President of the World Bank, were his personal friends, and therefore he could make use of his private connections in the world to produce a turnabout in the economy. Sadat said that the foreign experts he had called in would help him remedy Egypt's malaise and that he was ready to face problems and resolve them. Having taken control of the economic affairs of his country, he hoped that his second term as President would be marked by an economic recovery. After he had overflown the Egyptian oil fields in the Gulf of Suez, he wondered aloud 'how ships could find their way through that forest of rigs', but he grew confident that in the 1980s Egypt would become a sizeable exporter of oil. This, coupled with the new projections he received on the revenues from the Suez Canal, made him conclude that 'we shall have no more problems in the future'.

10
THE PEACE GAMBLE

The year 1977 began badly for Sadat: in January food riots broke out and his popularity began to wane. The high hopes Sadat had held for economic recovery and for democratization suddenly foundered when it became evident that he had underestimated the bitterness of the crowds and overestimated his own charismatic authority and popularity. Sadat was dismayed when he understood the extent of dissatisfaction and realized that the violent demonstrations were aimed at him personally. Hundreds of the rioters were killed or wounded and over a thousand arrested, in what was probably the worst domestic upheaval since Sadat had come to power. The immediate cause of the riots was the Government's decision to face economic problems head-on and to reduce government subsidies on such basic food stuffs as oil, sugar, flour, rice and cooking gas. However, it was soon apparent that all the hates and fears, which had accumulated over the years, were now being brought into the open. The people were bitterly opposed to the open-door policy and disgusted with Sadat for allowing a few 'fat-cats' to flourish at the expense of the starving many.

The disturbances, which began in Alexandria on 18 January, soon spread to Cairo and other cities. Buses were set ablaze, windows were smashed and violent clashes occurred between hundreds of marchers and the police. Sadat, who was in Aswan awaiting the arrival of President Tito of Yugoslavia on a state visit, was kept informed of what was happening by Vice-President Mubarak from Cairo. Jihan, who had stayed behind in Cairo, telephoned him to let him know about the mounting discontent and to voice her concern, but found her husband as calm as ever. He boarded a plane to Cairo airport and then was lifted by helicopter to his home. He assessed the situation and decided to broadcast to the nation to assuage their anger. His economic advisers explained that there was no way of escaping a rise in food prices because of the country's catastrophic fiscal situation and the need to cut subsidies to cope with the price rises on the wholesale food markets abroad. Some of them suggested that prices might be held while the produce sold to the masses was adjusted to lessen its intrinsic value, for example, butagas bottles could be made lighter or loaves of bread less bulky. But Sadat, hard-pressed as he was by the public demonstrations, refused to be so dishonest. He said he preferred straight talk, and if the prices had to be raised, he would face his people and tell them the truth. But he also knew that the Egyptians were tired of making sacrifices and therefore he opted to restore food prices to the pre-riot level.

He announced his 'response to the people's needs' in his broadcast, but he also used this opportunity to accuse the 'Leftists and Communists', the remnants of the supporters of the long-defunct 'foci of power', of having used the misery of the people for their own political purposes. He said that violent demonstrations could never have been launched simultaneously in all major Egyptian urban areas unless someone had organized them and co-ordinated their timing. He lashed out at those who had no scruples about exploiting the country's difficult economic situation and branded them *haramiyyeh* (thieves), hence the *Intifad al-haramiyyeh* (Tremor of the Thieves), the name he gave to the riots. 'Tremor' or 'shudder' was Sadat's way of suggesting that he hoped this was the dying spasm of the troublesome opposition group; he was reluctant to go so far as to call them the leaders of an 'uprising', 'revolt' or 'rebellion'. His acute political sense told him that it was time to retract tough measures and appease his people; to confront and blame the opposition, rather than to entrench and isolate himself and give rise to widespread popular disturbances which might topple his regime. The violence receded, but Sadat was shocked by the extent of the unrest revealed; in view of the evidently deteriorating economic situation, his fear of more upheavals to come was very real. A new policy was needed, something radical, revolutionary, that would provide both a real breakthrough in some direction other than the open-door policy, and a means to hold the people's attention until that breakthrough was accomplished.

Sadat also became painfully aware of his tarnished personal image and of the growing grudge among the poor against what they perceived as the extravagances of their President: foreign travels, expensive suits, lavish palaces, numerous villas and resort-homes, the very symptoms that they so hated in the lifestyle of the *nouveau-riche munfatihun*. Crowds of tens of thousands marched in Cairo, shouting 'Nasser! Nasser!', 'down with Sadat!', and 'with our blood and our spirit we shall bring down the prices!'; Sadat understood only too well that they had had enough of him and his policies. They longed for a leader of the Nasser type, and were prepared to fight and die for their aspirations. It was a bad omen for Sadat – who thought he had upstaged Nasser and surpassed him in leadership – that his predecessor's lasting popularity should be vaunted amid his own sinking fortunes. What was more, Sadat saw that his open-door economic policy, the entire reorientation towards the US and the West, and the new commitment to technology and modernization were all now at stake. The protestors had not only shouted him down, but had also attacked American and German cars and ransacked bars and night-clubs which were frequented by businessmen and technical experts from the West. This anti-Western furore was as much leftist-Nasserite inspired as it was Muslim fundamentalist. Sadat was caught in a bind: he had, in the past, attempted to control and counter-balance the Left by giving some leeway to Muslim fundamentalists and allowing the Muslim Brothers to surface and propagate, but now both seemed to have run out of control.

The riots of January 1977 must have depressed Sadat in yet another way: having invested much face in the 'State of Institutions' (a term coined by Sadat to differentiate his form of government from a dictatorship) and the 'rule by law' which he had set up to supersede his predecessor's crude dictatorship and autocracy, he now found himself constrained to resort to the old ways which he had so outspokenly condemned. Political arrests, emergency rules, curtailment of the press and use of the army to crush civilian demonstrations were all symptoms of the tyrannical rule that he liked to think he had brought to an end in Egypt, and yet he now had recourse to each and every one of them in his desperate quest to stabilize his country. The military broke up the demonstrations, thus illustrating once more how dependent Sadat was on their loyalty; he removed what he regarded as 'leftist elements' from the editorial boards of *Rooz al-Youssef* and *Al-Tali'ah*, which had dared to criticize both his economic policies and the explanation he offered as to the origin of the 'Tremor of the Thieves'; he threatened new legislation, to be endorsed by a referendum which would make demonstrations, strikes and pickets punishable by hard labour; and he reimposed official uniformity, sanctioned by a stringent censorship, on the Egyptian press. The excuse for this last measure was that two respected editors of *Rooz al-Youssef* were arrested while actively participating in a demonstration, an accusation denied by the chief editor who claimed that the two men were in the office or at home at the time of the clashes. Another 'justification' offered by Sadat, this time to placate fundamentalists, was that he was determined to 'purge the state machinery of atheists'.

Severely shaken by his failure at home, and by the criticism and ridicule that he had to endure as a result, Sadat desperately looked abroad for a way out. He gave a great deal of thought during long days of isolated retirement to a new direction, to some spirited initiative which might produce a dramatic new development in an otherwise hopeless situation. He knew full well that without such a lifeline he would be doomed to sink deeper into the murky waters of his domestic quagmire. Obviously, once his Friendship Treaty with the Soviets had been irreversibly abrogated, and he had commited himself to the American-sponsored peace negotiations with Israel, his best hope for a solution lay with the United States. However, the second disengagement agreement of 1975 would have run its course by September 1978, and the Americans still had not seemed able to extract further territorial concessions from Israel. Sadat threatened that if the Geneva Conference did not materialize and Israel failed to withdraw from all Arab territories, he would have to take the military option again. But was he capable of venturing once more into a military operation which held no promise? In 1973, despite the support of his allies and the advantage of surprise, he had fallen short of achieving his war aims. Now that he had lost Soviet support, the Syrians had become his harshest critics, and Israel was constantly on her toes to ward off any repetition of the 1973 calamity, what chance did he stand? His economy was still so feeble that the further pressure of a new war effort might deal it a devastating *coup de grâce* from which it would never recover. And what would happen to all his guarantees of Egyptian stability, without which foreign visitors would not have risked their investments in his programme? A war would only lose investors and halt or destroy the new development projects, thereby exacerbating even further the already difficult economic situation.

At the international level, therefore, Sadat had only the Americans to lean on. They had given him generous economic aid since the end of the war, but he could hope for major and steady commitment only if he proved that he was definitely heading for a peaceful settlement. Moreover, in any major war, he would be dependent on sophisticated equipment that he could only obtain in the West, in particular from the US, and he was fully aware that the American Congress would not vote massive military aid to Egypt if there were any indications that such military hardware was to be used against Israel. Again, only the Americans could help avert a Soviet encirclement of Egypt, which Sadat feared was a real possibility, for Libya, on his western border, was gradually becoming a store-house of Soviet weapons which might be used against him. The Soviets were also cultivating a Marxist government in Ethiopia, while at the same time backing Libyan and Communist attempts to topple Numeiri's rule in the Sudan. For Sadat that would have constituted a deadly blow, not only because of the threat of hostilities on his southern front, but also because the Nile, the life artery of Egypt and the Sudan, drew two thirds of its waters from the Blue Nile which flowed down from the Ethiopian Plateau. Were the Soviets and Ethiopians to tamper with that vital source of water, Sadat would be embroiled in a struggle that he was not sure he could undertake single-handedly.

To stand up to those challenges, it was essential to pacify the Israeli front and to elicit a deeper American commitment, both military and economic, which alone would balance the Russian threat from without and support a sustained recovery from within. It boiled down to the necessity of some sort of American-sponsored settlement with Israel. But what sort of settlement? Sadat would have preferred to retrieve Arab territories, tackle the Palestinian problem and accept American military and economic aid without having to pay the price of recognizing and making peace with Israel. But he also knew that Israel was adamant about formal recognition, on direct negotiations, and on a full contractual peace treaty which would provide for diplomatic relations between her and her Arab neighbours. Would such a price be acceptable to Egyptians and to other Arabs? Would the Israeli Government be receptive to an initiative along these lines? Was the whole idea feasible?

Sadat thought the problem over for several months. He could foresee many obstacles and was taken aback by the implications of peace, which had begun to occur to him. The more he considered the issue and the more awesome and challenging it became to him, the more he grew obsessed by it. He realized that those Arab states and bodies which were solidly in the Soviet orbit, like Libya, Syria, Iraq and the PLO, were certain to condemn any move towards a direct contact with Israel as an act of treason. Others, like the Sudan, Saudi Arabia, Kuwait, Morocco, Jordan and Oman, whose political leanings were deemed pro-Western, might be more amenable to understanding such a breakthrough in Arab thinking, if not outrightly favourable towards it. After all, Saudi Arabia had been attempting to effect a *rapprochement* between Egypt and the US since the 1970s, and therefore it stood to reason that the Saudis would not disavow such a step. If they in turn could be brought to use their mounting influence in the Arab world, might they even persuade other Arabs to follow suit? For Sadat was not sure he alone could sway Egyptian public opinion completely to his new thinking, if, and when, he decided to make his thoughts public. There were hardliners in Egypt who continued, even after the October War, to advocate stepping up Arab pressure until Israel yielded to new demands. Admittedly, a few voices were heard favouring some sort of settlement with Israel, but their hesitant murmurs were soon drowned.

In March 1975, the foremost contemporary Egyptian writer, Naguib Mahfuz, commended the President's policy in an interview with a Kuwaiti newspaper. He said that Sadat 'was trying to extract recognition of Egyptian rights from Israel and the US without bloodshed', despite the wave of criticism raised against him by 'domestic vampires'. Mahfuz said that those who wanted to pursue the path of war indefinitely ought to know that war was the antithesis of civilization and progress. He argued that Arab oil-wealth would dry up within a generation or two; unless the Arabs prepared a new cultural and scientific infrastructure now, they would not survive the post-oil era. Culture, insisted Mahfuz, could not be constructed by weapons and war, which are instruments of destruction, but only by peace. He pleaded for the 'silencing of voices that advocated extremism and war', since those voices served only the interests of 'colonialists who were interested in keeping the Arabs in a state of backwardness'. Mahfuz then declared himself in favour of peace, even if that entailed 'yielding part of the territories'. Land in itself had no value for him, he said; he would prefer a state of peace where people no longer had to fight and die. If culture was the ultimate goal, and culture could only be attained by peace, it made much more sense to sacrifice land than to sacrifice people's lives in further wars. When pressed by his interviewer, Mahfuz conceded that by 'yielding lands', he did not mean those occupied by Israel in 1967, but part of those originally Arab territories. From that interview and from later clarifications that Mahfuz gave to Egyptian newspapers, it soon transpired that he was willing to settle for a truncated Israel, whose borders he did not specify, but who would have to shrink behind her pre-1967 boundaries. He was prepared to make such 'concessions' only because 'American and Israeli long-term aims were in favour of a continuing war in order to sap Arab power'. This position, which was echoed by other Egyptian intellectuals and writers, such as Toufiq al-Hakim, did not reflect acceptance of Israel's right to exist, but only recognition of the necessity of scaling down the Arab–Israeli conflict in order to allow Egypt and the Arab world some breathing space.

Predictably, the ideas of Mahfuz and his allies generated a flurry of protest both within Egypt and throughout the Arab world. The most violent responses from without were expressed in Syria, where the mouthpiece of the Ba'th regime, *Al-Thawra*, jeered at Mahfuz's 'distorted mind' which preferred culture over territory. *Al-Thawra* particularly denounced Mahfuz's comparison of the Arabs to the Carthaginians who had relentlessly but hopelessly fought against Rome until their own demise and destruction. For the Syrian critics the Arabs were comparable to great and victorious Rome, while it was Israel that was doomed to suffer the Carthaginian fate. Mahfuz and his colleagues were condemned for their inability to distinguish between 'noble and just wars', which justified any sacrifice, and 'oppressive and reprehensible wars', presumably the epithets which Israel's wars deserved. It is noteworthy that these attacks against Egyptian 'moderates' came in the wake of the second disengagement between Israel and Egypt (September 1975), almost a full year after the interview with Mahfuz was published by *Algabas* (Kuwait, March 1975). Egypt's 'submissive writers' were now charged with 'treason' and lumped together with Sadat, in the eyes of Arab rejectionists, as the paradigm of 'collaboration with Israel'. *Al-Thawra* also claimed that a gathering of intellectuals at the prestigious *Al-Ahram* publishing house in Cairo had discussed the question of peace and coexistence with Israel, which was another indication of the Egyptian intellectuals' sell-out to Sadat's regime. More ominous, from Sadat's point of view, was the three-part article that Hassanein Haykal, the hard-line Nasserite who had been dismissed by Sadat from the editorship of *Al-Ahram*, published in Lebanon's *Al-Anwar* (3, 4, 6 January 1976). The article, which reverberated throughout the Arab world, called upon Sadat to abandon his policy of separate settlement with Israel and to take up the leadership of the Arab world once more. Sadat was urged to co-ordinate a new strategy, to arrest Israel's advances in the occupied territories, to bolster up the weakening stance of the Arabs, and to launch a new campaign to retrieve the lost rights of the Palestinians. Above all, he should realign Egypt with the Soviet Union, the only superpower both able and willing to provide the necessary war-gear for such a strategy. In those articles, and in interviews that he gave to Kuwaiti newspapers, Haykal denounced Sadat's pro-American stance, which was the corner-stone of the President's new strategy for a settlement with Israel.

221

Sadat never liked to form his policy exclusively around the themes or the hypotheses professed by intellectuals whether of the Right or of the Left. But Haykal had been both popular and powerful before his dismissal from *Al-Ahram*, and in view of his criticism of the disengagement agreements with Israel, Sadat probably felt comforted by the relatively moderate thoughts that were voiced by liberals and self-proclaimed leftists such as Mahfuz (who declared in a press interview in February 1976: 'I am a friend of the national forces in Egypt and part of the Left. I do not understand why my statements were distorted'). It is hard to speak about an interaction or a dialogue between Sadat and Egyptian intellectuals during the preparatory stage which preceded the launching of the new policy towards Israel, although it may sometimes seem that Sadat borrowed some of their vocabulary, or followed in the footsteps of new thoughts that they occasionally dared to voice independently of the establishment. For one thing, Sadat was flanked by intellectuals on the Left and the Right, and whatever policy he pursued would of necessity be identified with one or the other. Thus, it is almost impossible to determine when Sadat was following one school of thought or rejecting another, since he would always act to the liking of someone and to the disappointment of the opposite view. Intellectuals were never unanimous in their view of the Arab–Israeli conflict and even the non-conformists among them, such as Mahfuz, tended to dilute their independent thinking if they came under sustained attack as 'deviationists'. The worst thing that could happen to an Egyptian intellectual writer was to lose readers in his own country and in the Arab world as a whole, therefore very few of them were audacious enough to risk their own personal future for the ideas they believed in. Haykal was one of those few; he remained at odds with Sadat and aligned himself with the hard-liners of the Arab world; therefore, he is not counted among the intellectuals that some researchers have identified as having 'paved the way for Sadat's new moves' in 1977. Be that as it may, the fact is that Sadat's post-war conciliatory policy towards Israel came under heavy fire from prominent Egyptian hard-liners such as Haykal and al-Khuli, who pressed for a continued armed struggle with Israel until a decisive victory was achieved. Sadat, however, due to the constraints of his position, found himself aligned with those who favoured disengagement from the Arab–Israeli conflict, a continued dependence on American aid and mediation, and an internal reorientation in order to solve the staggering socio-economic problems of the country. Nothing illustrates Sadat's lack of concern with the positions taken by the intellectuals of all creeds so much as his contemptuous disregard for their views before the war, when he labelled some of them as 'defeatists' for their 'dovish' beliefs. Therefore, his embracing the option of peace, while at the same time doing nothing to discredit the hardcore hawks among the Egyptian intellectuals, ought not to be construed as a conversion to dovish intellectual thought, but simply as an expedient coincidence of his perceived interests with their views.

As Sadat was pondering his options, two major developments hastened his decision: the installation of a new administration in Washington, and the meteoric rise to power of the Likud Party in Jerusalem. Sadat was wary of the fervent preacher of civil rights, Jimmy Carter, who unexpectedly wrested power from Gerald Ford, the man that he trusted and with whom he had established an amiable relationship since their Salzburg Summit in June 1975. He waited for the election dust to settle and for the new president to become acquainted with the complicated affairs of the Middle East. No less worrying for Sadat was the unknown quality of Secretary of State Cyrus Vance who had come to replace Sadat's best and most venerated friend in the American administration – Henry Kissinger. Carter's initial declarations, which favoured a 'Homeland for the Palestinians' and condemned Israeli settlements in the occupied territories, sounded an optimistic note in Sadat's oversensitive ears, but it was too early to conclude in which direction American foreign policy was heading. Geneva remained a distinct possibility and the new American administration seemed committed to it, but inter-Arab dissensions and the question of PLO representation made it less hopeful.

In Israel, a new Prime Minister, Menachem Begin, took power in June 1977, after almost thirty years of Labour-dominated coalition governments. Golda Meir, the once adulated leader, had been held responsible for the reversals of the Yom Kippur War and forced to resign. The Rabin Government, which followed her, had been viewed with disdain by Sadat, who considered the ruling elite in Israel as 'weak, divided and indecisive'. The 'Troika' of Rabin–Peres–Allon were seemingly unable to make crucial decisions or to take controversial or otherwise unpopular measures. For Sadat, collective rule, such as the one he perceived at the helm of Israeli politics, was an unmistakable expression of lack of leadership and resolve. He could not strike a deal with such diffuse leadership. He needed to respect a man in order to be able to measure up to him, challenge him, haggle with him and finally come to a deal with him on the basis of parity. Moreover, it took a strong leader, as Sadat believed himself to be, to take the necessary hard decisions that he intended to extract from Israel during the forthcoming negotiations. Finally, only a stable and decisive leader, respected by his people, could be expected to deliver whatever he pledged. As Sadat saw it, Begin, the former chief of an underground organization, who had occasionally resorted to terrorism, and who had acquired prominence in the Israeli political system by sheer resilience and tenacity of character, was exactly the kind of hero Sadat liked to deal with. Sadat regarded his own past as strikingly similar to Begin's, given the broad differences in the political traditions in which the two leaders grew up; he believed that Begin was his kind of man. When Sadat went to Romania in October 1977, he had his feelings about Begin confirmed by President Ceaucescu, who had welcomed the Israeli Prime Minister to Bucharest that summer and had had time to sum him up. Sadat was assured that Begin was indeed the right kind of man for him.

While Sadat was preparing his diplomatic surprise, he did not neglect routine channels of diplomacy, particularly continued contact with the American administration and with prospective Arab participants in the Geneva talks. One might push Sadat's astuteness to the limits and claim that he pursued the diplomatic beaten-track publicly in order to cover the real master-stroke that was in the making. But it is more likely that Sadat, like any other cautious statesman, was preparing to deploy a back-up move in case his new ideas did not come to fruition. Whichever is true, in the summer of 1977, Sadat adopted a 'two-pronged' approach and embarked simultaneously on both the revolutionary avenue of direct contact with Israel and the traditional and slow-moving road of diplomatic contact via the US. The Americans seemed to opt for the abandonment of the previous administration's step-by-step policy, which had run its course in September 1975, and began looking for a comprehensive settlement, to be achieved at one stroke, between Israel and all Arabs. Moreover, it soon became apparent that President Carter, unlike his predecessors, was willing to involve himself personally in tedious, time-consuming and controversial negotiations over the Middle East, thus risking his prestige and political future. As early as February 1977, Vance had visited Cairo and met Sadat in an attempt to set the Geneva talks in motion and reach a comprehensive Middle Eastern solution. However, divisions of opinion persisted between the parties in the conflict about the terms on which the conference should be reconvened. The official united Arab position, which President Sadat and his Foreign Minister Fahmi had adhered to in the talks with Vance, was clear: in return for Israeli withdrawal from all territories occupied in 1967; for the recognition of the PLO as the sole representative of the Palestinians; and for the establishment of an independent Palestinian state, the borders of which were never specified, the Arabs would be prepared to sign 'peace agreements' with Israel, which would merely end the state of belligerency between the warring parties. Fahmi stated that this kind of 'peace' would not mean normalization of relations between the Arabs and Israel 'until the completion of a long transitional period during which Israeli behaviour should be kept under close scrutiny and observation'.[37] And it was the Arabs who would determine whether Israel had behaved herself well enough to deserve full recognition of her right to exist and normal relations with her neighbours. Fahmi, with Sadat's backing, made it clear that the Geneva peace would only 'recognize the existence of Israel' (de facto recognition), not her right to exist (de jure recognition).

Much of 1977 was spent by the American administration seeking a formula agreeable to all parties, both in order to convene the conference and to formulate a prima-facie framework for its final outcome. These efforts continued throughout the summer and early autumn of 1977, with the parties submitting draft treaties, agreements, memoranda and messages, which the

US sorted out, synthesizing some of their more constructive elements and eventually coming up with a draft proposal of her own. The conference was to convene, if everything else was agreed upon, in December 1977, with all Arabs represented by one unified delegation which included members of the PLO. President Carter invited the Foreign Ministers of Egypt and Israel to Washington in late September 1977 to facilitate the drafting of formulae acceptable to both parties, accelerating the whole process by his personal involvement. At one of those meetings, Carter told Foreign Minister Fahmi, according to the latter's account,[38] that he was unable to fulfil President Sadat's demand that he exert major pressure on Israel to make her accept the Arab conditions for the peace conference. Carter reportedly said that he could not do so because it would entail 'personal political suicide'. Fahmi shared Sadat's impression that Carter was unable to force the Israelis' hand; Fahmi hoped to sway his President towards introducing other actors, such as the USSR and the Europeans, into the peace process rather than relying exclusively on the US. At that point, Fahmi, Sadat's trusted Foreign Minister, began to suspect that his President was in direct contact with Israel. Fahmi, who feared that such contact might undermine Egypt's commitment to a comprehensive settlement and sink the prospects of peace at Geneva, disapproved of any separate dealings. His reaction was to stiffen the official Egyptian stance towards peace with Israel. In his speech at the UN General Assembly, on 28 September 1977, Fahmi introduced a new element that had not been included in the draft peace proposal that Sadat had handed to Vance in August in Cairo: he demanded not only that Israel should withdraw to her 1967 frontiers and allow a Palestinian state to be born, but that she should also 'recognize the right of the Palestinian people to return', which meant in effect the destruction of Israel from within. Moreover, Fahmi's 'plan for peace' made no mention of Israel's right to exist beyond a general 'recognition of the right of every state in the area to live in peace', a formula which laid itself open to differing interpretations. Fahmi, furthermore, advanced his own personal view about the peace he sought with Israel: he wished her to be weakened and constricted, and to end her policy of allowing Jewish immigration from all parts of the world, lest that 'trigger further aggression and expansion at the expense of Arab countries'. Such candid comments set out, for the first time, what Egypt thought to be the 'right behaviour' which would entitle Israel to advance from non-belligerency to normal relations.

Fahmi's remarks, which did not pass unnoticed by either Americans or Israelis, added to the complications over the reconvening of the Geneva Conference in December. However, the Americans did not give up their quiet diplomacy. The Israeli draft peace proposal, which had been submitted to Vance on 19 September 1977 by Foreign Minister Moshe Dayan, and which insisted, in forty-two Articles, on a contractual peace between Israel and each of the Arab countries, to be followed by a total normalization of relations between them, was denounced by Fahmi as an attempt by Israel to 'impose its will on Egypt and other Arabs'. On 25 September, Vance handed to both parties a compromise draft-proposal, which left some ambiguities open to further discussion. As the parties were haggling over the details, the US and the USSR issued a Joint Declaration on 1 October 1977, without either Egypt or Israel being consulted beforehand. Predictably, both sides rejected the declaration and the American administration had to make great efforts to prevent the painstaking negotiations returning to square one. President Carter tried to mend the fence by convening a meeting between Fahmi and Dayan in Washington but Fahmi flatly refused to attend, for fear that the meeting might make other Arabs less willing to go to Geneva. Sadat was well aware of Fahmi's dealings with the Americans; on 19 October 1977, he sent a detailed letter to President Carter about the coming Geneva Conference, confirming his basic commitment to the substance of the 'working paper' submitted by Vance to Fahmi in Washington and intimating that he had had discussions with the PLO leader, Arafat, and other Arab statesmen about the Conference. It seemed as if Sadat was all set, despite the major differences that remained to be discussed, to join the negotiations in Geneva, and that the problems which remained to be elucidated, such as the representation of the various parties, the composition of the Arab delegation, and the procedural methods, had all been finally agreed upon, as specified in a further letter by Carter to Sadat on 28 October, and another by Vance to Fahmi on 9 November 1977.

While all this was going on, Sadat was deeply involved in secret, direct negotiations with Israel, which he hid from his inner circle, including his Foreign Minister, and from the Americans, who trusted Foreign Minister Fahmi to represent the policies and the thinking of President Sadat. The Americans knew, for example, that Sadat had opposed the 1 October Joint Declaration on the grounds that he was reluctant to see the Soviets reintroduced into the peace process, but they interpreted Fahmi's continued striving on behalf of the Geneva Conference as a sign that Sadat had swallowed the pill and had become reconciled to the idea, especially as it held promise for the participation at the conference of all Arab countries bordering Israel; they could not know that contact had begun between Israel and Egypt as early as July 1977. Available sources now show that on 23 July (Revolution Day in Egypt), the Mossad, Israel's highly thought-of intelligence service, alerted Sadat to a plot against him by Qadhafi of Libya. The information was passed via the US to Sadat, with details about terrorists being trained by Libya at an oasis near the Egyptian border. Prime Minister Begin took the opportunity to request a meeting with Sadat, or for some lower-level contact between the two countries. Sadat was not averse to the idea and, when he learned in August 1977 that Prime Minister Begin was to visit Romania, he sent his trusted representative, Sayyid Mar'i, the Speaker of the Egyptian Parliament and a personal friend and relation, to Bucharest to listen to Begin's views. That contact made President Ceaucescu of Romania a mediator of sorts between Begin and Sadat, and paved the way for further contacts in Morocco between the Israelis and Egyptians. The Israelis, it was clear, were seeking for a direct means of conveying to Egypt their thoughts about a settlement. Some Zionist leaders in the US and in Europe had attempted to see Sadat during August to inform him of Begin's desire for contact with Egypt, but because of Fahmi's strong objections, Sadat had declined. Then King Hassan of Morocco, who was renowned for his close contacts with world Jewry, agreed to act as a go-between and even offered his country as a venue for such meetings. He may have offered his services because, if the terms of a prospective agreement between the parties were acceptable to the Arabs, whoever was the mediator would overnight acquire a prominent position in the Arab world.

On 16 September 1977, while Moshe Dayan was visiting Brussels, ostensibly to meet with the then NATO Commander, General Alexander Haig, he suddenly 'vanished' from the sight of the newsmen and photographers who had been trailing him. He flew to Zurich and then on to Tangiers in a Moroccan plane. There, he encountered Hassan al-Tuhami, Egypt's Deputy Prime Minister and Sadat's emissary. It is not clear what they concluded there, but there is reason to believe that the Egyptians made further contact, and that Egypt was signalling her readiness to negotiate directly with Israel, provided that Israel was prepared to withdraw from Sinai.

It was evident that even at this point, Sadat had not definitely decided whether he would meet Begin in person; the idea of going to Jerusalem had perhaps occurred to him, but he was as yet uncertain whether such an astounding enterprise was feasible.

In October, Sadat set out for a tour of Romania, Iran and Saudi Arabia. On the 28th he was received by Ceausescu and the two leaders proceeded to the resort town of Sinaia, which Sadat was particularly fond of because of its tranquillity, the beauty of its countryside and its name, which evoked the Sinai that he longed to retrieve from Israel. Ceausescu briefed Sadat on Begin's August visit to Bucharest and assured his guest of the favourable impression that the Israeli Premier had left on him. Sadat spent many hours meditating and mulling over his thoughts, before making up his mind: yes, he was prepared to meet Begin and was willing to circumvent all the procedures of Geneva, the mediation of the Great Powers and the impotence of the UN. Rather than let others determine the rules of the game for him (as they had done with the 1 October Soviet–American Declaration, the superpower co-chairmanship of the Geneva Conference, and in the inter-Arab disagreements), why should he not take 'his fate into his own hands', as he often liked to say, and act in person? Why should he drift down a course charted by others, rather than launch his own 'initiative', which would attract international attention, stun statesmen and countries around the world, and give the Israelis such a jolt that they would be rid of their fears and suspicions for ever?

The pre-conditions laid down in Morocco by al-Tuhami seemed to be acceptable to the Israelis, and Begin looked both willing and able to come to a settlement. If all that the Israelis wanted was recognition and peace, what better place to offer it to them than in the Knesset, their parliament, in the heart of Jerusalem, their capital city? But then, he would not be understood by other Arabs; even his own Foreign Minister, Fahmi, with whom he shared some preliminary thoughts on the subject in Sinaia, was apprehensive of the outcome, and attempted to dissuade him from such an audacious step. Sadat was taken by the idea of going to Jerusalem, but he did not want to appear to be 'going to Canossa', to submit to his arch-enemies. No, he would not see Begin, nor beg for anything, nor ask the Israeli Government for concessions. He was going to address the Knesset, to tell the Israeli people that they had nothing to fear, and that in return for their evacuation of Arab territory he would be prepared to make peace with them. In a way, he saw this step as an act of defiance against the Israeli Government, a *beau geste* towards the Israeli public and a bold manifestation of statesmanship and vision on his part, which he was sure the world would appreciate. He knew, and admitted to his inner circle, that Egypt was unable to beat Israel militarily, so why not retrieve lost Arab territories by a stroke of peace rather than pursuing the fruitless and costly path of war?

After that, events began unfolding rapidly. On 9 November Sadat announced to his Parliament, in the presence of Yasser Arafat, that for the sake of peace he was prepared to go 'to the end of the earth', even to the Knesset, which lay, as far as he and his audience were concerned, well beyond 'the end of the earth'. Dumbfounded, the members of the Parliament, and the guests in the Assembly's lobby, applauded Sadat's speech, as was their wont, probably without realizing either what the President had in mind or the long-term significance of his statement. Admittedly, that stunning note was mentioned almost as an afterthought, an oral addition at the end of a long prepared text, and was meant as a first low-key probe to test Egyptian and Arab response. The headlines in the following morning's Cairo papers, *Al-Ahram* and *Al-Akhbar*, drew the public's attention to the 'challenge' that their President had made to Israel by his willingness to go to the Knesset. No less prominent in those headlines, however, was Sadat's readiness to 'go to Geneva, regardless of the procedural problems' which had plagued and delayed the reconvening of that conference. But as soon as the Israeli leadership picked up the gauntlet and responded favourably to Sadat's declaration, he demanded that a formal invitation be sent to him via the US. When the Israelis complied, Egyptian teams were sent to Israel to begin preparations in earnest for the incredible visit. Sadat was drowned in reactions which varied all the way from enthusiasm to condemnation. His coming visit was labelled as 'imaginative and heroic' by most of the Egyptian media, while the opposition press urged him to call it off. His Foreign Minister, Isma'il Fahmi, and his Deputy, Muhammed Riad, resigned in protest. The Arab world was divided: Sudan, Oman and Morocco welcomed the initiative; others, like the Jordanians and the Saudis, made a neutral response, waiting on the sidelines to see where it would all lead; but Libya, Syria, Algeria, Iraq and the PLO were violently opposed, despite Sadat's visit to Damascus to brief Assad on the reasons for his trip and on what he was hoping to accomplish with his master-stroke.

Internally, Sadat presented his 'journey of peace' to Jerusalem as a courageous risk-taking attempt to break the impasse in the Arab–Israeli conflict. Immediately his shattered domestic image and all the ridicule surrounding him since the 1975 riots were forgotten as the Egyptian media launched a campaign of praise and adulation for the 'hero of peace', who was willing to defy the enemy and to lecture the people of Israel, over the heads of their own Government, on the subject of peace. To Egyptian Muslims, who were as shaken as all the rest of the Arabs, he simply explained that he was going to pray in the Al-Aqsa Mosque in Jerusalem during the *Id al-Adha* (Holy Feast of the Sacrifice). An Arab head of state, who was prepared to go into the 'lion's den' to pray in Islam's third holiest place, something that many Muslims would have liked to do, could only elicit adulation and popular support.

Sadat himself appeared calm, almost careless of the storm he had raised. For this major decision had not been born suddenly, in a vacuum; he had conceived it, struggled with it, been tormented by it, and kept it to himself while everyone around him, including his own wife, was ignorant of it. Jihan was surprised, like all Egyptians, by his speech in Parliament; when she asked him about his stunning revelation, he admitted that he had been pondering over this issue for months and had come to the conclusion that such an initiative was the only way to regain Sinai and to remove the psychological hurdles that separated Jews and Arabs. Jihan received many telephone calls at the President's residence, from notables, friends and well-wishers, who, bewildered by her husband's decision, were inquiring whether he was *really* going to Jerusalem and almost unanimously expressing their doubts about the entire idea, predicting failure. But he would not be swayed from his course; he was sure of himself and of his mission. He had brushed aside his Foreign Minister's insistence that the *démarche* would be detrimental to Arab unity and damage prospects for Geneva. For a while, he considered the idea of calling an international peace conference in East Jerusalem, so as to be able to claim an initiative on his part without necessarily seeming to recognize Israel, but eventually that was discarded, apparently because of American disapproval. This exasperated Fahmi, who had favoured the idea as doing less harm than a talk to the Knesset, if nothing could prevent Sadat's visit to Jerusalem.

In early November, Sadat was still encouraging his Foreign Minister to continue to work towards Geneva; he exchanged a few personal messages with President Carter on the subject, and he showed personal interest in the Arab Foreign Ministers' Conference in Tunis, which convened on 12 November to prepare for an Arab Summit Conference to discuss a united Arab strategy for Geneva. At the same time, however, he restated his intention of going to Jerusalem at every possible opportunity. When he convened his National Security Council on 5 November, in order to report on his trip to Romania, Iran and Saudi Arabia, he mentioned the Israeli 'autonomy plan' for the Palestinians which Prime Minister Begin had explained in detail to President Ceausescu just before Sadat's own visit. Suddenly, Sadat astonished all those present by stating that he was prepared to speak to the Israeli Knesset if it 'could save the blood of my sons'. General Gamasi, the consummate military man, who had collaborated with Sadat since the 1973 war and had been rewarded with the position of War Minister, alone raised his voice in dissent, which cost him his post. Others were too stunned, or too frightened, to speak up. On 15 November, Sadat ordered his press secretary to make an official statement regarding the forthcoming visit, but after a vehement argument with Fahmi on the telephone, he was persuaded to postpone it. Then, on 16 November Sadat flew to Damascus, where he had a violent exchange with Assad, who totally condemned the peace initiative. Sadat told the press corps trailing him that he *was* going to Jerusalem despite Assad's opposition. This was the first time that he himself had made an official statement on the subject. Sadat did not return to Cairo from Damascus. Instead, on 17 November, he went straight to Isma'iliyya, in order to prepare himself for his trip by prayer, solitude and meditation. It was there that he got Isma'il Fahmi's letter of resignation, which had been handed to Vice-President Mubarak in person.

The peace initiative was making headlines around the world. Now that the Jerusalem trip had become official, Sadat was at the centre of attention. Speculation was rife about his motivation in the face of the disapproval of his closest associates in Egypt and the Arab world. Even his 'friend', President Carter, had been taken by surprise. Sadat himself stuck to his 'explanation' that by going to Jerusalem, he would resolve '70 per cent of the conflict' and smash the 'psychological barrier' which had separated Jews and Arabs over the past century. According to Sadat, that 'psychological barrier' consisted of two elements: the conventional Arab–Muslim conception of Israel as a 'foreign body' transplanted into the Arab world which was therefore to be rejected; and the simultaneous feeling in Israel of being under constant threat, hence the 'siege mentality' and 'garrison-state' mode of life that had developed there. Sadat also saw that Israel's obsession with survival, self-defence and security, which were the result of a long history of persecution, of confinement to ghettos and of the horrors of the Holocaust, could be satisfied if he stated openly that he was recognizing Israel and her need for security; in return Israel should withdraw from all occupied Arab lands and accord the same measure of recognition to the Palestinians. That was to be the thrust of his address in Israel. He also thought that by pledging that there would be 'no more war after October', he would alleviate Israel's fears and at the same time he would reassure the international economic community that he was determined to create a situation of peace and stability on his borders, which he hoped would encourage foreign investors to embark on development plans for Egypt. He was desperate to convince the world that he was concentrating on internal stability in order to resolve his difficulties, and entertained no further prospect of armed struggles.

Having created an atmosphere of suspense and drama which attracted the attention of all major media networks in the world, and having shown defiance and contempt for his critics at home and abroad, Sadat was in his element. Neither apologetic nor defensive, Sadat was evidently delighted with the mayhem he had created around him. He presented his trip not as a response to a need, not as a submission to constraints, but rather as a 'holy mission', inspired by his burning desire for peace. He wanted the Arabs and the Muslims to view his journey to Jerusalem as a daring and imaginative onslaught against the lethargic diplomatic bumblings which had led nowhere. In the heart of the enemy's capital city, movement would be forced on world events, under Arab terms and in conjunction with a pilgrimage to the third holiest site of Islam. Above all odds, at the least expected time and place, he would obtain some kind of revolutionary, comprehensive and hitherto unthought-of solution which would be in line with his other great feats of the past. And in so doing, he would overcome nearly all the taboos that had dominated Arab policies towards Zionism since the 1930s: the Arabs had sought to wipe Israel out, now he was prepared to recognize her; no Arab had agreed to talk directly to the Jewish state, now he would initiate a new era of direct negotiations; the Arabs had always dreamt about imposing directly, or via the great powers, a solution acceptable to them, now Sadat was accepting the notion that Jerusalem was a crucial venue for any settlement with Israel; all agreements with Israel in the past (armistice, truce, cease-fire, disengagement) had been labelled by the Arabs as 'military agreements' of a temporary nature, now Sadat was seeking a permanent political settlement; instead of war being the sole legitimate means of Arab communication with Israel, Sadat was now offering a channel of peace.

Sadat landed at Ben-Gurion airport on 19 November at 8 p.m. He was conscious that in a flight of less than one hour from the military base at Abu Sweir to Tel Aviv, he had spanned almost a century of Arab–Zionist enmity. When his Boeing 707 plane touched down, every historically-minded person around was immediately struck by the irony of the President of Egypt, the most powerful and dangerous of Israel's enemies, entering the country at the Ben-Gurion airport, named after the founder of Israel who was regarded as one of the most formidable enemies of modern Arab nationalism. More of those ironies would unfold in Sadat's way: the first handshake with Golda Meir, 'the old lady' in Sadat's parlance, whom he had insulted and ridiculed from 1970 to 1974, and with General Sharon who had contributed so much to the undoing of Sadat's plan during the October Crossing; Herzl Avenue in Jerusalem, which he took on his way to Yad Vashem, the memorial for the Holocaust victims. Sadat had on many occasions lashed out at 'Herzl's plan' of expansion 'from the Nile to the Euphrates' and had helped spread the story that 'Herzl's map' was hanging on a Knesset wall. Now, he was going to see for himself; in the meantime, every person he saw and every street he passed through was a reminder of the extraordinary situation in which he found himself. Without transition or preparation, he was immersed in a world that he had always imagined to be satanic, pernicious, devious and full of vice. What was even more unreal to him was the warmth with which he was greeted by the President, Prime Minister and entire Government of Israel. He was evidently enchanted by the Egyptian flags which flew everywhere, by the huge signs, in Arabic, which welcomed him to Israel, and thrilled by the Egyptian national anthem flawlessly played by an Israeli army band. On his entrance into Jerusalem, in the Israeli President's car, he came close to tears at the sight of the masses of Israelis of all ages who lined the streets, enthusiastically waving Egyptian and Israeli flags. He had been wrong, he thought to himself, to have imagined the Israelis to be warmongers, and he was delighted that he had taken this step, which vindicated his gut-feeling that the era of peace had dawned. At Yad Vashem, Sadat was visibly shaken by the documentation of Nazi war-time horrors and the Holocaust. His visit to the Al-Aqsa Mosque was a moment of deep religious experience, and he found his meetings with the Israeli top leadership and the major factions of the Israeli parliament exciting and rewarding. But the high point, and the purported *raison d'être* of the entire initiative, was his speech in the Knesset on 21 November. The atmosphere was both festive and tense when Sadat was invited to the rostrum to deliver his long-awaited address.

What was remarkable about Sadat's speech was that he pre-empted any possible Israeli condemnation of the Arabs' conduct towards the Jewish state, by himself enumerating all the past wrongs that Arabs had meted out to Jews: he admitted that, yes, the Arabs had rejected the Israelis, had refused to meet them anywhere, had denied or ignored their national existence and had avoided negotiating with them directly. All that would change now. He was willing to accept the Israelis and live with them in lasting peace, provided justice was done to the Palestinians and Arab territories, including the Arab part of Jerusalem, were restored. He castigated the Israelis for establishing a country in land that 'was not their own', while denying Palestinians the right to nationhood on land that was undeniably theirs. Sadat regarded his own sacrifice, his trip to Jerusalem, as so significant and far-reaching that he likened it to the sacrifice that Abraham, the 'father of Arabs and Jews', was prepared to make for the sake of the Lord. Exactly as Abraham had become reconciled to the sacrifice of his son, not out of submission, fear or oblivion, but out of a spiritual strength fed by faith and personal choice, so did he come to Jerusalem on *Id al-Adha*, the Festival of the Sacrifice in the Muslim Calendar, which commemorated Abraham's dramatic offering on the rock of Moriah. He emphasized that his quest for peace emanated from a position of strength, not of weakness, hence the credibility of his initiative which was an act of choice and generosity, not compelled by constraint or necessity. Then, obliquely referring to the storm his trip had caused in the Arab world, he reiterated that Egypt would not sign a separate peace with Israel, because that would be a recipe for continued confrontation between Israel and the Arab world. Nor would he consent to an agreement between Israel and all Arabs which would leave the Palestinian problem unresolved. He stated that he was not expecting to sign another disengagement agreement in the Sinai, but wished to establish a permanent and true peace that would rule out further wars and bloodshed. Finally he emphasized once more the need to produce a reasonable national solution for the Palestinian people, since Palestine remained the 'core of the Arab–Israeli conflict'.

Sadat's speech also covered the history of Arab–Israeli conflict. Having admitted that the Arabs had wronged Israel in some respects, he then lashed out at the wrongs and injustices Israel had committed. He accused Israel of sustained psychological warfare aimed at convincing the Arabs that they were a 'dead corpse', suffering one defeat after another but unable to react. He said that the 1973 war had shown the Arabs' mettle on the battlefield and had shattered the old image. However, the psychological hurdle remained, founded on mutual suspicions, fears and delusions which accounted for '70 per cent of the conflict'. He urged Israel to abandon the 'road of conquest and expansion' and to shed the idea that force was the best way to deal with Arabs. For all Arab land was holy, and no Arab could renounce one inch of it. He could understand Israel wanting to live in security and peace, he was prepared to grant 'any guarantees the Israelis wanted'. Therefore, he demanded that Israel should withdraw from all Arab lands, including 'Arab Jerusalem'. He invoked the spirit of 'Umar Ibn al-Khattab and Saladin, respectively the second caliph of Islam, who had won Jerusalem for the Islamic world, and the great Muslim hero who had recaptured the city from the Crusaders. Since Sadat had often likened Israel to the Crusader state of the Middle Ages, signalling that he thought of it as a passing episode, he may have seen himself as the third link in the chain of Islamic heroes who had conquered or restored Jerusalem to Islamic rule. In fact, shortly after the Camp David accords were signed in 1978, a new tapestry was seen on Sadat's office wall, conspicuously inset with the names 'Umar, Saladin and Sadat. He clearly wished to be remembered in Arab–Islamic history as the man who brought Jerusalem back into *Dar al-Islam* (the Islamic Realm), although he had to content himself with a somewhat less glorious *reconquista* than the military feats of the previous two heroes.

Sadat made it clear that he did not come to Jerusalem to *ask* for Israeli concessions, but to *demand* that Israel should withdraw from all Arab territories occupied in 1967. He said that this demand was unequivocal and non-negotiable, since it was a vital step towards establishing a 'just and lasting peace'. In return, he would 'recognize the right of all countries in the region to live in peace within secure and defensible boundaries' and would 'put an end to the state of belligerency in the region'. The fact that in the operational clauses of his speech Sadat mentioned Israel only in the context of 'ending the Israeli occupation', but not in the general context of peace, raised queries in some Israeli circles. In fact, Sadat only recognized the 'right of all countries in the region to live in peace', which meant to some observers that he, or others, could always claim that Israel 'was not a state'. Similarly, his omission of 'peace with Israel' as a final goal, instead of merely 'terminating the state of war', was seen by the same observers as a further corroboration of their suspicions. Furthermore, even in the preamble to his speech, where he declared that 'we are now willing to accept you in our midst', Sadat did not mention Israel by name, and 'you' could be construed as 'Israelis' or 'Jews' living in 'peace and security' among the Arabs. Sadat concluded by mentioning his great concession for the sake of advancing the cause of peace, his willingness to talk with the Israelis even though they continued to occupy Arab lands, something that he had consistently refused to do in the past. He implied that his sense of mission for peace had outweighed all other considerations.

Whether Sadat meant his historic speech to the Knesset as a long-term political programme, or just as an opening statement towards the peace process, is hard to judge. It stands to reason, however, that he had Arab rejectionists in mind, since he only made cautious peace advances towards Israel, and fell short of suggesting a full contractual peace treaty to be followed by normalization of relations. He also emphasized that the idea of a comprehensive peace conference was not dead, and that the current peace effort should culminate in the signing of peace agreements between Israel and the Arabs, including the Palestinians, in Geneva. Begin's rather harsh response to Sadat's speech might have been, paradoxically, something of a relief to Sadat. He needed to show his countrymen and the Arab world that he went to Jerusalem to confront the Israelis and to challenge them, not to yield or submit to their demands. It was *he* who had laid a set of demands at *their* door, and in so doing he had not deviated in the slightest from the Arab consensus. He could not even be accused of having 'negotiated directly' with them, a 'crime' that the Arabs would not let pass with impunity, for all he had done was to go and lecture to the Knesset and to the Israeli people about Arab interests. Israel's tough response only attested to Sadat's uncompromising stance in his presentation of those interests. However, one breakthrough that had been accomplished in Sadat's eyes was his declaration: 'no more war, no more bloodshed', a resolve which signalled his readiness to embrace henceforth the road of negotiation (direct or indirect) instead of pursuing the path of war. But even in that seemingly major concession, Sadat could claim that it was *he* who had gone to Israel of his own free will and who had, in a gesture of generosity, foresightedness and supreme leadership, bestowed on the Israelis the option of peace. He was not talked or dragged into it, he did not submit to pressure and therefore he could not be said to have relinquished, like a coward under duress, an all-Arab tenet. To crown his achievement in Israel, Sadat could wave his joint communiqué with Begin, issued at the end of his visit, in which both parties committed themselves to the reconvening of Geneva and the negotiation of a comprehensive peace between Israel and all Arabs.

Sadat departed from Israel on 21 November, leaving behind him a trail of euphoria; Israelis were pinching themselves in disbelief, asking each other whether it had all really happened. Hope ran high in Israel and Sadat attained a peak of popularity that overshadowed even Begin. Although nothing practical emerged from the highly publicized visit, a great 'psychological barrier' had indeed been overcome and the new 'road of peace' occasioned much expectation. The arena of action had definitely shifted from Washington, and other world capitals, to Cairo and Jerusalem. At one stroke, all the behind-the-scenes American efforts to produce an agreement between Israel and her neighbours, from the 'shuttle-diplomacy' years of Kissinger to Vance's valiant attempts to reconvene Geneva, were made to seem petty, superfluous, even ludicrous. Hence, the derision with which the American–Soviet Joint Declaration of 1 October came to be regarded. It was seen as a weak, inappropriate and altogether unwarranted attempt to provide the wrong remedy to a festering sickness. Sadat was now regarded, particularly in the US and the West, as a hero of international stature who had achieved the impossible. To Arabs, however, despite Sadat's protestation that his initiative had given the Middle East its best chance of peace, he became the centre of much controversy. He had pushed Syria and other rejectionists to the margin of international affairs, and by claiming to speak on behalf of the Palestinian people, he also implied that the PLO did not necessarily stand as their sole legitimate representative. Sadat was confirmed in this belief when many Palestinians from the West Bank and Gaza began to look to him for a solution to their plight. Rejectionist Arabs rapidly responded to Sadat's challenge by gathering together in the 'front of steadfastness' in Tripoli (3–5 December 1977) and the 'front of rejection' in Algiers (2–5 February 1978).

Sadat reaped his greatest reward in Egypt. Although opposition voices continued to denounce his initiative, he could find consolation and comfort among the masses who now hailed him as the 'hero of peace', a far cry from the hostile slogans chanted by the same crowds during the food riots of January 1977. It seemed as if Sadat's gamble for peace had indeed paid off and shifted the people's attention from his Government's domestic inadequacies and impotence to his great feats on the world's stage. Sadat was evidently thrilled by the people's enthusiastic response, which went much further than he had hoped. Israelis, who had been regarded in Egypt as creatures from another planet, only encountered in textbooks or on the battlefield, were now made welcome; Israeli diplomats, journalists and other functionaries streaming into Cairo were well received by their Egyptian counterparts. Everyone appeared to be immersed in the same sweet dream; the 'shock treatment' he had reserved for the Israelis had touched the Egyptians as well. What was particularly appealing to Egyptians was the new credibility that Sadat's peace rhetoric seemed to take on. His new slogans 'no more war', 'no more widows and orphans', and the 'civilized road of peace', echoed arguments which famous Egyptian writers, such as Mahfuz, had been putting forward for the last two years. Newspapers in Egypt were full of articles and editorials singing the praise of peace and of its hero; the bureaucracy, the army, the media and the state institutions were all united in support of Sadat's new road to peace. This meant, of course, that Sadat's political future, and perhaps survival, would hinge upon the success of his peace initiative. For if it were to fail, he would not only have tarnished his record with yet another major flop, but would have to admit to his rivals in the Arab world that their rejectionism was sound and that his vision of peace had been no more than a pipe dream. Sadat's mouthpiece, the *October Magazine* of 11 December 1977, branded rejectionists such as Qadhafi of Libya, Boumedienne of Algeria and others, as 'mice and monkeys, dwarfed in Sadat's sight'; it remained to be seen whether Sadat's inflated stature could remain dominant in the days to come.

Before long the euphoria began to fade. Sadat, following up his trip to Jerusalem, called in December 1977 for a peace conference in Cairo (the Mena House Conference, named after the posh guest-house in Giza). The conference, which was to prepare for Geneva, was to include the superpowers as well as all countries bordering Israel, and the PLO. However it soon turned into a triangular Egyptian–Israeli–US meeting, with all the others either opposing or shunning it. Sadat was trying to maintain the momentum of his initiative, lest the new opportunity he had opened to the world sink into oblivion. He wanted the peace issue to remain at the top of the international agenda; even a truncated conference was better than none. However, the Egyptian and Israeli delegates restated the conventional positions of their respective Governments so that one began to wonder what the entire peace initiative had been about. When Israeli Defence Minister, Ezer Weizman, visited Sadat on 20 December, he found the Egyptian President still euphoric about a forthcoming settlement. Sadat wisely led the discussion round to the subject of aviation, aware that as former Chief of the Israeli Air Force, this was Weizman's first love. Sadat wished to charm Weizman, whom he regarded as an open, spontaneous and enthusiastic fan of his, for he needed an ally of calibre and standing to weigh against the calculating and somewhat obnoxious Prime Minister Begin. Weizman spoke Sadat's down-to-earth language, and was warm and forthcoming in his approach, unlike the inscrutable and bombastic Begin, who seemed to hide behind legal phrases and Latin terms with which

Sadat did not feel at ease. Sadat sized up his guest and found him amiable; they exchanged jokes and compliments and indulged in open and unrestrained laughter. When at length they turned to serious matters, Sadat expressed his desire to speed up the entire process and pledged that he would be prepared for full normalization of relations with Israel if Begin agreed in principle to evacuate all Arab territories and provide a solution to the Palestinian problem. Sadat, who was being attacked on all sides by the Arab world, and was personally indulging in a shouting-match with the 'front of steadfastness and confrontation', desperately needed to emerge rapidly from the painful peace process and prove to the 'dwarfs' of the rejectionist Arab world that his policy had proved successful and produced the very solutions to the problems of the Palestinians and the occupied territories that the Arabs had all agreed to aim for.

Sadat asked Weizman to 'take a walk' with his Egyptian counterpart, General Gamasi, and try to resolve the differences between Israel and Egypt. He wanted quick results and cared little about how those intricate problems would be smoothed over at the technical level. However, whether for fear of being implicated in an agreement which was sure to be rejected by the rest of the Arabs, or because of their uncertainty as to Sadat's ultimate aims, senior Egyptians, including Gamasi, were reluctant to go into specifics and relied completely on their President's decisions. It soon became evident that a meeting between the leaders of Egypt and Israel was essential to thaw the stalemate.

On 25 December, Begin arrived at Isma'iliyya, a lovely city on the Suez Canal, where Sadat maintained one of his hideaway resorts. Sadat could not yet afford to welcome Begin to Cairo, with the pomp and ceremony due to a Prime Minister, as that would have necessitated hoisting Israeli flags in the Egyptian capital and playing the Israeli anthem at the international airport. A 'working visit' outside the capital city would avoid all such embarrassment. When Begin's plane landed in Isma'iliyya, no Israeli flags were in sight and no welcoming ceremony was in evidence. He and his party were taken by helicopter to Sadat's resort, where the talks started immediately, after Sadat had introduced his new Foreign Minister, Ibrahim Kamel, a former Egyptian Ambassador to Bonn and a close friend of the President. Sadat was apparently pressed to come to a quick settlement if the Israelis agreed to evacuate Sinai and state something that would seem to protect Palestinian rights. However, Sadat's advisers dissuaded him from rushing into any agreement that might prove disastrous to Egypt's standing among the Arabs. When, much to Sadat's disappointment, the negotiations led nowhere, he asked Begin to suspend the talks and join him in a drive to see the Suez Canal. Sadat sat at the wheel of his black Cadillac with Begin at his side, and Israeli ministers Weizman and Moshe Dayan in the back seat. All participators in this 'historic' drive, chauffeured by Sadat in person, were impressed by Sadat's restlessness and his yearning for quick results. If Sadat had his way, one of them later reflected, an agreement could perhaps have been signed during that brief encounter with Begin in Isma'iliyya. Suddenly Sadat realized that he was going too fast, riding too high, and had left his Israeli counterparts and Egyptian aides out of breath, and his Arab rivals dumbfounded. He said in an interview with the *October Magazine*, on that 25 December, that while others may ride horses, he rode a rocket and left all the rest lagging behind. But he was confident, he asserted, that his people were 'riding ahead of him' and that he was on the track of their desires.

The only practical outcome of the Isma'iliyya Summit was an agreement to convene two bilateral meetings in January, to be attended by the US: the Foreign Ministers would discuss the political aspects of the desired peace agreement in Jerusalem, while the Ministers of Defence would take care of the security aspects of the settlement in Cairo. It was clear from the outset, however, that the focus of the talks would be on the diplomatic angle and therefore much publicity was given to the Jerusalem Conference. Moshe Dayan, the Israeli Foreign Minister, and his novice counterpart, Ibrahim Kamel, met at the Jerusalem Hilton, with the Secretary of State Cyrus Vance participating, and serious negotiating began. It soon became evident, however, that Israel wished to cling to the Israeli settlements in northern Sinai and to the two strategic air bases (Etzion and Eitam) which she had built at immense cost in northern and central Sinai. Again, a war of words ensued, which began to spoil the optimism generated in November and December 1977. The tension became critical when, at a dinner given by Prime Minister Begin in honour of the Egyptian delegation, the Israeli Premier tactlessly referred to Foreign Minister Kamel as 'my young colleague', a slight in Arab tradition where age is associated with wisdom. On 19 January, just two days after the opening of the Jerusalem Conference, Sadat released a communiqué announcing the withdrawal of the Egyptian delegation from the talks. The communiqué strongly castigated Begin and Dayan for 'blurring the issues' and raising 'partial solutions' which were not conducive to permanent and comprehensive peace in the region. Egypt's twin commitments of Israeli withdrawal from all Arab territories and recognition of the 'legitimate rights of the Palestinians' (including self-determination) were spelled out once again as a *sine qua non* starting-point for any further negotiation. Sadat also made the point that Israel's security could only be ensured by a peace settlement not by 'settlements or air bases here and there'. Thus, the communiqué stated, Egypt would not pursue the road of 'haggling and intrigue', implying that Israel had embarked along that road. The People's Assembly was called to an emergency meeting on 21 January 1978 to hear a report from the Egyptian President on the unexpected snags.

After the disappointment of the Isma'iliyya Summit, the Egyptian media began an orchestrated attack on Israel, Zionism and especially on Prime

Minister Begin. But now, after the recall of the Egyptian delegation from the Jerusalem talks in January 1978, the campaign was stepped up, outdoing even the pre-November 1977 peace-initiative days. Begin was likened to a Shylock, a stereotype of the greedy Jew who would bargain and deceive endlessly to make some gain. He came to personify, according to the Egyptian propaganda machine, all the evil that had ever been imputed to Israel, Zionism and the Jews. A clear attempt was made to incite the Israeli public, which 'genuinely wanted peace', against their elected leader, who was represented as having deviated from his people's will. Begin's past as an underground fighter against the British in Palestine was conjured up to 'prove' his present-day 'terrorist propensities', and his 'blowing up the peace process' was likened to his acts of sabotage against the British mandatory authorities. This attack against the Israelis was coupled, for some time, by equally vitriolic accusations against the PLO, following the murder in Nicosia, Cyprus, of Yussuf Sibai, the chief editor of *Al-Ahram* and one of Sadat's close associates and confidants. The Egyptian attempt to mount a commando operation against the murderers ended in disaster, and in their frustration, the Egyptian Government and people turned against the Palestinians. Many of the media accused PLO officers of living it up in European capitals while sending their men to commit acts of terror against innocent civilians. What is remarkable, however, is that neither these U-turns in the media treatment of Israel and the Palestinians, nor Sadat's personal fury at this turn of events, had any visible effect on his commitment to carry on with his peace initiative. On the contrary, he seemed determined to prove to the rejectionists that he was right to have launched his peace drive and to defy the PLO by providing a solution for the Palestinian people that would pull the carpet from underneath their leadership. Back in December 1977, when he was vilified and condemned by Syria and the PLO for his peace initiative, Sadat retorted by accusing Assad and the other rejectionist leaders of holding their personal positions of leadership above the interests of their nations. He asserted that he was different: if he should realize that his peace initiative was a failure, he would not hesitate to resign from office. Thus, all his personal future hinged on his success and he would not easily admit to his own shortcomings or accept any reverse upon the road to peace. On the contrary, he redoubled his efforts to convince the Israelis that he 'really meant peace', asserting that since the Egyptians had taken their revenge in October 1973, they were now free of any complexes and prepared to be flexible.

A new complication emerged in early 1978, when Prime Minister Begin, in an effort to circumvent Sadat's adamant stand on the Palestinians, came up with his 'autonomy plan' for the West Bank and Gaza, which was designed to remove the possibility of returning those territories to Arab rule, be it Jordanian or Palestinian. Begin travelled to Washington and London to 'sell' his idea for the Palestinians, and advanced the claim that Security Council Resolution 242, which was still the magic password for any negotiation about the Middle East, did not apply to the West Bank and Gaza. On the other hand, Begin had assured Sadat that 'everything is negotiable except for the elimination of Israel', and Sadat publicly endorsed that approach in an interview he gave to three American networks on 5 January 1978. Sadat was hoping that the Jerusalem Conference would come to a joint declaration of principles for a settlement between Israel and the Arabs, something he had sought to achieve in Isma'iliyya but failed. However, the Jerusalem 'political committee' had also failed to make progress in that direction, despite the Israeli peace plan which had initially been welcomed by Sadat and discussed in both Isma'iliyya and Jerusalem.

As the Carter administration was studying Begin's 'autonomy plan', a dramatic PLO act of terror occurred in Israel, in March 1978, when a group of terrorists commandeered a civilian Israeli bus and, in the shoot-out which ensued, many Israelis and a number of PLO fighters were killed. In reprisal, Israel launched a raid against PLO bases in southern Lebanon. While the Israelis were mopping up Palestinian camps in this 'Litani Operation', Sadat could not appear to condone their raid. He dutifully condemned the Israeli counter-attack, thereby further cooling off the peace process, the more so since Sadat's enemies in the Arab world were claiming that it was Egypt's 'copping out' of the war which was enabling Israel to grow more intransigent. So, despite his personal outrage at what the PLO was doing to innocent Egyptian and Israeli civilians, Sadat went on record as still being champion of the Palestinian cause, although he might have led the Israelis to understand that he was now more amenable to a separate peace.

On 31 March 1978, Sadat received in Cairo the Israeli Defence Minister Ezer Weizman, the only man in the Israeli Government whom he was willing to talk to during those tense days of bitterness and frustration. While they discussed the current state of affairs, Sadat made no secret of his exasperation at the slow pace of progress, at the sight of his great vision of instant peace dissipating into petty negotiations over matters of detail, into bickering about words and formulae of the forthcoming peace treaty. Sadat also complained that while time was being wasted on side-issues, the PLO and other Arab countries were escalating their attacks against him, and even the domestic support he was enjoying was now being increasingly diluted by protests from opposition groups. He insisted that Israel's rejection of all his proposals to break the deadlock put him in a tenuous situation *vis-à-vis* the other Arab states, because anything he would agree to now would be construed as 'submission to Israeli *diktats*'. This time Sadat looked bitter and sounded pessimistic. He was more withdrawn and less forthcoming than in previous encounters, and his waning self-confidence was reflected in the number of body-guards who surrounded him. It seemed that an ebullient and radiant Sadat had given way to a dejected and desperate man who saw his dream crumbling before his eyes.

Sadat's meetings with Israel's opposition leader, Shimon Peres, late that summer in Vienna, and the hopeful signals he was getting from the growing 'Peace Now' movement, which pressed Begin not to 'waste the peace initiative', did not change his mood. For the balance-sheet looked grim: the Jerusalem–Cairo Axis, which was to become the focus of the peace initiative, was short-lived and soon gave way to a renewed American involvement in the peace process. So much so, that Sadat himself came to regard America 'as a partner', and not merely as an observer or catalyst. Sadat's instant rapport with Begin in Jerusalem had also been transformed into suspicion and discord. What was worse, he realized that neither party seemed to be pleased with the progress of the talks so far: Israel was claiming that in return for her vast concessions and her preparedness to give up most of Sinai, including the oil wells and the strategic passes, Sadat was being inflexible with regard to continued Israeli presence in the northern Sinai settlements and the military air bases, and was even making demands over Palestinian self-determination which were beyond his authority or call of duty. Sadat retorted that Sinai was 'his territory' and Israel was doing him no favour in evacuating it in its totality. Therefore, it was he who awaited Israeli generosity towards the Palestinians, in return for the tremendous risks he had taken in launching his peace initiative and in defying the Arab consensus against negotiation with, and recognition of, Israel. Recriminations that Sadat exchanged with Begin through the media, where strong anti-Jewish sentiments were sometimes barely hidden, did not help ease the tension in the least. In mid-1978 Sadat returned to bellicose statements against Israel, thus compromising his pledge of 'no more war', especially after the failure of the Leeds Conference in July, when Egypt produced another peace formula unacceptable to Israel.

Fortunately for Sadat, President Carter too was exasperated by the slow pace of the peace process. Sadat's initiative had come as a total surprise to Carter and he reluctantly went along with it, being unable either to oppose or ignore it. Now, Carter was himself beleaguered at home, with inflation and un-employment rising and his own popularity plummeting. The peace initiative became his best bet and his central preoccupation. In addition, he had himself invested so much time and energy in the peace efforts and had made so much of his role of 'mediating between Sadat and Begin', that he might well have to pay the full price of failure if the Egyptian–Israeli peace process were not brought to fruition and presented as his own personal achievement. In August 1978, Carter sent sealed letters to both Sadat and Begin inviting them to come to the presidential retreat at Camp David, Maryland, 'to seek a framework for peace in the Middle East'. For thirteen consecutive days (5–17 September) the three leaders and their aides were closeted in Camp David, which was declared out-of-bounds to the media, and in an atmosphere of haggling, bargaining, cajoling and threats, in which President Carter played the major role, an agreement was finally produced. The few indications which emerged from the conference sounded rather gloomy. Word leaked out that at a certain point, Sadat had begun packing to leave, and only Carter's personal intervention had averted disaster.

The breakthrough apparently occurred in the final two days of the talks, when a double framework for peace, instead of the one the conference had set out to achieve, was signed at Carter's insistence. Begin could then claim that the two frameworks, the first regarding the Egyptian–Israeli treaty and the second on the question of Palestinian 'full autonomy', stood independent of each other and permitted Israel to fulfil the one while negotiating the other until it satisfied her requirements; Sadat had a face-saving package whereby he could argue that what he had achieved was the beginnings of a comprehensive peace with Israel, and that he had refused to be bought off with a quick and comfortable separate peace for Egypt. What was more important, from Sadat's point of view, was that Israel had agreed to a total evacuation of the entire Sinai Peninsula, and to enter into negotiations regarding Palestinian autonomy and the ultimate status of the occupied territories, in conjunction with Jordan and representatives of the Palestinian people. The two parties had also given their word that they would do their utmost to sign a final peace treaty 'within three months', *i.e.* by December 1978. This was, obviously, less than Sadat had hoped for, but since he had become a pariah in the Arab world, he could either repent his initiative and go back into the Arab fold or defy them and go all the way. The latter was more like Sadat. He could also console himself that under heavy pressure from Carter, Begin had finally given up all Israeli settlements in Sinai and was prepared to evacuate the air bases, under the understanding that the US would help build new ones within Israel's frontiers. In the process, Sadat had to accept the resignation of a second Foreign Minister, Kamel, who thought his President had yielded well beyond what was acceptable. Sadat apparently had to overrule Kamel and many of his other aides during the critical phases of the conference; he argued that he had not caved in to Begin, but was merely responding to the urgings of 'his friend', Carter, who needed as desperately as Sadat a successful end to the conference. Sadat calculated that if he responded to Carter on this score, it would later enable him to demand increased American aid and modern US-made weapons. He was dreaming of a 'Carter Plan', along the lines of the Marshall Plan which had followed the Second World War. Indeed, Sadat gave in on all matters relating to Israeli phased withdrawal from Sinai, demilitarization of the Peninsula and normal-ization of relations with Israel. Sadat had also agreed to an 'autonomy' formula which deviated only slightly from Begin's plan.

There has been much speculation about Sadat's adamant refusal to exchange his claims on the Israeli settlements and air bases of northern Sinai for an equal portion of the Negev in southern Israel. Sadat's own feeling was that he could not allow an inch of Egyptian soil to remain under occupation. His entire peace initiative was founded on the equation between land and national honour, and by extension his own honour as Egypt's father. Only if he could prove to his people and to the world that he was capable of redeeming Arab rights in their totality, could he claim to have redressed the wrong inherent in the Israeli occupation of that land. Exchange of lands, as Israel had suggested, or leaving Israeli nationals within Egyptian territory, as some of the settlers had begged, could be interpreted to mean that Sadat could not deliver his responsibility and therefore had had to compromise with Israel on a *quid pro- quo* basis. Sadat might have been amenable, after the signing of the peace treaty and the Israeli evacuation of Sinai, to some territorial exchanges, but these would have had to emanate from him, as reflections of his own initiative and generosity, like the *beau geste* he made in 1978 in Haifa, when he suggested that water surpluses from the Nile River might be channelled to irrigate the Negev. Anything extorted from him while under occupation was out of the question. What was more, no matter what recompense he got for it, Sadat could not bear the prospect of being accused by the Arab states of having 'traded away' parts of Sinai to Israel or of ceding sacred Egyptian and Islamic territory to the Jewish state. As it was, his consent to demilitarize Sinai brought him under attack from Egyptian and Arab alike for having 'signed away' Egyptian sovereignty. Thus, it is too simplistic to claim, as some naïve Israeli writers and politicians did, that had Israel insisted on extracting territorial concessions, or had she refrained from establishing 'dummy' settlements in the Sinai during the peace talks in order to 'create new facts' which ended up infuriating Sadat, he might have been more amenable to territorial exchanges. Sadat, by temperament, rejected ultimatums, and if he were faced with such a demand, he would probably have toughened rather than softened his stance. His violent reaction against Ariel Sharon's sham settlements in northern Sinai was only an illustration of his fury when confronted with a *fait accompli*. He would not take anything that appeared to have been dictated to him; on the contrary, his instinct would be to revolt and undo it. And to the extent that he made concessions, he did so at second hand, via the Americans, for it was 'respectable' and understandable to give in to a friend who is also a great power, while submission to Israeli demands amounted to surrender and humiliation; and he would have none of that.

Against the backdrop of gloom which swept the Arab world in the aftermath of Camp David, the Egyptian press raved about the 'great achievements' won by negotiation, both for the Egyptians and the Palestinians. The media hailed Sadat as a hero and his accords as a feat of extraordinary acumen and political wisdom. From now on, they promised the Egyptian populace, Egypt could turn to work for construction instead of remaining immersed in war and bloodshed. A new messianic era of prosperity and plenty was proclaimed under the aegis of Sadat, who was now basking in splendour and glory and had probably reached the highest point in his political career. However, despite Egyptian protestations that the Palestinian autonomy was to become, with

American support, a fully-fledged Palestinian state, the Arab world continued to attack Sadat for 'selling-out' the Palestinian and Arab causes. The Arabs slated Sadat for the Camp David accords, accusing him of having signed away the sovereignty of Egypt by agreeing to limits on the presence of his troops in Sinai. What was worse, from the rejectionists' point of view, was that Sadat had consented to what he had vowed never to agree to, *i.e.* peace with Israel, while his own territories, let alone other Arab territories, were still under Israeli occupation. Even Jordan, Morocco and Saudi Arabia, the 'moderates' and 'friends' of the US, who were expected to come out in support of Camp David, feared to expose their own regimes to extremist Arab and PLO onslaught. Sadat's isolation was almost total, except for the murmurs of encouragement that he heard from the Sudan and Oman. Sadat responded by saying that in his generation that was the best possible deal he could extract from Israel, and that the 'coming generations' would be free to act as they deemed fit. He also contended that Egypt and the Sudan alone constituted '60 per cent of the Arab world', and therefore he had the 'majority' of the Arab world on his side. But the Iraqis, who saw Sadat's retreat as a golden opportunity to wrest the leadership of the Arab world from Egypt, called an emergency Arab Summit in Baghdad and obtained a unanimous Arab condemnation of Camp David. However, in a last-ditch attempt to lure Egypt back from the 'trap of Camp David', before the peace treaty was signed, the Baghdad Summit decided to budget large funds to assist the economy of Egypt, which was understood to be one of the major reasons why Sadat had embarked on his peace initiative in the first place. But Sadat refused the offer with disdain, arguing that Egypt, unlike other Arab countries, 'was not up for sale' to the highest bidder. At that point, not only would reneging on Camp David have been fatal to his personal prestige and sense of honour, but he felt he could get much more from his 'friend' Carter, and on a more constant and reliable basis, than from erratic Arab regimes who gave or withheld aid according to their shifting political whims. Instead of accepting their offer, Sadat poured scorn on the Arabs at Baghdad, dismissing them as 'myopic' and 'backward' and understanding little or nothing of international politics.

But Sadat found no consolation in the Camp David accords either. In the face of continued Israeli settlement in the West Bank and Gaza, he reiterated the 'linkage' between Frameworks I and II which had been signed simultaneously, as one package, and meant, to his mind, that Israel should not take any unilateral step that might prejudice the future of the 'autonomy'. Sadat was under pressure from his critics and from his aides in council to resist the Israeli *fait accompli* by refusing to sign the peace treaty by 17 December, unless the Israelis mended their ways. Despondent and in the middle of controversy, he elected not to go to Oslo to collect the Nobel Peace Prize which was awarded to him jointly with Begin. Instead, he sent Sayyid Mar'i to receive the prize. He dreaded the prospect of facing Begin, as the recriminations between Egypt and

Israel, which he hoped had been buried after Camp David, surfaced again. In addition, he was said to have felt personally injured by the Nobel Prize Commission's decision to share the Prize between him, who deserved it for his audacity and vision, and Begin, who he felt had taken the ride without paying for his ticket.

Having enlisted the full support of the American administration for his stand regarding the Israeli settlements, Sadat could only count on an equally frustrated and bitter Carter to make some new breakthrough, without which all the efforts invested at Camp David would be in vain. In March 1979, Carter went to Israel and Egypt to try his own hand at shuttle diplomacy, realizing that if he failed, the only bright point of his presidency would be dimmed. With a tenacity that won him much praise, Carter extracted a new 'understanding', anchored in a series of letters that were to be appended to the text of the long-awaited peace treaty, and which provided that Israel and Egypt would begin the process of negotiating the details of running elections in the West Bank and Gaza one month after the treaty was signed. Those talks were to be completed within one year, to be followed immediately by the agreed elections. Sadat was not content with what he viewed as the dilution of the 'comprehensive spirit' of Camp David. However, President Carter, who saw the Shah of Iran fall in February, merely ten months after his own declaration that 'Iran was an island of stability in the Middle East', was hard pressed enough to prevail on Sadat to accept the terms. On questions connecting diplomatic relations with Israel's demand that Egypt undertake to continue to supply Israel with Sinai oil, now that her link to Iran was severed, Sadat was reluctant to give way. However, as in Camp David, when all the effort seemed doomed, a new formula was worked out: Sadat agreed to open immediate diplomatic relations with Israel, and the US guaranteed oil supplies to Israel in the years to come.

In mid-March 1979, Sadat sent a message to all Arab heads of state, to report to them on the current progress of his peace initiative, on the basics of his talks with President Carter in Washington in February, and on Carter's visit to the Middle East in order to narrow the gap between Egyptians and Israelis. In his message Sadat gave vent to his frustration over the pace of progress of the talks and to his belief that unless the US exerted heavy pressure on Israel, there was no chance of obtaining any agreement. Sadat claimed in his message that he had attempted to persuade the Americans to abandon Israel, in return for which the Arabs, if provided with the necessary hardware, would be able to defend the Middle East, a job that Israel was supposedly doing with American blessing. Sadat said that he had based his offer to the Americans on the community of interest that he found between them and the Arab world over the solution of the Palestinian problem and the firm American opposition to Israeli settlements in the occupied territories. Therefore, Sadat counselled his colleagues in the Arab world to accept 'self-government' for the Palestinians, confident as he was that with American support it would necessarily strengthen the grip of the Palestinians on the West Bank and Gaza, arrest the process of Israeli settlement and ultimately lead to a Palestinian state. Sadat also reiterated that Israel, in demanding that an Egyptian–Israeli peace treaty should supersede any obligation Egypt had towards the Arab world, was interfering in matters that were none of her business. However, Sadat stated that he was not opposed to 'normalization' of his relations with Israel, at the latter's insistence, which won strong support from President Carter. Sadat also recounted the outcome of Carter's negotiations in Israel and Egypt and stressed that all major clauses of the coming agreement with Israel were Sadat's own doing. He insisted that he had discussed and agreed on all points of controversy with Carter before the latter went to Israel to elicit her consent. Thus, Sadat ensured that he could not be charged with having caved in to Israeli demands or been outmanœuvred by Carter's supplications and pledges. Sadat also stressed that he refused to give in on the issue of oil supplies to Israel, a matter of considerable sensitivity in the Arab world due to the strategic importance of oil, and the blow that a guaranteed flow from Egypt to Israel would constitute to the Arab economic boycott against the Jewish state. Above all, Sadat assured the Arab heads of state that he had obtained guarantees from President Carter that the American administration would persist in its efforts to resolve the Palestinian problem. The message, of course, was that Egypt was not going to sign a separate agreement with Israel. Furthermore, Sadat pledged to his Arab colleagues that the Palestinians would participate in the forthcoming 'autonomy talks' and that the 'Palestinian people would take direct part in the shaping of the final settlement without any mediator speaking on their behalf'.

With the last hitches removed, the peace treaty was signed on the White House lawn on 26 March 1979. Solemn, Sadat went to Washington to apply his signature to the treaty, together with the exuberant Begin and jubilant Carter. Upon the exchange of the ratified treaty, the state of war between Egypt and Israel came to an end, the timetable of Israeli withdrawal was set (three years), diplomatic relations would be established immediately and ambassadors appointed within six months. Multilateral forces were to be stationed in Sinai to monitor possible violations of military limitations in the demilitarized zone, and methods of establishing economic, trade and cultural relations, freedom of movement and communications between the parties were sketched out. The treaty expressed all the stipulations that legalistic Begin wished to entrench in the peace document so as to make it irreversible, before he committed Israel to the evacuation of Sinai. And the evacuation would be gradual so as to impress upon Sadat that he could lose parts of Sinai if he abrogated the treaty or reneged on some of its major clauses, such as Article Six, which stipulated that neither party should enter into any agreement in conflict with the treaty. The idea was that if a clash between Israel and a third Arab party should occur (say with Syria, over the Lebanese civil war), Israel was assured of Egypt's neutrality, the assumption being that Sadat would not endanger the Israeli evacuation of the rest of the Sinai. According to this line of reasoning, by the time three years had elapsed, and Israel had completely evacuated the Sinai, Sadat would be so deeply committed to the treaty, and bilateral relations between Egypt and Israel would have developed to such an extent, that abrogation of the treaty would be unthinkable. Sadat, unlike the rest of the Arab world, understood Israel's desires for safeguards and security, and he was willing to grant them as long as he had the Carter administration's support for the next stage of reconstruction that he was envisaging. In his address at the signing ceremony, Sadat lavished praise on Jimmy Carter, who had 'single-handedly brought about the miracle of the Agreement' and had achieved 'one of the greatest feats of our generation'. Sadat, who did not mention Begin in his speech, did allude to the Palestinian problem and expressed his hope that the Palestinian people 'would be able to establish a state of their own', because 'when the Arabs retrieve their domination of the West Bank and Gaza, our common strategic interests will be served'. He also emphasized that Egypt would remain loyal to her inter-Arab obligations despite making her peace with Israel. This was as far as Sadat could go in contradiction of the treaty he had just signed, pending the return of all Sinai to Egyptian sovereignty. But he did not live to see the last stage of the Israeli retreat, in April 1982.

11
TRAGEDY

The writing was on the wall for Sadat for two reasons: domestically, he had ushered in an era of peace and high expectations, which if unfulfilled would inexorably give rise to bitterness and opposition; and on the inter-Arab scene, the peace treaty left Sadat with the stigma of treason. The grapes of peace turned sour. This was reflected in Sadat's personal conduct in the final two years of his rule. He became withdrawn, aloof, irritable and paranoid. He increasingly indulged in religious piety and in mystical dreams, sensing that he had come to the end of the road. He had often told his wife that, once he attained peace with Israel, he would seek peace with himself. He would probably have retired from public life in late 1982, at the end of his second term of office, when he would have lived to see all Sinai retrieved from Israel. But before his term was up, Sadat was gunned down by Muslim fanatics. They represented a growing trend towards Muslim fundamentalism: people who opposed Sadat both for his domestic policies and for his peace with Israel, and they were encouraged, some say financed, and at any rate applauded, *post factum*, by the Arab rejectionists. Sadat's murder by Egyptian fanatics also sadly, if dramatically, illustrated the contention of many Egyptians that the peace treaty had been signed by Sadat and Israel, not Egypt and Israel. With Sadat gone, many envisaged the reversal of his political programmes and a return to the *status quo ante pacem*.

Ironically, Sadat's 'Era of Peace', which won him world recognition and international acclaim, brought about his demise at home and on the inter-Arab scene. We are accustomed to politicians who, in order to retain their popularity at home, adopt measures unpopular on the international scene. Sadat did quite the reverse: in order to win world prestige, he sacrificed his popularity at home. He hoped, of course, that his people would follow him, but he miscalculated the depth of the feeling he would stir up in the Arab world and the violent repercussions that inter-Arab rejectionism would have at home in Egypt. Ironically, his Egyptian and Arab leadership, which had brought him world-wide recognition, was lost in the acquisition of that recognition.

Sadat marked the 'Era of Peace' by reshuffling the Egyptian Government. General Gamasi, who had served as War Minister, became Sadat's Counsellor, and was replaced by General Kamal Hassan Ali, another hero of the 1973

248

October War, who was this time given the title of Defence Minister. Softly-spoken, Western-educated and free-market-orientated, Mustafa Khalil was appointed as Prime Minister and Foreign Minister, thus filling the gap left by Ibrahim Kamel's resignation at Camp David. Khalil's task was formidable: to represent Egypt in the autonomy talks and to try to steer a new course as Egypt now found herself isolated on the eve of the peace treaty with Israel. Indeed, a second Baghdad Conference was convened to carry out the previous confer-ence's warnings that, if Sadat proceeded, he would find himself excom-municated from the Arab community. The proceedings were swift: Egypt was thrown out of the Arab League, whose headquarters were transferred from Cairo to Tunis; all Arab countries were ordered to cut diplomatic relations with Cairo, all Arab financial aid was discontinued, and Egypt found herself economically and culturally boycotted by the Arab world. But Sadat would not budge. Instead, he stepped up his attacks against 'moderate' heads of state, like the Saudi and Jordanian monarchs who had 'betrayed' him, choosing to align themselves with the rejectionists in order to buy time and 'insurance' for their shaky regimes. He declared that Egypt remained the centre and focus of power in the Arab world and insisted that no major decision for war or for peace could be taken without Cairo. He ridiculed the 'blindness' of the Arab rejectionists and vowed that in the end they would come to see the light and follow in Egypt's footsteps. In the meantime, he set out to convince the Arabs that he was intent on lending true significance to the Second Framework Agreement by pursuing in earnest the autonomy talks, and on strengthening his ties with Israel and the US in order to prove the worth of his peace policy. He sailed into Haifa harbour in what used to be King Farouq's royal yacht. There, he was cheered with unabated enthusiasm by the Israelis, an experience which brought him and his wife close to tears, especially in view of the hostility and outright hatred he was encountering among his brethren in the Arab world. He must have reflected on the imponderables and ironies of politics, as he found himself thrust from a position of leadership to the unpleasant margins of the Arab world where he was lumped together, as a pariah, with hated and boycotted Israel. In Haifa he also announced that he would sell Israel two million tons of Sinai oil annually (25 per cent of Israel's consumption) and gave his approval to twinning Alexandria with Haifa. It was on that emotional occasion that he also spoke of his vision of the Nile waters irrigating not only the barren Sinai Peninsula but also the southern desert of Israel – the Negev.

Mustafa Khalil now started to get the autonomy talks under way. Meetings were held successively in Alexandria and Herzlia (near Tel Aviv) and sub-committees were formed to deal with particular questions arising from the talks, but it soon transpired that the gap between the parties was too wide to bridge. There were differences of opinion on almost every single issue that was raised: Jerusalem ought to remain united under Israeli rule, contended the Israelis, while Egypt insisted on a special status for an Arab Jerusalem; the

Egyptians pushed for a legislative council on the West Bank and in Gaza, while Israel refused to recognize anything beyond an administrative council; Israel expanded her settlements on the West Bank and in Gaza and constructed new settlements, while Egypt wished to arrest that process; Israel wanted autonomy for the inhabitants of the territories, while Egypt insisted on autonomy for the territories themselves. And so it went on with the issues of water resources, land, security, police, the redeployment of Israeli forces, the fate of existing Israeli settlements, etc. Even the nature of the coming elections, whose arrangement had been agreed upon in the Camp David accords, was widely disputed between the parties. The bottom line of all this was simple: the Egyptians, with American backing, wished to create an infrastructure, legislative and executive, that could and would take over power in the West Bank when the three-year interim period expired; the Israelis wished to give to the Camp David accords a more limited interpretation that would ultimately prevent the establishment of a fully-fledged Palestinian state on the West Bank and in Gaza and would enable Israel to perpetuate her military rule and her settlements there. The talks soon reached an *impasse*. The failure of Jordan to join them on the one hand, and Israel's refusal to talk to the PLO on the other, gave the *coup de grâce* to the negotiations, despite attempts made at the highest levels to revive them.

It was not until September 1981, just one month before Sadat was assassinated, that Israel unilaterally announced the abolition of military government on the West Bank and in Gaza and the institution of a civilian government in its stead, a step that was seen as preparatory to the forthcoming Israeli-style autonomy. To exacerbate matters further, most Palestinian leaders on the West Bank and in Gaza, either because they were intimidated by the PLO or because of genuine concern, rejected the autonomy plan out of hand. Sadat himself soon became discouraged at the prospect of this autonomy, since the beneficiaries of the arrangement rejected it, the PLO was not a partner to the talks, and Israeli rule seemed to be strengthening as the days passed. Israel's attempts to cultivate a new Palestinian leadership on the West Bank, through 'village leagues', which were supposed to provide an alternative to the PLO, were also bogged down owing to the inability of the leagues to attract much following despite, or rather because of, their vocal support of the peace process between Egypt and Israel and their favourable attitude towards the autonomy plan.

Sadat's exasperation at the turn that the peace process had taken was expressed in the bitter messages he exchanged with Begin on 13 and 17 August 1980. Sadat wrote to Begin that the failure to produce a plan for coexistence and reconciliation between Israel and the Palestinians might backfire on Israel and on the entire peace accords. Sadat said that he had been hoping to complete the autonomy talks by 26 May 1980 (one year from their beginning), but that he was appalled by the continuing wave of Israeli settlement and by Israeli 'acts of oppression' against the Palestinians of the West Bank and Gaza. Sadat was particularly incensed at the announcement by the Israeli cabinet of the transfer of some government offices, including the Prime Minister's, to East Jerusalem. Sadat rejected that measure not only as an 'insult to 800 million Muslims', who had as much right to Jerusalem as the 'eighteen million Jews', but also as a 'breach of confidence' on the part of Begin. The breach of confidence was in respect of discussions that Sadat and Begin had had in Haifa, in Alexandria and later in Aswan, where Begin had gone to see Sadat at his winter resort. In all of these meetings, Sadat had confided in Begin his feelings about Jerusalem and had attempted to impress upon him the importance of the holy city to all Muslims. Sadat assumed that Begin had accepted his concern. Sadat had come to believe, especially after his visit in May 1979 to Al-Arish, the city in northern Sinai which Israel had evacuated ahead of schedule to enable Sadat to boast an immediate achievement from the peace treaty, that the treaty would be smoothly implemented and that he could confide in Begin his wishes and concerns and expect them to be acted upon. When Sadat was met in Al-Arish by exuberant Egyptians waving the slogan 'peace and prosperity', he recognized that his people had high expectations of the peace treaty, and that they would remain highly supportive of his peace initiative provided it showed quick results. Since he could not produce instant prosperity, the best he could do was to instil in Begin some understanding of Arab feeling on the issues of Jerusalem and the Palestinians. In his letter of 13 August to Begin, Sadat contended that, without redividing Jerusalem, a way could be found to ensure peaceful coexistence between Muslims, Christians and Jews through the 'restitution of the Arabs' historical and legal rights in the city'. Sadat also counselled Begin to desist from his policy of further settlements on the West Bank, which he described as 'a lost battle' for the Israelis, and he reiterated his generous offer to provide water from the Nile for Jerusalem and the Negev which would enable Israel to build new settlements for its citizenry. Sadat suggested that if Israel and Egypt were to reach an agreement over autonomy, he would be prepared to implement it first in Gaza. Sadat warned, however, that if no progress was made in this direction, the entire peace process might disintegrate. In his answer, Begin repeated the Israeli position and implied that the new Israeli settlements and policies in Jerusalem did not run counter to his interpretation and understanding of the Camp David accords and the peace treaty; and he vowed to fulfil Israel's obligations as he believed them to be formulated in those documents.

All Sadat could do was to write another message to Begin on 17 August, this time claiming that his ideas had occurred to him as he was praying and reading the Holy Quran on the summit of Mount Sinai. He said that he had realized during his meditation that his peace initiative was a 'sacred mission' and divinely inspired; the Almighty was to bring full circle the history of the Hebrews, which had begun on Egyptian soil. Sadat contended that Jerusalem could not be monopolized by Israel, and that it was, geographically and politically, part of the West Bank, and therefore ought to be included in the autonomy. Sadat warned that unless the Jerusalem problem was resolved in a way which took into account the national needs of the Palestinians, tension and conflict would continue to prevail and a great historical opportunity to settle the matter would be irretrievably missed. Sadat also referred to the settlement problem and pledged that if Israeli settlers were evacuated from the West Bank, he would supply the water from the Nile necessary to resettle them in the Negev desert. Sadat also pressed Israel to recognize the 'legitimate rights' of the Palestinians – an issue Begin seemed to ignore – and to desist from vowing that no Israeli settlements would be dismantled, since this might be construed as a precondition to future negotiations. Sadat put the blame for Palestinian reluctance to participate in the autonomy talks squarely on Israel, who, to Sadat's mind, had so fiercely pursued her policy of settlement and oppression on the West Bank, and continued to lay such a pressing claim to the occupied territories, that even moderate Palestinians were deterred from entering the negotiations. Sadat rejected Begin's accusation that the state-controlled press in Egypt was mounting a vitriolic anti-Israeli propaganda campaign despite the fact that Israel had scrupulously implemented her obligations under the peace treaty. Sadat retorted that he was proud of his 'democratic system where everyone is free to express his view according to his liking'. In the end, Sadat concluded that there was no point in resuming the autonomy negotiations, as their failure would only erode the faith of the Egyptian and Israeli peoples in the peace process.

Sadat aired his frustration in an interview given to the Israeli newspaper *Ma'ariv* on 22 August 1980. He admitted, for the first time, that in May 1971, during the Rogers initiative, he had been ready to sign, in effect, a cease-fire, not a peace agreement with Israel. He explained that, when challenged by Golda Meir to sign a peace agreement, he had said that he was prepared to accept such an agreement, but normalization could begin only five years later. Sadat complained that all the steps he took towards strengthening the peace process were misinterpreted by the Israelis; normalization with Israel had not resolved all the problems. He claimed that even his invitation to Israeli President Navon to visit Egypt, which was extended *bona fide* with a view to furthering normalization, was misconstrued by Israel as 'a measure to undermine Begin's authority'. He said that his efforts to further the peace process went well beyond his obligations under the treaty and that he had 'taken ten steps forward for each single step that the Israelis have made'; he also contended that Israel's activities on the West Bank and her repeated attacks in southern Lebanon did not help the situation. At the same time, Sadat praised Israel's decision to advance *ex gratia* her withdrawal from parts of Sinai ahead of schedule. He said that he appreciated this step which helped him placate those Arabs who had opposed his initiative on the grounds that Israel would never withdraw from the Sinai. Sadat repeated his conviction that no more wars would mar relations between Egypt and Israel and that all existing differences could and should be resolved by negotiation.

While Sadat was desperately attempting to resolve the stalemate with Israel, he did not lose sight of the trouble brewing at home. A restive opposition, which was critical of both his home and foreign policies, was now openly and menacingly joined by Muslim fundamentalists. Communal disagreements between Copts and Muslims had surfaced again, and the perennial economic problems made the promised 'age of prosperity' seem more remote than ever. The multi-faceted opposition had begun to institutionalize itself; paradoxically Sadat's liberalization had allowed it, since 1976, to grow into platforms and then organizations within the ASU, and ultimately into fully-fledged parties. To the Right, the Liberal-Socialists were no great threat, since they supported free enterprise and the open door; but to the Left, Sadat faced an array of Marxist and Nasserite groups, headed by Khaled Muhyi-a-Din, who, though a small minority in the Assembly, were vocal and openly hostile. Following the 1976 elections, Sadat had declared that *he* was allowing the various groups to turn into fully-fledged parties. The move was as much directed at controlling the dissidents through recognition and institutionalization as it was aimed at breaking the monopoly of the ASU on political life. In fact, the Centre platform, the mainstream of the ASU, which was loyal to Sadat and which had run for the 1976 elections under Prime Minister Salem sweeping up some 280 out of the 350 seats in the Assembly, also grew into a fully-fledged political party when, at the end of 1978, Sadat announced the creation of his 'National Democratic Party', of which he became the chairman. In May–June 1977, the final touches were put to the new 'Parties Law', which was passed in the Assembly. It actually signalled more restrictive control, rather than continuing liberalization, in Egyptian politics.

At the end of 1977, the Wafd Party, which had been dominant in pre-revolutionary Egyptian politics, applied and obtained permission to re-emerge as the 'New Wafd'. It was constituted by some twenty members of the Assembly who had run, for the most part, on independent tickets in the 1976 elections (there were forty-eight independents altogether). However, rather than being an indication of a more 'liberal' attitude on the part of the regime towards plurality in the political system, the resuscitation of the Wafd after the elections, by members of the House already elected, represented a continuation of the same policy of institutionalizing existing factions into parties, and thereby making it an easier task to identify and control them. All factions, except for the right-wing group, stood in vocal opposition to Sadat's domestic economic policy and to his peace initiative with Israel, and all of them were equally ridiculed, harassed and at times even persecuted. The democratic game had limits, as far as Sadat was concerned; however, opposition disenchantment with the 'multi-party system' was not only mounting, but also taking the concrete form of vocal groups who commanded some popular following and who were represented in the Assembly. Sadat's response was swift and devastating: in May 1978 he put to the people, by referendum, the question of the 'political rights of individuals who were corrupt'; when approved by the populace, as the President knew it would be, the referendum gave the President a 'democratic' *carte blanche* to throw out of the House anyone who did not fall in line. The New Wafd Party dissolved itself, protesting that Sadat's 'limited democracy' could not stand the test of criticism and independent opposition. It was then that Sadat launched his National Democratic Party, which not only advocated the usual 'modern state based on science and faith', 'national unity and social peace' and a 'striving for Arab unity', but also outflanked the Muslim fundamentalists in its vow to 'cultivate spiritual values' and to adopt *Shari'a* (Holy Law) as the main source of legislation in the future.

In the summer of 1979, not long after the inauguration of the Khalil Government in October 1978 (following Camp David), and the referendums of April and May 1979, which were held to approve the peace treaty with Israel and the new domestic political measures, Sadat held new elections, and his new Democratic Party won a landslide of 330 seats (out of 392). Only Ibrahim Shukri, a former Minister of Agriculture in Sadat's Government, who had been encouraged by the President to form a new 'honest opposition' party (the Socialist Labourites), was able to make a sizeable dent (twenty-nine seats) in the Democratic Party majority. The vocal opposition, notably Khaled Muhyi-a-Din, was virtually wiped out – at any rate, within Parliament. It was yet another clear message that Sadat would not allow any opposition to infringe upon what he regarded as 'national unity'. However, Shukri, the leader of what was to be a 'tame opposition', began to show signs of independence. So again, Sadat went to the people: in May 1980 a new referendum approved sweeping measures that gave Sadat extraordinary powers. Firstly, he could seek re-election as often as he wanted. It is evident that he had seriously considered leaving office in 1982, when the last stretch of Sinai was due to be returned, but how could he quit in the midst of the pandemonium that his policies were causing in Egypt? It would be humiliating to depart unless he was riding high, basking in success, admiration and prestige and likely to leave a noticeable hiatus behind him, which would make him greatly missed. He saw the example of his friend, the Shah of Iran, unfolding before his eyes: a powerful leader giving in to opposition and domestic pressures, quitting and finding himself turned instantly into the personification of Satan. Sadat did not want that to happen to him. He would stand up and fight. Secondly, to silence the increasing protests of Muslim fundamentalists, the referendum now approved the proposition that the *Shari'a* would become the *sole* (no longer the *main*) source of legislation. Thirdly, he obtained approval for creating a legislative council, a kind of counterweight to the Assembly, where he could eliminate the remnants of any opposition to him. Finally, he passed the *Qanum al-'aib* (Law of Shame), which enshrined in law the spiritual and ethical values that he had embodied in his new NDP. In June 1980, many notables signed a petition lashing out at Sadat's new style of rule by referendum and decree, but he would not budge. Nor was he moved by the widespread indignation against the *Qanum al-'aib*. Unperturbed, he took over the prime ministership from Mustafa Khalil at the moment when the autonomy talks with Israel were suspended and Khalil ceased to be of use in the negotiations. In late 1980, most of the opposition labourites, sensing that they could no longer serve any purpose, resigned. So, very much resented, Sadat was left as the supreme, seemingly unchallenged and unchecked ruler of Egypt.

In the face of strident criticism from the castrated and disbanded opposition groups, Sadat took comfort in the 'evidence' of his popularity provided by the various referendums, which were all passed with a majority of 90 per cent or higher. Sadat realized full well that the harsher his crackdown against his critics, the greater his tacit acknowledgment that they posed a threat to him; accordingly, he confined himself to dismissing, vilifying and harassing the opposition, with, he supposed, the overwhelming support of the Egyptian populace. In a way, it was the same pattern of behaviour he had adopted with the Arab countries who had criticized him over his peace with Israel. When they had threatened his and Egypt's supremacy in the Arab world, he had dismissed them as 'dwarfs', while claiming that in so doing he had the absolute support of all Egyptians and other 'sane' Arabs. Sadat regarded his opponents at home and abroad as badly behaved children who did not realize what they were doing; when they were taught a lesson, they would return to the harmonious family fold, of which he was the patriarch. He constantly told other Arab leaders that one day they would realize their own short-sightedness and would recognize his statesmanship, which they were unable to emulate. They would repent, he thought, when they realized that they were isolating themselves from Egypt, rather than isolating Egypt from the Arab world. However, Sadat's critics, both inside and outside the country, did not seem to be intimidated by his campaigns of deprecation, nor impressed by the popular support he claimed to command. When the opposition parties dissolved, opposition members continued to express their dissent, either in public, or under cover through underground organizations. The primary outlet for their criticisms were the newspapers, which had been allowed to operate during the height of the liberalization drive, but which were now either subjected to harsh censorship or temporarily banned when they became too outspoken. The weekly *Al-Ahali*, the party organ of the *Al-Tagammu* (Nationalist Progressive Union Party), for example, which voiced harsh criticism of Sadat's policies, only managed to survive for six issues before it was banned in 1978, and did not resume publication until Sadat's murder in late 1981.

Criticism from the opposition covered a wide range of issues. The leftist

255

opposition in particular were greatly disturbed from the outset by Sadat's pro-American orientation, and their sentiments grew fiercer as Sadat became more firmly committed to this. They also criticized Sadat's socialist rhetoric, which they felt was no more than lip service and slogan-making, and they pointed to his implementation of socialism as a complete and dismal failure. The economic situation also brought wide criticism: nothing seemed to have improved for the vast majority of Egyptians; peace did not seem to yield any tangible results for them either. There was no more food on the tables than before and what there was was more expensive and subject to fluctuating world market prices. Services, such as transport and communications, were still in a shambles.

These criticisms concerning the economy, though they were articulated by limited segments of the population, actually reflected a concern shared by many Egyptians, who could recognize the disastrous path their country was following. For not only were the long-standing promises about prosperity not being fulfilled, but there was apparently no likelihood of their being fulfilled in the foreseeable future. Much scorn was again poured by Sadat's critics on his open-door policy. Even though some opposition members (especially on the Right and in the Centre) did not rule out some form of *infitah*, they had become exasperated at the failure of the policy to work as planned. Only the rich were benefiting from it, while to the masses it remained a closed door. Large-scale corruption on the part of entrepreneurs within Egypt and the economic exploitation of Egypt by foreigners seemed to be the visible results of the open-door policy. Domestically, for example, there was outright cheating in the production of sub-standard concrete and steel, which occasioned the collapse of many a building during, or shortly after, construction, resulting in loss of life on more than one occasion. Ironically, one of the major *infitah* constructors, whose iron and steel construction rods were found deficient, and who was later imprisoned for his misdemeanours, was named *Al-Hadidi* ('the Iron Man'). Somebody had made an easy profit, without Sadat's direct knowledge and even, conceivably, against his will, but since this rampant corruption and quick profiteering were seen as the outcome of the *infitah*, the blame was quite often laid at Sadat's feet. Another reason for harsh criticism by the opposition was that the *infitah*, which had been designed to strengthen Egypt's infrastructure, had become oriented towards the acquisition of consumer goods rather than towards investment in industry. The flow of foreign capital that Sadat had promised would begin to pour into Egypt in the form of investment seemed to be swallowed up by exhibitionist and superfluous consumerism. This served to deepen Egypt's economic dependence on outside sources rather than to launch Egypt into economic independence. Some opposition groups claimed that this process was introducing into Egypt a new kind of foreign domination and exploitation. They contended that where the open-door policy was necessary, it should be pursued selectively and with far greater supervision.

Sadat was also severely criticized for his 'democratic' ways, particularly during 1981. The opposition argued that democracy was simply another of Sadat's 'inflated balloons'. They contended that there was neither democracy nor freedom of expression in Egypt, despite Sadat's insistence to the contrary. For newspapers could be banned, censorship enforced, and people arrested and jailed for expressing ideas that were considered to exceed the bounds of free expression, whether in newspapers, books, films, plays, on television or at public gatherings. They also claimed that the election process, let alone the public referendums, were a total farce, and they spoke with scorn of the 'eternal 99.98 per cent' figure in favour of Sadat and the representatives of the governing party. More specifically, they denounced the 1979 elections as having been rigged, with ballot-box stuffing, unsupervised counting of votes and so on. The result had been that the non-government party candidates, who clearly enjoyed majority support in certain districts, were pushed out of the picture altogether, with the familiar 99.98 per cent count in favour of the government candidates. One notable exception widely and bitterly reported, despite censorship, in the opposition press, was the case of Mumtaz Nassar, who was running on an independent ticket for Parliament in the town of Assyut in Upper Egypt, where he reportedly enjoyed fiercely staunch support. After the voting had taken place, officials came to remove the ballot boxes in order to 'count' the votes *in camera*; a group of Nassar's supporters, armed with guns, successfully demanded that the ballot boxes be opened in their presence. Predictably, Nassar won by a landslide, and he was one of the few candidates who made it to the 1979 Parliament on a non-government ticket. Other candidates, who did not have the political acumen, the determined following of Nassar, or the guts to take drastic measures, simply lost the 'elections'.

The cumulative effect of these criticisms, which were aimed directly at those policies Sadat prided himself on – democracy, economic progress and the *infitah* – were to make it increasingly difficult for the proud President to dismiss them as the mischievous conduct of incorrigible children. Sadat remained most sensitive to criticism of his peace accords with Israel. On this issue, Sadat was unequivocally intolerant; he had put up with such a barrage of criticism from the Arab world that he felt similar criticism at home was tantamount to betrayal. He could not bear the idea that Egyptians were allying themselves with his enemies, eroding his prestige and denigrating his honour.

For Sadat, the Camp David accords and the ensuing peace treaty with Israel were his greatest achievements, the culmination of his life's effort to bring a brighter future to Egypt. He believed his daring and visionary action would earn him a place in the annals of history as the man who brought peace to the Middle East, who brought off a *tour de force* that no one before him, not even the revered Kissinger, had been able to achieve. Sadat treated the peace accords as an intimate part of himself and felt intensely that criticism of them was criticism of him. At the outset, Sadat dismissed, even pitied, those who failed to see the magnificence of his step. In view of the world-wide recognition in which he basked, he must have believed that his critics in Egypt and the Arab world were simply blind, ignorant, unworthy or unable to see the light. But as the criticism persisted and mounted, Sadat could no longer deal with it summarily or calmly; the accords were too bound up with his own being and therefore the criticism was too intensely personal. In early 1979, he had attempted to 'institutionalize' approval and acceptance of his peace initiative by adding a stipulation to the laws regarding the formation of legitimate political parties in Egypt: all political parties had to endorse officially the peace agreement as one of the prerequisites for their legal recognition; but opposition persisted. Initially Sadat had only taken action against opposition when it had been particularly trenchant, as in the case of the *Al-Ahali* weekly which was closed down because of its virulent condemnation of the peace initiative; but as time went on, Sadat began to take harsher action in response to the slightest hints of disapproval or doubt about his policies. His desperate course of action reached its lowest ebb when, during the last months of his life, Sadat ordered the arrests of thousands of people, including many public figures, suspected underground Communists, members of the opposition parties and even of his own government party, as well as writers, journalists, Copts, Muslim fundamentalists and others. A variety of reasons were presented to justify these arrests, but judging from the multifarious political, and non-political, causes the detainees represented, scepticism, opposition or benign doubt regarding the greatness of the Camp David accords lay behind the arrests.

It became increasingly difficult for Sadat to fend off the combined attack of the domestic opposition and the Arab world. He might dismiss his domestic opponents on the grounds that he enjoyed popular support and that *he*, not they, represented the legitimate aspirations of the Egyptian people; but in the Arab world, he constituted an aberration rather than an accepted norm and he, the hero of 1973, was now branded as a 'traitor', the 'saviour of Zionism', 'Begin's stooge' and an 'American running dog'. He could scorn the Ba'th Party of Syria as unrepresentative of the Syrians, and he could denigrate the PLO leaders for their excesses, but he could not ignore the near unanimity of the Arab world in their opposition to his policies. The more he protested that the other Arabs would come to grasp the significance of his historic move in the Middle East, the more he insulted his Arab opponents; and the more evident his agony at his isolation, the more self-elevating, ascetic, 'spiritual', remote, mystic and given to daydreams he became. Even after the second Baghdad Conference, Sadat had anticipated that the rupture of political, economic and diplomatic ties with the Arab world would be short-lived. For it was clear to him that his visionary nature had enabled him to 'see the light' before others, but that the light was so bright that the others could not remain blind to it indefinitely. It was their return to the fold, rather than his own, that he expected in the foreseeable future. But time passed and there was no improvement in Arab attitudes towards him. It was ironic (and injurious to his pride) that as the man who had restored Arab unity on the eve of the 1973 war, he now became its most conspicuous victim; Arab hostility towards him was harsher, more persistent and continued much longer than he had expected and it did not seem to be receding. Sadat boiled with anger and frustration at those who could not see the greatness of his feats. Diplomatic isolation and the cutting of the purse strings by the Arabs delivered heavy blows to Sadat's ambition to retain Arab leadership and to his tottering economy; but it dealt no less a blow to his ego. To have lost the image of benign father at home and to be dubbed 'traitor' abroad tormented Sadat. He preferred to fight on one front where he could concentrate his forces and win: but combined pressures from more than one quarter and from the least expected directions made him nervous and withdrawn. It was his past supporters who now seemed to be his enemies, vilifying him, delegitimizing him and setting him up as a target for any good and conscientious Egyptian, Arab or Muslim. What he believed to be the adulation of the West was now his sole source of comfort. He felt that the deeper the gap between him and the Arab world, the more he should be pampered and supported by the West. He thought that what had turned out to be the tremendous personal price he had paid for peace should be made up for by unconditional loyalty to him on the part of the US. However, even on this front, Sadat felt thwarted. The Americans were engaged in a new election campaign in 1980 and seemed unable to prevail on Israel to yield on the autonomy talks. President Carter, on whom Sadat had pinned so many hopes, was not re-elected. When Sadat heard the election results, he reportedly burst out in exasperation: 'This will be the fourth American President I will have to educate!'

Doubts raised in the West regarding Sadat were not over Camp David. Attacks against him in the Western media, which started intensifying in 1980–81, were directed at the 'sacred image' Sadat still held of himself as the 'man of democracy', an image he was desperate to continue projecting to the West. Sadat, himself an erstwhile journalist and writer, knew and was sensitive to the power of words. He once said that the pen is the most potent of weapons. In Western newspapers, articles began to appear in noticeably growing numbers exposing the numerous limitations on freedom of speech and expression in Egypt, the dubious nature of the elections, censorship and arrests without due recourse to legal processes. For Sadat, this was not simply another criticism like the ones he was weary of facing in Egypt and the Arab world. For him, this signified supreme disloyalty and betrayal on the part of the West. He painfully absorbed Western criticisms in his daily readings of the world press; indeed, during his visit to the US in 1981 he was sharply confronted by them: he came across many an article, a wording, an insinuation which attacked the image he had projected of himself abroad. What was worse, however, was the full-page announcement in the *New York Times*, paid for by the Copts living in America, voicing their protest over what they felt were his oppressive policies towards the Copts of Egypt. Even in America, his last 'natural reserve' of popularity, he could find little comfort.

Before this trip to America, Sadat was already spending much of his time in Mit Abul-kum, where he was detached from family, government and hostile Cairo. It was there that his daughter Camellia, about to take a study trip to the US, came to see him in early August. She found him despondent, extremely irritable, ascetic and losing weight. Her queries about his health were brushed aside, but he intimated that this situation could not go on much longer. When Camellia and her daughter Eqbal took their leave of Sadat, after taking a three-generation family picture, the President bade them farewell, said that he was going to the US shortly and suggested that he might not live to see them again.

When Sadat came back from the US, he again spent much of his time at Mit Abul-kum. In September he held a press conference for foreign correspondents in his native village, and delivered what sounded like a final message to the world. He was aggressive and explosive, but rather than responding to the substance of the various claims that were hurled against him, or defending himself or correcting what he considered to be a distorted image of his policies, he spent much of his address yelling, 'How can you write these lies about me?' He would quote large sections of articles from the London *Times* and other newspapers, which had called into question various aspects of his practice of democracy in Egypt, repeating again and again, 'These are vicious lies! How can you write these things?' To many of the correspondents, the sight was pitiable, but as the conference went on they became increasingly indignant. He began waving a tape in his hands saying: 'I am going to have you listen to this tape, to make you hear the truth about the vicious lies that are being spread about me and about Egypt.' The tape was a recording of an interview with a British correspondent, David Hirst, who had been expelled by Sadat in 1977, made by an ABC correspondent. The original recording had been secretly monitored by the Egyptian security apparatus. The correspondents were filled with consternation at this blatant violation of privacy and freedom of speech, by a President who was trying to defend his democratic ways. It was during this press conference that a correspondent asked Sadat if, in view of the timing of his recent trip to the US and the subsequent mass arrests on his return, it was reasonable to assume that there had been some sort of implied or explicit approval on the part of the American Government for these actions. Sadat exploded, speaking with a fury and a lack of control the like of which nobody had ever seen. Sadat had always been calm in moments of distress; he had never wept in private or in public, and had always looked like a consummate and rational statesman who would never let emotions overtake him. Now he reportedly screamed: 'I have the right to shoot you for asking such a question, but this is a democracy.' He went on to protest that Egypt was independent and needed no permission or approval from any outside country or entity regarding its policies, internal or foreign. The press conference became, to its participants, a frightening indication of Sadat's state of mind in the final weeks of his life. One of Sadat's daughters, who was watching the press conference on television, was stunned by her father's performance.

Sadat had ordered mass arrests; he sensed he was losing his grip; he seemed continuously restless, tormented, persecuted, wary of people and events around him; something seemed to have snapped inside him. Faced with a crescendo of criticism from all directions, he felt attacked, isolated and forlorn. He was no longer the master of events. His willingness to fight was giving way to a deep feeling of anti-climactic emptiness. He felt he was being hounded and harassed for reasons he could ill understand. This, in turn, generated further alienation between Sadat and the Egyptian people, an alienation that was seen in his growing remoteness and which was fed by his deepening paranoia. Sadat's frame of mind was also demonstrated by a series of oppressive measures against the Copts and the Muslim fundamentalists, two elements that he had attempted to placate before, but who now contributed to the siege that he felt was closing in on him.

Sadat had been aware of the Coptic problem in Egypt since his first involvement in Egyptian politics. He had always regarded the issue as one of inter-communal accommodation between the majority Muslim culture and the minority Coptic culture, although he understood, but never articulated, the Coptic resentment of the historical twist which had turned them from the host culture into a guest culture in their own land: from the proud heirs of the ancient Egyptian, Hellenistic and Christian traditions and cultures into a community tolerated in the midst of a Muslim, and at times hostile, environment. Sadat had had to deal repeatedly with the Coptic problem during his presidency, but as his personal situation worsened, he came to perceive the Copts as yet another faction contributing to his predicament. He particularly resented the term 'Coptic nation' which was used by some militant Copts and which implied that Egypt's unity, and consequently Sadat's authority, was disputed. The 'divisive' nature of Coptic 'nationalism' was what incensed Sadat most, and he tried throughout his presidency to stress that Copts would be tolerated and accepted as equal citizens in the country, but at the same time that they should entertain no doubts as to who ruled the land and should not challenge the predominance of Islam in the Egyptian polity. This message, which Sadat had hammered home on several occasions, was nothing new to the Copts. They had become accustomed to maintaining a low profile, resigned to their status as a tolerated minority, and did their best not to arouse the wrath of their Muslim masters or provide them with an excuse to question the loyalty of the Copts to the Arabs and to Egypt. The Copts had usually succeeded in going about their business without attracting too much attention. As long as they were not pushed to the wall and provided their basic freedom of worship was respected, they would accept humiliation, job discrimination, cultural slights and sometimes open persecution. Many of them envied the Jews, who had thrown off their minority status and had established a state of their own, but they never entertained illusions of reaching statehood or even an autonomy of sorts, and certainly laid no plans for such a thing. The Copts had to endure the condescending attitude of the dominant Muslims, who could not understand their religio-cultural obstinacy, and to put up with their own denigration in the teaching of Egypt's history. For example, the 1919 Revolution in Egypt had counted a disproportionate number of Copts among its heroes, and in 1922, towards the end of the formal British mandate in Egypt, seven Copts had died for their patriotism. The rise of Islamic fundamentalism in the 1970s, which in many ways had encouraged Muslim–Coptic confrontation in Egypt, had also contributed significantly to the process of eliminating from historical writings and records the prominent role of the Copts in the liberation of their country.

The submissive role of the Copts in Egyptian society and their often heroic efforts to secure Egyptian independence had not diminished the suspicion and slurs directed at them over generations. Under Nasser's regime, as a result of the policy of nationalization of merchant banks and other financial services, the Copts had probably suffered more than their Muslim compatriots. So when Sadat assumed power and declared the democratization of Egypt and the liberalization of the economy, Coptic expectations were raised. Sadat seemed to pursue a more or less impartial course with respect to the Copts, whom he considered as his children like all the rest. Islamic fundamentalists, however, began inciting the Egyptians by accusing the Copts either of having turned their churches into arsenals, or of being ready to subvert the state and 'kill Muslims', or of collusion with Israel in their struggle against the Muslims. Following the euphoria of 'victory' in October 1973, and the accounts which abounded in the Egyptian press of 'supernatural events' allowing Egyptian forces to cross the Canal and defeat Israel, a note of sobriety was introduced when the first reports of the Israeli counter-attack came in. The military were embarrassed by the Israeli success, achieved in spite of the 'supernatural forces' supposed to be at work on the Muslim side, and reports spread in Egypt that the Egyptian unit which had allowed the Israeli counter-attack to succeed was commanded by a Copt field officer. Making scapegoats of the Copts was not a new phenomenon and the logic of collusion between Copts and Israelis, Christians and Jews, against the Muslims, made sense to many Egyptians. These reports were compounded by rumours that Christian doctors were refusing to treat dying Muslim patients in Egypt, or were viciously administering incorrect treatment which brought about the patients' deaths. By the 1970s the Copts were suffering constant persecution: churches were broken into and sometimes set ablaze; Copts were publicly humiliated, insulted or even killed, and those who protested against the rampages, notably Coptic priests, were thrown into jail. Their Pope, Shenouda III, was deposed, and at the height of anti-Christian sentiment, in Khanqa (1972), in Miniah (1980), and in Zawiya al-Hamra, Cairo (1981), many churches were burned and Coptic property looted or destroyed.

Sadat's relations with the Copts deteriorated steadily after the election of Pope Shenouda III in September 1972. Sadat suspected that the vigorous and opinionated spiritual chief was willing to take advantage of the seeming weakness of the pre-October 1973 Government to press for the fulfilment of Coptic demands. Absorbed in the preparations for the war, Sadat chose not to take the offensive against the Copts, but instead to reassure them (after the 1972 Khanqa incident) and to placate their leaders. Unity was his paramount concern. In July 1976, a Coptic committee was formed, with Pope Shenouda among its members; it sought to provide one unified organization so that all Copts could better resist the campaign against them by Muslim fundamentalists. The first meeting led to a much more formal and widely attended meeting of the 'Committee for the Coptic people' in December 1976. The Copts, while reiterating their unfailing loyalty to Egypt, of which, they believed, they were the original masters, stated in no uncertain terms their unflinching support for the independence of the Coptic Church, which they regarded not only as a spiritual institution, but also as the only accepted means of expressing their separate identity. In January–February 1977, the Copts launched a campaign of fasting and Coptic solidarity, which only exacerbated the suspicions of the Muslim population. When in September 1977 the Egyptian Government announced its intention of reinstating capital punishment for Christian converts to Islam who reneged on their new faith and returned to Christianity, a five-day fasting period was again declared by the Coptic Church in protest. Sadat, who had attempted, during the October War, to dismiss the vicious rumours about Coptic 'traitors', made a new effort to maintain contact with the Coptic leadership in order to avert the escalation of inter-communal clashes. In October 1977, while pondering over his peace initiative, Sadat attended a Coptic wedding, and as a gesture of reconciliation invited the Patriarch to join him in prayer. The Copts greeted Sadat's benevolent, and quite unusual, gesture with great excitement and gratitude. However, in 1978–9, the Muslim fundamentalists' violence against the Copts escalated, and Sadat was unwilling or unable to crack down on them. The Copts again felt abandoned. The burning of churches, the murder of Coptic priestly families and the bombing of the Damshirieh Sanctuary in Cairo prompted new and vigorous protests by the Coptic Pope. He cancelled the Easter celebrations of 1980, suspended his participation in official ceremonies where members of the Egyptian Government took part, and he rejected the idea, promulgated by Sadat's Government, that the *Shari'a* should be the basis for legislation in Egypt.

Coptic protests against Muslim fundamentalists and the Sadat regime mounted, culminating in the 1980 advertisement in North American newspapers, which so angered Sadat that he vowed he would discipline Shenouda when he returned home. From May 1980, a co-ordinated campaign was conducted by the Egyptian media against the Copts; the Copts were accused of being responsible for all Egypt's ills. Even the Muslim fundamentalists' excesses were traced back to Coptic provocation. Shenouda, who was now accused by Sadat of having plotted to turn the Coptic movement into a political organization that would challenge the legitimacy of the Egyptian Government and push for Coptic secession from the Egyptian state, published the text of the telegram he had sent to the Copts in the US during the President's visit there. The cable in effect declared the unswerving loyalty of the Copts to Egypt and their interest in promoting a favourable image of Egypt abroad. The Coptic Patriarch stressed that he would conduct his struggle for Coptic rights in Egypt with 'wisdom and spirituality so as not to damage Egypt's reputation'. In addition, the Pope exhorted his followers to greet Sadat respectfully and to give him credit for all he had done for Egypt, the Copts and the cause of peace. However, Shenouda's call to his people to 'withdraw into the desert' in order to protest at the current state of affairs was construed by Sadat as a sure sign that the Copts were preparing for autonomy in the part of the country most difficult for the Egyptian Government to control.

The hatred and suspicion between Muslims and Copts brought about one of the worst inter-communal struggles in modern Egypt. In June 1981, Zawiya al-Hamra, a Cairene suburb where Muslims and Copts had lived together for centuries, erupted. The clash arose over who had the right to use a parcel of land belonging to a Copt. Muslim fundamentalists took over the plot 'in order to build a mosque' and the Copt proprietor, who ran armed to the place to enforce his ownership, found himself surrounded and threatened by a horde of Muslims. He opened fire 'in self-defence', which was immediately construed as a blatant attempt to 'kill Muslims'. Supporters of both faiths rushed to the plot and a real battle ensued, resulting in dozens of deaths and injuries and the burning and destruction of many houses and some churches. Nabawi Isma'il, Sadat's Minister of the Interior, who sent in the police to quell the rioting, was reportedly slow to respond, and it was rumoured that he wished to use the opportunity offered by the battle to identify and incarcerate the militants in both the Coptic and the Muslim fundamentalist camps, which were equally threatening to the Sadat regime. At the end of this three-day on-and-off battle, there were many casualties among the Muslims as well as among the Copts. The fact that the Copts had defended themselves added to the suspicion that they had indeed been stockpiling arms for a more far-reaching enterprise.

The events of Zawiya al-Hamra represented only the tip of the iceberg. Mounting beneath was not only the long-standing animosity between Copts and Muslims, but also the Muslim fundamentalism which had been gaining in Egypt since the late 1960s. While devastating Coptic churches and houses, and in some cases throwing Coptic children from windows and burning houses with all their Coptic occupants inside, fundamentalist Muslims also waved virulent slogans attacking Sadat and his 'godless rule'. Sadat, a pious Muslim himself, was well aware of the Islamic revival in his country. He recognized that the more liberal and democratic he wanted to be, the more attentive and responsive he had to become to the popular demand to revert to Islamic tradition. The Islamic establishment was tame and could be relied upon to justify Sadat's policies of domestic modernization and peace with Israel, but it could not satisfy the public desire for an Islamic renaissance. Fundamentalism, which criticized the ossified and subservient Islamic establishment, posed a new problem. Fundamentalism was apparent not only among the disaffected masses, whose revolutionary potential was becoming more and more evident, but also among the intelligentsia, the urban bourgeoisie, the student population and those in the bureacracy. It was clear that not all fundamentalists were necessarily engaged in a new quest for Allah, nor were they interested in the practical tenets of Islam; their fundamentalism was an indication that many were frustrated by their inability to cope with modernity and by the isolationist stance that their President was taking with respect to the Arab world. The wave of fundamentalism was manifest in the press, in the Friday sermons in the mosques and in the massive sales of religious works, not least of which was the *Al-Da'wa* magazine, the mouthpiece of the Muslim Brothers, on street stands. These publications usually coupled a stern demand for restoration of the *Shari'a* with a violent refutation of modernization, technology and Western norms in general. The sermons of the Brotherhood, and of the *gama'at* (revivalist groups), called publicly for the 'rescue of the Abode of Islam from Zionist occupation' and for the extermination of Israel. These exhortations obviously ran counter to Sadat's peace initiative, which had been motivated primarily by his obsession with Western-orientated modernization and by his drive for economic recovery.

At first, Sadat did not move against the extremist Muslim groups. He was unable to follow the example of Nasser, who had quashed the Brotherhood with great cruelty: perhaps because of his own religious convictions; because of his fear that in general the Egyptian people were too much in favour of Islam to tolerate such repression in days of relative freedom; because of the possible backlash from Muslim fundamentalists abroad; or because he intended to harness fundamentalism to his own ends. Whichever it was, Sadat was caught in the contradiction that modernization also meant a certain liberalism, and that this in turn meant that opposition groups such as the Brotherhood and other religious fanatics were able to operate openly. Sadat was also well aware of the cautionary example of the Shah of Iran, another champion of Westernization, who had repressed Islamic and other opposition groups, only to be cast out by a popular revolt. Sadat obviously dreaded that this might happen to him, hence his desperate attempt to cultivate a conservative and tame Islam reconcilable with modernism and pro-Westernism. Though Sadat's public image was that of a devout Muslim, he warned that the Brotherhood held no monopoly over Islam. He allowed Islamic legislation and paid lip service to Islamic predominance in Egypt, but he also stressed 'democratic' ways and the necessity of avoiding fanaticism and intolerance. However, there was little Sadat could do to stem the rise of fundamentalism. After 1974, when an attempt was made on his life at the Technical Military College by a young doctor of philosophy, Saleh Sarrieh, who headed a fundamentalist group called the Islamic Liberation Party, Sadat became concerned about the physical threat posed to him. Fundamentalists spoke up in the streets of Cairo and elsewhere and, encouraged by the prevailing ambiance of freedom, won landslide victories in the student elections in 1975 and again in 1979. Sadat, who had hoped to use the fundamentalists to thwart the Marxist and Nasserite Left, was now witnessing with horror the uncontrollable growth of Muslim revivalists. These groups demanded that separate teaching for men and women be instituted in universities, that amusement centres on campus be closed down and that hours of prayer take precedence over the school curriculum. In some cases, their demands were met. Many women students, who absorbed this new trend and at least partly contributed to its momentum, now wore the *zay-shar'i*, the traditional garb which covered up their sexuality and announced their unavailability. The circulation of the *Al-Da'wa* and *I'tisam* magazines, which some say was encouraged by Sadat in order to offset the biting criticism of the Left, became so widespread that the regime began questioning the wisdom of permitting their distribution.

The fundamentalists were not merely seeking reforms of an Islamic nature within the existing system, they demanded a total overhaul of Egyptian society, the scrapping of the existing base and the adoption of the 'Islamic alternative'. They contended that Egyptian society was basically corrupt, violent and degenerate and that the state machinery was plagued by embezzlement, neglect, bribery and nepotism. The state institutions, they claimed, were unable and unfit to remedy the malaise of Egyptian society. Nor could education be counted upon to bring about a spiritual and moral turnabout: the present educational system was defective and encouraged apostasy rather than belief, and subversive Western thinking rather than constructive faith in Islam. Under the prevailing system in Egypt, argued the fundamentalists, imperialistic thinking, the ultimate goal of which was to weaken and eliminate Islam, was advancing in great strides via the educational system and the media. Worse still, in their view, was the Marxist threat. By contrast, being a holistic religion, Islam offered a system which, if implemented in letter and spirit, provided all relevant answers to the pressing problems of the day. Moreover, the very values that were treasured in Western society, such as liberty, sovereignty and the supremacy of law, could best be realized under the Islamic system: Islam encouraged generosity, solidarity and social responsibility, while Western societies fostered individualism and egotistic pursuits. The fundamentalists advocated a radical reversion to *Shari'a* law, not the partial and gradual reversion advocated by Sadat. The expression of fundamentalist principles in *Al-Da'wa* was coupled with the demand that the movement should be allowed to operate as a political party, so that it could compete for the establishment of a just and egalitarian Muslim society. Sadat was rightly concerned that a political party based on Islamic fundamentalist ideas might shatter the monopoly of power that his own party had held since the 1976 elections. While the Brotherhood was prepared to play the democratic game, and was usually opposed to violence, other more extremist groups, such as the Repentance and the Holy Flight, the Muhammedan Youth, the Islamic Liberation Party and the Jihad Group, resorted to kidnappings and terror to force their fundamentalism upon society. However, their ideas about the 'Islamic alternative' did not significantly vary from those of the Brotherhood, except for their yearning to resurrect the caliphate as the true expression of the Islamic state. Most members of these extremist groups were young and deeply committed to the cause of Islam, and while the membership was drawn from all walks of life, a disproportionate number of them came from student circles and from the military.

Part of the thrust of the fundamentalists' argument was that a true Muslim life could only be conducted within the *Umma*, the universal congregation of all Muslims; hence the demand for a return to the caliphate. The fundamentalists' position was strengthened by the vitriolic response of world Islam to the Camp David accords which were rejected on Islamic as well as on political grounds. Although Sadat had been the hero of the 1974 Islamic Summit Conference in Lahore, Pakistan, because of his 'victory' over Israel, and although he had continued to have a major influence at subsequent Islamic gatherings before his signing of the peace treaty, he was now cast out by the world Islamic community. Egypt was excluded from Islamic conferences after 1979. Moreover, the Islamic Conference of February 1981 in Ta'if, Saudi Arabia, not only condemned the peace treaty again but called for an outright *Jihad* to redeem the occupied holy land from Israel. A link was thus established between Islam as an international political force and opposition to Sadat in Egypt on the issue of Israel. In matters of domestic policy, the Brotherhood and other extremist groups sought to emulate Libya and Iran, where Islamic norms had taken over most aspects of life. There is reason to believe that opponents of Sadat in the Arab–Islamic world were playing up the affinities between the opposition at home and his critics abroad in order to pressure him to change his stance on the peace issue. For the Muslim opposition in Egypt led the Muslim world to believe that a reversal of Egypt's aberrant policies was possible and that not all Egyptians were as solidly behind their President as he pretended. Sadat had tried to stem the tide by recruiting some moderate fundamentalists, like Sheikh Sha'rawi, into the establishment. During Ramadan in 1980, Sadat organized a nationally televised debate with the Muslim *'Ulama* and Omár Talmasani, one of the leaders of the Muslim Brothers. Sadat tried to placate Talmasani, who was also the editor of *Al-Da'wa*, by remarking that he was allowing the magazine to appear although he could shut it down at any moment. Talmasani outwitted Sadat by insinuating that Allah was above both of them and that he who had committed no sin should have reason to fear neither God nor any human being. Sadat had to concur before the cameras, and thus to concede that Allah, not the President of Egypt, would determine the course of things to come.

Sadat's last few months seemed to be a microcosm of his long history of past troubles. He spent much of 1981 in isolation in either Aswan or Mit Abul-kum reflecting upon the *impasse* in which he found himself. He also went for a few days' prayer and meditation on Mount Sinai, hoping perhaps for some inspiration that would generate a new breakthrough. While in Aswan, he announced that he was giving asylum to the deposed Shah of Iran, his friend, who had been unable to find refuge for himself and his family elsewhere. There was certainly an element of defiance in this, a feeling that *he* would do what all other world leaders had not dared to do and *he* would teach all others the virtue of loyalty to a friend. But it was more than that: he was in search of a dramatic and worthwhile event that would revive his waning self-esteem and return him to the centre of world attention. He also felt an instinctive empathy for a pursued and disgraced man, who had so recently lived in glorious splendour; he may well have sensed a community of fate with him. When the deposed Shah became terminally ill, Sadat personally gave daily medical bulletins to the press about his guest's state of health and, upon the Shah's eventual death, he ordered a state funeral. This was probably the way he would have liked to be treated had he encountered the same misfortune. Sadat's stately hospitality towards the Shah did not escape the opposition. The Left, or what remained of it, viewed Sadat's move as yet another despairing gesture by a ruler who had lost touch with reality. They resented the fact that Egypt had been used as a haven for what they viewed as a corrupt, oppressive, imperialistic and reactionary monarch. The Muslim fundamentalists were infuriated by Sadat's blatant affront to the venerated Khomeini and to the Islamic revolution in Iran, which they held in high esteem and considered a model to emulate.

About this time, Sadat ordered the release of some Muslim fundamentalists who had been jailed after a renewed wave of rampages against the Copts in the summer of 1981; this brought about a new wave of protests from the Coptic patriarchate. Sadat reacted by removing Shenouda III from office and exiling him to the Libyan desert, much to the resentment of the Coptic community, which grew more restive than ever before. Sadat's strong-arm policy against the Copts evidently pleased Muslim fundamentalists, but was not enough to outweigh what they considered to be his continuing crimes on the question of relations with Israel. Sadat not only swallowed the 'Jerusalem Law' passed by the Israeli Knesset in July 1980, which caused a great uproar throughout the Islamic world, but in June 1981, just before the Israeli elections, Sadat agreed to meet with Begin in Sharm al-Sheikh (Ophira to the Israelis). A few days later, Israel bombed and destroyed the Iraqi nuclear reactor near Baghdad. It was assumed by many Egyptians and other Arabs that Sadat had approved this action beforehand. Begin would not have dared to attack a nuclear plant in the heart of an Arab capital, clamoured many Arabs, if he did not have the assurance either that Egypt would support this act or at least that she would not react to it. The escalating battles between Israel and the PLO in southern Lebanon, which culminated in the devastating Israeli bombing of the PLO headquarters in Beirut in the summer of 1981, were also blamed by the Egyptian opposition on Sadat's peace treaty, which had in effect neutralized Egypt's military power and enabled Israel to act freely on all other fronts. Sadat and his subordinates alone defended his peace policy; even the 'honest opposition', the Socialist Labour party, decided to desert him in 1981. Then came Begin's triumph in the elections of June 1981 and another meeting between him and Sadat, in Alexandria in August. This signified to Sadat's critics that the Egyptian President had given his *post-factum* approval to what were considered Israel's 'rampages' in the Middle East: Jerusalem, Lebanon, Iraq, the settlements on the West Bank and in Gaza. The announcement at the end of the Alexandria meeting between the two leaders about the imminent resumption of the autonomy talks was taken as yet another whitewash of a rather grim political deadlock. Sadat further inflamed the Muslim opposition when he publicized his plan to erect an inter-denominational complex which was to house a mosque, a church and a synagogue on Mount Sinai. Nothing could be more offensive to Muslim fundamentalists than the sight of houses of prayer belonging to the Christian and Jewish 'people of the book' side by side with the house of Allah. The cup of grievances against Sadat was full to the brim and ready to spill over.

September 1981 was Sadat's last month. People who were close to him and who managed to see him from time to time during that last month, in private or in public, attest that he seemed to have been in an extremely fragile and unstable psychological state. He gave the impression, not unlike Nixon in his last weeks in power, that he had grown impatient with people, extremely edgy, impulsive and that he was on the verge of collapse. All the old calm and self-control for which Sadat had become famous, all his charm, his charisma, seemed to be vanishing; in place of the old Sadat was a paranoid, confused, inconsistent, restless and erratic man. He began sweating more profusely than before, and gave way to outbursts of shouting of surprising violence. His incoherence and the disorganization of his thoughts were baffling to his entourage. The final *coup de grâce* to Sadat's morale was delivered by the corps of foreign correspondents who, up until then, had handled him as if he were a 'media doll'. He had enjoyed one of the most positive images that Western correspondents had created of anyone anywhere. He had been depicted to the West as the daring hero of peace, as a man of charm and finesse, a founder of democracy in his country and a new champion of Western values in the Middle East. Suddenly, in the wake of his domestic problems and his crackdown on the foreign press, he lost his last allies in the world; his larger-than-life image was damaged, his mystique was unravelled and his charisma was 'routinized'. The foreign correspondents, who had helped him transcend the gloomy reality at home by burnishing his image abroad, now cruelly pushed him to the abyss. Sadat was akin to the witch in a fairy tale who was constantly told that she was the most beautiful woman in the world; when she finally looked in the mirror and saw the wrinkles on her face, she thought they were cracks on the mirror. Sadat was now forced to look at his wrinkled image in the Western mirror; he did not like, nor could he accept, what he saw. But all he could do was to lash out verbally in all directions. His last press conference with foreign correspondents (10 September 1981) at Mit Abul-kum, when he told a western correspondent that he could have him shot for his question about whether or not he had Reagan's approval for the mass arrests in Egypt, was also revealing in many other ways. He expressed his disgust with the democracy he had built. He said, 'I would have shot you, but this is a democracy. I am suffering because of it as much as I am suffering because of the opposition.' His manner of speaking at that conference, as preserved on a tape recording, was a far cry from his calm, charming, self-confident manner of yesteryear. He stumbled for words; his train of thought was inconsistent, almost incoherent, jumping and darting from one subject to the next without completing his thoughts; he flitted back to past subjects, and repeated almost verbatim things he had already said. When he wanted to put the questioner in his place, he assumed a very sarcastic tone of voice, but this would suddenly give way to a pathetic diatribe in which all his anger, indignation, sense of hurt and betrayal would surface. Then he would begin to shout and yell.

The image Sadat had built up of himself was one of his greatest assets. Throughout his presidency, in nearly all his public utterances, he made statements such as 'in front of my people and in front of the whole world'. He very seldom went into detail when responding to criticism directed against him at home and abroad. Instead, he would positively stress his (and Egypt's) image for the benefit of his world audience. In his last press conference, he did not attempt to create a positive image of himself by stating his own views, but simply read long excerpts from critical articles recently written about him in the Western media; it seemed like a sado-masochistic trip. He felt, as he told reporters, that he was 'responsible not only to the people of Egypt, but also to those who have supported me in Britain, the US, Europe, abroad'. But his link with his universal audience was the press and the press now 'betrayed him' by conveying to his audiences what he viewed as a 'distorted image'. Rather than recognizing that his image had perhaps been irreversibly tarnished abroad, he shouted at the foreign media: 'I want you to clarify the situation, because they supported me, and they still support me, and they fill me with pride, your people.' He pathetically begged:

> Tell them, frankly, the facts. Tell them, for you live among us. *I* have asked for opposition, because opposition is the main fact in democracy. . . . Tell them that *I* have asked for it, that *I* made the amendment, that *I* asked the Assembly . . . that this kind of political system be instituted here. Why do you forget this? I want you to tell everyone about this!

On 3 September, Sadat had ordered the arrest of some 3,000 students, fundamentalists, leading politicians, journalists and prominent religious leaders. He ordered the eviction of some foreign journalists who had reported the details of his new oppressive measures and in particular details of the incident of Zawiya al-Hamra. It seemed that anybody who had spoken against Camp David, criticized corruption, reported inter-communal unrest or complained against the crackdown on the opposition found himself incarcerated. Troops were used to carry out these massive arrests, where people were pulled out of bed in the middle of the night or dragged from their houses or offices with little or no notice. An atmosphere of emergency, fear and expectation descended on the country. No one knew or could guess what the next step would be. It was evident, though, that something momentous would have to happen, and soon, for Egypt could no longer function normally in this atmosphere. All avenues seemed blocked and the political game appeared to be at stalemate. Only a cataclysm of some sort could bring about a new beginning. These thoughts crossed the mind of Lieutenant al-Islambouli, a young artillery officer who belonged to the fundamentalist splinter group of the *Gama'a al-Islamiyya* (the Islamic Association) and who was entrusted with the task of leading an artillery column during the 6 October military parade in Cairo, held to commemorate the eighth anniversary of the October crossing. Since the beginning of the year, his group had considered disposing of Sadat as part of an Islamic take-over of Egypt, but the first practical opportunity presented itself on 6 October, when the President and all his retinue were certain to be watching the parade. Al-Islambouli and his fellow conspirators planned meticulously, and arranged that, upon the assassination of Sadat and his entourage, an announcement would be made by a radio station in Assyut that the Islamic era had dawned in Egypt after the disposal of the 'tyrant'.

On 5 October 1981, Sadat was at home in Giza with Jihan. He got up early on the morning of 6 October, put on his new field-marshal's uniform and prepared for the parade. He reached the stands, where hundreds of notables and foreign guests were seated, just across from the 'Tomb of the Unknown

Soldier' in Nasser City, where a new monument had been erected to commemorate those who had fallen in battle against Israel. The parade began at noon. It was reviewed by Sadat, who was flanked by his Vice-President and Minister of Defence. Shortly before 1 p.m., the air display started with low-flying aircraft passing overhead and everyone, including Sadat, looked up to the sky. At that moment, al-Islambouli and his fellow conspirators charged with sub-machine-guns and grenades, intent upon wiping out the entire top brass of Egypt. Eye-witnesses who were on the stand said that Sadat stood up, thinking that al-Islambouli was about to salute him. Sadat was fatally wounded and died before he reached the Ma'adi hospital by helicopter a few minutes later.

12
POST-MORTEM

The last book which Anwar Sadat wrote, or had ghost-written for him, was published posthumously and entitled *Wasiyati* (my legacy or my last will). A brief scrutiny of the book, and the context in which it was written, may provide some insight into Sadat's state of mind just before he was assassinated.

The title itself is revealing, giving the impression that these were the parting words of a man who had accomplished his mission in life, was ready to retreat from the world and had begun to walk inexorably towards his fate, towards the return to his Creator. It is as if, whilst moving towards his end, he had stopped for a moment, looked back and summed up the most important events and turning-points of his life and left them as a legacy to his 'children', the Egyptian people, and the world at large. Indeed, from Sadat's wording in his book, which said: 'The sum total of my life's experience has brought me to understand . . .', one gets a clear indication that he felt that his race had been run, that he was in a position to draw conclusions about his life and that for him the end of that life's experience was close at hand.

The range of topics that Sadat addressed in his 'legacy' was indicative of his removal from the pressing events of the day, amounting to a rather lofty commentary on such issues as 'faith – the gift of security', 'love – the most wonderful of God's favours', 'the Spirit, the mind and the body', 'the meaning of inner success' and such like. Sadat's remarkable introspection certainly deserves a close examination, for it seems to indicate his gut reaction in the face of desperation and isolation which had peaked during the last six months of his life. Admittedly, Sadat had confided in his wife, Jihan, back in 1979, that after the conclusion of the peace treaty, he really had a sense of having fulfilled his role as Egypt's President. He also remarked to his wife, on various occasions, that a leader should know when to step down and hand things over to the next generation. For he sensed that the string of accomplishments that he had attained during his presidency, and which he referred to with relish as his great 'annual breakthroughs' (1971 – 15 May 'Corrective Revolution'; 1972 – the expulsion of the Soviets; 1973 – the October War; 1974 – the *infitah*; 1975 – reopening the Suez Canal, etc.), had culminated in his visit to Jerusalem (1977), then the Camp David accords (1978) and the peace treaty (1979). Nevertheless, he had not resigned his post, despite the fact that at some point he had given it serious consideration. The reason he gave in his book and to his wife was that he wanted to remain in office until the return of Sinai was completed (April 1982), to ensure that all went as he had planned. It seems, however, that Sadat's imminent and urgent sense of his end as president did not surface until early 1981, during his last difficult few months in office. It is also true that Sadat had always been seen by his friends and family members as an eccentric dreamer, who was somewhat inclined to bouts of 'inward and upward' reverie. He had himself mentioned his fasting and meditation in Cell 54 in the 1940s, and he was often seen withdrawing into isolation throughout his presidency. Jihan attested that in the last three years of his life, her husband used to fast every Monday and Thursday and he became more ascetic, mystical and 'elevated' than before, often invoking his close communion with God. His family, friends and acquaintances also noticed that his propensity for withdrawal had markedly increased during the last six months of his life.

In his 'legacy', extolling the virtues of divine love and the necessity of love between people, Sadat exhorted his readers to 'come and listen to a Sufi poet' who said:

> It is my Lord whom I worship
> It is my Lord whom I love
> It is my Lord for whom I want
> To suffer and be tormented
> And want to be in agony,
> And for whom I want
> To be split, to be torn and die.[39]

In a different context this quotation might be viewed as innocuous verbosity. But considering the circumstances in which Sadat chose to quote it, it seems poignantly relevant to his own immediate predicament and state of mind at the time. The next section of the poem goes on to describe a variety of images of union, of darkness and light, ending with:

> we shall remain wretched on this earth, and we shall remain on struggling and contending paths; we shall not enjoy this life unless we rise up above ourselves to think about the creation of the heavens and earth.

This state of transcendence described by the poet seems to have coincided with Sadat's own transcendence and retreat during the last phase of his life. And, as though revealing to his readers his own way of dealing with the fear and insecurity that must have been generated by the widespread opposition he faced towards the end, domestically, on the inter-Arab arena and from the West, Sadat wrote: 'And when divine life abounds in the heart, all fears subside, just as darkness is dispelled when invaded by light.'[40] His torment and agony, which were noticeable to almost everyone with whom he had to deal on state affairs, could no longer be relieved by his 'dialogues' with the huge audiences who used to gather to hear him and in whose response he had always sought and found comfort. Now he was alienated and isolated from his people as well. He sank into long periods of withdrawal, whereas before his times of meditation had not lasted long. His wife, Jihan, who described him as 'never having lost his calm or composure' during his last months, was perhaps one of the few people in whose presence he could safely withdraw into himself without having to account for anything. When others were present, he was liable to explode, to get excited and to begin justifying his role in 'this world'. At home, he was alone and could be left alone; in public he felt an outsider and he could no longer bear his surroundings. He would rather vanish than put on an act in front of those who had betrayed him and in whose company he felt ill at ease.

It is not surprising, then, that a famous Egyptian psychiatrist from Al-Ahzar University, Dr Muhammed Sha'alan, tried to grapple with the question of whether Sadat's death was an act of 'self-chosen martyrdom or a public execution' by the Egyptian people. He came to the conclusion that in some way it was both of these. According to Sha'alan, Sadat had ruled and lived selflessly until 1977, sacrificing his life for what he felt was the greater good of Egypt. However, from 1977 on (possibly as a result of the food riots), Sadat moved to a mode of almost total self-assertion and near despotism. This was an image that he detested and could not accept for it was the antithesis of what he believed he stood for. But once he did change to this mode of self-assertion, he became so entrenched in it that he lost his perspective of himself and of events around him. And from this mode of self-assertion, which brought with it self-loathing for what he had become, he moved to martyrdom. In some deep sense, Sha'alan feels that, once it became evident that there was no turning back, Sadat was just as anxious to get rid of the man he had become, to die, as were those who suffered from his despotism. Sha'alan wrote of Sadat:

> He constantly ignored security measures despite warnings of plots to assassinate him by Muslim fundamentalists. He refused to wear his bulletproof vest on October 6 and even dismissed the guards surrounding him. When he was shot he stood up and faced the assassins, rather than shy away or stoop. He chose to be a martyr and a hero rather than a despot. When a man becomes identified with a given role and faces the choice of giving up that role or dying, he often chooses death.[41]

At the same time, however, Sha'alan also asserts that, yes, indeed it was a public execution, but that the condemnation and execution was not of Sadat himself, but rather of an image that had been falsely projected upon him. He feels that the real, deep-rooted tension was not in fact between Sadat and the masses, but between the corrupt Egyptian elite and the masses; the elite had always succeeded in diverting the anger of the masses away from themselves and onto Sadat, who, in many other ways, was becoming more and more suitable as a scapegoat. The Egyptian elite was itself in the firing line and worked in concert with the masses to oppose and publicly execute Sadat, who had become a sacrificial scapegoat. Sadat 'co-operated' by fostering this same image of himself, thereby offering himself up for sacrifice on 6 October, the day of his glory and death in martyrdom.

Naguib Mahfuz, perhaps the foremost living Egyptian writer, offers a quite different perspective on Sadat's life, in *In Front of the Throne*. The theme of his book is that the past rulers of Egypt from Pharaonic times onwards, beginning with King Mennes and ending with Anwar Sadat, are called upon to account for their accomplishments and failures, before the judgement throne of the goddess and god of Egypt's mythology: Isis and Osiris. Isis and Osiris then decide whether they should dwell among the eternal or be sent to Hell. All those who had already been judged were free to question or comment upon the rulers that came after them. The main criteria for establishing good deeds were: ridding Egypt of foreign invaders, uniting Egypt politically, enhancing social cohesion, avoiding excessive wars and killings in neighbouring countries, and preventing oppression and exploitation of the Egyptian masses. The criteria for defining evil deeds were basically the inverse of those virtues. In Mahfuz's scenario, perhaps surprisingly, nearly all rulers were admitted to dwell among the eternal. The examination of Nasser's life was harsh; by the end of it even the lenient Osiris could not accept the idea of letting him dwell with the eternal ones, until he underwent a further trial which would seal his ultimate fate. Then came Sadat's judgement. The review of his life is interesting as it discusses some of the major criticisms levelled at the deceased President during his lifetime, as well as those hurled against him post-humously. In view of Mahfuz's general support for Sadat and his peace policies, this criticism is particularly revealing: it has a strong feeling of legitimacy about it, not only because of its moderation but because Mahfuz represents a broad segment of the Egyptian public, rather than the small but vociferous groups who were screaming their criticisms of Sadat in an unbalanced way before his death, and even more so afterwards.

When Sadat came up for review before the gods, the 'peanut gallery' was already full of all Egypt's past leaders who were free to question their successor. First, several of the kings praised him for his efforts in war and in peace, despite the fact that he had been labelled a traitor for his *démarche*. Amenhotep III told Sadat that he saw a similarity between them in that he too sought prosperity and wealth for his people and for himself, and that both of them had a taste for pomp, ostentation and castles. The only difference, he said, is that 'in my time, I was permitted to pursue this without worry, but doing so in *your* time made you taste the bitter along with the sweet'. This was perhaps one of the kinder ways in which one could present the common charge, made so often against Sadat, that he lived extravagantly and lavishly, acquired too many official residences, spent too much on expensive clothes and elaborate uniforms. Such an ostentatious public display of wealth made people consider him to be a 'fat cat', which was looked upon with suspicion. The next

Pharaonic King admitted that Sadat had accomplished some great deeds during his rule but he also castigated him: 'You neglected to punish corruption so that you almost turned the victories you accomplished into defeats.' This referred in particular to the case of Sadat's brother, Esmat, who made a fortune through criminal means during Sadat's rule. A commission that had reported on this case had been dissolved by Sadat and the case was ignored. It was only after Sadat's death that the case was taken up again, and Esmat was indicted, convicted and imprisoned on a number of criminal counts. After Sadat's death, newspapers would delight in revealing some new detail about the misdeeds of his brother. The magnitude of his criminal activities and the wealth he illicitly amassed shocked the people; what shocked them even more was that such misdemeanours had been ignored during Sadat's lifetime. From then on, people came to assume that any new case of corruption that was exposed and was shown to have gone on during Sadat's rule, was attributable to Sadat. Because of Esmat's case, people unjustly reached the conclusion that Sadat must have been negligent about cracking down on corruption in general, thus tacitly sanctioning it or even encouraging it, and in any case bearing the ultimate responsibility for it. As time elapsed, this tendency to place all of Egypt's evils at Sadat's door gained momentum, as fewer Egyptians, including people who had worked closely with him, became inclined to stand up in his defence. As in other spheres of life, decency had yielded to fashion; people found out that it was much easier to be critical than to be correct.

As Sadat's judgement before the gods continued, Nasser asked him how he could have been so disloyal to him. Here, the book voiced the sentiments of the Nasserite groups in Egypt as well as broader public opinion about Sadat's policy of de-Nasserization. Nasser went on to claim that he had laid all the groundwork for Sadat's later achievements, especially the October War, while Sadat did nothing but 'pluck the fruits of Nasser's labour'. Sadat bitterly retorted: 'You are the man who led us into defeat; I returned honour and freedom to the people and then went on to victory.' Nasser charged Sadat with having fatally 'stabbed Arab unity and sentenced Egypt to isolation and elimination from the Arab world', a common reproach against Sadat. Sadat answered that the Arab world was actually quite indifferent to the interests and well-being of Egypt and only wanted it to remain in a submissive position, ever begging for Arab mercy and money, and therefore he had no qualms about the decision he took. Nasser also attacked the policy of *infitah* saying that it had produced a wave of corruption and that while, during his own rule, he had ensured the security of the poor, Sadat had boosted the security of the rich. Sadat, in self-defence, contended that it was all the work of opportunists operating behind his back. Mustafa Nahhas, the Wafd leader of pre-revolutionary Egypt, joined in and attacked Sadat's kind of democracy which amounted, in his mind, to 'ruling with dictatorial authority over a democracy'. Sadat responded that he wanted a democracy that would adhere to, and protect, the manners of the village and the rights of the family father. Nahhas chided: 'That is tribal democracy!' Nahhas also accused Sadat of having let things get out of control, neglecting them as though they did not concern him and then suddenly erupting into activity, jailing thousands of people, in the process angering Muslims, Christians, extremists and moderates alike. As in the case of Nasser, Sadat's sentence was that he might sit among the Eternal Ones but only until the next trial, which would determine his ultimate fate. So, according to Mahfuz's allegorical account of Sadat's rule, criticism weighed quite heavily against the deceased President. However, despite the non-committal nature of the judgement, Sadat was awarded a place among the eternal, temporary as it might be, until a later verdict was arrived at by history.

Another view, which has attempted to explain Sadat's assassination in terms of the mistakes committed by the entire system, was advanced by the prominent Egyptian historian, Dr Ibrahim Abaza, in his book *The Ten Errors: From Nasser to Sadat*. He made the claim that the bullet which killed Sadat was not intended for Sadat himself but was aimed at the tyranny cultivated by the revolution since its inception, of which Sadat had become the living symbol. The bullets expressed absolute rejection of the entire revolutionary experiment because it had been a dismal failure. Abaza claimed that the Sadatists had a short-sighted view of the assassination, seeing it as an isolated incident, without deeper roots. He felt that the Nasserites had entertained a similarly short-sighted and fragmentary explanation of the assassination, because they took its roots to stem from early 1977 when the people's impatience at Sadat's policies erupted into violence and culminated in the 6 October murder. According to Abaza, both views were deficient, because the 'autumn of fury' of 1981 had been preceded by the 'spring of deception' of Nasser's rule where lies, delusions, false rumours and deceptive propaganda had led to the devastating defeat of June 1967. To that cataclysmic event Abaza traces back the genesis of Sadat's 'autumn of fury'. He claims that the anger of the fatal bullets of the assassination stemmed from the same source as the 'ten errors' which lay at the base of the failure of the revolution, the major one of which was autocratic despotism pursued first by Nasser and then by Sadat. But Abaza's 'kindness' to Sadat, in making him divide the blame with his great predecessor and in exonerating him because he was the product of a deviant system, is not widely shared in post-Sadat Egypt. Even today, a continuous stream of vituperation against Sadat appears in Egypt's newspapers; these only fade from view when some more pressing occurrence dominates public attention; attacks on the Sadat era then return with renewed vigour.

The people's obsession with Sadat, the intensity of the diatribes against him, the persistence and longevity of the 'Sadat tales', suggest more than a mere interest in gossip, or fascination with a departed Pharaoh. The range of attacks on Sadat has been very broad, digging back into his pre-presidential past, indirectly implicating him – though claiming to expose his family and friends –

in corruption, and going into great detail in the process. During his brother's trial, newspapers were full with the daily progress of the case and constantly alternated between amazement and indignation at how such illicit activities, on such a large scale, could have gone on right under the President's nose. Tacit in all of these newspaper reports was the linking of Sadat to those crimes. Although it was clear that 'fat cats' were specifically to be indicted and punished, a large portion of the blame was laid at the 'system's' door, and finally came to rest on the leader of that system as the 'perpetrator' of those improprieties, Anwar Sadat. As the paradigm of corruption Sadat has been encapsulated in yet another of those compact expressions in which the Egyptians are accustomed to vent their sentiments: 'With the first [Nasser] it was austerity; the second [Sadat] taught us corruption; and the third [Mubarak] doesn't do a thing.'*

Then newspapers began to focus on members of Sadat's family other than Esmat: other relatives were found to be connected with all sorts of shady business dealings, and a full campaign was launched against Jihan, the President's widow, who was accused of not having rightfully earned her university degree. She was brutally attacked and condemned. Her Western image, her prominence and visibility in public life and even her beauty were deemed as 'inappropriate behaviour' for the First Lady of Egypt. They claimed that she had interfered in political affairs, directly and indirectly, and accused Sadat's son, Gamal, who had been named Abd al-Nasser, of receiving his degree without having fulfilled the necessary requirements. Sadat was even attacked for having written a revisionist history of the 1952 Revolution and his role in it, because in his autobiography he had virtually claimed responsibility for having formed the Free Officers, which later led the 1952 *coup*, saying that Nasser stepped in as head of the group only later when he himself was jailed for his political activities. Sadat's critics contended that he had falsely assumed a major role in organizing and recruiting the Free Officers and in planning and launching the revolution.

Sadat's posthumous detractors are united in wishing to push him to the periphery of Egyptian history, in claiming that he rose to power, and then became a deviant aberration rather than a model of leadership. If Sadat could be vilified, dehumanized, stripped of his achievements and attributes, then the remnants of his policies could be easily disposed of. Thus, some critics, including former members of the Free Officers, who had watched Sadat overtake them and leave them on the side-lines, now claimed that not only had he not established the Free Officers, but that he had barely been active in that organization; some of them specify that he had attended only two meetings. Others went even further, saying that he was a double agent, not only keeping

---

*This expression has a catchy rhyme in Arabic: '*Ma'a al-awwil akalna al-mish; wa-ttani 'allamna al-ghish; wa-ttalet la bi-hish wa-la bi-nish.*' Literally: 'With the first we ate "mish" [a crude salty cheese], the second taught us corruption and the third does not move one way or another.'

tabs on the royal palace, for the Free Officers, but that he was also spying, for the palace, on the activities of his fellow Free Officers. That, they explained, was the 'real' reason that Sadat was at the cinema with his wife till after midnight, on the eve of the revolution. He was waiting to see how events would turn out: if the *coup* seemed to be succeeding, he would join it; but if it was failing, he had an alibi and could move into the fold of another allegiance – the palace, or the British, or both. A far-reaching accusation even linked him with the CIA, as a spy for the United States. Charges against Sadat also covered such areas as the rigged elections which had provided a cover for his 'democracy', and dozens of court cases were reported demonstrating as unconstitutional a host of laws, presidential decrees and amendments made during Sadat's presidency. Al-Gizawi, an ex-Free Officer himself, is one of several attorneys who have specialized in initiating court cases against Sadat's laws governing political parties, such as the Law of Shame. Attacks were also launched against Sadat for his peace agreements with Israel.

Sadat's harshest critics, among whom were Isma'il Fahmi and Ibrahim Kamel, his two successive Foreign Ministers, who had resigned during the peace process, were particularly incensed by those agreements, which had tied Egypt's hands and isolated her from the Arab world. Israel's incursion into Lebanon in June 1982 seemed to prove that Israel was pursuing a policy of destroying Arab states one by one, having neutralized her major Arab antagonist, thus indicating critical charges against Sadat. Even many Egyptians who had been supportive of Camp David felt that Israel had betrayed her Egyptian ally now that the peace treaty between them had been finalized. The manner in which these reservations were expressed in the newspapers again put the blame squarely on Sadat's shoulders. Even the hitherto universally acclaimed 'October victory' began to be queried. Some Egyptians were now claiming that the so-called 'victory', which had ostensibly restored Egypt her land, honour and self-esteem, was in fact no victory at all. They contended that the war had been handled recklessly and that Sadat's 'military expertise' had been faulty. What was worse, they claimed that when time came for negotiations, he had proved to be weak, playing into the hands of Kissinger and Begin. Fahmi's book, *Negotiating for Peace in the Middle East*, on the way in which Sadat had 'negotiated away' Egypt's sovereignty, coming from an acknowledged authority on Egypt's foreign relations, added credence to Sadat's Camp David detractors. Hassanein Haykal's book, *Autumn of Fury*, attempted to build a far-fetched case against Sadat by claiming that the deceased President used to drink alcohol frequently, that he was lazy and had a psychological complex about his skin colour. Although officially banned in Egypt, a chapter of this book was printed in the *Al-Ahaly* newspaper and later, after the banning came into effect, the contents of the book were roughly paraphrased and summarized in a series of newspaper interviews with Haykal; smuggled copies of the book were also circulated in Cairo. The suspense and intrigue which surrounded the book added to its appeal among Egyptians. It became fashionable to get hold of the book, to 'exchang with other clandestine readers about its contents and then to outwit t. ridicule of Sadat. All the accusations hurled at Sadat during his lifetime, after, seemed to be concisely summed up by Haykal and to provide 'conclus evidence' for all past rumours.

Some time will have to elapse before one can, with the benefit of hindsight, sort out legitimate criticism from exaggerated and often distorted accounts which seem more like vituperative vendettas than expressions of scholarly concern or of the 'search for truth'. It is very difficult to determine conclusively at the moment the validity of a considerable amount of the criticism voiced against Sadat, although much of it contains at least some truth. Sadat was no saint, but he was certainly not the incarnation of Satan either. The controversies about Sadat's role in the revolution, for example, or his leadership during the October War, can only be brought to rest when state archives are made public and documents can be evaluated with a broader historical perspective and stringent scientific circumspection. Other events, like the peace accords or the *infitah* policies, may take many years to assess, because we are all still living under their impact; whether they have been, or will come to be, regarded as beneficial or disastrous to Egypt, only time will tell. But already some serious students of Egypt, such as John Waterbury, have been revising their initial indictments of Sadat's economic policies; and others maintain that the Camp David process, incomplete in itself, has achieved a true breakthrough in so far as it has ushered in a new era of negotiations between Israelis and Arabs. Certainly the merits of any of Sadat's policies, external or internal, will remain, like beauty, justice or wisdom, in the eyes of their beholders. His personality, which, in the mid-1970s, was virtually worshipped throughout the Arab and Western worlds, has now been destroyed in a bout of iconoclastic fervour nearly as repulsive as the previous hysteria of the personality cult. It is useful to remember, however, that much of the criticism originated from a relatively small, if vociferous, segment of the population spearheaded by the legitimate organized opposition of Sadat's rule. Only later were they joined by the cacophony of Sadat's supporters who felt that they had been wronged by Sadat or his regime, as well as by Sadat's former loyalists who were trying, after his death, to gain favour with the new regime which felt it had to dismantle the former leader's image.

De-Sadatization, however, does not seem to provide the entire answer to the current backlash against Sadat, nor is the dismantling of Sadat's image comparable to the de-Nasserization campaign under Sadat's rule. De-Nasserization was a deliberate policy, carefully directed from the top and systematically implemented down through Egyptian society. As we have seen, Sadat had begun his rule under the almost total grip of his predecessor and it took him years to grow and disengage, to launch his own blueprint and then to begin to question the past. That procedure was necessary in order to point out mistakes and learn not to repeat them. After the October 1973 war, Sadat was strong enough to denounce some of Nasser's policies publicly, and his move was obediently followed by a wealth of books, articles and films which set out to 'document' all the ills and evils of Nasser's rule, in contrast to the new glorious course charted by Sadat. Such a carefully orchestrated campaign was not repeated by Mubarak. For apart from allowing people to write or say or publish what they wished about Sadat, Mubarak took no active role in establishing a policy of de-Sadatization. It happened spontaneously; those who have been the most outspoken against Sadat are not particularly supportive of Mubarak either, and they continue to find their niche, by and large, in opposition parties, which further removes the possibility of a state-initiated de-Sadatization.

Several explanations are called for. Firstly, Sadat had fallen into the trap of the 'guided democracy', believing that if he was improving upon his predecessor in terms of civil liberties, he could make the Egyptians grateful to their 'father' for his generosity. He was unaware that he was falling into the 'half-way democracy syndrome', which means that when people are given a taste of freedom, they begin demanding, in the name of that freedom, to go all the way, unaware of the limitations of an autocratic regime. Under Nasser, both the political dissidents and Muslim fundamentalists knew exactly where they stood, and where the *Rais* stood. The slightest voice of criticism was immediately construed as a 'plot against the regime' and dealt with harshly. Sadat had the gallantry to allow 'a hundred flowers to bloom', but when they began burgeoning, he had to crack down on them before they posed a serious threat to his autocratic regime. So, paradoxically, the more liberal the ruler, the more he stands to be criticized and then the harder he has to clamp down on his critics, who subsequently turn against him as soon as they can, either during or after his reign.

Secondly, what happened after Sadat's death was an explosive over-compensation by the Egyptians, who needed to express openly the grievances that had been accumulating under Sadat's rule. With threats of censorship, arrest and an ambiance of fear during Sadat's last year, criticism against the President had been repressed, for fear of retribution.

Thirdly, the intensity and longevity of this criticism made it evident that it was not simply a one-time escape-valve to vent Egyptian frustrations, but rather a cumulative and deep-rooted dissatisfaction − whether directly attributable to Sadat or not − not only on the part of the small vocal opposition but also on the part of the masses. There had not been in recent memory such an atmosphere of high expectation, of promise that abundance was around the corner, and of peace and prosperity, as the one that prevailed in Egypt at the height of Sadat's rule. Instead, over-population, an overblown bureaucracy, poverty, inadequate services, faulty education, health and communications, and a disastrously decaying economy, all made the promises evaporate and Sadat's image crumble. Sadat was the second *Rais* of the revolution, and the people who remembered the euphoria of July 1952 would wait no longer.

Fourthly, in Egypt the population has been traditionally submissive to the ruler. The *Rais*, even when harshly criticized by the urban press, remained generally respected and held in awe by the millions in the countryside (hence the 99.8 per cent in election returns and referendums, even allowing for some improprieties in the system). In any case, it is not 'done' to aim one's frustrations and criticisms at the current leader or regime. Some 'polite' and restrained criticism, or some good-humoured anecdotes are permissible, but deeply-felt hostility is usually directed at a more distant and intangible entity which cannot strike back. Now that Sadat is gone, he is past and harmless, remote and unreal, and therefore all anger and frustrations can be safely vented on him, rather than on existing rulers.

If this is the case, then why not Nasser? Why was he not humiliated or vilified even at the height of the de-Nasserization period under Sadat? If anger is felt for the long-term failure of the revolution, at the previous rulers who are now gone, and is a compensatory over-reaction to the repression of the bygone regime, then Nasser could have been 'credited' with all these attributes. He was not. Many observers have noticed that the Egyptians genuinely grieved at Nasser's death, seeming lost without their leader, but at Sadat's funeral no one seemed to care much; his death looked like an expected and 'natural' course of events. Two years after Sadat's death, most of the newspaper articles are still harshly critical of him, whereas most on Nasser are still laudatory, to the point of nostalgia. Bookstores are still stocked with books, old and new, singing the praise of Nasser, while books on Sadat are very scarce and for the most part critical.

In some very real sense, the Egyptian people never really blamed Nasser, not even during the de-Nasserization period. They never consciously allowed themselves to hold him personally responsible, or rebuked him with the full intensity of the hostility, frustration and humiliation that they had suffered at his hands. They never, even after his death, aimed their anger at him for his failure to develop a viable and stable economy, for the repressive and dictatorial nature of his regime, or for any one of the issues which seemed to beg critical or angry reaction, such as the terrible defeat of 1967. On the contrary, when Nasser had announced that he would resign in the wake of the rout, the masses flooded the streets, screaming their support for him and their determination to fight. The Egyptians had come to identify strongly with this forceful and charismatic ruler, because he had established Egypt as the leader and centre of the Arab world, and had made all Egyptians feel important and heroic. If they had rejected him that would have meant their own demise. Ernest Becker, in his book *The Denial of Death*, explains this relationship between a ruler and his people:

283

If the leader loses, they too perish; they cannot quit, nor does he allow them to. . . . This gives an added dimension, too, to our understanding of why people stick with their leaders in defeat, as the Egyptians did with Nasser. Without him they may feel just too exposed to reprisal, to total annihilation. Having been baptized in his fire, they can no longer stand alone.[42]

After Nasser died, as Sadat himself had to admit, he lived on as the embodiment of the spirit of Egypt, the symbol of self-esteem for Egyptians with his 'lift up your head, brother!': the symbol of Egyptian power and Arab unity. The reality crumbled in his wake (it had, in fact, begun to crumble during his lifetime), but Nasser the symbol lived on virtually untarnished by failure, representing the ideal of the 'all-good'. Sadat, on the other hand, was by no means as symbolic and pristine a figure as Nasser. At his best, Sadat had been only second to Nasser and the second after Nasser; he had had to institutionalize the revolutionary charisma of the founding father of the new Egypt, a sort of Paul, Caliph '*Umar*, or Stalin following in the footsteps of the great spiritual founding figures of Christ, Muhammad and Lenin. It seems that as well as their dissatisfaction with Sadat's rule, the Egyptian people were able to vent on him not only their accumulated feelings of anger and frustration with the revolution but also all the intense resentment that they had never expressed for Nasser. This transfer of 'displaced punishment' from Nasser to Sadat combined with the long-standing frustration of the revolution, as well as some legitimate criticism that Sadat certainly deserved, all account for the intensity and severity of the anti-Sadat sentiments and the virulent writings after his death. Furthermore, the fact that Sadat was 'chastized' by public execution, unlike Nasser who died from illness, was in itself 'indicative' of the evil nature of Sadat in popular belief. So, upon Sadat's brutal death at the hands of Muslims who had reproached him for his 'ungodliness', the 'pure' Nasser could be used as a whip by folk imagination to administer public flagellation to 'Westernized and corrupt' Sadat.

Was Sadat's 'legacy' his painful admission that he was leaving no legacy behind? Can Sadat's rule be construed as an era unto itself? A cynic may say that Sadat had three phases in his presidency: the first three years, when as a mere nobody, he hopelessly tried to follow the trodden path of his predecessor; the next three years, when he tried to be his own man, haplessly emulating the village '*umda*; and the final four years, when he became so enamoured of himself and his delusions that he acted like a Pharaoh. Although there was undeniably much of each of these elements in Sadat's presidency, the '*umda* theme stands out as the most genuine. Sadat was basically a very simple man, who felt at ease with simple people and with the rural environment. Regardless of whether we accept or reject the objective authenticity of his *fellah* identity, it is evident that he *felt* himself to have deep-rooted peasant and village values. They seemed to be a source of strength to him and a source of lucidity: in a rural setting things are black or white, happen in winter or summer; one works during the day and retires to the family at night; there were the profane and the sacred, Allah and his creatures, good and bad people; and one could tell those who ruled and gave orders – the wise, the smooth, the well-born – from those who received the orders and carried them out – the common people, the rough, the less fortunate. The village also gave Sadat a clear, though admittedly simplistic, notion of what leadership was all about and the dynamics between leader and people. Sadat was not born to an *'umda* family, he belonged to the less fortunate. But he had always held the *'umda* in awe, he married a daughter of the *'umda* family and when he took over power, he tried to be the *'umda* of all Egyptians.

Sadat conceived of the *'umda* first of all in terms of demeanour. Even when Sadat seemed to his critics to be departing from the very norms of rural simplicity that he had himself praised so highly, he was in fact playing the *'umda* as he understood it. An *'umda* had to be respected, respectful, and well-dressed, to represent the 'face' of his village. He was usually informal, but ceremonious when necessary. On the outside, the *'umda* must present a prosperous façade, offer the best food to his guests and be somewhat distant from his people. Inwardly, he must be accessible, simple, frugal, one of the people. This interpretation may explain why we are told so many seemingly contradictory things about Sadat. Jihan and others told us that he often fasted, always insisted on simple furnishings in the rooms where he slept, and ate only fruit, vegetables or a little lean meat. He would go for long walks, do exercises and take a daily massage. He would often gaze at the ceiling or the sky and sink into meditation, or sit in the garden of his house and read or write. Jihan describes him as a man of phenomenal memory, who liked to memorize his material. He was very intense in everything he did and that was reflected in his profuse sweating. But even in time of extreme adversity he would come home, put on his *galabiyya* and retreat into himself. He hated jewellery and other 'superfluous' additions on his body (his wife, in fact, was angry with him when he removed his wedding ring from his finger). His watch was a simple one with a Quranic verse carved on the back. When alone, or with his family, either at home in Giza or in one of his residences, he would sit on the floor. He did not have many clothes, but what he had was always of good quality, neat and clean. His wife insists that all his suits were made in Egypt. He did not talk much at home and kept calm even in the face of adversity and imminent danger. When everyone seemed to be ganging up against him (as in May 1971, November 1977 or September 1981), he would state his faith in Allah and in his own capacity to pull things through. He loved his children, cared for them, and had time for each one of them. He never cried in his life, not even in the presence of his wife and children. In everything he did, in every job he filled, Sadat felt like a king in his kingdom. Whether he was being a journalist, the Speaker of the House, Vice-President or President, he gave each job his all, performing each with the same enthusiasm. The only job he had not liked was serving as a minister in Nasser's cabinet. Apparently, to be one of many, rather than a king in his little realm, did not appeal to him, for he feared that he could not bring his talents and desires to full fruition within the confines of a team. He needed to be a head-man, and as *'umda*, the facet that we know best in Sadat, he was exuberant, talkative, ceremonious, formal, well-dressed, distant and princely, looking and sounding more sophisticated than he really was.

To be an *'umda* was also to have values. The 'village values' that Sadat seemed to be touting were not mere ideological slogans, although at times, as in the case of the 'Law of Shame' (May 1980), he did not hesitate to use the 'rural values' imperative to quell his opponents. But even then, the text of the law unequivocally called upon the Egyptians to return to, and maintain, the lofty religious, moral and social values of the traditional Egyptian families in the village. And the fact that many Egyptians griped: ' *'aib, 'aib, Qanun al-'Aib'* ('shame, shame, the Law of Shame') did not detract from Sadat's resolve to enter the new law as a constitutional amendment. Regardless of what people said of Sadat's 'fake rural identity', he did not measure it by the number of years he had stayed in the village, and was not swayed by the state ceremonies which he attended or the lavish palaces where he lived. Such pomp and extravagance were external frills which gained much attention, but internally he craved the simple and informal setting. *That* was authentic from Sadat's viewpoint. In addition to what he saw as the simplicity of the peasant existence, the honesty and generosity that he felt characterized relations there, and perhaps the somewhat idealized and romantic notion of the hard toil of the peasant, Sadat most admired the unity and social organization of the village. The village became the context in which Sadat could devise, develop, test and reinforce his system of thought, or his system of constructs, without which the world would not be comprehensible but become instead an overwhelming swirling mess of disorganized details, complexities and traditions, a world in which it was impossible to act. The simplifying quality of the village way of life helped him to impose order on what was otherwise a very disconcerting reality.

For Sadat, the Egyptian village was a filter, and his notions of the traditional Egyptian village and family structure became constructs against which he would evaluate the dynamics of leadership. When he was suddenly placed in the position of leader, it was a totally new experience for him. He was acutely aware of the tremendous responsibility of being at the helm, surrounded by a morass of domestic and foreign problems which had to be resolved. The notion of the traditional family structure as a model for cohesive leadership was attractive to Sadat: the extended family was analogous to the Egyptian nation; the family head was not unlike his position as President; and all were bound together, like the villages and the *'umda*, under the wise guidance of the latter, with the due respect and obedience on the part of the former. This neat metaphor not only helped Sadat to weed out disturbing details and inconsistencies, but it also gave him a familiar construct to nurture and elaborate upon throughout his presidency. It is interesting to note that Sadat's construct of the family as a model for leadership did not appear in any of his writings, books or articles before he became President. On gaining power, he found he needed some basic system of values to which he could cling, which would help him to grapple with all the problems he had to face; out of necessity he drew on the concept he knew best: the family.

Many of Sadat's acquaintances and close associates said that he did not have patience for detail. His supporters concluded that he preferred to deal with broad, far-reaching and exciting visions rather than with boring details. His adversaries alleged that he simply neglected to flesh out his ideas, and that was why they were diluted and the people, for whom he could not be bothered to think or plan, ended up as the losers. Be that as it may, Sadat's aversion to detail could also be linked to his use of the 'family construct'. For example, the multitude of issues which arose in the realm of leadership, such as the various opposition groups ranging from the Communists to the Muslim Brotherhood, were reduced by Sadat to one simple problem to allow the cohesive and smooth 'family life' of Egypt to continue: fundamental values had to be observed. Those rules required, according to tradition, that the father remain the all-wise and undisputable figure-head. The perpetrators of any of the various forms of opposition that might hinder the smooth flow of family life were largely perceived by him as impetuous disobedient sons, children who had to be sternly disciplined and reminded of their place. One must emphasize, however, that while the family construct had helped Sadat understand the dynamics of leadership and his relationship with the people, and had allowed him to act upon his perceived world view, it appears in retrospect that he over-used it. For when applied to an increasingly complex and differentiated opposition, against the background of a worsening economic situation and a decaying social cohesion, the simple construct became ineffective and began to operate against him, particularly during the fateful 'autumn of fury' of 1981, leaving Sadat mentally ill-equipped to deal with the new situation. His tenacity in clinging to his construct, despite the mushrooming negative consequences, reached a peak in September 1981 when he arrested thousands of opposition, or suspected-opposition, members. At that point, he seemed to have lost his ability to distinguish between various shades of opposition, merely lumping them all together as a group of rebellious sons who had dared to question the judgement, wisdom and authority of the head of the family.

Another example of Sadat's abhorrence of 'details' which brought about his demise were the food riots of early 1977, dismissed by Sadat as the 'Tremor of the Thieves'. By giving them that simple label Sadat categorized events into a construct he knew, which was obviously at odds with their inherent complexity. His 'simplifying construct' was incapable of dealing with Egypt's long-standing economic, political and social problems, which were now made worse by the Government's decision to remove subsidies on primary food staples. While the masses rioted in anger and desperation, Sadat attempted to belittle the magnitude of the phenomenon and to discredit the participants by calling them thieves: if the participants and their outburst could be dismissed as insignificant, then the entire issue would be rendered unimportant. Sadat eventually made cosmetic changes: he removed the subsidies. But having treated the entire matter as peripheral, he felt under no obligation to look at the underlying reasons for the riots. This was not to be the last time that Sadat's use, or misuse, of labels was to prove counter-productive. For with the repeated usage of labels, Sadat came to identify the simplification with the reality. In his mind, the label 'tremor of thieves' divided the problem into 'them' and 'us', excluding 'them', including 'us'. 'Thieves' are obviously excluded from the family, rejected and rendered, in effect, non-family. Exclusion is a step further than chastizing misguided sons of the family who need correction: it is a desperate and ill-advised step that the father of the family undertakes with reluctance, for he has *ipso facto* disrupted the 'family cohesion', alienating some of his children at the very moment he is also trying to reinforce family cohesion. In conclusion, Sadat's often innocent and well-intended use of simple constructs to deal with complex situations, a tendency that was viewed by some as 'impatience with detail', eventually produced enough oversight and miscalculation to bring about his loss of control and his eventual murder.

The problem, of course, is whether Sadat should be judged for what he did or what he thought, or perhaps not be judged at all. For one thing, we have already remarked that it is too early to come to any conclusive judgement of the Sadat era. But there is much more to it than that, in a biography of this sort. Admittedly, the years of Sadat's rule were, for better or worse, marked by his personal imprint, and one cannot disassociate him from Egypt's successes and failures in the 1970s. However, if we purport to describe *his* life, we ought to limit ourselves to the way *he* regarded or constructed the world, not to events which occurred around him. His life unfolded on various levels, but only the spheres of his life that he consciously touched upon, thought about and acted upon, would count as part of his biography – the story of *his* life. For example, what good would it do if we analysed the 1973 war for its own sake, with all its causes, military and strategic considerations, deployment of forces, consequences and aftermath? For Sadat, it was a Ramadan war that *he* had to fight for his own reasons. He influenced and directed it as best he could and tried to salvage from it whatever was afforded to him, but the term 'October War' (a 'neutral' description of the war), or 'Yom Kippur War' (the Israeli description), remained completely irrelevant to him, except perhaps that the Islamic Ramadan was up in arms against the Jewish Yom Kippur. Similarly, no purpose would be served if we proved that the economy of Egypt, or certain social problems, were not resolved by Sadat. His world did not necessarily consist of all those things, and what remains as an important part of his life experience is *his* participation, at his own level, in the making or the unmaking of something. For there were numerous acts done in his name or under his aegis (on the battlefield or in the economy) that he was never aware of. Yes, he might be deemed responsible for all those deeds; however, this was not an *existential* but rather a *formal* or jurisdictional responsibility. Corruption there was in Sadat's time, for example, but can we label him 'corrupt' because of that? There is no evidence that he ever took, solicited, accepted or condoned bribery or corruption in his household. So, *he* did not live a corrupt life even though Egypt, the Egyptian system, the regime that Sadat had helped build, might have been immersed in corruption.

Sadat had been simultaneously tormented by many problems. He was constantly preoccupied and his mind wandered from one issue to another, from personal to public matters, from domestic to external policies, from the Arabs to the West. His mental torment was erratic and the variety of the problems which preoccupied him crossed his mind in a disorganized manner. How does one form that whirlpool of the mind into a coherent life story? If we do not reproduce his thoughts, his actions, or the way others treated him, minute by minute, we would not give a true representation of his life. But if we did, would we be writing a biography or a 'secondary' diary? A compromise has to be found, therefore, between the 'truth' as it unfolded and the constraints of rendering that 'truth' into a consistent story. For the sake of Sadat's 'truth', we have based the text almost exclusively on his thinking, his hesitations, his fears, his images and the reasoning behind his acts. But for the sake of organization and order, we have tried to capture the meaning of Sadat's life in a series of generalizations, analyses, questions and conclusions, without, however, delving into value judgements of any sort. Bad or good is not the issue. The issue is *why* Sadat did what he did, thought what he thought, accomplished what he accomplished, what his vision was and what made him tick.

One way of penetrating Sadat's personality would be to dissect it and to expose his motivations to psychoanalysis. Such a psychologically inclined account would not serve any purpose, however, in the same way that no purely political narrative could unravel what crossed Sadat's mind at any given moment. For political scientists are interested in deeds and their results, while psychoanalysts seek the motivation that caused the deeds. An intersection of the two disciplines could probably provide the best result, as Paul Roazen put it: 'The study of psychology can sensitize the political scientist to an additional dimension of human experience while reminding him of what we cannot know or assert.'[43] For example, if we examine the criteria set by the American Psychiatric Association[44] for the narcissistic personality, one is amazed to find almost all of them in Sadat: self-importance and usefulness, preoccupation with fantasies of unlimited success and ideal love, requiring constant attention and admiration, feelings of shame, inferiority or humiliation in response to criticism, and the like. In a sense one may say that all, or most, politicians carry some of these traits, but why is it important to categorize someone as narcissistic? Psychologists claim[45] that one of the chief reasons politicians have a lust for power and success, resist criticism and need to be constantly admired, is that they seek compensation for early blows, deprivations and feelings of helplessness in their childhood. We could certainly trace Sadat's characteristics as a politician to his early days when, deprived of his mother, he was brought up under the dominant guardianship of his grandmother. Charisma, which Sadat acquired, or externalized, after he became President, could also be cited as a quality which could be linked to his background. In psychological terms, charisma is identified as the 'product of a person who is often manic, highly active, aggressive, authoritarian, with a gift for oratory or the behaviour which makes people – especially the unsophisticated – perceive him as Big Brother or Father, and attribute to him superhuman qualities'.[46] In Sadat's case, as in those of other politicians, it was his 'unconscious but festering rage which gave rise to his charismatic behaviour'. His rage, which in his early years was not outwardly obvious, must have been occasioned by his years in prison and then the tension of waiting on the side-lines in Nasser's shadow. His frustrations accumulated, only to erupt violently once he came out on top and assumed the presidency. Sadat's personality may be said to have been enhanced, at least in the eyes of the Western media, by what L. Schiffer called the 'charisma of imperfection', that is the powerful attraction of someone who is not totally without fault. In the case of Sadat, his dark skin, which he and many Egyptians viewed as a stigma, was certainly an added ingredient in his exotic appeal to the non-Arab world.

Political scientists, on the other hand, would probably rather lean on the 'hard facts' in order to conjecture on what Sadat had in mind, on what was his reasoning. But can one really judge motives according to results, or extrapolate intentions from hard data? If we study policies and their repercussions, then this method is probably the best available; but if we put our emphasis on men, can we hope to tap the essence of their lives without delving into their minds and their inner selves? And there is yet another factor that we cannot disregard – that is history as a record of the past. Sadat, as we have seen, was as obsessed with history as any of his contemporaries. His world was fixed on historical situations that appeared to him analogous, or parallel, to the situations he faced. Thus, understanding the historical background of Sadat's culture, the roots of his nationalistic sentiments, the burden of history on him and his generation and the prevailing trends in his country and the Arab world, would also seem essential for the complete comprehension of the man. Take this 1941 description of the 'ideal leader' who is needed to bring about the realization of the aims of Arab nationalism:

The mind of the masses is very much like that of a child, preoccupied with frivolous things, easily swayed by emotions. . . . Such a lack of a critical faculty makes necessary the existence of a powerful and violent leader who can arouse the masses of the people by appealing to their emotions, controlling and directing them. Thus, the leader must equip himself according to the intellectual condition of his people, in order to be spiritually united to them; he must set himself up as an example to his people, because the mass requires its leader to be a living and acting ideal, and not an immobile statue or a talking machine. He must have confidence in himself and he must also have an attractive, penetrating personality able to influence and control men's thoughts. In addition, he must be ascetic in his habits, because asceticism and sanctity go together, and he must have suffered in a way which has left a positive mark on him, because suffering is strength. . . .[47]

When this modern 'mirror for princes' was written and published in 1941, Sadat was embroiled in his struggle against the British and, although there is no clear indication anywhere that he had read this particular passage, the Arab nationalist mood was imbued with notions of this sort. Small wonder, then, that Sadat, perhaps unconsciously, complied almost to the letter with these prescriptions. An even older 'mirror' can be found in ancient Pharaonic tradition, in the form of instructions by a Pharaoh to his son, dating back to the twenty-second century BC:

Do not be evil, for patience is good; make your lasting monument in the love of you. . . . Make your magnates great that they may execute your laws. . . . Great is the great one whose great ones are great; valiant is the king who owns an entourage; and august is he who is rich in magnates. Speak truth in your house so that the magnates who are on earth may respect you, for a sovereign's renown lies in straightforwardness; it is the front room of a house that inspires the back room with respect. . . . Do justice that you may live long upon earth. . . . Beware of punishing wrongfully. Do not kill, for it will not profit you, but punish with beatings and with imprisonment, for thus the land will be set in order.[48]

This is, of course, the benevolent obverse of the preceding Machiavellian prescriptions; both could very well have been read and internalized by Sadat, and contributed to his multi-faceted personality. The point is that no matter how much ground one covers, how much material and data one digs up to substantiate the biography of a man, no absolutely conclusive picture can be expected to emerge. If it is understood that we have merely attempted to illuminate some aspects of this fascinating man, to comprehend components of his immensely complex personality, we will feel completely rewarded. Now more than ever, after many arduous years of data gathering, of hesitation between various theses and of writing all this into one coherent account, the task of encompassing all facets of the man seems daunting if not utterly impossible.

SOURCE NOTES

1 For these little-known facts about Gandhi see the fascinating account/critique by Richard Grenier, 'The Gandhi Nobody Knows', *Commentary*, March 1983

2 Raphael Israeli, *The Public Diary of President Sadat* (Brill, Leiden, 1978), Vol. I, p. 33; Vol. II, p. 915

3 *Ibid.*, Vol. I, pp. 234–5, 334, 356

4 *Ibid.*, Vol. III, pp. 1041, 1081

5 *Ibid.*, Vol. I, p. 197; Vol. II, p. 922

6 *Ibid.*, Vol. II, p. 457

7 *Ibid.*, p. 452

8 *Ibid.*, Vol. I, pp. 218, 245

9 *Ibid.*, Vol. I, pp. 17, 102; Vol. III pp. 1148, 1068–9

10 Address on Revolution Day at the University of Alexandria, 26 July 1976

11 Address to the People's Assembly, 14 March 1976

12 Address to the Arab Socialist Union (ASU), 27 March 1976

13 Address on Nasser's Memorial Day, 28 September 1971

14 Israeli, *op. cit.*, Vol. II, p. 554; Vol. III, p. 1220; Vol. I, pp. 24, 48, 209

15 *Ibid.*, Vol. III, p. 1100; Vol. II, pp. 55, 557; Vol. I, pp. 31–2

16 *Ibid.*, Vol. I, p. 193

17 *Ibid.*, Vol. II, p. 948

18 Speech to the ASU, 28 September 1975

19 Israeli, *op. cit.*, Vol. I, p. 274

20 *Ibid.*, pp. 23, 26

21 *Ibid.*, p. 352

22 Interview with Yugoslavian newspaper, 27 May 1973

23 Interview with *The Times*, 4 June 1976

24 Interview with *Al-Usbu al-Arabi* (Lebanon), 6 October 1974

25 Address to the ASU leadership, 15 September 1975

26 Israeli, *op. cit.*, Vol. III, p. 1167

27 *Ibid.*, Vol. II, p. 30

28 *Ibid.*, Vol. III, p. 1049

29 *Ibid.*, pp. 1080, 1024, 1155, 1216, 1195

30 *Ibid.*, Vol. I, p. 251; Vol. III, p. 1195

31 Broadcast by CBS (New York) on 7 or 8 January 1971

32 Israeli, *op cit.*, Vol. III, pp. 1110, 1118

33 *Ibid.*, p. 1027

34 Henry Kissinger, *The Years of Upheaval* (Little Brown, Boston, 1982), pp. 638–41

35 *Al-Nahar* (Beirut), 17 June 1975

36 Interview to *Sawt al-Jami'a* (Cairo), 22 December 1975

37 Isma'il Fahmi, *Negotiating Peace in the Middle East* (Johns Hopkins, 1983), pp. 192–3

38 *Ibid.*, p. 196

39 Anwar Sadat, *Wasiyati* (Cairo, 1982), pp. 645

40 *Ibid.*, p. 66

41 Dr Muhammed Sha'alan, 'Sadat's Death: Self-Chosen Martyrdom or Public Execution?' (unpublished article, 1982). Dr Sha'alan graciously agreed to be interviewed and to make this article available to us. We are deeply grateful to him.

42 Ernest Becker, *The Denial of Death* (Free Press, New York, 1973), p. 140

43 Paul Roazen, *Psychology and Politics, Contemporary Psychoanalysis*, Vol. XXII, No. 1, 1975, pp. 156–7

44 R. Spitzer (edn) *Diagnostic and Statistical Manual*, 3rd edn (American Psychiatric Association, DSM-III)

45 See, for example, Avner Falk, 'Moshe Dayan: Narcissism in Politics', *Jerusalem Quarterly*, No. 30, Winter 1984

46 This quote and the following are based on *ibid*.

47 Abdulleh al-Alayili, *Duslur al-Arab al-Qawmi* (Beirut, 1941), quoted by Haim, Sylvia (ed.), *Arab Nationalism: An Anthology* (University of California Press, Berkeley), p. 42

48 W. K. Simpson, *The Literature of Ancient Egypt* (Yale University Press, Connecticut, 1973), cited by Robert Dankoff, *Wisdom of Royal Glory* (University of Chicago Press, Chicago, 1983), p. 4

BIBLIOGRAPHY

Many books and articles were written about Sadat during his lifetime and especially after his assassination. We have used a considerable number of them, both in Arabic and Hebrew, and in English and other Western languages. However, since this work was meant to be an 'inner' psycho-biography, a special emphasis had to be lent to Sadat's own writings and speeches, under the assumption that they best reflected his thinking. Indeed, Sadat expressed himself abundantly, on a great variety of occasions, and his statements were significant, both for their substance and for learning about his state of mind.

Some aspects of Sadat's personality and private life, as well as those relating to his political conduct, could be fathomed only with the help of people who were close to him, worked with him and watched him during his moments of euphoria and depression, stress and relaxation. Therefore, we have supplemented our sources with a long list of interviewees who were willing to talk about him. However, some of them agreed to talk only provided they were not tape-recorded; others did not even consent to be cited; still others were reluctant to be mentioned as a source even when not specifically quoted. In view of this situation, we have decided to cite only Sadat's own words, or others' statements when we were specifically permitted to do so. Otherwise most of the narrative of the book is drawn from the various sources, some of which are in the public domain, without attributing every piece of information to its particular source. Thus, we could do away, for the most part, with the heavy apparatus of footnotes. But the complete list of the most important interviewees figures as part of this bibliography.

Newspapers and magazines, Arab, Israeli and Western, were our most vivid and up-to-date sources. However, with a few exceptions, we have not used the same publications consistently. We have relied on selections of the most important Egyptian, Arab, Israeli and Western sources to cover particular developments and events – the 1973 war, the Camp David accords, etc. Many of the newspapers and magazine reports were used not merely for their chronology but for their feature articles about Sadat's personality and policies. Some of the Western reporters or interviewers who wrote about Sadat were so well-informed and perceptive that they could extract statements and reactions he would not otherwise have uttered 'voluntarily'. Others got so close to him that they could record his spontaneous remarks or register the slightest nuances in his thinking and conduct. It goes without saying that the Arab press, and to a lesser extent Arab television and radio, were our main sources for Sadat's public addresses and statements, while his interviews to the media could be found interspersed in almost every major medium in the world: from the US and Israel to Iran, from Yugoslavia to the Sudan, through most Arab countries' state-controlled press.

Finally, a great many scholarly books on Sadat, modern Egypt and psychology helped us set the general context in which events were unfolding. Our debt to these secondary sources is immense, and our borrowings from them are unmistakable, although we did not always adopt their interpretation or see eye-to-eye with them over the relative importance of events. They are all listed below. Less emphasis was put on personal accounts and memoirs which mentioned Sadat *en passant* while their main focus was elsewhere.

Books in Arabic and Hebrew

Abaza, Dr Ibrahim Dussuki, *al-Khataya al-ashar min Abd al-Nasser ila as-Sadat* (Misr Printing House, Cairo)

Abu Taleb, Sufi, *Ishtirakiyatuna al-dimuqratiyya, Idyulujiyyat thawrat Mayu, 1971* (University Press, Cairo, 1978)

Abu al-Magd, Sabri, *al-Masira at-Tawila ma'a a-Sadat 'ala Tariq a-nidal* (Dar al-Hilal Publications, Cairo)

A-Sadat Min al-qariya ila a-Thawra (Dar al-Hilal Publications, Cairo, 1977)

Baghdadi, Abd al-Latif, *Mudhakkirat Abd al-Latif al-Baghdadi* (Cairo, 1977)

Foda, Dr Faraj, *Al-Wafd wal-Mustaqbil* (Cairo, 1983)

Israeli, Raphael, *Anwar Sadat 'al Milhama ve-Shalom* (Magnes Press, Jerusalem, 1981)

Labib, Fomil, *As-Salam a-Sa'ab* (Dar a-Ta'awun Publishing House, Cairo, 1978)

Mahboun, Ali, and others, *Misr ba'ad al-'ubur* (Cairo, 1975)

Mahfuz, Naguib, *Amam al-'arsh* (Misr Printing House, Cairo, 1983)

Mar'i, Sayyid, *Awraq Siyasiyya* (3 Vols), (*Al-Ahram* Publishing House, Cairo, 1978)

Raghib, Nabil, *Anwar al-Sadat: ra'idan li-tta'sil al-fikri* (Dar al-Ma'azif, Cairo, 1974)

Sabry, Abd al-Mun'im, *As-Sadat wa Thawrat a-Tashih* (Cairo)

Sabry, Musa, *Wathaiq harb Oktober* (Cairo, 1974)

Sadat, Anwar, *Asrar a-thawra al-Misriya* (Dar al-Qawmiya Printing House, Cairo, 1965)

Sadat, Anwar, *Qissat a-thawra al-Kamilah* (Al-Qawmiya Printing House, Cairo, 1965)

Sadat, Anwar, *Qissat al-Wahdah al-'arabiyya* (Dar al-Hilal, Cairo, 1957)

Sadat, Anwar, *Ya waladi, hadha 'ammak Gamal: Mudhakkirat Anwar a-Sadat* (Cairo)

Sadat, Anwar, *Wasiyati* (Cairo, 1982)

Sarrag-a-din, Fuad, *Limadha al-Hizb al-Jadid* (Sharq Publishers, Cairo, 1977)

Shamir, Shimon, *Mitzrayim Behanhagat Sadat* (Dvir, Tel Aviv, 1978)

Shamir, Shimon (ed.), *Yeridat Hanasserism 1965-70* (Tel Aviv University, Tel Aviv, 1978)

Shumays, Abd al-Mun'im, *Anwar a-Sadat: Sirat batal harrar ruh Misr* (General Agency of Information, Cairo, 1974)

Abd al-Qawi, Samir Zaki, *al-Sadat, bayna Yawmihi il-awwil wa Yawmihi al-akhir* (Cairo, 1981)

'Uthman, Ahmad, *Safahat min Tagribati* (Cairo, 1981)

Articles in Arabic and Hebrew

Al-Maghribi, Jihan, 'The Free Officers and Memories of the Revolution' (in Arabic), *Rooz al-Yussuf* (Cairo), 25 July 1980

Altman, Israel, 'Islamic Opposition Groups under the Sadat Regime' (Shiloah Institute Publications, Tel Aviv, 1980)

Altman, Israel, 'The State of the Shari'a and Islamic Legislation in Egypt under Sadat' (Shiloah Institute Publications, Tel Aviv, 1980)

Ben, David, 'The Confrontation with the Muslim Brothers 1965-6', in Shimon Shamir (ed.), *Yeridat Hanasserism 1965-70* (Tel Aviv, 1978)

Kramer, Martin, 'The Egyptian Religious Establishment in Crisis' (in Hebrew) (Tel Aviv University, Tel Aviv, 1983)

Rejwam, Nissim, 'Nasserism and Islam: The Ideological Dimension' (in Hebrew), *Hamizrah Hehadash*, No. 3, 1974

Shamir, Shimon, 'Egypt Searching Her Soul', *Ha'aretz* (Tel Aviv), 31 July 1980

Toledano, Ehud, 'Egypt: The Four Streams of the Opposition', *Ha'aretz* (Tel Aviv), 29 October 1980

Zarai, Oded, 'Egypt Discovers the Other Facet of Israel', *Ha'aretz* (Tel Aviv), 2 May 1982

Newspapers and Magazines in Arabic and Hebrew

Al-Ahali (Cairo), 1982-3
Al-Ahram (Cairo), 1970-81
Al-Akhbar (Cairo), 1977-81
Akhbar al-yaum, 1977, 23 February 1980
Al-Gumhuriyya (Cairo), 1955-60, 1977
Al-Musawwar (Cairo), 18 September 1953, 9 October 1981
Al-Nahar (Beirut), 1970-76
Al-Ra'y (Jordan), March 1976
Al Usbu' al-'Arabi (Lebanon), 6 October 1974, 17 October 1977
Filastin al-Thawra, 1976
Ha'aretz (Tel Aviv), 1970-82
Kotereth Rashith (Israel), October 1983
Ma'ariv (Tel Aviv), 1977-81
Mayu (Cairo), 1981
October Magazine (Cairo), 1977-83
Rooz al-Yussuf (Cairo), 25 July 1983, 18 July 1983
Saw al-Jami'a (Cairo), 1975

Books in European Languages on Sadat and Modern Egypt

Baker, Raymond, *Egypt's Uncertain Revolution under Nasser and Sadat* (Harvard University Press, Cambridge, Mass., 1978)

Carpozi, George, *Anwar Sadat, A Man of Peace* (Manor Books, New York, 1977)

Eideberg, Paul, *Sadat's Strategy* (Dawn Books, Quebec, 1979)

Fahmi, Isma'il, *Negotiating for Peace in the Middle East* (John Hopkins, New York, 1983)

Haykal, Hassanein, *Autumn of Fury* (André Deutsch, London, 1983)

Hirst, David, and Beeson, Irene, *Sadat* (Faber and Faber, London, 1981)

Indyk, Martin, *To the Ends of the Earth: Sadat's Jerusalem Initiative*, Middle East Papers, Modern Series, No. 1 (Harvard University Press, Cambridge, Mass., 1981)

Israeli, Raphael, *I, Egypt: Aspects of President Sadat's Political Thought* (Magnes Press, Jerusalem, 1981)

Israeli, Raphael, *The Public Diary of President Sadat* (3 Vols), (Brill, Leiden, 1978–9)

Masriyya, Y., *A Christian Minority: The Copts in Egypt* (Vol. IV), report from Case Studies on Human Rights and Fundamental Freedoms (Martinus Nijhof, The Hague, 1976)

Nutting, Anthony, *Nasser* (Constable, London, 1972)

Peroncel-Hugoz, Jean-Pierre, *Le Radeau de Mahomet* (Lieu Commun., Paris, 1983)

Sadat, Anwar, *Révolte sur le Nil* (Pierre Amiot, Paris, 1957)

Sadat, Anwar, *In Search of Identity* (Collins, London, 1978)

Shamir, Shimon (ed.), *Self-Views in Historical Perspective in Egypt and Israel* (Tel Aviv University, Tel Aviv, 1981)

Shazli, Sa'ad, *The Crossing of Suez* (London, 1980)

Stephens, Robert, *Nasser* (Simon and Schuster, New York, 1971)

Vatikiotis, P. J., *The History of Egypt from Muhammed Ali to Sadat* (Weidenfeld and Nicolson, London, 1980)

Waterbury, John, *Egypt, Burdens of the Past, Options for the Future* (Indiana University Press, Indiana, 1978)

Waterbury, John, *The Egypt of Nasser and Sadat* (Princeton University Press, New Jersey, 1983)

Auxiliary Books

Becker, Ernest, *The Denial of Death* (Free Press, New York, 1973)

Copeland, Miles, *The Game of Nations: The Amorality of Power Politics* (Simon and Schuster, New York, 1969)

Dankoff, Robert, *Yussuf Khass Hajib: Wisdom of Royal Glory* (University of Chicago Press, Chicago, 1983)

Dayan, Moshe, *Breakthrough* (Weidenfeld and Nicolson, London, 1981)

Eban, Abba, *An Autobiography* (Weidenfeld and Nicolson, London, 1978)

Edelman, Murray, *The Symbolic Uses of Politics* (University of Illinois Press, Illinois, 1976)

Eisenstadt, S. N., and others (eds), *Socialism and Tradition* (Van-Leer, Jerusalem, 1976)

Graber, Doris, *Verbal Behavior and Politics* (University of Illinois Press, Illinois, 1976)

Haber, Eitan, and others, *The Year of the Dove* (Bantam, New York, 1979)

Haim, Sylvia (ed.), *Arab Nationalism: An Anthology* (University of California Press, Berkeley, 1962)

Hamady, Sania, *Temperament and Character of the Arabs* (Twayne, New York, 1979)

Handel, Michael, *Surprise and Change in Diplomacy* (Harvard University Press, Cambridge, Mass., 1980)

Kelly, George, *The Psychology of Personal Constructs* (Norton, New York, 1955)

Kissinger, Henry, *The Years of Upheaval* (Little Brown, Boston, 1982)

Lapidus, Ira, *Contemporary Islamic Movements in Historical Perspective* (University of California Press, Berkeley, 1983)

Meiring, Desmond, *Fire of Islam* (Wildwood House, London, 1982)

Patai, Raphael, *The Arab Mind* (Charles Scribner's and Sons, New York, 1976)

Rabin, Y., *The Rabin Memoirs* (Weidenfeld and Nicolson, London, 1979)

Rabinovitch, Itamar, and others (eds), *From June to October: The Middle East between 1967 and 1973* (Transactions, New Jersey, 1975)

Rahman, Fazlur, *Islam and Modernity* (University of Chicago Press, Chicago, 1982)

Rostow, Eugene (ed.), *The Middle East: Critical Choices for the US* (Westview, Boulder, 1972)

Schacht, Joseph, *The Legacy of Islam* (Oxford University Press, Oxford, 1979)

Schiffer, I., *Charisma* (University of Toronto Press, Toronto, 1973)

Sheffer, Gabriel (ed.), *Dynamics of a Conflict* (Humanities Press, New Jersey, 1975)

Simpson, W. K., *The Literature of Ancient Egypt* (Yale University Press, Connecticut, 1973)

Wallace, Anthony, *Culture and Personality* (Random House, New York, 1961)

Weizman, Ezer, *The Battle for Peace* (Bantam, New York, 1981)

Scholarly Articles

Adams, Phillip, 'Sadat's Egypt', *British Society for Middle East Bulletin*, Vol. 3, No. 2, 1976

Adelman, Howard, 'Sadat's Death', *Middle East Focus* (Canada), Vol. 4, No. 4, November 1981

Ajami, Fuad, 'The Struggle for Egypt's Soul', *Foreign Policy*, Summer 1979

Altman, Israel, 'Islamic Movements in Egypt', *Jerusalem Quarterly*, No. 10, Winter 1979

Aly, Abd al-Muneim, and Wenner, M., 'Modern Islamic Reform Movements: The Muslim Brotherhood in Contemporary Egypt', *The Middle East Journal*, Vol. 36, No. 3, Summer 1982

Baer, Gabriel, 'The Interests of Significant Groups in Arab Society in a Peace Settlement with Israel', in G. Sheffer (ed.), *Dynamics of a Conflict* (Humanities Press, New Jersey, 1975)

Bailey, Clinton, 'A Note on the Bedouin Image of 'Adl as Justice', *Muslim World*, Vol. LXVI, No. 2, 1976

Baker, Raymond, 'Political Vision of an Age: Uthman Ahmed Uthman and the Arab Contractors': paper delivered at the conference on *Egypt: The Sadat Decade in Perspective*, SUNY, Binghamton, New York, 6–7 April 1984

Ben-Elissar, Eliahu, 'Two Years after the Signing of the Peace Treaty Israel–Egypt',

Research Project on Peace, Tel Aviv University, 1981

Bowie, Leland, 'The Copts, the Wafd and Religious Issues in Egyptian Politics', *Muslim World*, Vol. LXVII, No. 2, April 1977

Cantori, Louis, 'Egypt at Peace', *Current History*, January 1980

Cooper, Mark, 'The Leftist Opposition: Retrospective and Prospects': paper delivered at the conference on *Egypt: The Sadat Decade in Perspective*, SUNY, Binghamton, New York, 6–7 April 1984

Cuno, Kenneth, 'The Origins of Private Ownership of Land in Egypt: A Reappraisal', *International Journal of Middle Eastern Studies*, No. 12, 1980

Davis, Eric, 'Islamic Military and the Leftist Void': paper delivered at the conference on *Egypt: The Sadat Decade in Perspective*, SUNY, Binghamton, New York, 6–7 April 1984

Dekmejian, Richard, 'Anwar Sadat: In Search of Legitimacy': paper delivered at the conference on *Egypt: The Sadat Decade in Perspective*, SUNY, Binghamton, New York, 6–7 April 1984

Eilts, Herman, 'Camp David in Perspective': paper delivered at the conference on *Egypt: The Sadat Decade in Perspective*, SUNY, Binghamton, New York, 6–7 April 1984

Falk, Avner, 'Moshe Dayan: Narcissism in Politics', *Jerusalem Quarterly*, No. 30, Winter 1984

Finver, Frank, 'Prudence in Victory: The Case of Anwar Sadat and the October War' (unpublished paper), 1980

Ghali, Boutros, 'The Foreign Policy of Egypt in the Post-Sadat Era', *Foreign Affairs*, Spring 1982

Grenier, Richard, 'The Gandhi Nobody Knows', *Commentary*, March 1983

Hakki, Muhammed, 'The Egyptian Press in the Nasser and Sadat Eras': paper delivered at the conference on *Egypt: The Sadat Decade in Perspective*, SUNY, Binghamton, New York, 6–7 April 1984

Hamed, Osama, 'Egypt's Open-door Economic Policy: An Attempt at Economic Integration in the Middle East', *International Journal of Middle Eastern Studies*, No. 13, 1981

Handel, Michael, 'Surprise and Change in International Politics', *International Security*, 1980

Harkabi, Yehoshafat, 'Obstacles in the Way of a Settlement', in Sheffer, G. (ed.), *Dynamics of a Conflict* (Humanities Press, New Jersey, 1975)

Ismael, Tareq, 'Egypt and the Arab World': paper delivered at the conference on *Egypt: The Sadat Decade in Perspective*, SUNY, Binghamton, New York, 6–7 April 1984

Israeli, Raphael, 'Sadat between Arabism and Africanism', *Middle East Review*, Vol. 11, No. 3, Spring 1979

Israeli, Raphael, 'The New Wave of Islam', *International Journal*, Vol. 34, No. 3, Summer 1979

Israeli, Raphael, 'The Role of Islam in President Sadat's Thought', *Jerusalem Journal of International Relations*, Vol. 4, No. 4, 1980

Israeli, Raphael, 'Sadat's Egypt and Teng's China: Modernization versus Revolution', *Political Science Quarterly*, Vol. 95, No. 3, Fall 1980

Israeli, Raphael, 'Comparative Notes on Islam in Egypt under Nasser and Sadat', in M.

Heper and R. Israeli (eds), *Islam and Politics in the Modern Middle East* (Croom Helm, London, 1984)

Kelman, Herbert, 'Overcoming the Psychological Barrier: An Analysis of the Egyptian–Israeli Peace Process': paper delivered at CFIA 25th Conference, 10 June 1983

Kimche, Jon, 'The Riddle of Sadat', *Midstream*, April 1974

Kupferschmidt, Uri, 'The Muslim Brothers and the Egyptian Village', *Asian and African Studies*, Vol. 16, 1982

Lachine, Nadim, 'Class Roots of the Sadat Regime', *Middle East Research Institute (MERIP)*, April 1977

McDermott, Anthony, 'Sadat: The Art of Survival', *Middle East International*, No. 53, 1975

Merriam, John, 'Egypt after Sadat', *Current History*, January 1982

Mitchell, Gertrue, 'Education in Egypt: Coping with Numbers', *American Education*, June 1979

Moench, Richard, 'Plunder on the Right: Bleeding the Public Sector': paper delivered at the conference on *Egypt: The Sadat Decade in Perspective*, SUNY, Binghamton, New York, 6–7 April 1984

Mohsen, Safia, 'Laws without Sovereignty: The Culture of Corruption': paper delivered at the conference on *Egypt: The Sadat Decade in Perspective*, SUNY, Binghamton, New York, 6–7 April 1984

Muhammed, Akbar, 'Egypt's Changing Role in Africa': paper delivered at the conference on *Egypt: The Sadat Decade in Perspective*, SUNY, Binghamton, New York, 6–7 April 1984

Myers, Amy, 'Ideology in Post-Revolutionary Egypt' (unpublished thesis), Princeton University, May 1980

Owen, Roger, 'The Rise and Fall of A. Sadat' (review article), *The Middle East*, February 1982

Peretz, Don, 'Egypt and US Foreign Policy': paper delivered at the conference on *Egypt: The Sadat Decade in Perspective*, SUNY, Binghamton, New York, 6–7 April 1984

Ralaman, Uri, 'The Soviet Union and the Middle East', in Eugene Rostow (ed.), *The Middle East: Critical Choices for the US* (Westview, Boulder, 1972)

Reed, Stanley, 'Dateline Cairo: Shaken Pillar', *Foreign Policy*, Winter 1981/82

Rejwam, Nissim, 'Culture and Personality: Building the New Egyptian Man', *New Middle East*, No. 4, February 1972

Roazen, Paul, 'Psychology and Politics', *Contemporary Psychoanalysis*, Vol. 12, No. 1, 1975

Rubin, Barry, 'America and the Egyptian Revolution', *Political Science Quarterly*, Spring 1982

Rubinstein, Alvin, 'Egypt's Search for Stability', *Current History*, January 1979

Scobie, Grant, 'Government Policy and Food Imports: The Case of Wheat in Egypt', International Food Policy Research Institute, *Research Report 29*, December 1981

Sha'alan, Muhammed, 'Sadat's Death: Self-Chosen Martyr or Public Execution?' (unpublished manuscript), 1982

Shamir, Shimon, 'Some Arab Attitudes Toward the Conflict with Israel 1967–1973', in G. Sheffer (ed.), *Dynamics of a Conflict*, Humanities Press, New Jersey, 1975

Shamir, Shimon, 'Nasser and Sadat (1967–1973)', in I. Rabinovitch and others (eds), *From June to October* (Transactions, New Jersey, 1975)

Shamir, Shimon, 'Arab Socialism and Egyptian–Islamic Tradition', in S. N. Eisenstodt and others (eds), *Socialism and Tradition* (Van Leer, Jerusalem, 1976)

Shamir, Shimon, 'Two Years after the Signing of the Peace Treaty Israel–Egypt', *Research Project on Peace*, Tel Aviv University, 1981

Springborg, Robert, 'Patrimonialism and Policy-making in Egypt: Nasser and Sadat and the Tenure Policy for Reclaimed Lands', *Middle Eastern Studies*, Vol. 15, No. 1, January 1979

Stork, Joe, 'Bailing out Sadat', *Middle East Research Institute (MERIP)*, April 1977

Stork, Joe, 'Sadat's Desperate Mission', *Middle East Research Institute (MERIP)*, February 1978

Suleiman, Michael, 'Changing Attitudes towards Women in Egypt', *MES*, Vol. 14, No. 3, October 1978

Vatikiotis, P. J., 'After Sadat', *Policy Review*, Winter 1982

Waterbury, John, 'The Political Economy of Infitah, 1974–84': paper delivered at the conference on *Egypt: The Sadat Decade in Perspective*, SUNY, Binghamton, New York, 6–7 April 1984

Yadlin, Rivka, 'The Egyptian Personality: Trends in Egyptian Character Literature', *Asian and African Studies* (Israel), Vol. 14, No. 1, March 1980

Newspaper and Magazine Feature Articles

Allen, Robin, 'Sadat Plays a Writing Game', *MEED*, Vol. 23, No. 27, 6 July 1979

Al-Lozi, Salim, 'Sadat: Hope and Determination', *Events*, Vol. 33, 30 December 1977

Al-Lozi, Salim, 'My Friend Anwar', *Events*, Vol. 34, 13 January 1978

Bassiouni, Cherif, 'Sadat's Grand Design for Egypt', *New Outlook*, No. 7–8, November–December 1978

Beeson, Irene, 'Sadat's Egyptian Inquisition', *Jerusalem Post*, 18 September 1977

Beeson, Irene, 'Why the Copts are Rebelling in Egypt', *Jerusalem Post*, 9 October 1977

Borsten, Joan, 'A Day with Mrs Sadat', *Jerusalem Post*, 22 June 1979

Boulare, Habib, 'Le Sadatisme à l'épreuve', *Jeune Afrique*, No. 839, 4 February 1977

Brown, William, 'Isolating Sadat – what does it mean?', *Christian Science Monitor*, 30 May 1979

Brown, William, 'The Calculated Non-Settlement', *Washington Post*, 15 September 1980

Charoub, Akim, 'Qui croit en Sadate', *Jeune Afrique*, No. 615, 21 October 1972

Dimbleby, Jonathan, 'Sadat's Solitary Hand', *New Statesman*, Vol. 94, No. 2421, 12 August 1977

Dishon, Daniel, 'Sadat's Time for Decision', *SWASIA*, Vol. II, No. 5, 7 February 1975 (reprinted from the *Jerusalem Post*, 24 January 1975)

Dorwey, William, '1968 Revisited: Student Power in Cairo', *New Middle East*, No. 40, January 1972

Eilon, Amos, 'Egypt after Sadat', *Ha'aretz*, January 1982

Fouad, Ahmed, 'A Call to the Egyptians and the World', *Middle East Research Institute (MERIP)*, Vol. 8, no. 1, February 1978

Glubb, Faris, 'Sadat's Fading Hopes', *Middle East International*, No. 85, July 1978

Goell, Yosef, 'Anwar Sadat: Master of the Unexpected', *Jerusalem Post*, 20 November 1977

Gonbus, Martin, 'Depression on the Nile', *The Nation*, 5 April 1980

Gran, Judith, 'Impact of the World Market on Egyptian Women', Middle East Research Institute (*MERIP*), No. 58, June 1977

Haykal, Hassaneim, 'Frankly Speaking', *SWASIA*, Vol. 3, No. 15, 16 April 1976 (reprinted from *Al-Ra'y*, [Jordan] 12 March 1976)

Hertzberg, Arthur, 'The View from Cairo', 26 June 1980

Herzog, Haim, 'The Recurring Scenario', 11 April 1980

Hirst, David, 'Sadat's Slogans Wearing Thin', *Guardian*, 18 January 1975

Hirst, David, 'Sadat's Impossible Two-way Stretch', *Guardian*, 12 July 1975

Kapeliuk, Ammon, 'Student Unrest in Egypt', *New Outlook*, Vol. 15, No. 1, 1972

King, Christabel, 'Woman behind President Sadat', *Jerusalem Post*, 4 June 1978

Kipper, Judith, 'A Long Way to Go', *Jerusalem Post*, 20 April 1976

Kirkpatrick, Jeane, 'Dishonoring Sadat', *New Republic*, 11 November 1981

Kissinger, Henry, 'They Are Fated to Succeed', *Time*, 2 January 1978

Kraft, Joseph, 'Letter from Egypt', *New Yorker*, 28 May 1979

Mackie, Alan, 'Peace Marathon brings Little Joy to Sadat', *MEED*, Vol. 24, No. 23, 6 June 1980

Mansfield, Peter, 'Has Sadat's Democracy Failed?', *Middle East International*, No. 84, June 1978

Mansfield, Peter, 'Sadat's Controlled Experiment', *Middle East International*, No. 66, 1976

Mansfield, Peter, 'Mr Sadat's Egypt', *New Statesman*, 30 July 1976

Marcus, Yoel, 'Throw Sadat a Rope', *New Outlook*, Vol. 14, No. 5, 1971

Martin, M., 'A note on Worker Agitation in Egypt', *CEMAM*, 1975

Martin, M., and Labib, S., 'Nasserism Today', *CEMAM*, 1975

Michaels, James, 'Sadat to Israel: We are ready for normalization etc.', *Forbes*, 27 April 1978

Mitgang, Herbert, 'A Writer with Steady Work under Sadat's Aegis', *New York Times*, 8 August 1978

Mondesir, Simone, 'Sadat and Democracy', *MEED* (Arab Report), No. 2, 14 February 1979

Morris, Willie, 'Sadat, Another Assessment', *Middle East International*, 29 January 1982

Mortimer, Edward, 'Sadat Stifles the Opposition', *Middle East International*, 14 September 1979

Oweiss, Ibrahim, 'Egypt's Economy: Room for Optimism', *Middle East International*, July 1978

Pattir, Dan, 'Sadat and Camp David', *Kotereth Rashith* (Hebrew), 5 October 1983

Reed, Stanley, 'Egyptian Assembly Elections: Sadat does it again', *MEED* (Arab Report), No. 11, June 1979

Rejwam, Nissim, 'Culture and Personality: Building the New Egyptian Man', *New Middle East*, No. 41, February 1972

Rogers, David, 'Becoming Irritant', *Jerusalem Post*, 14 December 1980

Rouleau, Eric, 'Egypt from Nasser to Sadat', *Survival*, No. 14, No. 6, 1972 (reprinted from *La Monde*), 9 August 1972

Rubin, Barry, 'What Mubarak Inherits', *New Republic*, 28 October 1981

Sadat, Anwar, 'A Last Interview', *Encounter*, Vol. LVIII, No. 1, January 1982

'Sadat or the Emergence of a New Egyptian Leader', *Bulletin of the Africa Institute of South Africa*, No. 3, 1974

Salem, Yussef, 'The Sadat Quandary', *Israel and Palestine*, No. 65, 1978

Samak, Qussai, 'The Politics of Egyptian Cinema', *Middle East Research Institute (MERIP)*, No. 56, April 1977

Samuelson, Maurice, 'Sadat, the Stayer', *New Statesman*, Vol. 90, No. 2325, 10 October 1975

Schanche, Don, 'Eilts – the Ambassador who Knew Too Much', *Jerusalem Post*, 15 May 1979

Shapiro, Sraya, 'Sadat Helping Expose Nasser's Torture Methods', *Jerusalem Post*, 30 April 1978

Sharon, Moshe, 'Mohammed Must Go to the Mountain', *Jerusalem Post*, 28 September 1979

Sharp, Jonathan, 'The Egyptian Fair Lady', *Jerusalem Post*, 24 October 1976

Sheehan, Edward, 'The Real Sadat and the Demythologized Nasser', *New York Times Magazine*, 18 July 1971

Sheehy, Gail, 'The Riddle of Sadat', *Esquire*, 30 January 1979

Sheehy, Gail, 'Portrait of a Pathfinder', *Pathfinders*, 19 October 1981

Steinem, Gloria, 'Two Cheers for Egypt: Talks with Jihan Sadat etc.', *Ms Magazine*, June 1980

Stevens, Janet, 'Political Repression in Egypt', *Middle East Research Institute (MERIP)*, Vol. 8, No. 3, April 1978

Stewart, Desmond, 'An Ominous Trial', *Middle East International*, No. 111, October 1979

Tanner, Henry, 'Shrewd and Intuitive Egyptian President', *New York Times*, 27 October 1978

Tucker, Judith, 'Economic Decay, Political Ferment in Egypt', *Middle East Research Institute (MERIP)*, Vol. 8, No. 2, March 1978

Vashitz, Joseph, 'Heir to Nasser', *New Outlook*, Vol. 14, No. 5, 1971

Walters, Barbara, 'Personal Portraits of Peacemakers', *Ladies Home Journal*, June 1979

Whitaker, Jennifer, 'They Don't Miss Sadat', *The Atlantic*, January 1982

Wren, Christopher, 'Sadat Remains Loyal Son of a Nile Village', *New York Times*, 14 May 1978

Younger, Sam, 'Sadat Ignores his Critics', *Middle East International*, No. 108, 14 September 1979

Newspapers and Magazines used for their News Chronology

Africa (London), No. 75, 1977

Afrika (Germany), Vol. 25, 1971

Afrique Nouvelle (Senegal), No. 1399, 21–27 April 1976

Afriscope, Vol. 9, January 1979

American Annual (New York), 1973–80

American Education (Washington), 1 June 1979

Asian and African Studies (Haifa), Vol. 14, March 1980; Vol. 161, July 1982

Atlantic Magazine (Boston), Summer 1980, January 1982
Britannica, Book of the Year (London), Biography, 1972
British Society for M-E Bulletin (London), Vol. 3, 1976
Bulletin of the Africa Institute of South Africa (Johannesburg), No. 3, 1974
CEMAM (Beirut), 1974
Christian Science Monitor (Boston), 1979–81
Commentary (New York), March 1983
Current Biography (New York), 1971
Current History (New York), January 1979, January 1982
Department of State Bulletin (Washington), May 1980
Economist (London), 22 May 1971, 1977–9
Encounter (Los Angeles), Vol. 58, No. 1, January 1982
Esquire (Chicago), January 1979
Events (New York), 1977–8
Forbes (New York), 1978–9
Foreign Affairs (New York), Spring 1982
Foreign Policy (New York), Summer 1979, Spring 1981, Winter 1981–2
Guardian (London), January–July 1975
Guardian Weekly (London), Vol. 12, No. 4, 25 January 1975
Israel and Palestine (Paris), No. 65, 1978
Jerusalem Post (Jerusalem), 1976–81
Jeune Afrique (Tunis), No. 615, 21 October 1972; No. 839, 4 February 1977; No. 886–
    7, 28 December 1971; January 1978
Jewish Observer (London), 19 September 1975
Ladies Home Journal (Philadelphia), June 1979
Macleans (Canada), June 1979, September 1981, October 1981
Mainstream (New York), March 1974
MEED (London), No. 2, February 1979; No. 11, June 1979; No. 27, July 1979; No.
    23, June 1980
MERIP (Cambridge, Mass.), April 1974, No. 56, No. 58, June 1977, February 1978,
    No. 64, March 1978, Vol. 8, No. 2, April 1978, Vol. 8, No. 3
MES (Washington), Vol. 14, October 1978; No. 3, Vol. 15, January 1979, No. 1
Midstream (New York), April 1974
The Middle East (London), Vol. 40, February 1978; Vol. 56, June 1979; February 1982
Middle East International (London), No. 53, 1975; No. 66, 1976; No. 84, 1978; No. 85,
    1978; September/October 1979; No. 111, 1982
Middle East Review (New York), September 1975
Le Monde (Paris), August 1972, 1977–81
Ms Magazine (New York), June 1980
Muslim World (Hartford, Connecticut, USA), Vol. LXVII, No. 2, April 1977
The Nation (USA), 24 March 1979, 5 April 1980, October 1981
New Outlook (Israel–Paris), 1971, 1972, 1978
New Middle East (London), January and February 1972
New Republic (New York), 1979, October 1981, 11 November 1981
New Statesman (London), October 1975, July 1976, 12 August 1977
Newsweek (USA), 1970–81
New York Times, 1970–71, 1973, 1977–9

New York Times Magazine, 18 July 1971, 25 November 1979, 21, 28 January 1979
New Yorker, 1979
Pathfinders (Washington), October 1981
Policy Review (Washington), 1982
Political Science Quarterly (New York), Spring 1982
Progressive (Wisconsin, USA), July 1981
Survival (London), Vol. XIV, 1972; Vol. XVII, 1975
SWASIA, Vol. II, February 1975; Vol. III, April 1976
Time (USA), 1973–4, 1977–81
The Times (London), 5 November 1975
US News and World Report (Washington), August–October 1981
Washington Post, September 1980
World Press (Cambridge, Mass.), August 1981

Interviewees

Abu Taleb, Sufi – Professor of Law, President of Cairo University, and Deputy of the Parliament under Sadat

Afifi, Madame Eqbal – Sadat's first wife

Al-Gizawi, Abu al-Fadl – Ex-Free Officer, now a lawyer in Cairo

Azzam, Hamdi – Egyptian Press Attaché in Bonn during Sadat's presidency; accompanied Sadat and interpreted for him during his visits to Germany and Austria; now active in the Arab League

Ben-Elissar, Eliahu – Former Director-General of Prime Minister Begin's office; a key participant in the Israeli–Egyptian negotiating process and the first Israeli Ambassador to Cairo; then Chairman of the Knesset's Foreign Affairs and Defence Committee

Ben-Elissar, Nitza – Wife of Eliahu Ben-Elissar; maintained close contacts with Sadat's family and inner circle

Kamel, Hassan – Sadat's *Chef de Cabinet*, now a businessman

Kamel, Husam – Labour Party activist, leader of miners' syndicate, and lawyer

Khalil, Mustafa – Prime Minister and then Counsellor to Sadat; he headed the Egyptian delegation for the autonomy talks with Israel; now Deputy Chairman of the National Democratic Party and Chairman of the Arab–Africa Bank

Laniado, Eli – Press Attaché to the Israeli Embassy in Cairo; had interviewed Sadat for Israeli television

Mansur, Anis – Editor of *October Magazine* and one of Sadat's confidants

Mar'i, Sayyid – Speaker of Parliament under Sadat and Sadat's in-law

Murad, Hilmi – General Secretary of the Socialist Labour Party, one of the major opposition parties in Egypt

Ottaway, David – Foreign correspondent in Cairo, met Sadat on many occasions

Sadat, Jihan – Sadat's widow; she graciously agreed to give three tape-recorded interviews in her house at Giza

Sadat, Camellia – Sadat's daughter from his first marriage; now settled in Boston, USA

Sadat, Rawiya – Camellia's older sister; she provided us with some insights into the family and Sadat's native village, Mit Abul-kum

Sa'ad al-Din, Mursi – Director of State Information Service under Sadat; spokesman

for Egypt's Foreign Ministry and Cultural Attaché for the Foreign Ministry
Shafi'i, Hussein – Ex-Free Officer, Muslim Brother, and Vice-President under Sadat
Shakir, Amin – writer
Sha'alan, Dr Muhammed – Psychiatrist and Professor at Al-Azhar University

INDEX